On This Rock

On This Rock

When Culture Disrupted the Roman Community

E. A. Judge

EDITED BY
A. D. Macdonald

CASCADE *Books* • Eugene, Oregon

ON THIS ROCK
When Culture Disrupted the Roman Community

Copyright © 2020 E. A. Judge. All rights reserved. Except for brief quotations in critical publications or reviews, no part of this book may be reproduced in any manner without prior written permission from the publisher. Write: Permissions, Wipf and Stock Publishers, 199 W. 8th Ave., Suite 3, Eugene, OR 97401.

Cascade Books
An Imprint of Wipf and Stock Publishers
199 W. 8th Ave., Suite 3
Eugene, OR 97401

www.wipfandstock.com

PAPERBACK ISBN: 978-1-7252-6038-2
HARDCOVER ISBN: 978-1-7252-6037-5
EBOOK ISBN: 978-1-7252-6039-9

Cataloguing-in-Publication data:

Names: Judge, E. A., author. | Macdonald, A. D., editor.

Title: On this rock : when culture disrupted the Roman community / by E. A. Judge ; edited by A. D. Macdonald.

Description: Eugene, OR: Cascade Books, 2020 | Includes bibliographical references and index.

Identifiers: ISBN 978-1-7252-6038-2 (paperback) | ISBN 978-1-7252-6037-5 (hardcover) | ISBN 978-1-7252-6039-9 (ebook)

Subjects: LCSH: Church history—Primitive and early church, ca. 30–600. | Rome—History—Empire, 30 B.C.–476 A.D.

Classification: DG276.5 J83 2020 (print) | DG276.5 (ebook)

Manufactured in the U.S.A. 10/12/20

For Macquarie's Alanna Nobbs,
who pioneered the history of Late Antiquity.

Contents

Preface | ix

Chapter 1: Diversity under Galerius and the Body Corporate under Licinius | 1

Chapter 2: Christianity and Society by Late Antiquity | 8

Chapter 3: Synagogue and Church in the Roman Empire: The Insoluble Problem of Toleration | 22

Chapter 4: Group Religions in the Roman Empire | 38

Chapter 5: Rethinking Religion from Hellenistic Times | 52

Chapter 6: On This Rock I Will Build My Community | 56

Chapter 7: Christian Innovation and its Contemporary Observers | 103

Chapter 8: The Conversion of Rome: Ancient Sources of Modern Social Tensions | 127

Chapter 9: The Absence of Religion, Even in Ammianus? | 149

Chapter 10: Did the "Flood of Words" Change Nothing? | 163

Chapter 11: Destroying the Gods | 167

Chapter 12: Why No Church Schools in Antiquity? | 171

Chapter 13: What Makes a Philosophical School? | 182

Chapter 14: The "First Monk" and the Origin of Monasticism | 190

Chapter 15: The Impact of Paul's Gospel on Ancient Society | 215

Chapter 16: Athena, the Unknown God of the Churches | 227

Bibliography | 231
Index | 263

Preface

The "conflict of cultures" around the mission of the apostle Paul, and the legacy of that conflict in the transformation of modern culture, provided the two-stage focal theme for the collection of Judge essays edited by James R. Harrison and published by Cascade in 2019. Harrison introduced that collection with a wide-ranging study of his own, focused on the rediscovery of Pauline thought in modern intellectual discourse. It is not surely a mere coincidence that Harrison was in the same year elected a Fellow of the Australian Academy of the Humanities, the public authority committed to what it defines as "the new humanities."

But Harrison spans a two-thousand-year gap in the historic reception of Paul's gospel, from the first century until now. The main bridging point between those times lies in the fourth century, with the revolutionary establishment of the church as an autonomous civil institution. In the disciplines of classics and ancient history this epoch has come to be called "Late Antiquity." The standard classical reference works internationally have been systematically expanded not only to connect with the ancient Near Eastern and biblical culture, but also to incorporate the ongoing reception of our two-sided tradition down to the present.

Volume 13 (1998) of the new Cambridge Ancient History, entitled *The Late Empire, AD 337–425*, for example, introduced two newly dominant themes of the fourth century: "Orthodoxy and Heresy" by Henry Chadwick, and "Asceticism: Pagan and Christian" by Peter Brown. The issue was how to accommodate the Pauline gospel within the rational concert of philosophy (Chadwick), or how the activist church life could meet the serene ethical restraint of the Classics (Brown). Both these provocative themes are reflected in the present seventh collection of my historical essays.

The apparently seamless web of multiculturalism, commonly assumed among interpreters of ancient history, may be symbolized by

Bishop Pegasius of Troy.[1] But the philosophically defined creeds of the Roman and Orthodox churches and their practical moral commitments remain anchored in the demonstrative vision and life-giving care of the Pentecostal gospel.

A. D. Macdonald has assessed, arranged and edited these interpretative arguments at Macquarie University, with the more extensive essays in the middle after "On this Rock" (chapter 6) and briefer pieces before and after. Hitherto they have only been seen in often obscure places in Australia or Germany (the latter now of course in English). Their assembly celebrates the fifty-year fostering of late antiquity at Macquarie by Alanna Nobbs, to whom this collection is dedicated.

Wherever possible, this volume follows the abbreviations set out in the 2014 *SBL Handbook of Style*, 2nd edition. In some cases abbreviations were required for items not included in the SBL list. In those cases, abbreviations have been taken from the 1996 *Oxford Classical Dictionary*, 3rd edition.

E. A. J.

---

1. For Pegasius of Troy see chapters 6, 7, and especially 16 below.

1

Diversity under Galerius and the Body Corporate under Licinius

In 311 and 313 respectively, Galerius and Licinius issued the two pieces of legislation that would define the legal status of Christians in the fourth century. This chapter attends to the details and background of these edicts. It first considers the meaning of Galerius's ruling that Christians may operate "on divergent principles," praying for the empire (*res publica*) but not participating in customary contractual sacrifice. Attention turns thereafter to Licinius's (and Constantine's) Edict of Milan, and especially its ruling on the restitution of confiscated property, which granted legal recognition to Christian assemblies rather than individuals—a phenomenon explored here in light of the third-century history of Christian corporate bodies. This chapter was first published as "Diversity Versus the Body Corporate," in *St. Mark's Review* 225.3 (2013), and is reproduced here with minor revisions.

THE FIRST OFFICIAL TOLERATION of a collective choice to live differently, in spite of the law, was granted to "the Christians" by Galerius on April 20, AD 311. On June 13, AD 313, Licinius defined "the churches" as having corporate status in law. These two truly epoch-making rulings lean in opposite directions. The one reluctantly implies an open society (as we might now say). The other grandly exploits it by insulating the churches as bodies corporate apart from the legal status of their individual members. In the twenty-first century we are still distracted between the rival options, both internally amongst church members and externally across the tides of public debate.

Galerius: A Conditional Toleration

For the better part of a decade Galerius had been promoting the public campaign for everyone to sacrifice to the gods. He was himself now the senior Augustus in Diocletian's tetrarchy. His decision to excuse the Christians from sacrificing was made on his death-bed. The edict is our only surviving official definition of what had been wrong with the Christians.

> Among all the other arrangements which we are always making for the advantage and benefit of the state (*res publica*), we had earlier sought to set everything right in accordance with the ancient laws and public discipline of the Romans and to ensure that the Christians too, who had abandoned the way of life (*secta*) of their ancestors, should return to a sound frame of mind; for in some way such self-will (*voluntas*) had come upon these same Christians, such folly had taken hold of them, that they no longer followed those usages of the ancients which their own ancestors perhaps had first instituted, but, simply following their own judgement and pleasure, they were making up for themselves the laws which they were to observe and were gathering various groups of people together in different places (*per diversa varios populos congregarent*). When finally our order was published that they should betake themselves to the practices of the ancients, many were subjected to danger, many too were struck down. Very many, however, persisted in their determination and we saw that these same people were neither offering worship (*cultus*) and due religious observance to the gods nor practicing the worship of the god of the Christians. Bearing in mind therefore our own most gentle clemency and our perpetual habit of showing indulgent pardon to all men, we have taken the view that in the case of these people too we should extend our speediest indulgence, so that once more they may be Christians and put together their meeting places (*conventicula sua*) provided they do nothing to disturb good order. We are moreover about to indicate in another letter to governors what conditions they ought to observe. Consequently, in accordance with this indulgence of ours, it will be their duty to pray (*orare*) to their god for our safety and for that of the state and themselves, so that from every side the state may be kept unharmed and they may be able to live free of care in their own home.[1]

The term *secta* ("way of life") clearly embraces both moral "discipline" and intellectual "frame of mind," as now abandoned by the *voluntas* of the

---

1. Lactantius, *De mortibus persecutorum* 53, trans. Creed.

Christians. Creed translates this as "self-will", rightly capturing the outrage of Galerius. (We might have said "commitment.") Eusebius reports that the edict was published "in each city," and translated it seems by himself, "as well as may be" (*kata to dynaton*).[2] He gives for *voluntas* the Greek *pleonexia* ("presumption" perhaps), and for *secta* of course *hairesis*. Both "sect" and "heresy" were to become pejorative in Christian usage, but not yet. In the fourth century one spoke easily of "the Catholic *secta*."

It is intolerable to Galerius that people should presume to make up laws for themselves to observe merely at their own discretion. He had no doubt been briefed on the argument of Origen that even the "common law" of civilized humankind might be rejected in the name of truth.[3] Yet it was not the philosophical issue that concerned him, but the social one. The Christians were undermining national solidarity before the gods. Creed's translation of *per diversa varios populos,* however, leaves Galerius with a fatuous anticlimax, it seems. Eusebius rendered both Latin adjectives with the Greek *diaphoros,* which should not imply "different" in the sense of "various", but rather in the more contrastive sense of "differing," hence "divergent," or pejoratively "divisive" or "deviant." So "diversity" (our contemporary ideal) may have had a bad start. The fourth-century Christian term for "heresy" was in Latin *diversitas*. We might then translate *per diversa* as "on divergent principles." Creed's translation has assumed a locative rather than an intellectual reference ("places" is no more implicit in the Latin than "principles"). Other translations into modern languages typically do the same. The source of this consensus is no doubt the Latin version of Rufinus, whose approximate life-span is given as AD 345–410. Translating the Greek text of Eusebius, Rufinus has introduced the term *loca* ("places"), *in locis diversis plebs diversa concurrit*.[4] He had presumably not consulted Lactantius. Ammianus Marcellinus, a contemporary of Rufinus used the phrase *per diversa* of defeated soldiers who fled "in different directions."[5]

In AD 1659, Eusebius was again translated into Latin, by H. Valesius. He judged it necessary to spell out the meaning: "they were forming divisive communities, deviant in life and thought" (*in diversis sectis atque sententiis diversos cogerent coetus*).[6] In AD 1679, the missing text of Lactantius

---

2. Eusebius, *Hist. eccl.* 8.17, trans. Oulton.

3. Origen, *Contra Celsum* 1.1, trans. Chadwick.

4. Rufinus ap. Eusebius, in Schwartz et al., *Eusebius Caesariensis Werke*, 795.

5. Ammianus Marcellinus, *History* 17.13.19, trans. Rolfe. A geographical scenario often carries other overtones, for example disloyalty (27.8.10), alienation (31.2.15), or alternative ethnicity (31.7.7).

6. De Valois (alias Valesius), "Eusebii Pamphili: Ecclesiasticæ Historiæ," 10–44. Translation above is that of E. A. Judge.

was at last published. But it has been a mistake to think that Galerius was being careless with his words.

For three centuries the imperial power had followed a generous multicultural policy. It did not matter which divinity one cultivated, yet one must not fail to secure such protection to the national good. The system was contractual. One must pledge one's "vow" by "supplication" (literally "sacrifice"). This the Christians refused absolutely. The idolatry was anathema. Roman Jews of course were officially exempted from classical supplication in as much as it was banned by their older heritage. The Christians however were only betraying theirs. Galerius was no doubt not the first ruler to hear that they guaranteed their own alternative. They could not supplicate, but they would intercede constantly by advocacy (*oratio*) before the Almighty for the protection of Caesar, pleading his cause. Christian "prayer" was neither cultic nor contractual, but forensic. Galerius does not deserve the malevolent contempt of Lactantius. He was the first (so far as we know) to recognize and concede the validity of such prayer (*orare*). They need not supplicate after all, but they must still intercede.

Licinius: An Alternative Body Politic

After the death of Galerius his place as senior Augustus in the East was taken by Licinius. The latter's colleague Maximinus authorized the cities to seek from himself an apartheid ruling against the Christians. They must clearly still have the freedom to be such and to form conventicles. That, however, had explicitly been granted subject to their doing nothing against *disciplina* ("good order").

The rescript of Maximinus to such a request for ethnic cleansing confirms that the Christian *superstitio* had contaminated Colbasa, a city of Pisidia. The stain (*macula*) of impiety must be removed by segregation. It is not only the city proper (*civitas*), but the whole of the dependent countryside (*territorium*, where a quiet retreat might have been found?) that must be cleared.[7]

In the same year (AD 312) Constantine had taken Rome by force (at the Milvian Bridge). He assumed the senior rank within the tetrarchy. Licinius met him at Milan (the northern headquarters), sealing their agreement by marriage with Constantine's daughter. After the defeat of Maximinus, Licinius published in Nicomedia (the eastern headquarters) the so-called "edict of Milan."

7. Mitchell, "Maximinus."

This, though proclaimed like an edict, is in the form of instructions sent in writing to a provincial governor. It reports the agreement made between Constantine and Licinius. The toleration of Christians is confirmed. Conditions previously imposed (by Maximinus?) are cancelled. The practice of any other *religio* or observance is likewise protected (against Christian activism?). Confiscated property is restored. Referring explicitly to the *persona* (Greek *prosōpon*) of the Christians, it adds the following explanation.

> And since these same Christians are known to have possessed not only the places in which they had the habit of assembling but other property too which belongs by right to their body— that is, to the churches not to individuals (*ad ius corporis eorum id est ecclesiarum, non hominum singulorum, pertinentia*)—you will order all this property, in accordance with the law which we have explained above, to be given back without any equivocation or dispute at all to these same Christians, that is to their body and assemblies (*id est corpori et conventiculis eorum*), preserving always the principle stated above, that those who restore this same property as we have enjoined without receiving a price for it may hope to secure indemnity from our benevolence. In all these matters you will be bound to offer the aforesaid body of Christians (*supra dicto corpori Christianorum*) your most effective support so that our instructions can be the more rapidly carried out and the interests of public tranquility thereby served in this matter too by our clemency. In this way it will come about, as we have explained above, that the divine favor towards us, which we have experienced in such important matters, will continue for all time to prosper our achievements along with the public well-being.[8]

The mandate seems explicitly to be proposing a principle of corporate personality. Such a doctrine was not systematically entrenched in Romanist law until the Middle Ages. Neither classic Greek law nor sharia law developed such a concept.[9]

In the third century the Roman jurist Ulpian had asserted that individuals were not credited with the dues owed to any *universitas* ("collectivity"?), nor liable for its debts.[10] This did not however apply to a *societas* ("partnership," formed for commercial gain). The case with a *collegium* ("association")

---

8. Lactantius, *De mortibus persecutorum* 48.9–11.

9. Katz, *Oxford International Encyclopedia of Legal History*, 1:69–72 (ancient Greek law) with 2:70; 7:357–58 (sharia law) with 4:64–65.

10. *The Digest of Justinian* 3.4.7.1 citing Ulpian (Mommsen et al., *Digest of Justinian*, 97.

no doubt varied with its purpose (cult, funeral, trade, the last becoming obligatory in late antiquity). The "ecumenical synod of Dionysiac artists" (along with its athletic parallel) was an empire-wide organization securing tax-privileges for prize-winners. It was centrally regulated by the state.[11]

The churches were never brought under any of these legal forms, nor did they seek that. They did not charge fees, nor publish lists of members. They did not have constitutions, annual meetings, or secretaries. Yet they multiplied at large in parallel with the civil order as a whole, using the same civil terminology, but repudiating totally its cultic and sacral aspects.

After the capture of Valerian by the Persians (AD 260) the bishops of Egypt applied to Gallienus for restoration of their *topoi threskeusimoi* ("reverential sites"). This novel epithet will hardly have been invented by the government to suit them. It was surely their own attempt to formulate a collective stake in law. Were commemorative meetings already being held over the graves of the martyrs?[12]

In AD 272 a much more dramatic bid for state recognition was made. At Antioch the charismatic and dominant bishop Paul (of Samosata) was presenting himself in the style of an imperial procurator (he was in touch with the independent magnate, Zenobia of Palmyra). A synod of other bishops attempted to depose him, but he had control of the *oikos* ("house") of the church. The bishops appealed to Aurelian, who ruled (at their suggestion?) that the bishops of Italy and Rome should prevail.[13]

A generation later (AD 303) Galerius had instigated the destruction of the church buildings now multiplying, with confiscation of all property. The mandate of Licinius on restitution now finds it necessary to clarify the issue of collective ownership.

The "places" (*loca*) where the Christians used to "assemble" (*convenire*) are to be given back, but not to individuals (who presumably had been their owners in law, as with Paul of Samosata?). Instead, the owner will be their "body" (*corpus,* Greek: *soma).* These "bodies" are described by Licinius as the "churches" (*ecclesiae*) or at another point as the "assemblies" (*conventicula*). The Greek version of Eusebius uses "Christians" or "their synod" respectively. He first uses *ekklēsiai* for buildings in his enthusiasm for the boom leading up to 304.[14]

11. Judge, "Ecumenical Synod," 67–68, at *Jerusalem and Athens*, 137–39.

12. Judge, "Synagogue and Church," 40 (*Jerusalem and Athens*, 53 and 33 in the present volume), citing Eusebius, *Hist. eccl.* 7.13.1.

13. Judge, "Synagogue and Church," 41 (*Jerusalem and Athens*, 53 and 33–34 in the present volume), citing Eusebius, *Hist. eccl.* 7.30.19.

14. Judge, "On This Rock," 18 (*First Christians*, 656 and 95 in the present volume), citing Eusebius, *Hist. eccl.* 8.1.5.

Arnold Ehrhardt proposed that the repeated explanatory phrases ("that is, to the churches ... ," "that is to their body ... ") will have arisen from the need of Licinius in Nicomedia to explain to the East what in the West may have already been taken for granted during his negotiation with Constantine.[15] Lactantius had been professor of rhetoric in Diocletian's capital of Nicomedia. He would have understood the need there for clarification even in the Latin. The slight awkwardness of the translation used by Eusebius in Caesarea may well suggest more unfamiliarity in the case of Greek.

So the strange quasi-state works out its identity within the body politic, yet soon beyond it and even over it. Such a phenomenon must surely be unique in our history. There is no parallel in the Roman world of its time, whether in the cultic life of the cities or in the intellectual world of philosophy.

Winning the prize of long-suffering and peaceful intransigence, the privilege of toleration threatens to limit the freedom of others. It is the insoluble paradox of toleration. Corporate identity pulls against diversity.

---

15. Ehrhardt, "Das Corpus Christi."

2

Christianity and Society by Late Antiquity

This chapter consists of two short articles on "Christianity and Society" first published as "Gesellschaft und Christentum III: Neues Testament" and "Gesellschaft und Christentum IV: Alte Kirche" in *Theologische Realenzyklopädie* 12 (1984), and appearing here in English for the first time. They address first the social context and social vision of the New Testament communities, considering Graeco-Roman concepts of society, the development of social-historical approaches to the New Testament, and the outlook of the churches which maintained rank while denouncing status. The second section addresses the development and recognition of the church as an alternative community with a divergent lifestyle. It refers to the ideologies of church and society adopted by such figures as Tertullian, Origen, Eusebius, and ultimately Augustine, noting the social consequences of the conversion of Rome.

New Testament

AS WITH OTHER ANCIENT WRITINGS, the New Testament has no conception of society in the sense of a comprehensive system. Social connections were seen as personal relationships. The social setting of the New Testament communities moreover cannot be simply specified as proletarian. Their break with the traditional basic underlying patterns, together with their expectation of a new order, was nevertheless the precondition of their working out for the first time something like a structural understanding of social relationships.

1. Ancient Environment

Life in the community (*koinōnia*) belonged, according to Aristotle, to the essence of human nature, which could not therefore subsequently be disencumbered of it.[1] The individual was not sufficient on his own, and consequently those major social structures which necessarily provided for his well-being were predetermined for him by nature, namely the household (*oikia*) and the state (*polis*). The family, which was built up on the superiority of the master over the servant, the husband over the wife, and the father over the child, is historically older but the state took first place, since it alone was able to cater comprehensively for the well-being of all. Nevertheless Aristotle (in contrast with Plato, *Rep.* 5.457c–d) did not propose to abolish the family in favor of the state. It still satisfied essential human needs. A natural deficit in measured reason assigned many people to servitude; women certainly possessed reason, but not independently; for children, however, reason was attributed only potentially.[2] Men who did not by nature belong to a *polis* could in a similar way be classified as sub- or as superhuman.

These distinctions, together with the attitude to education on which they were founded, still represented the frame of reference for social policies in Paul's day, even though their validity was fundamentally restricted by him (Rom 1:14; Gal 3:18). The ancient world knew no comprehensive analytical system corresponding to our concept of society, as also with economy.[3] The social context of New Testament life can thus most appropriately be described as the connection between *polis* and *oikia*.

The democratic *politeia* had long represented the norm for civilized life, while tribal, priestly, or regal powers were increasingly losing ground to it (as in the Decapolis). Messianic movements in Judea formed a kind of counter-culture, especially since the Maccabees had prevented the attempt to turn Jerusalem into a *polis*. The kings who emphatically propagated this form of Hellenism for their subjects nevertheless developed for themselves the old Homeric style of family rule against which *polis*-democracy had originally developed. Their patronage already undermined the democratic system, since through this the increased power of well-to-do families was fostered within the democracy.

The intervention of Rome also strengthened this tendency through two decisive new impulses. The Roman *res publica* had always been dependent on its major families (property determined voting rights). On the other

---

1. Aristotle, *Pol.* 1.2.9.
2. Aristotle, *Pol.* 1.13.7.
3. Thraede, "Gesellschaft."

hand, the range of citizenship was increasingly expanded, incorporating the leading families of other states. Thus in New Testament times we have the power of one leading family (the Caesars) and the development of Roman rights into a kind of international elite ranking. In both cases their position rested on the possession of extensive landed estates. The income from these floated the welfare of the *polis*. So a subjugated peasantry fed the cities and contributed moreover to their wealth, while the latter rose proudly over their kindred through the common use of the Greek language and their ostensible independence (Acts 21:37-9).

The modern analysis of ancient society focuses mostly either on the capital, Rome, or on Egypt. Yet neither can provide the life setting of the early Christian communities. The imperial society of Rome (giving precedence to the senatorial or equestrian classes, or even the Caesarian freedmen) lies far above their experience. The Egypt of the papyri on the other hand presents a unique non-urban, but nevertheless centralized economic system, an *oikia* at the national level. The New Testament communities belong however to the world of the normal Greek *polis*, such as we find in the hundreds, especially in its heartland of Asia Minor. So long as their rich inscriptional material lies without systematic evaluation the connection of the communities with the society of their time will remain obscure.[4]

2. Social Setting of the New Testament Communities

At the beginning of the twentieth century the view prevailed that the communities had arisen from the lower classes, citing especially the fishermen's calling of the disciples, having their goods in common (Acts 2:44-5), Paul's critical remarks on his communities (1 Cor 1:26-8), and on his working with his own hands (1 Cor 4:12). Jesus spoke "as a proletarian to proletarians."[5] This verdict matched that of the ancient critics of Christianity (Origen, *Cels.* 3.55) and was soon confirmed by Adolf Deissmann's identification of New Testament Greek as the "popular" Greek of private

---

4. In relation to section 1 ("Ancient Environment"), see also: Alföldy, *Römische Sozialgeschichte*; Bolkestein, *Wohltätigkeit und Armenpflege*; Finley, *Ancient Economy*; Freyne, *Galilee*; de Coulanges, *La cité antique*; Gagé, *Les classes sociales*; Garnsey, *Social Status*; Hammond, *City-State and World-State*; Hands, *Charities and Social Aid*; Hengel, *Judentum und Hellenismus*; Hengel, *Die Zeloten*; Jeremias, *Jerusalem zur Zeit Jesu*; Jones, *Greek City*; Kippenberg, *Religion und Klassenbildung*; Kreissig, *Die sozialen Zusammenhänge*; Pöhlmann, *Geschichte der sozialen Frage*; Rostovtzeff, *Social and Economic History*; Sherwin-White, *Roman Society*.

5. Pöhlmann, *Geschichte der sozialen Frage*, 467.

letters, such as had recently been discovered on papyrus.[6] The first disciples also seemed to fit the role assigned for the proletariat by Karl Marx (Kautsky moreover had established that their setting was determined rather by consumption than by production).[7]

The development of form criticism ought to have given incentive for a better historical analysis of the social relationship under which the primitive Christian traditions arose. But for half a century biblical studies broadly lost interest in social history. Gerd Theissen explained this on the one hand by the concentration of Karl Barth on the theological content, and on the other hand by the existential interpretation of Rudolf Bultmann, who was himself the leading figure in form criticism.[8] Meanwhile in America the Chicago school continued to work in the old way at the investigation of the social questions, without taking account of the new German methodology.[9]

The significance of the *oikos* for community life was indeed affirmed,[10] but eventually it was an ancient historian who outlined the basic pattern of the social conditions, according to which the stereotypical view could be revised: "Far from being a socially depressed group, then, if the Corinthians are at all typical, the Christians were dominated by a socially pretentious section of the population of the big cities. Beyond that they seem to have drawn on a broad constituency, probably representing the household dependents of the leading members."[11]

A fundamental sociological investigation of the community in Corinth by Theissen brought the problem again into the center of New Testament research and was concerned to clarify methodological questions.[12] New references were discovered to the intellectual and cultural binding of Paul to Greek matters,[13] and the Greek language of the New Testament was no longer brought into connection with the colloquial speech of the papyri, but with the contemporary professional prose,[14] which was soon to be swamped by the rising of classicism.

---

6. Deissmann, *Das Urchristentum* and *Licht vom Osten*.
7. Kautsky, *Der Ursprung des Christentums*.
8. Theissen, *Studien zur Soziologie*.
9. Case, *Social Origins*; Schütz, "Introduction."
10. E.g., Filson, "Significance."
11. Judge, *Social Pattern*, 60.
12. Theissen, *Studien zur Soziologie*, 201–317.
13. Betz, *Der Apostel Paulus*; Malherbe, *Social Aspects*.
14. Rydbeck, *Fachprosa*.

That Paul worked with his own hands implied an intentional renunciation of status,[15] while the repudiation of private property and the sharing of goods presuppose basically secure economic conditions.[16] Even the Galilean fishermen belonged to a prosperous economic sector.[17] This "new consensus" gave rise to the claim of its resting on a strictly trustworthy conception of the social circumstances.[18]

But at the same time there was put to the test an important alternative method.[19] The long-neglected possibility that from the form of biblical writings conclusions might be drawn on the "social world" of their authors was brought to bear in that interpretative models were applied to these writings that had been developed from sociology and anthropology. Some of these models (charismatic leaders, the chiliastic movement) had originally been won from the New Testament itself. But once they had been built into the analysis of modern social forms there arose in fact from this retrospect the danger of an anachronistic procedure. In particular the supposition imposed itself that social discontent must be seen as a primary ground for conflicts noticeable in the New Testament. In this way the retreat from the proletariat as the early Christian driving force came together with the new postulate of the "relative impoverishment" of early Christian strata.[20] But that the rich patrons of Paul should have been frustrated because their high status in their home cities was not honored within the Roman class system would need much more conclusive material.

Stimulating examples have been presented, on the one hand in using contemporary data for the definition of social relations,[21] on the other hand for the historically reliable application of anthropological categories in coordinating the facts.[22] Before a secure answer can be given to the question of the social structure of the New Testament communities, these two methods must be brought into relation with each other. It is nevertheless certain that these communities were bound in a unique way to commit to a common cause people whose relations with each other were normally determined by

---

15. Hock, *Social Context of Paul's Ministry*.
16. Hengel, *Eigentum und Reichtum*.
17. Wüllner, *Meaning of "Fishers of Men."*
18. For the term "new consensus" see Malherbe, *Social Aspects*, 31.
19. Gager, *Kingdom and Community*; Theissen, *Soziologie der Jesusbewegung* and *Studien zur Soziologie*.
20. Gager, "Shall We Marry," 262.
21. Marshall, *Enmity*; Sampley, *Pauline Partnership in Christ*.
22. Malina, "Social Sciences and Biblical Interpretation."

the well-established rules of *oikos* and *polis*, and that these latter indeed were heavily shaken, while concurrently being upheld in the communities.

3. Contributions of the New Testament to the Theme "Society"

There follows an overview of what the New Testament as a whole might contribute to the theme "Society." For the statements of individual New Testament books as well as more particular details of the ancient world themes assumed there, see the *TRE* articles on Edification, Humility, Property, Slavery, State, Women, Work, etc.

The New Testament treats such social questions on the personal rather than institutional level. The ground for this is not simply a lack of abstract thinking, in which however for example John and Paul seem to be at home. Even without the advantages of our category of "Society," people always had a concept of socio-economic relations and they must, through a simple encounter, have first come to the insight that the responsibility for themselves as well as the final solution of their problems lay with themselves (e.g. Jas 4:13—5:9; Rev 18:19–20). Yet the New Testament (in contrast with the Stoa) does not call for a retreat into individualism. Its "dyadic" understanding of the person sees man from the standpoint of his commitments to his fellow man and to God (Rom 12:3–21).[23] This lends itself directly to the formulation of a social doctrine, yet one that arises from a personalistic basic perspective rather than a materialistic one.

The existing social order with all its class distinctions is to be invalidated under God's rule (1 Cor 12:13; Gal 3:28; Col 3:11). But precisely for that reason the New Testament avoids any attempt to anticipate this through institutional reform or revolution (1 Cor 7:17–24; 1 Tim 6:1–10). Instead of that the *polis/oikos*-structure with its class system is to be carefully preserved, for in the meantime it is that through which God rules the world (Rom 13:1–7; Eph 6:4–6, 9).[24] Believers must accept their place in it as assigned to them by God, and fulfill it in personal responsibility to him, as applies also to their rulers or masters, whether these know it or not (1 Tim 2:1–4; 1 Pet 2:11—3:7). This is the basis of the New Testament class doctrine. Hence the recognition of the tax-right and penal-right of the power-holder (Rom 13:4, 6), the rejection of private force (Matt 26:52), the maintenance of slavery, and the other traditional *oikos*-relations between man, wife, and

---

23. Malina, *New Testament World*, 53–60.

24. Editor's note: The original *TRE* publication erroneously cites Eph 5 rather than Eph 6 here and again later in this paragraph.

child (Eph 6:4-6, 9). On the other hand, the spirit in which these social commitments are to be fulfilled should lend emphasis to the fact that they are not only subject to the rule of God but are also due at the end to be disempowered by that (Gal 3:28). The New Testament lays down for now in particular a row of immediate and total confrontations with the ruling social spirit. Personal use and exploitation of wealth is continually rejected (1 Tim 6:9-10; Jas 4:13), as applies also with the legalistic refinement of Judaism (Rom 14:1-12, 17; Gal 3:1-5; Col 2:16-18; 1 Tim 1:3-8) and the aesthetic and intellectual ideals of Hellenism (Rom 1:5; 1 Cor 1:20-25; 2:1, 4; Col 2:4, 8). What is at stake here is a thoroughgoing rejection of any status aspirations, through which the ranking system had been perverted from being an obligation into the struggle for privileges (2 Cor 10:7-12; 11:4-6). Claims to personal honor and reputation most certainly do not belong to what God had intended for the good of humankind, even in the interim (1 Cor 4:6-13). From the moral point of view, they are injurious for others and at the same time dangerous, even for those into whose head the false security of pride arises (1 Cor 2:1-5). For the first time the Graeco-Roman world is here confronted with a positive ideal of humility (1 Cor 1:26-31; 2 Cor 11:12-32). The entire "agonistic" culture with its central values of honor and shame is turned upside down.[25]

The historic source of this radicalism, revolutionary for the individual, is clearly seen. The impulse comes from the paradox of the humiliated and rejected Messiah (2 Cor 1:3-7; Phil 2:3-11; 3:4-11). Both the itinerant radicalism of the first disciples of Jesus and the caring households of the early gentile congregations were based directly on the example of Christ. In this way it was possible that such very different social phenomena (as defined by Theissen) could be embraced within the common formula: renunciation of personal status within a temporarily recognized ranking system in view of its transformation in the coming kingdom of God. The inclination to identify the good life with prosperity, respectability, beauty, or wisdom was a fundamental element of Jewish and Graeco-Roman culture alike. The gospel calls believers to a radically alternative lifestyle. The long-term historical outworkings of this internal revolution have been foundational in the culture of the Western world, which has secularized the gospel call into such generally recognized values as personal responsibility, integrity, and service to others. That Paul used terms of physical labor (Rom 16:6, 9, 12; 1 Cor 16:16; 2 Cor 1:24) and servitude (1 Cor 3:5; 9:19; 2 Cor 4:5) to describe an occupation that on the other hand could have been seen as honorable leadership has turned the classical ideal of placid imperturbability into its

---

25. For the agonistic culture, see Malina, *New Testament World*, 25-50.

opposite. Although we know the names of at least 80 people from his network, it is hard for us to rank them in social terms, since the usual indicators are mostly replaced by a new language of mutual regard which points to the transformation of relationships that was underway. With the new-formed concept of edification (German "Erbauung")—the term *oikodomē* ("construction") was a solecism—a conception of society was being introduced which superseded the classical assumptions of the inalterability of the social order (Eph 2:19-22).[26] Every believer was newly endowed by the Spirit to contribute to the upbuilding of Christ's body (1 Cor 12:12-27; Eph 4:11-16). One might even see this as the first structural understanding of "Society," but a society that began and ended with personal relationships. Both the early Christian communities and those who observed them from the beginning saw in this event the creation of a new people that could not easily find room in the existing culture (1 Pet 2:9-12). The New Testament communities thus established their new way of life so firmly that it eventually must lead to the specific pluralism of the Western world.[27]

Early Church

1. The Christians as a New Nation (AD 100–250)

In the second century the Graeco-Roman ideal of civilization reached its fulfillment under the Antonines. Conditions were secure, the economy flourishing. The central Caesarian government on the one hand promoted local autonomy, and on the other hand increasingly extended Roman rights to the leading city elites.[28] Roman citizenship, which from 212 was possessed by all free inhabitants of the empire, became a bond of institutional

---

26. Pohlmann, "Erbauung."

27. In relation to sections 2 and 3 ("Social Setting of the New Testament Communities" and "Contributions of the New Testament to the Theme 'Society'"), see also: Alfaric, *Origines sociales du Christianisme*; Banks, *Paul's Idea of Community*; Elliott, *Home for the Homeless*; Grant, *Economic Background*; Grimm, *Untersuchungen zur sozialen Stellung*; Holmberg, *Paul and Power*; Horsley, *New Documents*, vol. 1 and subsequent vols.; Judge, *Rank and Status*; Judge, "St. Paul and Classical Society"; Judge, "Social Identity"; Keck, "On the Ethos"; Kee, *Christian Origins*; Knopf, "Über die soziale Zusammensetzung"; Kreissig, "Zur sozialen Zusammensetzung"; Mealand, *Poverty and Expectation*; Meeks, "Social Context"; Meeks, *Social World*; Meeks, *Zur Soziologie des Urchristentums*; Norris, "Social Status"; Ollrog, *Paulus und seine Mitarbeiter*; Schottroff and Stegemann, *Jesus von Nazareth*; Schottroff and Stegemann, *Der Gott kleinen Leute*; Schumacher, *Die soziale Lage*; Scroggs, "Sociological Interpretation"; Smith, "Social Description"; Troeltsch, *Die Soziallehren der christlichen*; Wüllner, "Ursprung und Verwendung."

28. Aelius Aristides, Εἰς Ῥώμην.

fellowship unparalleled in history. Admittedly, the more the old national distinctions were evened out, the broader did the gap become between those of no rank and those who had inherited rank. Yet as ever it was possible for an enterprising man, in military service, as a member of the Caesarian court personnel, or even through productive farming, to work his way up into the privileged levels of the social hierarchy.

Christianity drew its supporters from both sides of the social dividing line, as one can see from the different penalties in the sporadic local persecutions of this period.[29] Celsus criticizes the deliberate trouble taken by Christians over the uneducated, slaves, women, and children—as though they were not in the position to convince intelligent people.[30] Justin remarks on the internationality of the communities and shows that the number of non-Jews was meanwhile surpassing that of the Jews.[31] Tertullian cites the objection that the Christians had become a third race (*tertium genus*) after Romans and Jews, and reacts that they will soon outstrip the others, since there was no nation that was not Christian.[32] But even in 251 the proportion of Christians in the city of Rome was rated at only 3 percent.[33] The Roman community supported 150 office-bearers of various rank and 1500 widows or paupers.[34] To be able to maintain this unique charity one depended on rich patrons.[35] The appearance of a group of women, for whom rejection of marriage, or of a second marriage, was a commitment (a new social trend) may have been produced by the need for the recognition of women's independence, if the apocryphal Acts of the Apostles are to be understood this way.[36]

That the Christian communities were practicing a new form of life was one of the few points on which they and their critics agreed. It was not so much the church organization that caught attention—even though Origen (*Cels.* 8.75) describes that as an alternative to the city administration—but much more the deviant lifestyle of the Christians. Tertullian supported freedom of worship, such as existed for all nations.[37] For the first time in our sources Origen claimed the right, "for the sake of truth . . .

---

29. Grant, *Social Setting*, 23–25.
30. Origen, *Cels.* 3.44, 55.
31. Justin, *Apol.* 1.53.
32. Tertullian, *Nat.* 1.8.1–11, cf. *Apol.* 37.4.
33. Grant, *Early Christianity and Society*, 7.
34. Eusebius, *Hist. eccl.* 6.43.11.
35. Countryman, *Rich Christian*.
36. Davies, *Revolt of the Widows*.
37. Tertullian, *Apol.* 24.6–10.

to form associations contrary to the lawful order."[38] Thus the institutionalization of the Pauline church services had drawn the heavenly *politeuma* (Phil 3:20) into a structured confrontation with the secular social order. The tentative and various compromises of the apologists of the second century were overtaken by the provocative appearance of Tertullian and by the encyclopedic learning of Origen. It was more a matter of philosophy and lifestyle than of religion. Tertullian explains the name *christianus* in analogy with the terminology of the philosophical schools: it signifies the follower (*sectator*) of the *disciplina* of an authoritative teacher (*magister, auctor*). Cult-gods produced no such names for their worshipers.[39] From Tertullian's depiction of the *negotia Christianae factionis* it is clear that the meetings of the Christians still, as in the days of Paul, had as their centerpoint doctrinal and social concerns.[40] The Christian communities engaged society as a social movement and not as a cult. Insofar as they were propagating in society new ideas or new basic principles for the shaping of life (which in Roman eyes represented a highly irreligious activity), the Christians began to emerge as a particular nation.[41]

2. Confrontation between Church and State (AD 250–400)

By the middle of the third century it had become impossible to overlook the fact that the Roman empire was falling apart. The armies could no longer defend the frontiers. Without a stable succession practice the central government collapsed, and usurpers won regional autonomy. Economic collapse could be read from the clear decline in inscriptions and in the height of public buildings. After the restoration of order under Diocletian there followed a decided tightening of the state structure. The imperial rule was placed on a collegial basis which ensured a regular succession to power and anticipated the later division between East and West. A somber spirit of compulsion marked the rulers, who separated themselves from their subjects through an expansive ceremonial. The administration was intensified. Prices were

38. Origen, *Cels.* 1.1.
39. Tertullian, *Apol.* 3.6–8.
40. Tertullian, *Apol.* 39.1.
41. In relation to section 1 ("The Christians as a New Nation [100–250]"), see also: Andresen, *Die Kirchen*; Barnes, *Tertullian*; Fredouille, *Tertullien et la conversion*; de Ste Croix, *Class Struggle*; Grant, *Augustus to Constantine*; Gülzow, *Christentum und Sklaverei*; von Harnack, *Die Mission*; Judge, "Antike und Christentum"; MacMullen, *Paganism in the Roman Empire*; MacMullen, *Roman Social Relations*; Markus, *Christianity in the Roman World*; Simon, *La civilisation*.

controlled, and occupations made hereditary. A consequence was to fortify the social gap between *honestiores* and *humiliores*.

In the wake of the efforts at national reorganization there were now for the first time attempts to compel all inhabitants of the empire to conform to a public cult-ritual. Under Decius everyone had to submit a certificate of having sacrificed. The edict of toleration under Galerius terminated the principle of social solidarity that had lain behind such measures.[42] That Christians had given up the practices of their forefathers was a threat to public security. Under Maximinus Daia appear signs that the public cults, perhaps provoked by the social power of the churches, were for the first time to be organized as a national system. Comparable principles were applied across the whole fourth century. The Christians Constantine and Theodosius as well as the Hellenist Julian saw it indifferently as their self-evident duty as ruler to push through an official religion for the whole society. This conscious amplification of cultic worship into a dogmatic system with social consequences was an overflow from the proper drive of the churches for the complete integration of faith and life.

The official recognition of Christianity led no doubt to a considerable increase in conversions, but the process of Christianization of the Roman empire cannot be exactly defined, and certainly worked out differently according to time, place, and social rank. Only by the end of the fourth century was the turnaround in most cities in some sense complete, but still in no way was this the case everywhere in the countryside, and not consistently so in intellectual circles. A few groups of conservative scholars simply denied what was before their eyes, and no historian known to us offers a straightforward analysis. Only the Neoplatonic Porphyry towards the end of the third century and the *imperator* Julian in the mid-fourth (who had both in their youth had disagreeable experience of Christianity) recognized plainly the linkage of social organization and dogmatic drive which distinguished the church so fundamentally from Graeco-Roman society. For the first time in history a national society was governed by an ideological conviction that was in principle independent from that society. Never before were people of all social classes and levels instructed from the same books and seized by the same ideas as was the case with the great christological controversies. From this arises in our culture the possibility of orienting one's own life and practice aside from the state, or even in opposition to it. This is the origin of what today we understand by "religion" (though to its practical heirs in the meantime also convictions such as humanism and Marxism belong). Julian's impotent answer consisted in the attempt to change Hellenism itself

---

42. Eusebius, *Hist. eccl.* 8.17.3–10.

into such a committed basic institution. Even though his regime was only brief, the total lack of success which comes out in his letters shows how foreign this idea was to his contemporaries.

For Eusebius the conversion of Constantine meant the triumphal solution to the conflict between church and state. The Christian empire was for him one with the church. The earth is now again presented with a kind of Messianic kingdom. However, although Constantine was completely convinced of his mission of unity, the problems with the church were now only beginning. Unlike his precursors he had committed himself to a God whose identity was being defined by the authoritative teaching of bishops. Councils under imperial patronage demonstrated before the eyes of the world the new central meaning of doctrine for public order. But precisely through this patronage there were opened up conflicts over questions of church order. In Africa the strong Donatist communities were pushed aside. They drew in much from the nationalism of the barely Romanized levels of the population, while Arianism became the faith of the Germanic tribes who were later to settle in imperial territory. When Constantine overcame his last rival in Egypt, monasticism was arising there as a new form of withdrawal from society. Nothing demonstrated so visibly the social explosiveness of the words of Jesus and nothing repelled the critics of Christianity so much as the deliberate renunciation not only of a civilized lifestyle, but above all of the natural structures of life such as marriage and family. So powerfully did the social paradoxes of the gospel assert themselves in the attempt to erect the kingdom of God on earth.[43]

City of God and Earthly City (AD 400–550)

At the end of the fourth century the Roman empire was exposed anew to massive invasions; in 410 they reached a high point in the sacking of Rome by the Goths. The Vandals seized Africa in 430 and in 476 the imperial succession ended in the West, so that now even Italy fell to the Ostrogoths,

---

43. In relation to section 2 ("Confrontation between Church and State [250–400]"), see also: Brown, *Making of Late Antiquity*; Browning, *Emperor Julian*; Dagron, *Naissance d'une capitale*; Dodds, *Pagan and Christian*; Festugière, *Antioche païenne et chrétienne*; Frend, *Donatist Church*; Gaudemet, *L'Église*; Hornus, *Évangile et labarum*; Isichei, *Political Thinking*; Jones, *Later Roman Empire*, vol. 3; Judge, *Conversion of Rome* (reproduced as chapter 8 in the present volume); Judge and Pickering, "Papyrus Documentation"; MacMullen, *Constantine*; MacMullen, *Soldier and Civilian*; Matthews, *Western Aristocracies*; Momigliano, "Popular Religious Beliefs"; Monachino, *S. Ambrogio*; Nestle, "Die Haupteinwände"; Peterson, *Der Monotheismus*; Teja, *Organizacion economica*; von Haehling, *Die Religionszugehörigkeit*.

Gaul to the Franks, and Spain to the Visigoths. Constantinople kept the formal supremacy, and in the middle of the sixth century Justinian subjected parts of the West again to direct Roman rule. In Italy and Gaul especially, the old aristocracy maintained its place. Its members withdrew into their rich autonomous estates and often also occupied the local episcopal sees. By the early fifth century they had all gone over to the Christian faith and at the end of the century they presented themselves as true guardians of the ancient culture that had once appeared as the last bastion against the Christian flood. But the lower rank of city *curiales*, whose main duty had been to deliver the city finances, had broadly disappeared. Within the *humiliores* the difference between slave and free had lost significance through the binding of craftsmen to their trade and of farmers to their land. Nevertheless, such *coloni* still possessed their property and could lawfully marry. The decline of the international order delivered the elites to food shortage and the land to banditry. Yet it was no social revolution that marked the transition of the ancient world to the Middle Ages. The administration collapsed, as it became the heritage of the families that took office, under the growing corruption. The suppressed took refuge not only under the *patrocinium* of major landlords, but, as the Christian historians Orosius and Salvian report, also in the more free and more humane society of the Germanic settlements.[44] The formation of independent Germanic kingdoms in the territory of the Western empire finally delivered its death-blow.

For Augustine the dream of a Christian empire had already faded before Rome's burning. Although he remained to the last a supporter of the official Catholicism and even of state force against the Donatists, he shared more and more their skepticism as to whether the publicly organized church was to some extent a worldly body. Conversely the power of the state stood by no means simply in opposition to God but held, even from a higher viewpoint, a relative righteousness as a divine instrument for the well-being of humankind. The *civitas dei* and the *civitas terrena* correspond finally neither to church and state nor to heaven and earth. They are two social bonds which do not correspond with the church and the Roman empire. Even the conversion of the empire had not altered their relation to each other. In each organized body, whether church or state, the two *civitates* ("cities") intersect; but at the deepest level they exclude each other. They represent two antagonistic value systems. In his comprehensive discussion over this theme, appearing at a time when the Christian empire, as it stood since Theodosius, was unravelling around him, but still before the remnants of the old culture

---

44. Orosius 7.41; Salvian, *De gubernatione Dei* 5.5.

were gathered under the wing of the church, Augustine showed the radical incompatibility of the love of God with the values of worldly society.

Did the conversion of the Roman world then bring no kind of change in its social functioning? Patriarchy lost power. Through the recognition of the rights of children and the ban on rejection of children (sc. after birth) the *patria potestas* was further cut back. Slaves received better protection against mistreatment, and emancipation was favored. In the understanding of marriage love won larger significance, and the grounds of divorce were restricted. But the most important social effects of Christianity lay not in the realm of law. The impulse for benefaction, which had distinguished the classical cities, now brought good for the neediest through church charities. Above all, with the conception of the *civitas dei* there was given a fundamental position which was independent of worldly power, and from which the reconstruction of society in later times could be undertaken.[45]

---

45. In relation to section 3 ("City of God and Earthly City [400–550]"), see also: Adams, *Populus of Augustine and Jerome*; Brown, *World of Late Antiquity*; Claude, *Adel, Kirche und Königtum*; Diesner, *Studien zur Gesellschaftslehre*; Duchrow, *Christenheit und Weltverantwortung*; Markus, *Saeculum*; Savramis, *Zur Soziologie*; Seyfarth, *Soziale Fragen*; Steinwenter, "Corpus Iuris"; Vogt, *Kulturwelt und Barbaren*.

3

Synagogue and Church in the Roman Empire

The Insoluble Problem of Toleration

By collating and commenting upon a series of nineteen extracts from ancient sources (in the original, with independent translations), this chapter seeks to understand (I) the increase in Roman regulation of private associations, (II) the ongoing Roman toleration of Jewish customs and communities, and (III) the absence of such toleration for Christian lifestyles and communities. It is an edited version of the 2008 Library Lecture delivered at Moore Theological College in Sydney, and has been previously published (with the same title) in *RTR* 68.1 (2009) 29–45 and again in *Jerusalem and Athens*, 44–57. It appears now with only minor revision.

THE GREEK TERMS SYNAGOGE and *ekklēsia* were ordinary words for a meeting or assembly.[1] They were not cultic terms. Nor do they imply an association, let alone a community. But they have in either case come to do so, and the words also came to refer to the buildings where the community met.

The common ground between synagogue and church has been actively explored in recent decades, with emphasis on how gradual the parting of the ways must have been. But Roman observers seem not to have noticed such a parallel, even though Greek philosophy later understood the intellectual link between Moses and Christ.[2]

Synagogue and church both irritated the Roman state over several centuries, presenting in either case unique problems. From their earliest contact in the second century BC, the Jews enjoyed Roman protection. Yet between AD 66 and 135 they came into violent conflict with Rome three

---

1. Runesson et al., *Ancient Synagogue*; Levine, *Ancient Synagogue*; Berger, "Volksversammlung und Gemeinde Gottes"; Campbell, "Origin and Meaning."

2. Judge, "Judaism and the Rise of Christianity."

times, affecting not only Palestine but Egypt and other provinces. The protection, however, was only reinforced.

The Christians, by contrast, were total pacifists, avoiding conflict if possible. Yet they were given no guaranteed protection, nor even sought it. Across three centuries various attempts were made to break the momentum of their disconcerting growth. No one suggested a solution on Jewish lines.

Neither synagogue nor church fits the pattern of private associations in Roman law. The conditional freedom of these was established as early as 450 BC in no. 8 of the Twelve Tables. But the associations also proved contentious.[3]

I. Why Did Rome Limit Private Associations?

1. Gaius, *Ad legem duodecim tabularum* 4 (*Digesta* 47.22.4) (mid-second c. AD)

> Sodales sunt, qui eiusdem collegii sunt; quam Graeci ἑταιρείαν vocant. His autem *potestatem facit lex pactionem quam velint sibi ferre*, dum ne quid ex publica lege corrumpant.

> Associates are those who are of the same *collegium*, or *hetaireia* in Greek. *The law grants them power to make any rule they like for themselves*, subject to their not infringing any public law.

Gaius, Rome's earliest extant teacher of law, attributes the right of association to Solon, the sixth-century Athenian legislator. They were to have power in effect to make their own by-laws on a contractual basis, as the term *pactio* implies. It would be better translated "compact." Innumerable *sodalitates* across the empire set up stones giving their rules of association, frequency of meetings, and names of members. Neither synagogue nor church did this.

The inscriptions made clear that the associations functioned within legal limits. The government feared political activism. To avoid being taken as *hetaeriae* of this kind, the Christians in Bithynia stopped the predawn meetings they had been holding under oath (*sacramentum*, Pliny, *Ep.* 10.96.7).

---

3. Judge, "On this Rock," reproduced as chapter 6 in the present volume; Cotter, "Collegia and Roman Law"; De Robertis, *Storia delle corporazioni*.

2. *Senatus consultum de Bacchanalibus* 19–22 (186 BC)

Homines *plous V oinvorsei virei atque mulieres* sacra ne quisquam | fecise velet, neve inter ibei virei plous duobus, mulieribus plous tribus | arfuise velent, nisei de pr. urbani senatuosque sententiad, utei suprad | scriptum est.

No-one may choose to perform a sacrifice *with more than five men and women present in all*, a maximum of two men and three women, unless by decision of the urban praetor and senate, as stated above.

In 186 BC Italy was overrun by a mania for the cult of Bacchus. Instead of discreet priestesses celebrating the sacrifice at intervals on an annual cycle, men and women were thronging together frequently after dark, suspected of scandalous liaisons. There seem even to have been structures, since the senate speaks of their destruction.[4]

By permitting only two men to three women the senate no doubt hoped to stop the orgies, while allowing any traditional Roman cult duties to be maintained. The consuls told the senate that the trouble had arisen from using foreign rather than Roman rites. The danger had been that the assemblies of the Roman people could have been upstaged by the new populist movement, the consuls feared (Livy 39.15–17). A Julian law (of Caesar or of Augustus) later required senatorial approval for any new *collegium* (*praeter antiqua et legitima*, Suetonius, *Aug.* 32, cf. *CIL* 6.4416).

3. Augustus, *Res gestae divi Augusti* 9, 18–20 (AD 14)

Privati]m etiam et municipatim *univers[i* | *cives* unanimiter continente]r apud omnia pulvinaria pro vale|‖[tudine mea supplicaverunt]. |

Individually also and by municipalities *the citizens as a whole* unanimously, uninterruptedly and at every shrine for my health did sacrifice.

The serious matter of national solidarity in sacrifice is flourished by Augustus. The sixfold emphasis on the totality of it leaves no room for the slightest deviation or neglect. As normal, *supplicatio* here specifies actual sacrifice; the Greek translation is *ethusan*.

---

4. Pailler, *Bacchanalia*; Gruen, *Studies in Greek Culture*, 34–78.

4. Gaius, *Ad edictum provinciale* 3 (*Digesta* 3.4.1) (mid-second c. AD)

Neque societas neque collegium *neque huiusmodi corpus passim omnibus habere conceditur*: nam et legibus et senatus consultis et principalibus constitutionibus ea res coercetur. paucis admodum in causis concessa sunt huiusmodi corpora: . . . Quibus autem permissum est . . . proprium est ad exemplum rei publicae habere res communes.

No association or collegium *or any other body of this kind is permitted to everyone*, for it is restricted by laws, resolutions of the senate and the determinations of our leaders. For relatively few purposes are bodies of this kind allowed . . . For those to whom it is permitted . . . it is fitting for them to hold their common business on the model of the republic.

A century later than Augustus, Gaius registers the increasing restriction of *collegia*, reinforcing the point that any voluntary body should manage its affairs on the public model.

5. Gaius, *Institutiones* 1.1 (mid-second c. AD)

Quod quisque populus ipse sibi ius constituit, id ipsius proprium est vocaturque ius civile . . . quod vero *naturalis ratio* inter omnes homines constituit, id apud omnes populos peraeque custoditur vocaturque ius gentium.

What each people has determined to be right for itself, that is appropriate for it and is called civil law . . . but what *natural reason* has determined amongst all men, that is maintained equally among all peoples and is called the law of the nations.

Far above even the civil law lies the highest level in this pyramid, the common law of all nations, determined by natural reason itself. This is that rationality which constitutes nature as a whole. It is the *logos* which in Greek thought determines the coherence, perfection, and changeless eternity of the cosmos.

The same force of logic defines it as natural that men should live under law in a constituted state, which takes priority by nature over lesser units, notably the family (Aristotle, *Pol.* 1.1.8–12).

To say that an association should model itself on the republic locks it also into the cosmic whole. But how can a synagogue find a place in such a totalizing structure? The when, where, and why of its origin is unknown, but it clearly first appears under other names. The earliest referred to in Jerusalem is the "synagogue" of the Freedmen (Acts 6:9). The earliest buildings referred to as "synagogues" are those at Capernaum (Luke 7:5) and Corinth (Acts 18:7).

II. Why Were the Synagogues Tolerated?

6. Valerius Maximus, *Facta et dicta memorabilia* 1.3.3 (summary, on 139 BC)

> Chaldaeos igitur Cornelius Hispalus urbe expulit et intra decem dies Italia abire iussit, ne peregrinam scientiam venditarent. Iudaeos quoque, qui *Romanis tradere sacra sua* conati erant, idem Hispalus urbe exterminavit *arasque privatas* e publicis locis abiecit.

> The astrologers therefore Cornelius Hispalus expelled from the city and ordered to leave Italy within ten days, to stop them selling foreign science. The Jews also, who had tried to *pass on their sacrifices to Romans*, the same Hispalus excluded from the city, and removed their *private altars* from public places.

How Jews in particular could have been erecting altars publicly in Rome is a multiple puzzle. If the epitomizer has not botched it, we might conjecture a Hellenizing cult, perhaps sprung from the rededication of the Jerusalem temple in 167 BC to the Olympian Zeus. The Thracian cult of Zeus Sabazius might offer an easier explanation. The epithet Sabazius was taken as akin to Sabaoth or Sabbath, and the cult came under Jewish influence as a result. Either way it was not lawful for foreigners to convert Romans to their cult, as the colonists at Philippi well knew.

7. Acts of the Apostles 16:20–21 (AD 50?)

> Προσαγαγόντες αὐτοὺς τοῖς στρατηγοῖς εἶπαν, οὗτοι οἱ ἄνθρωποι ἐκταράσσουσιν ἡμῶν τὴν πόλιν Ἰουδαῖοι ὑπάρχοντες, καὶ καταγγέλλουσιν ἔθη ἃ *οὐκ ἔξεστιν ἡμῖν παραδέχεσθαι οὐδὲ ποιεῖν* Ῥωμαίοις οὖσιν.

> Bringing them before the praetors, they said, "These people are disturbing our town being Jews, and they are promoting customs *which it is not permitted us to accept* or practice, being Romans".

The same issue may best explain the accusation of the Corinthian Jews that Paul's way of worshiping God was "against the law." Although Gallio declined to intervene on the grounds that this was a matter for their own law, this last phrase shows that the Jews had actually argued that it breached Roman law. They would in any case hardly have sought Roman arbitration on an internal matter. It must surely relate to Paul's non-Jewish converts (many Corinthians, Acts 18:8), whom he urged not to seek circumcision (1 Cor 7:18).

8. *Acts of the Apostles* 18:13–15 (AD 51?)

Παρὰ τὸν νόμον ἀναπείθει οὗτος τοὺς ἀνθρώπους σέβεσθαι τὸν θεόν . . . εἰ δὲ ζητήματά ἐστιν περὶ λόγου καὶ ὀνομάτων καὶ νόμου τοῦ καθ' ὑμᾶς, ὄψεσθε αὐτοί.

It is *against the law* (the way in which) he argues people should worship God . . . if the question is one of definitions, terminology, and the law (that applies) amongst you, see to it yourselves.

The Jewish community *en bloc* (*homothumadon*, Acts 18:12) no doubt objected to any implication that their privileged exemptions from Roman sacrificing might also be applicable to the gentiles now claiming the heritage of Abraham (Rom 4:11). Paul was ready to reply (Acts 18:14), and might have defended himself, from the Roman point of view, in that his not circumcising them avoided that particular breach of Roman law.[5]

Since the original treaty granted to Judas Maccabaeus in 164 BC (Josephus, *A.J.* 12.417–19) Julius Caesar and others had extended its application to the Jews resident in Greek cities (*A.J.* 14.185–267). This remarkable recognition of an ethnic minority in other states that were nominally on equal terms with Rome highlights the privilege available to Jews living in Rome itself.

When Caesar had banned meetings of cult associations (*thiasoi*) in Rome he excepted the Jews (*A.J.* 14.215). All *collegia* were dissolved except old established ones (Suetonius, *Julius* 42.3). Provincial commanders then requested parallel enactments in the individual Greek cities. Their decrees sometimes cite the treaty with Rome as the model for their decision (e.g., Halicarnassus, Josephus, *A.J.* 14.247), or else their own past practice (e.g., Sardis, Josephus, *A.J.* 14.259). The Sardian Jews are granted a building where their "ancestral prayers and sacrifices (*thusias*)" may be offered, along with a

---

5. Winter, "Rehabilitating Gallio."

guarantee of kosher food in the market (Josephus, *A.J.* 14.261), as well as use of their own courts of law (*A.J.* 260).

Since thousands of Jews had been paraded in Pompey's triumph of 61 BC, and sold into slavery at Rome, their descendants would mostly by Paul's day (over a century later) have attained Roman citizenship. The Jewish exemptions had been explicitly provided to those who were at the same time Roman citizens (Josephus, *A.J.* 14.231–32). Gallio's brother, Seneca the philosopher, admired Jews because, unlike Romans, they had kept track of the origin of their rites (*causas ritus sui noverunt*, Augustine, *Civ.* 6.11). We may guess that Gallio's own liberalism led him to insist that the details of such matters were not actionable in a Roman court. Sosthenes, the Jewish leader, was then left to the rough justice of a resentful public, hostile to calumnious prosecution (Acts 18:17).

The temple in Jerusalem received an annual subscription from Jews abroad, expressly permitted by the Romans (Philo, *Legatio* 156–57, 311–16). After its destruction in AD 70, this *fiscus Judaicus* ("Jewish fund") was diverted to the reconstruction of the temple of Jupiter Capitolinus in Rome. Under Domitian it was imposed on people who had dropped out of Judaism and no longer wished to identify as Jews. An old man was stripped in court to see if he was circumcised. Suetonius personally witnessed this humiliation (*Dom.* 12.2). Others were charged with the tax who had never been Jews but chose to live the Jewish lifestyle. People at the highest level were incriminated. After Domitian's assassination the new government of Nerva declared this a calumny, and trumpeted its abolition on a coin.

9. Reverse legend of a sestertius of Nerva (AD 96)

FISCI IVDAICI CALVMNIA SVBLATA S. C.

Jewish tax misrepresentation abolished by resolution of the senate.

The consequences have proved historic. It turned out to be the watershed between Judaism understood as the national cult of the Judeans, a nation with its own homeland and temple, and a new Judaism that has rested on the desire to identify culturally with that now lost tradition. This Judaism has displayed an unmatched feat of continuity. It may be claimed as a major source of that complex shift which moved away from the cultic tradition of one's nation and created the modern sense of "religion." We now mean by that term a self-determined worldview and lifestyle which can be joined (or abandoned) through conversion.[6]

10. Tertullian, *Apologeticum* 18.9 (c. AD 197)

> Sed et Iudaei palam lectitant. Vectigalis libertas; vulgo aditur sabbatis omnibus.

> Even the Jews read (the Scriptures) publicly. Their freedom comes by taxation; they go in crowds every Sabbath.

It soon became apparent that the *fiscus Judaicus* was not so much a penalty for defeat as the safeguard for ongoing liberty of conscience. This must be why Tertullian speaks indignantly of Jewish privilege as "liberty through taxation".

We know from the Edfu ostraca that it was duly collected, and receipts issued, even during the Jewish revolt in Egypt (AD 115–117). The tax agents were themselves Jews. Even though also often Roman citizens, they were exempted from military service because of the idolatry involved in a soldier's oath.

11. Modestinus, *Excusationes* 6, *ap. Dig.* 27.1.15.6 (AD 222–235)

> Αἱ γὰρ διατάξεις ἐκείνοις μόνοις ἀνενοχλήτους αὐτοὺς εἶναι κελεύουσιν, δι' ὧν ἡ θρησκεία χραίνεσθαι δοκεῖ.

> For the rulings order that they should be unencumbered only in respect of those matters by which it seems *their worship would be contaminated*.

At grain distributions in Rome that fell on the Sabbath Augustus reserved their share for the Jews so that they would not lose their entitlement. Ordinary Romans admired and envied the Sabbath routine, while ethicists blamed it as laziness. Privileges once institutionalized are easily maintained, given the way Roman administrative practice was governed largely by the precedents cited by interested parties. The tax was clearly no handicap. Those who could produce a receipt could claim the privileges. The didrachm rate was never increased. It was still being collected in the third century, and possibly even in the fourth.

6. Goodman, "Nerva."

12. *Acta martyrum*, Pionius 13 (AD 251?)

Ἀκούω δὲ ὅτι καί τινας ὑμῶν Ἰουδαῖοι καλοῦσιν εἰς συναγωγάς.

And I hear also that Jews are *inviting* some of you *to synagogues*.

But surely the synagogue authorities also had an interest in listing those who were eligible. The complaint of the martyr Pionius perhaps implies that the Romans by mid-third century simply took it for granted that those whom the synagogue vouched for need not be required to offer the sacrifices. These proved a fateful stumbling-block for Christians. But why did the latter not request a tax license for themselves?

III. Why Were the Churches not Tolerated?

In contrast with the obscurity over the origin of the synagogue, we know quite clearly when, how, and why the churches came into being. Their highly unusual origin is the subject of a near contemporary history which calls itself "The Second *logos* for Theophilus." Its later misnomer, "The Acts of the Apostles," distracts attention from the point in favor of a pseudo-Hellenistic individualized encomium. The purpose of this *logos* is to explain how the gospel of Israel's Messiah came to be detached from Jerusalem and focused instead on the world capital of Rome itself.

We then enter upon a flood of internal documentation of the *Christiani*, as the Romans called them, but precious little from the Roman point of view. This goes also for the great successor to the "*logos* for Theophilus." Eusebius in the early fourth century amassed the documentary evidence for the re-focused movement, now reconciled with Rome, and forward-looking. But it is only an internal history. It must be unique in the discipline of history for us to possess such full and precise evidence for a veritably axial point in world history, yet largely untouched by external evidence.

13. Origen, *Contra Celsum* 1.1 (prior to AD 250)

Ἐπεὶ οὖν τὸν κοινὸν νόμον θρυλεῖ, παρὰ τοῦτον λέγων Χριστιανοῖς τὰς συνθήκας· . . . οὕτως παρ᾽ ἀληθείᾳ δικαζούσῃ οἱ νόμοι τῶν ἐθνῶν, οἱ περὶ ἀγαλμάτων καὶ τῆς ἀθέου πολυθεότητος, νόμοι εἰσὶ Σκυθῶν, καὶ εἴ τι Σκυθῶν ἀσεβέστερον. Οὐκ ἄλογον οὖν συνθήκας *παρὰ τὰ νενομισμένα* ποιεῖν, τὰς ὑπὲρ ἀληθείας.

Since he harps on *the common law*, saying this is infringed by Christians through their associations ... thus judged by (the test of) truth the laws of the nations, about images and godless polytheism, are laws of the Scythians, or whatever is more impious than them. It is not therefore unreasonable to form associations *against the (customary) law*, (when that is done) out of regard for truth.

The most extensive negative treatment survives only in the citations of Origen who aims to refute it. Celsus had written in the latter part of the second century, Origen's reply coming near the mid-third.

By "common law" Celsus is not appealing to our humdrum Anglo-Saxon system, but rather to that high Platonic doctrine of the universal law of reason which undergirds all civil institutions, binding humankind as a whole into a natural unity, "human rights" as we might now say. This unity is breached by the petty Christian associations.

Origen appeals to an even more elusive principle, that of "truth" itself. On this principle polytheism is indeed godless. So although it may be enshrined in custom, to reconstruct one's affairs to avoid it is not irrational (*alogos*, appealing to the same principle of *logos* as Celsus held) when "truth" itself is at stake.

This is the first explicitly attested instance of an appeal to the absolute rectitude of opposition based on personal conviction of what is right. It is now an unquestioned axiom of all Western polity; hence, for example, conscientious objection to military service, or the prosecution of generals for war crimes where they claimed they had been bound by their oath of loyalty.

14. The Formula of the Decian *libelli*, Distilled from Forty-Seven Copies (AD 250)[7]

Τοῖς ἐπὶ τῶν θυσιῶν ἡρημένοις· ἀεὶ θύων τοῖς θεοῖς διετέλεσα καὶ νῦν ἐπὶ παρόντων ὑμῶν κατὰ τὰ προσταχθέντα ἔθυσα καὶ ἔσπεισα καὶ τῶν ἱερείων ἐγευσάμην. ἀξιῶ ὑμᾶς ὑποσημιώσασθαί μοι.

To those selected (to be) over the sacrifices. *Always* have I continued sacrificing to the gods *and now* in your (pl.) presence according to what has been laid down I offered sacrifice, poured (the libation) and tasted the sacred things. I ask you (pl.) to certify below for me.

---

7. This total (47) is updated from the total of 45 *libelli* cited in the original publication of this chapter.

In the Roman world (and even in ours occasionally) the countervailing principle prevails. Whatever is part of inherited custom must be respected as sacred, especially when none of us really believe it any more. This is why cathedrals are precious and must not be touched, or why migrant groups must be praised for keeping up their primeval culture which we nevertheless hold to be misconceived.

Decius, like Augustus (no. 3 above), needed to be certain that everyone was performing their traditional sacrifices; only then will the thousand-year-old city be secure. But it was notorious that people had been neglecting their duty. To avoid conflict Decius has reduced it to the bare essentials. A pinch of incense and a drop of wine will do (you need not provide the sacrificial animal). No particular god is required. There will be no witch-hunt, since everyone simply asserts that they have not been in default.

Decius need not have spotted the crisis this was bound to cause for Christians. They would expose themselves as frauds in having professed loyalty to Christ. You also had actually to taste the sacrificial meat, the very thing bishops held to be physically incompatible with the Holy Communion. Worse, you had to do it in front of publicly appointed local officials who had to sign your petition, "I saw him sacrifice."

Many Christians, especially bishops since they could least afford falling into this trap, simply went into hiding. Others paid the officials to sign even though they had not actually tasted the meat—a de facto kind of "liberty through taxation" for which they might later be excused by their bishop. Perjury and bribery were not so bad as decisively to renounce Christ by tasting the idolatrous sacrifice.

15. *Acta proconsularia Sancti Cypriani*, Musurillo 1.1 (Valerian and Gallienus, AD 257)

> Qui Romanam *religionem* non colunt, debere Romanas *caerimonias* recognoscere.

> Those who do not endorse Roman *cultic usage* must (nevertheless) perform the Roman *ceremonial*.

Seven years later the government offered a sophisticated and classical solution. You no longer needed to perjure yourself nor to conceal your personal commitment (*religio*). It was not intellectual assent to Roman usage that was required, but the mere performance of the set ceremonies. Educated Romans (such as Cicero and many other philosophers) no longer believed personally in particular deities, but the divine element with which the cosmos as a whole was necessarily infused must be respected through customary safeguards. Valerian also dealt with the social reality of the Christian movement. Clergy were exiled (AD 257) and otherwise executed (AD 258). No more synods, no haunting the cemeteries where martyrs lay. Senators were to be downgraded, or if unrepentant deprived of Roman citizenship altogether. Matrons were exiled. Civil servants were sent in chains to the quarries.

16. Eusebius, *Historia ecclesiastica* 7.13.1 (AD 260)

Αὐτοκράτωρ Καῖσαρ Πούπλιος Λικίνιος Γαλλιῆνος . . . Σεβαστὸς Διονυσίῳ καὶ Πίννᾳ καὶ Δημητρίῳ καὶ τοῖς λοιποῖς ἐπισκόποις· τὴν εὐεργεσίαν τῆς ἐμῆς δωρεᾶς διὰ παντὸς τοῦ κόσμου ἐκβιβασθῆναι προσέταξα, ὅπως ἀπὸ τῶν *τόπων* τῶν *θρησκευσίμων* ἀποχωρήσωσιν . . .

Imperator Caesar Publius Licinius Gallienus . . . Augustus to Dionysius and Pinnas and Demetrius and the remaining bishops. The benefit of my concession I have ordered to be applied throughout the world, so that they must vacate those *places* that *relate to worship*.

Gallienus, son of Valerian, revoked all this after his father was captured by the Persians. He restored confiscated property, but the Egyptian bishops sought a ruling on the church buildings which now it seems had no individual owner. They spoke coyly of "places that relate to worship" (*topoi threskeusimoi*), picking up the harmless term used by the Jews in safeguarding synagogue life (no. 11 above). It avoided any identification with the polytheistic sacrificial system that was anathema. The adjectival form of the word *threskeia* is a hapax legomenon. It will not have been devised by Gallienus, but replays the formula supplied by the bishops to bring church life safely under a conventional rubric.

17. Eusebius, *Historia ecclesiastica* 7.30.19 (AD 272)

Βασιλεὺς ἐντευχθεὶς Αὐρηλιανὸς αἰσιώτατα περὶ τοῦ πρακτέου διείληφεν, τούτοις νεῖμαι προστάττων τὸν οἶκον, οἷς ἂν οἱ κατὰ τὴν Ἰταλίαν καὶ τὴν Ῥωμαίων πόλιν ἐπίσκοποι τοῦ *δόγματος* ἐπιστέλλοιεν.

On petition, (our) ruler Aurelian most opportunely settled the matter, prescribing that the house should be allocated to those with whom the bishops of the *doctrine* in Italy and the city of Rome were in correspondence.

Under Aurelian, bishops again appealed to the government over property. Paul of Samosata held the episcopal house at Antioch, running a charismatic movement which he ruled like an imperial procurator (he was in correspondence with Zenobia in Palmyra who had taken control of the Roman East). Seeking to depose him, the bishops of the region put to Aurelian (who was in Syria in AD 272) that their nominee had a prior claim to the church house at Antioch because he was endorsed in writing by the bishops of Rome and Italy. Across the following generation the churches boomed, with Christians entrenching themselves in the established circles of the army and government.

18. *Mosaicarum et Romanarum legum collatio* 15.3.2–3[8] (Diocletian and Maximian, AD 302)

> Maximi enim criminis est retractare quae semel *ab antiquis statuta* et definita suum statum et cursum tenent ac possident. Unde pertinaciam pravae mentis nequissimorum hominum punire ingens nobis studium est: hi enim, qui *novellas et inauditas sectas* veterioribus religionibus obponunt . . .
>
> For it is a very serious crime to revise things once *settled* and defined *by the ancients* that maintain their status and hold to their course. Consequently we are strongly committed to punishing the stubbornness of the perverse minds of evil men; for they, setting up *novel and unheard-of causes* against old-established obligations . . .

By contrast, the newfangled Manichaean missionaries, recently working their way westwards through the Mediterranean from their home base in Mesopotamia, provoked total rejection by Diocletian in AD 302. They were alien intruders, from across the iron curtain of the Roman Middle East. Mani had died only within living memory, and Diocletian had presumably not been told that he had presented himself on Pauline lines as an "apostle of Jesus Christ."

Diocletian's tirade was nevertheless ominous for the older denominations of this faith. After two and a half centuries they were hardly any longer an unfamiliar presence at home. In the Eastern Roman capital,

---

8. Riccobono et al., *FIRA*, 580.

Nicomedia (below the Bosporus), there was now even a central and conspicuous church building.

A year after the Manichaean edict this was suddenly demolished on imperial command. Valerian's policy of the disestablishment of the churches was nationally reinstated and pursued with several spurts of particular energy across the next decade. For the first time we find (in P.Oxy. 33.2673 of AD 304) the term *ekklēsia* applied officially to a church building. It is only now that we find Eusebius from the Christian side also using the word that way.

19. Lactantius, *De mortibus persecutorum* 34.2, 5 (Galerius, AD 311)

... ut etiam Christiani, qui parentum suorum reliquerant sectam, ad bonas mentes redirent, siquidem quadam ratione tanta eosdem Christianos voluntas invasisset et tanta stultitia occupasset, ut non illa veterum instituta sequerentur, quae forsitan primum parentes eorundem constituerant, sed pro arbitrio suo atque ut isdem erat libitum, ita *sibimet leges facerent* quas observarent, et *per diversa varios populos congregarent* . . . debebunt deum suum *orare* pro salute nostra et rei publicae ac sua . . .

. . . so that even the Christians, who had abandoned the cause of their parents, might return to a sound mind, given that such willfulness and stupidity had seized the same Christians, that they were not following those customs of their elders which perhaps their own ancestors had instituted in the beginning, but on their own discretion and as it appealed to them, they *made up laws for themselves* to keep, and *on divergent principles formed alternative communities* . . . they will be obliged to *plead* with their god for our safety and that of the republic and their own.

Lactantius claimed that the driving force behind the campaign of Diocletian was his deputy and successor, Galerius. On the latter's own death-bed he issued an order that was to solve the problem of the churches in an entirely novel way.

Down to this point there has remained no direct evidence from the government side of what was allegedly wrong with the Christians. Even Pliny's famous letter (*Ep.* 10.96) of AD 112 had only dealt with practicalities, taking the problem itself for granted. Eusebius for his part omits the rulings that tackled it head-on, giving us only those that reversed them.

But from Diocletian's complaint against the Manichees, and from the recantation of Galerius, we can see what was the insoluble problem with toleration. Galerius is presented by Lactantius as a monster. The first serious biographical appraisal of him is only now about to appear.[9] But he deserves a greater place in history as the one who (so far as our sources go) was the first to lay down a policy on the general toleration of social dissidents.

IV. Insoluble Toleration

Galerius formulated the essence of the problem. The Christians did not follow the customs of their own ancestors. This may sound banal in a world that has wholly abandoned the classic cosmology of the Greeks. We do not now see the universe as a perfect system where any appearance of change is only the endlessly repeated cycle of the unchanging whole. Modern science has only been built up through the experimental method validated and liberated by Genesis. Everyone now assumes there was a beginning, that every individual on earth is unique, and that we are yet ourselves answerable for the problems of the whole. Far from accepting that it is necessarily right to hold to the customs of our ancestors, we echo to the gospel promise that the old has passed away, and all things will be made new.

For Galerius, however, it was unthinkable that people should assume they might "make up laws for themselves to keep," and "form alternative communities on divergent principles." I am the only modern translator to render his words this way. Most simply say it means the Christians "formed various congregations in diverse places." They fall into the trap Latin sets for us: English has taken up the Latin terms, but the nuances shift. Even language is no longer immutable! Galerius can hardly have uttered anything so beside the point unless one thinks him more stupid even than Lactantius did. The phrase must be declaring what is wrong with making up laws for oneself. This was indeed how Eusebius understood it when he translated it into Greek (*Hist. eccl.* 8.17). The Latin text was only retrieved in quite modern times. Prior to that, in AD 1659, Valesius translated the Greek of Eusebius back into Latin in much the same sense as I apply to it.[10]

Galerius is well informed about Christians. He perhaps knew that *diversitas* ("divergence") was a term current with them (for the deviancy of heretics). He surely knew that *orare* was their distinctive term for prayer. In classical culture, prayer was a matter of begging or of contract (the vow). For the Christians prayer was "pleading," that is advocacy (as in law)

---

9. Leadbetter, *Galerius*.

10. Judge, "Diversity," reproduced as chapter 1 in the present volume.

or intercession. One "pleaded," typically on behalf of someone else, in a speech (*oratio*). Galerius has picked up this term, and asks the Christians to "plead" for him. They of course had been protesting all along that this was what they did. In particular, they had regularly been pleading for their earthly rulers, and only refused the contractual sacrifices because they were a blasphemy against divine truth.

Why were the synagogues tolerated? Because they had been a national institution. Classical thought held the republican state to have a priority by nature over its constituent parts, and within a national tradition the definitive truth had been laid down in the past. Detested though the Jews often were as aliens, they were nevertheless respected for their tenacious and articulated grip on their national heritage. The great military struggles against Rome confirmed the national status of the Jews. In defeat they were given a recognized place in the multi-national empire, their distinctive culture carefully safeguarded by a tax.

Why were the churches not tolerated? Because they were Roman, not part of a separate nation. They failed to uphold their national heritage. The churches had no place in the regular structure of the nation. To some extent they even provocatively parodied its pattern in structures of their own. The more this became apparent, the worse the threat to public order. The Christians seemed to be treating themselves as a new nation, within and against their own.

History offers no solution to the problem of toleration. Popper's "Open Society" was the twentieth-century answer to totalization whether messianic or Platonic (based that is on race or class). We may talk of freedom in a self-determined culture, but culture is carried by a shared language, and embedded in language are national values. Openness and values pull against each other. Both may be retrograde. Openness may break down into hostile tribalism. National values may retreat into nostalgic conformity. The dynamic progress of the West, for better or worse, is driven by the tension between the two as internalized within the minds of each of us. Our classical heritage (including its ecclesiastical adaptation) ties us to established order, but the gospel calls us to an open-ended future which we should anticipate now. Living in two worlds at once is our existential predicament. But trying to live in only one is a dangerous risk.

4

Group Religions in the Roman Empire

This review of J. Rüpke, ed. *Gruppenreligionen im römischen Reich*, a collection of papers by various contributors on "group religions" in the Roman world, was published first in *JAC* 51 (2008) and then reproduced (with modification) in Judge, *Jerusalem and Athens*, 32–43. Here Judge contends that the category of "group religions" is ill-conceived, and that the various successes and failures of the essays contained in Rüpke's collection demonstrate the inadequacy of the paradigms it employs. In doing so he comments on the merits of each individual piece, especially the contributions of Cancik, but also addresses the history of the (modern) concept of "religion," the recognition at the time that early Christian communities resembled philosophical schools more than cult-groups, and the significance of dogmatic truth for the way Christianity engaged with the Roman state. The present reproduction follows the modified version (from *Jerusalem and Athens*) with only minor revisions.

WHAT IS THE TERM "Gruppenreligionen" meant to suggest? For the Roman imperial period, Jörg Rüpke explains, the "classic question" of *Religionswissenschaft* over the "social forms of religion" has not been very effectively tackled by such classifications as "church" and "sect."[1] Even the term "cult" leaves open the question of what social formation might attach to the omnipresent sacral rituals.

Rüpke also means to avoid the old trap of positing a type of "oriental" or "mystery" religion that has been thought to have offered both personal salvation and a new community life. Likewise, the terms *collegium* or

---

1. Rüpke, *Gruppenreligionen im römischen Reich*, 1.

"association" have come to imply a lawful constitution that cannot in fact be substantiated. Instead, Rüpke hopes to use the sociological concept of the "group" to cover various phenomena without further classificatory regulation. Yet a strictly comparative study is also to be avoided.

But what are these groups? In his particular contribution to this collection, Rüpke cites his own earlier definition: A "group" is "a delimited number of people communicating with and thus influencing each other; such a social process (*Gemeinschaftshandeln*) involves a minimum of regulation and continuity."[2] (No doubt "minimum" here means "at least a little," rather than "as little as possible.")

As for "Gruppenreligionen," they are also to be taken as a given.[3] They appear as a "self-evident variant (*Spielart*) in the religious landscape of ancient cities." Hence the question of their relation to other forms of religious institutionalization with which they may come into conflict in a great city of the second to fourth centuries. The sub-title of the book is *Sozialformen, Grenzziehungen und Leistungen* ("Social Forms, Boundary-markers, and their Contribution"), while Rüpke's own article is entitled "Integrationsgeschichten: Gruppenreligionen in Rom."[4]

Observing certain details of five "cults" (so classified for this purpose),[5] namely Mithraism, the cults of Sol and of Jupiter Dolichenus, Christianity, and "Gebaute Religion" (the public temples), Rüpke distills five more general theses for future discussion:[6]

1. The groups cannot be shown to have followed any sustained calendrical timetable of their own (did the Christian reference to the Sabbath/Sunday, Rüpke asks, in fact reflect a "sociological reality"?).

2. The religious groups aim at integrating themselves into the structure of public religion (a competitive situation is implied, with *religio licita* referring not to a legal category but to the opportune and temporary success of a group).

3. New migrants die younger and had not been the primary leaders in their community of origin, so immigrant groups are very fluid in content and structure, quickly adapting to the ranking system of the host society.

---

2. Rüpke, *Gruppenreligionen im römischen Reich*, 113.
3. Rüpke, *Gruppenreligionen im römischen Reich*, 113
4. Rüpke, *Gruppenreligionen im römischen Reich*, 113–26.
5. Rüpke, *Gruppenreligionen im römischen Reich*, 118, 121.
6. Rüpke, *Gruppenreligionen im römischen Reich*, 122–23.

4. It is groups more than organizations that we see, hence the instability of their rapidly changing institutional forms, with the attractiveness of overlapping institutions perhaps pointing to group instability rather than organizational strength.

5. In public the groups are often seen only incidentally, for example in processions, without the permanency of prominent buildings, but it is not clear whether this lack reduces conflict or only provokes suspicion (how can a cult have no image of the divinity?).

The air of questing uncertainty which pervades these very condensed proposals must surely be deliberate. It matches the approach Rüpke has already adopted in his introduction, reviewing the contributions of his collaborators.[7] But before I comment on the historical shortcomings of setting such low-level sociological horizons, it is essential to recognize its place in the monumental enterprise to which Rüpke is committed.

I. Imperial and Provincial Religion

In his current position at Erfurt, Rüpke is responsible by professorial title for the study of comparative religion. While previously at Potsdam, he had already in 1996, with his senior colleague H. Cancik (then at Tübingen, now in Berlin), presided over an international and interdisciplinary conference sponsored by the Werner-Reimers-Stiftung (Bad Homburg) on *Reichsreligion und Provinzialreligion*. One purpose was "to clarify the concepts, methods and issues for further work in this area, and to find the criteria by which the place taken by Christianity in the multi-dimensional field of ancient religions can be determined."[8]

The book of this conference then lent its title to an elite "priority program" (*Schwerpunktprogramm*) of the national research funding body (Deutsche Forschungsgemeinschaft, henceforth "DFG"). A subtitle indicated a focal point different from that identified in the preface to the Bad Homburg volume: *Globalisierungs-und Regionalisierungsprozesse in der antiken Religionsgeschichte*. The website of the DFG program, coordinated from Erfurt by Rüpke, identified as its principal stimulus the analogous modern phenomena of colonization, Europeanization, and globalization. No reference is made to the place (if any) of religion in the modern processes, except by reference to their "fruitful tension" with the concept of imperial religion in the title of the program.

---

7. Rüpke, *Gruppenreligionen im römischen Reich*, 1–6.
8. Cancik and Rüpke, *Römische Reichsreligion und Provinzialreligion*, iii.

By the year 2000 alone twenty-two projects had been accepted into the program, giving it the scale of a "special research area" (*Sonderforschungsbereich*) under the DFG. In a national drive for research excellence that is geared to the natural sciences, this represents surely a unique achievement, both in the disciplinary field and in its geographically devolved character.

Ancient historians worldwide recognize the very substantial contributions to Roman antiquities both of H. Cancik (*Der neue Pauly*) and of Rüpke as DFG coordinator (*Kalender und Öffentlichkeit*, 1995; *Fasti sacerdotum*, 2005). Now this massive harnessing of German forces is delivering a great surge of strength in our field, strong also in its international collaboration. But amidst all its successes the present volume confronts us with a problem of definition common to ancient historians in general. It has already been faced in the DFG-sponsored symposium (at Eisenach in 2003) and recognized by Cancik and Rüpke alike in their contributions to the published papers.[9] It is the problem of a definition for antiquity of the term "religion" itself.

Concluding his study of "universal and local religion" in Tertullian and Minucius Felix, Rüpke states that their use of Varro's *Antiquitates rerum divinarum* (lost to us apart from such citations) might give the impression that Varro worked with our conception of religion classified as to its city, provincial or imperial frame of reference. But such an impression is illusory, Rüpke says. There is no such conceptual reflection to set alongside the new offer of a universal religion presented by the Christian writers. This indeed points to the heart of our misunderstanding.

II. The Definition of "Religion"

The modern sense of "religion" as "the quest for . . . the ideal life, [its] practices . . . and . . . world view"[10] developed only with the penetration of the Roman world by Christian belief and experience. The *Oxford Latin Dictionary*, confined to sources down to AD 200 (the time of Tertullian and Minucius Felix but excluding them), offers a tenfold definition of *religio*, which may be distilled in the following terms: "taboo," "scruple," "impediment," "sanction," "principle," "awe," "sanctity," "ritual," "cult," "punctilio."[11]

---

9 Cancik, "Wahrnehmung, Vermeidung, Entheiligung, Aneignung," 231; Rüpke, "Literarische Darstellungen," 221.

10. Delbridge, *Macquarie Dictionary*, 1486.

11. Glare, *Oxford Latin Dictionary*, 7:1605–6. Editor's note: The definition in question was published in fascicle 7 of the *OLD* in 1980, and republished in the single-volume *OLD* edition of 1982, at 1605–6.

The classification of a series of alternative "religions" arose only in the early seventeenth century when "paganism" and "Mohammedanism" were seen to stand in sequence with Judaism and Christianity.[12] It had been the proposal of W. Cantwell Smith that the first religion in the modern sense (i.e., of a movement operating internationally and offering an alternative lifestyle to that of any national community) was third-century Manichaeism.[13] But Mani saw himself as "apostle of Jesus Christ", and the phenomenon he represents is manifested by the Christian movement as a whole from the beginning. In Mani's own day, the boast of his Zoroastrian persecutor, Kirtir (or Karder), seems already to presume a sequence of rival religions: Jews, Buddhists, Brahmans, Nasoreans, Christians, Maktaks (Mandaeans, Manichaeans?), and Zandiks (Mazdaean heretics?).[14]

Our problem however arises not from the difficulty of defining the history of what we now mean by "religion," but from the arbitrary yet (in spite of Cantwell Smith) now almost unshakeable convention of applying that indiscriminately as a primary categorization of what we judge to be religion in pre-Christian times or cultures. Yet everyone knows that neither Greek nor Latin (nor other national languages presumably, such as Hindi) had any such term, nor any other generic category for the cultural phenomena we now aggregate under that heading.[15]

Julian the Apostate, having been brought up as a Christian, baffled his fourth-century admirers by attempting to compel Hellenism itself to imitate the self-consciously didactic and interventionist practice of those he put down as "Galileans." It is a striking if tacit indication of this incomprehension that Ammianus Marcellinus, though repeatedly attempting to characterize the Christians in this very epoch, and in general sympathetic to Julian, cannot see any link or parallel between them and Julian's religion of Hellenism, as we might put it. The distinctive terminology of the classical cults is never used by Ammianus with reference to Christians. The latter have no *deus*, no *templum*, no *sacra*.[16]

Those who work under the modern rubric of "Religion" are of course well aware of the conceptual incoherence of their discipline.[17] Everyone

12. Feil, *Religio*; Harrison, *'Religion' and the Religions*; Taylor, *Critical Terms*.
13. Cantwell Smith, *Meaning and End*.
14. Boyce, *Textual Sources*.
15. Judge, "Did the Churches Compete with Cult-groups?"; Oddie, *Imagined Hinduism*, 68–83.
16. Judge, "Absence of Religion," reproduced as chapter 9 below.
17. Rüpke, *Companion to Roman Religion*, 6; Rives, *Religion in the Roman Empire* 4–7 (esp. 5, "fundamentally misleading"), 13–14; Davies, *Rome's Religious History*, 7; Feeney, *Literature and Religion at Rome*, 12–13; Saler, *Conceptualizing Religion*, on the

understands (or should do) that this is not a universal anthropological category of human behavior (such as marriage, or language), but that its modern invention as a construct, presumed to apply universally, has arisen from the sharpening of the missionary character of Christianity with the Reformation and the opening of the rest of the world to European navigation. It is ironic that in the Rüpke handbook, C. R. Phillips III blames the Lutheran cause for saddling the ancient religion of Rome with the ritualism of its Catholic successor.[18] Such a reaction against Luther, not unfashionable in American religious studies, overlooks the origin of our concept of religion. It also misses the crucial place of dogmatic controversy in creating the modern discipline of History itself.[19] This no longer turns on the rhetorical presentation of the past as a guide to policy, but puts the truth of a matter to the test by appeal to its primary sources.

An unresolved dilemma over how we are to understand the world has likewise generated the modern concept of religion. Religion is now a source of authority that may be set against the civil order. The prophet speaks for God against the king. The gospel is for all nations. The old is only temporary, until the new comes in. Instead of a perfect and therefore unchanging cosmos, we look to the challenge of an open future. It will be different. We must see things changed.[20]

III. Christianity and Roman Religion

Why did it not occur to the Roman state over 250 years to accommodate Christianity within the time-honored variety of the classical cults? Because it was precisely that which the Christians threatened to destroy. They claimed as their own the intellectual heritage of Israel. The divinization of the natural order, expressed in idolatry, was anathema. True, the church fathers drew upon the sacrificial cult of Israel, using its priesthood as a metaphor of the teaching ministry in church life. But the high doctrine of creation, radically distinguishing the cosmos from its maker, who would bring it to its end, remained intact. Once this too was freed from symbolic interpretation in the classicizing mode, and the world taken literally as an artefact, the path was opened for experimental science, and an evolving

---

anthropology of the matter.

18. Phillips, "Approaching Roman Religion," 18.

19. Pocock, "Origins of the Study of the Past"; Momigliano, *Conflict*, 149, refers to "the Eusebian form . . . brought back in full force by the Reformation."

20. Kinzig, *Novitas Christiana*; Stroumsa, *Barbarian Philosophy*.

universe.[21] Likewise for proof from evidence in history, and for religion as an alternative order of society.

The term *christianoi* brands the believers as partisans, while *christianismos* marks off their culture as a whole from *ioudaismos* and *hellenismos* alike. All three traditions are carried by their own canonical literature, driven by an elaborate scholarly enterprise, as they explain and propagate their positions. In this fundamental characteristic the Christian project is not at all similar to the classical cults. The better analogy within the classical tradition is with the philosophical schools, as was noticed on all sides by the second century. Yet the closest comparison in that case, with the Epicureans, shows how considerable the difference still is, particularly in social terms. Given that the modern concept of religion is defined by a combination of features essentially unique to Christianity, it is in effect a category mistake to impose the term upon other ancient phenomena.

This may explain the frustration of C. R. Phillips III. Arguing for "a comprehensive history of the study of Roman religion," he advocates looking for "interpretive guidelines and comparative information from disciplines such as anthropology, religion studies, sociology."[22] But he seems unable to explain why their "various theoretical guidelines" have left us now "less sure than ever what Roman 'religion' is."[23] He has repeatedly dismissed the "empirico-positivist" concerns of classical studies. But, if the search for "the whole" has failed to discover what that might be, clearly it is time to go back to the texts and check again what they say. Often, of course, that will be nothing at all beyond the immediate particulars that are detailed. Not so, however, our translations, which habitually import the term "religion" that our own minds call for. Anachronism is the historian's version of this paradox of hermeneutics.

The assumption of a universal category of "religion" seems to be one of two reasons for keeping the term.[24] The other is the desire to avoid the confessional implications of the word "theology" (in the name of an academic department, for example). But, since the modern sense of "religion" is determined by the distinctive theology of Christians anyway, this covert evasion risks being charged with bad faith. *Theologia*, moreover, unlike *religio*, is a regular term of classical philosophy for academic discourse on the divine. In any case it is essential for non-confessional students to examine the momentum of theology if they are to gain a realistic understanding of

---

21. Harrison, *Bible*.
22. Phillips, "Approaching Roman Religion," 10–11.
23. Phillips, "Approaching Roman Religion," 26.
24. Cf. Pearson, *Emergence of the Christian Religion*.

the phenomenon of religion. There are various ways of providing for this, as well as alternative terms, such as "ideology" or "mentality."[25]

The current fashion for deprecating Christian "triumphalism" risks missing the historic significance of the conversion of Rome. According to the great historian of historiography, Arnaldo Momigliano, the son of Israel, we are all heirs to this.[26] In the work reviewed here, Rüpke has adopted a scattered approach, setting his own essay on "Integrationsgeschichten" midway between three on early Christian topics and three on classical cults.[27] It is not however his intention to develop this contrast, though he is well aware of it. Rather he means to link Christian and classical cases as examples of his category of *Gruppenreligionen*. The central question (amongst a diverse array of others) is how *Gruppenreligionen* (i.e., those functioning from place to place as part of a chain of groups with a common identity) interacted with the civic cults of a particular place.[28] In Rüpke's article this place is the city of Rome itself, and he treats both Christianity and certain of the classical cults. But the three preceding articles on Christian topics are not mainly concerned with Rome, while the following three discuss different cults in three different provincial settings. Thus the whole collection, while rich in detail from case to case, leaves the big questions hanging.

Even the meaning of *Gruppe* is put seriously in doubt when we find the opening article (by C. Schultz) devoted to "The Social Classification and Religious Practice of Women in the Roman Republic."[29] Rüpke states that in it "the concept of *Gruppenreligionen* enables us to see the complexity of traditional religion even within the structures of public cults."[30] In a carefully documented study, Schultz demonstrates that women's participation in cult practices (where required or permitted) was conditioned by social class and wealth in much the same way as men's, except that high personal reputation and probity were sometimes explicitly required. But for women to constitute a "group" for the purposes of this collection they were supposed

---

25. Theissen, *Die Religion der ersten Christen*; Markschies, *Zwischen den Welten wandern*; Schneider, *Geistesgeschichte des antiken Christentums*.

26. Brown, "Arnaldo Dante Momigliano," 414, translates Momigliano (from the Italian), "No fully self-aware historian of the ancient world ... can get away with the refusal to recognise that ancient history only makes sense when it is seen to evolve in such a way as to end naturally in the rise of Christianity."

27. Rüpke, "Integrationsgeschichten," 113–26.

28. Rüpke, *Gruppenreligionen im römischen Reich*, 2–3.

29. Schultz, "*Sanctissima Femina*," 7–29.

30. Rüpke, *Gruppenreligionen im römischen Reich*, 3.

to be "communicating with and thus influencing each other."[31] Was there no women's movement at that time?

IV. The Contribution of Hubert Cancik

H. Cancik follows with what is in effect a stimulating test of the main theme of the collection. He writes on the organization of "foreign religion" in Rome, first to third c. AD.[32] Disclaiming any sociological system, he looks for group formation under household, school, and association (*conlegium*).[33] In each of these three forms the case of the Christians is discussed separately. The household is counted as a group by nature. In addition to its biological, economic, and juristic functions it has a "religious" one. The head sacrifices daily to its guardian spirit (*lar*) before whom even the peasants on the estate are fed (Columella, *Agr.* 11.1.19). But the imperial calendar of sacrifice must also be observed (challenging for a Christian wife).

This in effect extends the definition of a group to any human society. But Cancik looks to more individually determined cultic practice that a household might take in. Cicero (*Sen.* 45) has Cato turn his dining routine into a club (*sodalitas*) in honor of the Great Mother of Phrygia, whose cult was introduced to Rome during his quaestorship of 204 BC. Ovid (*Pont.* 4.9.105-112) fitted out his house of exile as a shrine of the divinized Caesars. Within a year of the death of Augustus all the (leading) houses of Rome organized worshipers of him "on the model of the *collegia*" (Tac. *Ann.* 1.43). From Torre Nova outside Rome under Marcus Aurelius comes the Dionysiac cult-group of 411 initiates within a major senatorial family (*IGUR* 1.160). Yet in each of these cases the initiative is wholly within the domain of the household head.

As in Caesarea (Acts 10:24, 11:14), Philippi (Acts 16:34), and Rome itself (Rom 16:5, 10, 11), conversion to Christ might begin with house-based groups. Four generations later (under Commodus) "whole households and families" are said to have been converted amongst the "rich and famous" of Rome (Eusebius, *Hist. eccl.* 5.21). Several of the parishes there go back to family foundations prior to Constantine. Cancik sees no evidence that this unit of development was conceived in Roman law as a private association (*collegium*).

A house, however, was normally needed to provide the base for a school, Cancik's second type of group. But he finds no evidence for an

31. Rüpke, "Integrationsgeschichten," 113.
32. Cancik, "Haus, Schule, Gemeinde."
33. Cancik, "Haus, Schule, Gemeinde," 32.

ongoing philosophical school in Rome (prior to the second century, no doubt?). Little as we know of school routine, it was not surely linked with the sacral system. Temples were not schools, teachers not priests. But education embraced mythology and ethics through the study of literature. It was only Julian who thought of subjecting this to a confessional test.[34]

Paul had listed teaching amongst the ministries in church (1 Cor 12:28). During his final two years in Rome he kept open house in premises large enough to accommodate anyone who wished to hear his teaching (Acts 28:30–31). Cancik had already stressed Cicero's frequent hospitality to visiting philosophers.[35] He now suggests, however, that the self-consciously philosophizing stance of Christian teachers in Rome "could not have been foreseen."[36] He is referring of course to the presentation of Valentinus, Heracleon, and Marcion as philosophers in the second century, and sees the third century Neoplatonic school of Plotinus as matching that.[37] But at the same time the multiplicity of Christian schools and teachers, along with the house-churches, was being sidelined by the Catholicism which was soon to win privilege and public financial support. Led by bishops claiming orthodoxy, it drew strength also from organized charity.

Cancik's first two "groups" stretch Rüpke's definition, but in largely also sidestepping the theoretical tangles created by the historically ambiguous category of "religion," he makes telling gains in realism. Yet one should not underestimate the phenomenon of orthodoxy itself as a force in cultural development. On the one hand history often shows how a church that identifies too closely with its national culture may come to function like an ancient cult-group, merely underwriting conventional values, conservative and backward-looking. On the other hand, Catholicism in particular has demonstrated time and again how the entrenchment of orthodoxy still preserves the prophetic voice and strongly didactic mission that can break out into new life.

Cancik's third form of socialization, the "community" (*Gemeinde*), more neatly fits the category of *Gruppenreligionen*. He sees in the second-century Isis-cult at Cenchreae and Rome, as presented by Apuleius, an anticipation of much subsequent Christian practice. The cult procession, for example, clearly marked off clergy from laity. This Isiac fashion, unlike that of the oldest mysteries, reflected a local society complete, it seems, with pastoral care by "priests." Cancik cites evidence which leads him to

---

34. Cancik, "Haus, Schule, Gemeinde," 39n54.
35. Cancik, "Haus, Schule, Gemeinde," 38.
36. Cancik, "Haus, Schule, Gemeinde," 40.
37. Cancik, "Haus, Schule, Gemeinde," 41.

believe similar developments were occurring with the cults of Mithras, the Great Mother, and Hercules. I have concurrently made a case against such a view.[38] But Cancik is able to develop in that direction the contemporary allegation that the Mithras cult was merely imitating the Eucharist.[39] Only a monotheist of course would have been upset by such a parallel.

Tertullian's calculated use of technical terms suggestive of the Roman law of associations (*collegia*) sharpens his point that the Christians had never been so classified. Indeed it is precisely this point which gives force to Tertullian's provocative assertion that, far from being localized, they have occupied every place and institution. Their only *res publica* is the world.[40]

Cancik thus concludes that, while house, school, and community all offered a private framework for various groups, only the Christians carried this forward into an imperial or worldwide movement. They do not fit the ancient *Religionsmodell*.[41] But this persuasively demonstrated result puts the "model" itself in question. Cancik has needlessly tied his case to the framework of his previous very impressive analysis of the ancient historiography of culture.[42] There he approached the dual *logoi* of Luke as the history of an institution, namely the *ekklēsia*, and sought a pattern for it in a section on "The Historiography of Religion from Herodotus to Lucian."[43]

But Luke nowhere explains his belated and hardly extensive use of the term *ekklēsia*. It does not occur at all in the first *logos* (contrast Matthew 16:18; 18:17). The preface there, which covers both *logoi*, addressed to a well instructed reader, clearly identifies the theme as "an orderly account of the *pragmata* accomplished among us, as handed down by those who from the outset were eyewitnesses and servants of the *logos*" (Luke 1:1–4). In Acts as well this master-*logos* is frequently identified as "the word of God," "the word of the Lord," or (once, Acts 15:7) "of the gospel." The *ekklēsia* is indeed multiplied (Acts 9:31, Cancik's key text) but so is "the word of the Lord" (Acts 12:24). The whole of the second *logos* is structured around set speeches which show the origin and growth of this very particular *logos*, as it is led across entrenched cultural borders to culminate in the unrestricted preaching of the kingdom of God in the imperial capital (Acts 28:31, cf. 1:1–3).

---

38. Judge, "Kultgemeinde," 402–5; cf. Judge, "On this Rock," (at 629–33), reproduced as chapter 6 in the present volume. See especially pages 68–72 below.

39. Justin, *Apol.* 1.66.

40. Tertullian, *Apol.* 37–39, esp. 38.3, 39.1.

41. Cancik, "Haus, Schule, Gemeinde," 46.

42. Cancik. "The History of Culture."

43. Cancik, "The History of Culture," 682.

In spite of Cancik's interesting attempt to establish a genre of the historiography of religion, the treatment within it of Lucian especially points rather to the next genre he establishes, "The Historiography of Philosophy from Dicaearchus to Cicero."[44] This is where both Luke and Eusebius belong. The central problem with the category "religion" for the ancient world is that it fails to account for the massive and relentless drive for dogmatic truth which surely lies behind all the social and cultic apparatus of the church tradition it generated. It is the preaching of the word that has created the church, and that builds it up. The central gifts of the Holy Spirit are mediated orally. As the term *logos* requires, the worship of God is rational (Rom 12:1), leading to social transformation (12:2). This is why Jewish observers spoke of the school (*hairesis*, Acts 24:5; 28:22) of the *Nazoraioi*, parallel with Sadducees (5:17) and Pharisees (15:5), amongst the "philosophies" of Judaism as Josephus puts it.[45]

V. New Testament Churches and Classical Cults

In "Boundary Markers in Early Christianity" James Dunn treats the key practices (circumcision, food laws) that set Jewish identity apart, themselves sometimes less rigid than intended; the arguments within Christian groups over them; and the other Jewish principles that Christians inherited as non-negotiable (monotheism, strict sexual morality) together with their new markers (belief in Christ, spiritual gifts, baptism and the Lord's supper).[46] In passing he refers to "the new religion" but without turning to the implications of this phrase.[47]

M. Bachmann treats the peculiarly Pauline concept "works of the law," especially in respect of its reception across the following two centuries, and beyond.[48] Examining the formulaic characteristics of the expression, he finds that the Augustinian tradition of both Protestant and Catholic exegesis is partly anticipated in taking "works of the law" to refer to "concerns over religious performance."[49] But the so-called "new perspective" is also to a certain extent anticipated in taking the "works" rather as corporate "boundary markers."[50] As for the prior history of the Pauline formula, Bachmann sees

44. Cancik, "History of Culture," 687.
45. Josephus, *A.J.* 18.1.2.11.
46. Dunn, "Boundary Markers."
47. Dunn, "Boundary Markers," 61.
48. Bachmann, "Zur Rezeptions-und Traditionsgeschichte."
49. Bachmann, "Zur Rezeptions-und Traditionsgeschichte," 80.
50. Bachmann, "Zur Rezeptions-und Traditionsgeschichte," 81.

the recently identified phrase from Qumran, "Some of the precepts of the Torah" (4QMMT C27), as remarkably close, though inverted by Paul for the purpose of including gentiles within the corporate boundary.[51]

J. Woyke treats the demonizing of other cults ("polylatric monotheism") in Paul's argument over eating meat offered to idols (1 Cor 8 and 10).[52] The rational accommodation of 1 Cor 8:4-6 (the many so-called "gods" do not in fact compromise the one God and Lord) reflects Stoic popular philosophy mediated through Hellenistic Judaism, so that the identity-marker need not be itself a boundary-marker.[53] But Paul's demonization of the other cults (1 Cor 10:19-21) brings out the contradiction.

The detailed and subtle philological analysis in the three New Testament papers only highlights the basic difference between the classical cults and the Christian tradition. The latter is essentially a philosophical movement, pursued through argumentation and recorded in books. But the former are essentially procedural, documenting their routine in monuments. The remaining three papers turn upon the inscriptions and buildings of three different cults in three different provincial regions: Mithras on the Western rivers as at Mainz, Strasburg, Lyons, and Vienne; Dionysus in Asia Minor and in Dacia; Saturn in Roman Africa.

W. Spickermann ("Mystery Communities and the Public") argues that in Roman Germany and Gaul the cult of Mithras (as also with Cybele and Isis) did not stand aside from established local practice, but interacted with it.[54] Mithras in particular is frequently linked with other cults, especially that of Mercury. Yet Mithraism remained exclusive of women, reflecting its military origin. Spickermann's scenario is documented extensively with recent discoveries and fresh interpretations of the archaeological data, above all for Mainz which he sees as a centerpoint for the public promotion of the main mystery cults. The integrating impulse was no doubt the imperial cult itself.

A. Schäfer ("Dionysiac Groups as an Urban Phenomenon") similarly explores the private/public nexus.[55] At Ephesus the exceptionally large residence of C. Flavius Furius Aptus catered for the cult of Dionysus "before the city." The son of this family of asiarchs became a Roman senator. The house was expanded for hospitality. Various inscriptions of Ephesus attest the non-urban ethos of Dionysiac groups, yet the very existence of the

---

51. Bachmann, "Zur Rezeptions-und Traditionsgeschichte," 84.
52. Woyke, "Depontenzierung und Tabuisierung."
53. Woyke, "Depontenzierung und Tabuisierung," 98.
54. Spickermann, "Die Integration von Mysterienkulten."
55. Schäfer, "Dionysische Kultlokale."

documents implies their integration into the public scene. Similar questions are explored over the excavation of the Dionysiac sanctuary of Liber Pater at Dacian Apulum, where the author himself has been working.

G. Schörner ("The Cult of Saturn as a Group Religion") takes up the question, stimulated by the rarity of Mithraic documents in Africa, whether the great mass of detail available on the cult of Saturn reveals a comparable group structure.[56] Against the established opinion (based on Le Glay's analysis of the monuments) that Saturn attracted mystery-type processes, Schörner argues that they are rather family-based rituals. The prominent display of rolls and *capsae* (book-boxes) on the reliefs need not imply religious instruction. They belong rather to the boyhood of those depicted. Nighttime sacrifices of a lamb are offered by the parents. The boy is given center stage. This is not to be linked to the other series of documents for entry upon the priesthood. Rather we seem to be witnessing a family ritual of Roman cultural confirmation, attested in this form peculiarly in Africa.

Jörg Rüpke has drawn together these very different studies under the motif of "integration."[57] The last three cultic essays show in detail how the exact study of the evidence may well support this in terms of inter-cultic accommodation. But Rüpke himself has explicitly and rightly offered no answer to the last of his "general theses," that we cannot tell from the spasmodic character of our evidence whether lack of public presence reduces conflict or attracts suspicion.[58] The orderly gathering of data by itself too easily fosters assumptions of similarity.[59] An extra degree of care is needed to establish differences. And contradiction takes us closer to the truth of *Wissenschaft*.

---

56. Schörner, "Von der Initiation."
57. Rüpke, "Integrationsgeschichten," 113.
58. Rüpke, "Integrationsgeschichten," 123.
59. Rüpke, *Römische Priester in der Antike*, sets second-century Roman senators, whose inscriptions show priesthoods, alongside the shadowy bishops of the Roman church. Neither lot would have tolerated such a travesty of their place in the world.

5

Rethinking Religion from Hellenistic Times

First published in *The Journal of Religious History* in 1989, this chapter is a review of J. Podemann Sørensen, ed. *Rethinking Religion: Studies in the Hellenistic Process*, a volume of papers from a 1984 symposium of the Institute for the History of Religions in Copenhagen. In addition to specific points of critique or appreciation for each paper, the review articulates a working definition of "religion," noting some of the problems inherent in applying that category to ancient phenomena. The text of the review has undergone minor revision and a new title has been provided for the present reproduction.

As historians of antiquity we need to rethink what we mean by "religion." But this collection ignores that question. It looks rather to the ancient "process of rethinking and re-formulating traditional religion," which "goes on within any culture, meeting the demands of changing conditions, and often inspired by culture contacts."[1] In effect, therefore, it applies to the Hellenistic period the modern category of "religion," as established by the subsequent Christianization of the Roman empire (which Sørensen obliquely recognizes at the beginning).[2]

My own definition of "religion" is "an institutionalized set of beliefs and practices, supporting a general framework of life, which may mark us off in a social sense from those involved in other such sets."[3] Prior to Christianization there was no such phenomenon (though the gentile "Godfearers" around synagogue communities anticipate it). As is well known neither Greeks nor Romans used anything like our concept of

---

1. Podemann Sørensen, *Rethinking Religion*, 7.
2. Podemann Sørensen, *Rethinking Religion*, 5.
3. Judge, "Beginning of Religious History," 394.

"religion" (*threskeia* refers to "ritual observance," *religio* to "scruple" essentially). Ancient cult practice was not related closely to either theology or ethics, which both belonged to philosophy. How then may one speak of the process of "rethinking religion" in the Hellenistic period? This dossier arises from the papers of a symposium on the occasion of Ugo Bianchi's visit to the Institute for the History of Religions at Copenhagen in 1984. Bianchi's paper on "Mystery Cult and Gnostic Religiosity in Antiquity" is taken by Sørensen as showing "exactly such a process in Greek religious thought, leading from 'mystic trends' as early as the sixth century BC *via* mystery cults to Hellenistic mysteriosophy and gnostic religiosity."[4] But his distinctions between the "mystic" experience (through fertility ritual) of a god's fate, "mystery religion" (as in the best documented case of Eleusis) and "mysteriosophy" (Orphism) which "transcends" that by seeking life beyond the corporeal world are not presented by Bianchi as part of a historical "process." The last, in particular, is said to be commonplace from the pre-Socratics through to Gnosticism. Bianchi is distinguishing three levels of Greek experience or thought, not three stages in an historical development. He begins indeed by warning against any "historical-cultural explanation" which might make too schematic a contrast between Olympian and mystic "religion" by neglecting the functional coexistence in both of (e.g.) the Greek concept of destiny (*moira*).[5]

In the second paper, Sørensen treats "The Myth of Attis: Structure and Mysteriosophy." This explains "the essential concerns" of the myth by means of a structural analysis. Nothing is said about whether ancient people consciously understood it this way, or whether any process of rethinking can be discerned across the Hellenistic Age. Per Bilde's paper, "The Meaning of Roman Mithraism," explores a remarkable paradox. We are very amply informed about Mithraism from inscriptions and from the many excavated *mithraea*, underground dining-rooms adorned with depictions of Mithras slaying the bull. But nothing conclusively discloses why he did it or why a dining-room was used to celebrate it. Bilde proposes that Mithraism is not a dualistic mystery religion, delivering the soul, but "an optimistic, this-worldly and monistic religion."[6] It may have undergone a late platonization, but, curiously, there is in the literary sources no reference at all to bull-slaying. If Bilde is right to see the adherents of Mithraism as feeling "well at home in this world," perhaps they did not need to explain themselves through the cult. The Romans preserved the

---

4. Sørensen, *Rethinking Religion*, 7.
5. Sørensen, *Rethinking Religion*, 12–13.
6. Bilde, "Meaning of Roman Mithraism," 40.

rites of a multitude of gods, but even the great polymath Varro had to admit defeat in attempting to explain them all.

Søren Giversen's paper, "Hermetic Communities?", raises the opposite problem. Everything we know about the Hermetic movement relates to its ideas, but it is by no means clear that it has any social form at all beyond that. Giversen detects allusions to prayer, hymns, liturgy, baptism, a holy meal, temple, and holy books. But these need be no more than references to such activities in other connections or to the metaphorical application of them in Hermetic thought.

J. V. Hansen treats "Adamas and the Four Illuminations in Sethian Gnosticism." H. M. Schenke had interpreted these *phosteres* as four world-periods catering for the four stages of pneumatic humankind represented by Adam, Seth, the "original" Sethians, and the historical ones. But together the four also constitute a heavenly *ekklēsia*. This Hansen takes to have a counterpart in an organized Sethian community on earth. Their reintegration into Adamas (the heavenly Adam) represents salvation for the Sethians. Four angelic deacons assist the illuminators in this. Hansen assumes that the five rituals they perform will have been replicated as cult practice in the Sethian community. But again, we simply do not know.

In "Attis or Osiris?" Sørensen presents an extensive and detailed study of the mystery ritual described by Firmicus Maternus (*De errore* 22), the most clear-cut account of its type to survive. He concludes that it must refer to the cult of Osiris, and not to that of Attis, nor to a generalized version covering both the Egyptian and the Phrygian ritual. Yet he allows that our knowledge of the cult of Attis is so restricted that it is inescapably overshadowed by the much richer evidence for Egyptian practice.

Finally, Karin Weinholt, in "The Gateways of Judaism from Simon the Just to Rabbi Akiba," is able to proceed to much solider evidence. Yet Judaism can only be compared with the movements studied in the preceding papers insofar as it had come to embrace some who were not born to it as a national tradition. Like many before her, Weinholt assumes that Jewish proselytization was a feature of Roman life in the first century. More recently a strong case has been argued against that.[7] Nevertheless Judaism compelled attention for two reasons. The antiquity of Moses and the tenacity of Jews for the law ensured that Greeks saw them as "a people of philosophers."[8] On the other hand they mostly lived far from the locus of their national cult; their law had to be observed in the midst of communities

---

7. Editor's note: For this perspective see Goodman, "Jewish Proselytising." For a more recent survey and argument (against Goodman) that Jewish proselytism was taking place (especially in cities), see Carleton Paget, "Jewish Proselytism."

8. Weinholt, "Gateways of Judaism," 92.

to whom it was alien. It is of course also for these two reasons that we are amply informed about Jewish life and thought, and moreover that we find ourselves dealing with an intellectual community that we can recognize as a "religion" in our sense. It is not surprising that only the final chapter of this collection succeeds in matching its stated intention.

6

On This Rock I Will Build My Community

The cornerstone of the present collection, this chapter explores in detail a number of the arguments and conclusions that recur throughout the volume. Scanning a broad range of ancient cults and groups (Greek cults, philosophical schools, Roman collegia, Jewish sects, and so on), it searches for "cultic communities," groups with both cultic ties and the kind of didactic practice that constituted early Christianity. The rarity (and apparent undesirability) of such communities in antiquity undermines the assumption that Christian community and the Greco-Roman cults both fit the modern category of "religion." The latter half of this survey focuses on the development of the Christian "alternative" community through to the fourth century, and the often-overlooked impact this has had—especially in the modern world. This chapter is based on the 2005 Petrie Oration of the Australian Institute of Archaeology, first published as "On This Rock I Will Build My *ekklēsia*: Counter-cultic Springs of Multiculturalism?" in *Buried History* 41 (2005), adapted in Judge, *The First Christians*, 619–68, and in German as Judge, "Kultgemeinde (Kultverein)," in *RAC* 22 (2007).

THE TERM "MULTICULTURALISM" is first cited by the *Oxford English Dictionary* from a Royal Commission of 1965 on what was also called "the Canadian mosaic." It had arisen as a way of referring to the coexistence in one national state of three cultures (Inuit, French, and English) marked off by language, ethnicity, and territory. In Australia any distinctives of language and territory are breaking down, yet ethnic tradition is being entrenched. So we may not mock each other's inherited beliefs or lifestyle any more, only our own. We are however allowed to switch over to someone else's lot, with reactions ranging from strained endorsement to resentment or even vengeance. This is not quite how the Romans did it. They mocked other people's cults, while taking care formally to respect them, as well as sometimes making it unlawful for their own people to join in with aliens.

The term "counter-cultic" is devised by me to refer to cults in this sense. "Cult" is the cultivation of an inherited tradition, always focused on the correct way of worshiping the deity, the necessary safeguard of the existing order of things. Cult is thus conservative, and nothing should change. But Australian culture derives momentum from the assumption that difference is good and change may be better. So we are in a bind. Multiculturalism is supposed to create opportunity while entrenching tradition. The purpose of what follows is to explore the archaeology of this paradox.

The saying of Jesus (Matt 16:18) in the title confronts us with three novelties. The "rock" of course is Peter, under the nickname Jesus gave Simon son of John (John 1:42) when he was the first to salute Jesus as the Messiah. The novelty however lies not only in the name (Peter being the only uniquely Christian name to last the distance), but in the (unprecedented?) adoption of a theological confession as the basis for a new movement. The second innovation is to conceive of that movement as a building. Such a metaphor also seems unprecedented, in contrast, for example, with that of the body, which is freely used as a figure of the social order. The most intriguing novelty however is the unexplained appearance of the prosaic term *ekklēsia*.[1] It occurs in the Acts of the Apostles when things were already well on the way, but without comment. It is the ordinary word for a meeting. In spite of the huge weight of meaning built upon the community it came to denote, neither its members nor their critics seem to have thought the term called for any discussion.

It is tempting to project the New Testament concept of community onto the many Greek and Roman associations linked with the cult of a god. But since in classical culture any public or private activity, whatever its concern, had to be placed under divine auspices, the analogy with New Testament communities has little point where the effective (as distinct from formal) purpose is not centered in the cult. Offering sacrifice on the altar, in sight of the image or emblem of the god, was simply the guarantee of security. Thus we should not seek a parallel in those based on family, class or civil commitments, or serving mainly occupational, convivial, or funerary ends. In addition, to count as members of a community rather than a routine cult-group we should expect people to have joined it voluntarily,

---

1. Editor's note: Translated "community" in this chapter's title.

with a personal interest in the cult, and above all to be forming a new and shared pattern of life around that. It may not be easy to find parallels to the distinctively Pauline ethos of social reconstruction.

If the term community may seem implausible when applied to the classical cults, so should the term cult when applied to the New Testament communities. As with the synagogues, the *ekklēsiai* were primarily engaged with fostering the correct understanding of a learned tradition, and with moral behavior. Theology and ethics belonged to philosophy, not to cult, which was preoccupied with correct ritual procedure and with ceremonial purity. The *ekklēsiai* painstakingly distanced themselves from the cultic practice both of ancient Israel and of the Greeks, and denounced the latter as demonic. From the classical side equally the "meetings" were seen as foreign to proper cult, and indeed as atheist. It was only slowly, across the first four centuries, and not decisively until after Constantine, that the Christians began to accept some analogy with cultic attitudes (for example, over the securing of the established order), and to adopt some of the relevant practices and terminology. But in doing so they were creating a combination of forces alien both to classical and (to some extent) to biblical culture, enshrining an openly radical and didactic approach to social relations within the conventional security of cultic practice. From this hitherto unparalleled (and inherently ambiguous and unstable) compromise arose what came belatedly (in the seventeenth century) to be classified as a series of "religions," that is alternative commitments of belief and life potentially critical of the civil community. What we choose to call "religions" in antiquity are profoundly different in each of these respects. They made no great demand on belief or life, and were pursued primarily to safeguard the established order of things, not to question it.

Greek Cult-groups[2]

Private initiative in establishing cultic rites (*orgia*) at Athens seems to be implied when Suidas (*s.v.*) defines *orgeōnes* ("celebrants") as *hoi tois idiai ephidrymenois theois orgiazontes* ("those celebrating for gods set up on their own"). Ziebarth held that they were groups of citizens whose descent excluded them from the phratries that managed the cultic life of the civil community at the local level.[3] But they were clearly linked in some way with

---

2. For more on Greek cult-groups see: Fisher, "Greek Associations"; Nock, "Historical Importance"; Nock et al., "Gild"; Rauh, *Sacred Bonds of Commerce*; Ustinova, "*thiasoi*."

3. Ziebarth, "Orgeones."

the public system.[4] A law of Solon (*Digest* 47.22.4) alludes to them amongst the partnerships, including business ones, whose agreements are valid unless contrary to law. Athenaeus, *Deipnosophistae* 186a itemizes their dinners separately from those of both phratries and *thiasoi*. Ferguson shows from the inscriptions that they were at first devoted to the cult of heroes.[5] From the inscriptions also we know that the introduction of the Thracian cult of Bendis (with which Plato opens his *Republic*) was entrusted to *orgeōnes*, applied now for the first time to foreigners. There are a few other such cases, the goddess Belela being supported by *orgeōnes* as late as the early third century AD.[6] But Aristotle makes no mention of them when classifying the several forms of *koinōnia* ("community") that are subsets of the *polis*.[7] They may already have been subsumed under the *thiasoi* and *eranoi*, which arise "for the sake of pleasure" in the form of sacrificial "gatherings" (*synodoi*) combined with "companionship" (*synousia*).[8]

These three sorts of group were identified by Foucart as the main prototypes of the Greek cult-group.[9] The comprehensive term was *koinon*. Members used scores of other collective terms for themselves.[10] Although *thiasos* is supposed etymologically to allude to the god and *eranos* to the companionship, Aristotle seems to be treating the combination as applying indifferently to either. This is certainly the conclusion one is driven to by any attempt to distinguish them historically.[11] Could the same group (as implied in Athenaeus, *Deipnosophistae* 8.64, 362e) be referred to as an *eranos* in relation to their club-like functions (membership, shared funding, entertainment) and as a *thiasos* in relation to the cult?[12] It is certainly not easy to envisage an *eranos* without the patronage of a god. *Thiasos* became the customary term for the associations of foreigners that became more frequent at Athens in the third century BC, some largely composed of slaves.[13] By the second century groups with mixed citizenship became common. The term *thiasos* goes out of currency at Athens by the first century. A common way of referring to the members of an association however was by the name derived from their

4. Parker, *Athenian Religion*, 109–11.
5. Ferguson, "Attic Orgeones."
6. *SIG*3 1111.
7. Aristotle, *Eth. nic.* 1160a.
8. Arnaoutoglou, *Forms and Legal Aspects*.
9. Foucart, *Des associations*.
10. Poland, *Geschichte des griechischen Vereinswesens*, 5–172.
11. Parker, "Private Religious Associations."
12. Cf. Poland, *Geschichte des griechischen Vereinswesens*, 30–31.
13. Mikalson, *Religion in Hellenistic Athens*, lists 24 such cults.

patronal god. Already by 1908 Poland had registered over 50 such names, the most frequently attested being *Hermaistai, Aphrodisiastai, Dionysiastai, Asklēpiastai,* and *Panathēnaistai.*[14] Athens, Delos, and Rhodes are the places where such groups are most often found. They seem all to be strictly localized, mostly with small memberships (say 30 on average).[15]

From across the 600 years of the Macedonian and Roman imperial hegemony we possess the commemorative inscriptions of many hundreds of such cult-groups. The uncertainty over what they were mainly doing persists.[16] A stele of AD 250 from Pydna in Macedonia records "the assembled worshipers (*thrēskeutai*) of the god Zeus Hypsistos."[17] Five office-bearers are named (*logistēs, archōn, archisynagōgos, prostatēs, grammateus*), with twenty-nine others. There are 20 Aurelii, 3 Aelii, 2 Claudii and 7 more with Roman citizenship in different families. Most have Greek *cognomina*. Three are women. Two will have been in slavery. They have Greek names only, their occupations being *oikonomos* and *oiketēs*. The cult of Zeus Hypsistos can hardly have required such elaborate administration. Common funds and detailed records are implied. They want and can afford a standing monument. This is not a men's drinking club, nor is it tied to any family or occupation. The recording of the names implies that one paid to belong, and that there were benefits. But there is no hint of any broader interests such as might have justified our calling this group a community.

Of the 400 epigraphic (and often fragmentary) cult-rules assembled in the three volumes of Sokolowski hardly more than 20 preserve evidence of an accompanying association (5 called *orgeōnes*, 7 *thiasos*, 2 *eranos*; other terms, partly overlapping, include 6 *koinon*, 6 *synodos*).

This need not imply that there was no such group in most cases, but it does imply that a club was not essential to the cult. What had to be prescribed in the cult-rule were such necessities as the selection and qualification of priests, the calendar of sacrifices, the ritual cleanliness of those who offered them, and the division of the meat amongst those with a claim to it. The cult-group, if any, is not primarily responsible for these vital matters. In two cases of the fourth century BC from Piraeus and Axos (Crete) restrictions are placed on meetings of any *thiasos*.[18]

---

14. Poland, *Geschichte des griechischen Vereinswesens*, 57–62.

15. Poland, *Geschichte des griechischen Vereinswesens*, 287.

16. See in general Freyburger-Galland, "Les associations religieuses," and Price, *Religions of the Ancient Greeks*.

17. Horsley, *New Documents*, 1:26–27.

18. Sokolowski, *Lois sacrées des cités grecques*, 36, 145.

Certain *orgeōnes*, however, of Bendis in fourth-century Piraeus were allowed to sacrifice without charge, while they ruled that private individuals doing so must assign part of the meat to the priestess or priest. All *orgeōnes* had to contribute by a fixed date to the monthly gathering (*agora*). Anyone was invited to enroll.[19] Thracians were at first the only ethnic group permitted to own land and set up a sanctuary at Piraeus. A third-century decree of their *orgeōnes* granted privileges to the Athenian ones in return for a share in their procession.[20] One group let out their hero's sanctuary, with related buildings and grounds, for ten years.[21] The common funds provided loans, and family members were allocated shares in the sacrificial meat.[22] Second-century orgeonic decrees from Piraeus provided benefits to the priestesses of the Great Mother of Phrygia (Cybele).[23]

Third-century BC *thiasoi* are mentioned in cult-rules from Chalcedon, Miletus, and Halicarnassus.[24] A third or second-century *thiasos* from Piraeus imposed on its members an elementary form of the *Kanon der zwei Tugenden*.[25] The interests of relatives as well as members are protected, along with those of "all our friends, so that everyone may know that we show piety both to the gods and to them." Nothing is to take priority over this law. Anyone acting or speaking against it may be prosecuted by any member and subjected to a fine.[26] A Dionysiac *thiasos* of the second century AD from Physcus in West Locris was, like any ordinary association, concerned to stop its *maenads* and *boukoloi* from provoking or abusing each other, a far cry from the libertarian ecstasies of the literary sources.[27]

In second-century AD Attica, the Lycian slave (of a Roman citizen), Xanthus, who worked in the mines at Sunium, founded a cult of Men Tyrannus. His national god had chosen him for this, and he was to name his own successor. The cult-rule specified conventional tests of ritual purity. The usual sharing out of the meat is prescribed. No one is to sacrifice unless Xanthus is present (it would not be accepted by the god). But Men is easily propitiated by those who cultivate him in "singleness of soul." It was open to those who

---

19. Sokolowski, *Lois sacrées des cités grecques*, 45.
20. Sokolowski, *Lois sacrées des cités grecques*, 46.
21. Sokolowski, *Lois sacrées des cités grecques*, 47.
22. Sokolowski, *Supplément*, 20.
23. Sokolowski, *Lois sacrées des cités grecques*, 48.
24. Sokolowski, *Lois sacrées de l'Asie Mineure*, 2, 48, 72.
25. Dihle, *Der Kanon der zwei Tugenden*: the two virtues were piety and philanthropy.
26. Sokolowski, *Supplément*, 126.
27. Sokolowski, *Lois sacrées des cités grecques*, 181.

so wished to form an *eranos*, on the usual condition of providing the god's share when they dined.[28] It has been said this may have been an emancipation society, but nothing is recorded about the financing of that. Another second-century Attic *eranos*, however, publicly sought benefactions. It was formed by a group of "friends," under the patronage of the trustee of a man's tomb (the opening section of the inscription is lost). No one was to attend their *synodos* without being examined and found honest (*hagnos*, sc. financially clean?), pious (*eusebēs*), and respectable (*agathos*). For fighting and uproar a fine was prescribed, or a double flogging (for servile members?). This was presumably a burial society.[29]

The moral tone of these rules need not imply that the members constitute a community. They are not seeking to reconstruct their lives and have no mission to the wider society. Their ethical stance is strictly conservative, protecting a carefully regulated island of convivial goodwill for limited purposes. But one may argue for a more critical and active ethos in the case of the late second or early first-century cult inscription from Philadelphia in Lydia.[30] The usual purity rules are perhaps implied in *ta patria* (covering the need for a lapse of time between certain activities and the offering of sacrifice, no doubt).

But the added *parangelmata* given by Zeus to Dionysius in his sleep impose a strict and wide-ranging commitment to good behavior in the future. Moreover, those seeking access (to the monthly sacrifices?) must inform on any delinquents. The main constraints relate to drugs and promiscuity. There is a visible signal of one's having met the standard. On entering the *oikos* one must touch the inscription itself. Barton and Horsley class this "as moral propaganda on the one hand, and as private discipline on the other."[31] They cite the authority of L. Robert as well as of Sokolowski for their argument that the inscription documents a cult-group, and that the term *oikos* can imply that. But Stowers argues that the apparent universalism (embracing slaves and women) simply reinforces the traditional household order.[32] Dionysius is extending the hospitality of "his own" *oikos* but within its familiar norms. Whether so serious a disciplinarian would have allowed his guests to form a dining club may be doubted. None of the usual marks of a cult-group is indicated. He has however looked beyond such narrow horizons. In binding everyone to show their hand at the door he is not only

28. Sokolowski, *Lois sacrées des cités grecques*, 55.
29. Sokolowski, *Lois sacrées des cités grecques*, 53.
30. Sokolowski, *Lois sacrées de l'Asie Mineure*, 20.
31. Barton and Horsley, "Hellenistic Cult Group," 11.
32. Stowers, "Cult from Philadelphia."

relying on their watching each other. The goddess Agdistis also guards the house. For each of them she will "supply the good intentions" needed if they are to "have confidence in themselves." This sounds more like the ideals of a philosophical community, presented as it is in a "carefully written, educated *koine*," or of a mystery cult. In two passages stating its intentions, editors have restored the term *mystēria* to the inscription (11.13, 41).

Mystery Cults[33]

From the social point of view one may adapt the threefold categorization of Greek *mystēria* proposed by Bianchi in the following way: those tied to a given site, those practiced wherever the cult was celebrated, and those whose practice centered on a written philosophical tradition.[34] The primary focus of all *mystēria* is individual: the *mystēs* is to be personally initiated, and to keep the details to himself. In spite of the huge variety and interest in mystery practice in antiquity, the secrets have been well kept. The Eleusinian mysteries, celebrated at Athens for 1200 years, are the prototype. Honoring Demeter and Kore (Persephone), goddesses of harvest and spring, they formed part of the annual calendar of public festivals. Most Athenians probably took initiation. Greeks also came from all over the world for it. Yet we do not know exactly what they saw or heard at the ritual climax. This secretiveness, however, did not give rise to any Eleusinian group or community. The benefit was presumably existential. There was no change of life.[35] If Dionysius of Philadelphia had indeed included *mystēria* in his *oikos*-cult, that would not of itself have constituted it as a cult-group. But, as noted in Plato's Seventh Epistle (333e), *myēsis* ("initiation"?) and *epopteia* ("observance"?) help to forge the bonds of *hetaireia* ("loyalty"?) that tie political action groups. He proposed to ban sanctuaries in private houses (*Leg.* 10.909d–910c).

Second only to the Eleusinian mysteries in sanctity, according to Pausanias 4.33.5, were those of the Great Goddesses (Demeter and Kore?) of Andania, in Messenia. In 92/91 BC a revised set of rules was published.[36] The festival is now under public control (through the *synagōgēi tōn synedrōn*, line 49). Elaborate procedures are laid down for its administration, including the appointment, dress, and behavior of the various officials. (The details

33. For more on Mystery cults see Metzger, *Classified Bibliography*.
34. Bianchi and Vermaseren, *La soteriologia*, xv.
35. Mylonas, *Eleusis*, 280.
36. Sokolowski, *Lois sacrées des cités grecques*, 65; English translation Meyer, *Ancient Mysteries*, 52–9.

of the actual rites are of course not given.) There is no allusion to any association or other social bond that might be formed amongst the participants. In the sanctuary of Demeter and Kore at Corinth, however, fifty-two small dining rooms have been excavated. Exactly how these were linked with the cult has not been determined.[37]

The most famous mystery site after Eleusis was the sanctuary of the Great Gods at Samothrace, with whom Demeter also came to be associated. Across 1,000 years it attracted many foreigners. Unlike those initiated at Eleusis, they appear sometimes to have kept their link by making dedications elsewhere to the "Samothracian gods" or *Kabeiroi*.

Eleven groups (*koina*) of *Samothrakiastai* are attested amongst over fifty such inscriptions.[38] No. 48, from second-century BC Teos, bears fourteen titles set in wreaths, each apparently recording a group. Some of these are identified by their patron's name; one lot are called *orgeōnes*, one *mystai*, and one *Samothrakiastai*, in each case under the same patron. A *thiasos* is registered under a different patron. No. 42, another second-century BC inscription, from Karpathos, listed the names of up to 39 priests of the Samothracian gods. It is not to be assumed, however, that the mysteries were celebrated outside Samothrace. Commemorations extend from the Black Sea to the Nile. The gods were valued in particular by those in peril on the sea (no. 57, Koptos). Later a third of the *mystai* were Romans, and Samothrace even went bilingual.[39]

The fact that *mystērion* was rendered in Latin by *initium* is taken by Turcan to imply that the rite sanctioned reception into a particular group.[40] The privilege of group membership is rated first in his list of the benefits of initiation. While this may not be easily demonstrated for mysteries established at a national site, it is more plausible for those that multiplied themselves abroad.[41]

Dionysus / Bacchus[42]

In one version the son of Kore (Persephone), later identified at Rome with Liber Pater (himself linked cultically with Ceres, the Latin counterpart of

37. Bookidis, "Ritual Dining."
38. Cole, *Theoi Megaloi*, 78. The inscriptions are reproduced at pages 139–68 of the same volume.
39. Cole, "Mysteries at Samothrace."
40. Turcan, "Initiation," 90.
41. See in general Burkert, *Ancient Mystery Cults*.
42. For more on Dionysus/Bacchus see Beard et al., *Religions of Rome*.

Demeter), Dionysus occupied a conspicuous and ancient place in Athenian public ritual, with seven annual festivals. Wine, ecstasy, drama, and the afterlife were his four main provinces.[43] They mark him as the god who takes people beyond normal limits. But the *thiasoi* of frantic maenads who took to the hills and ate flesh raw existed primarily in the literary imagination. The risk of life imitating art, however, haunted the imagination of observers when a cult-group was formed with initiatory rites (inspired no doubt by the concern of Dionysus with the afterlife). Plato dismissed the dancing of Bacchus (cult-name of Dionysus) as not civil (*Leg.* 7.815c). Demosthenes ridiculed Aeschines for having helped his mother at night with her initiations, and with the daytime processions of her *thiasos* (*Cor.* 259–60). He led the chorus, crying *ephugon kakon, heuron ameinon* ("I fled from evil and discovered good"). This profession of a converted life was demeaning. But the vitality of the cult produced very diverse manifestations.[44]

In 186 BC the Roman senate gave the consuls authority to suppress an alleged Bacchanalian conspiracy. Livy (39.8–19) says 5,000 people were involved. The key complaint was that young men were being enticed by women into obscene rites practiced after dark. Instead of the three annual festivals observed when the women had kept it to themselves, there were now clandestine sessions at weekly intervals. The long bronze inscription of the *ager Teuranus* in southern Italy (*ILLRP* 511, the oldest extant record of senatorial policy-making and oldest lengthy display of legal Latin) confirms the fact that the crisis was pursued throughout the peninsula.[45] The senate had perhaps seized on the scandal to entrench its collective ascendancy nationally.[46] The cult was plainly well-established. The senate respected the *sacra*, but ordered demolition of the *bacchanalia* (presumably conventicles) within ten days. Women who were cultically dedicated to the priesthood might be permitted to continue their rites. But no man could be a priest, and no more than two men and three women could be present and then only with explicit permission of a quorate senate. There were to be no oaths, no elections, no common fund. The point of this precisely calculated ruling is clear. No association could be added to the cult because it had turned into something that challenged the community as a whole—the first recorded cult-community. The consular rhetoric reflected

---

43. Henrichs, "Dionysus."

44. Reviewed at the "round table" introduced by de Cazanove, *L'association dionysiaque*.

45. Full discussion in Pailler, *Bacchanalia*.

46. Gruen, "Bacchanalian Affair."

in Livy's speech dramatizes the threat. The public assembly (*contio*) of the Roman people will face a rival assembly (39.16).

In 176/5 the Dionysiasts of Piraeus met to appoint a new priest.[47] The previous one had provided the *orgeōnes* with premises for their monthly celebration, and with their statue of Dionysus. They now resolve to appoint his son, also for his lifetime. Such an effortless succession in the patronal family ensures regular fellowship within safe conventions. Even the second-century AD rule from Physcus solemnly maintaining night-time rites in the hills, found it necessary to impose fines on those who failed to attend.[48]

A very different kind of *koinonia* is seen in *IGUR* 1.160 from Torre Nova near Rome.[49] On three sides of a statue base were recorded the names of 411 *mystai* honoring Agrippinilla as priestess. They are grouped under 22 different titles, in descending (processional?) order of cultic rank, some attested in Bacchic circles elsewhere. Just over a quarter of the initiates are women. Agrippinilla has been identified as a descendant of Theophanes of Mytilene, married to Gallicanus the consul of AD 150 and proconsul of Asia in 165. He, their daughter, his father, and Agrippinilla's brother and nephew all appear, the first five names on the list. Four-fifths of the others bear Greek names. Everyone has only the single name, except for two women with Roman *gens*-names as well. It is likely that many will have been of freedman or servile rank, for this must surely be a domestic cult practiced amongst the staff of a large suburban estate. Nothing suggests that they had constituted themselves as a cultic association, and if the cult is being applied to reinforce the household structure it can hardly be called a cult-community either. The Villa dei Misteri at Pompeii offers vivid murals that show how such an *oikos* might literally envelop itself in scenes of Dionysiac initiation.[50]

At much the same time as Agrippinilla was honored, the ancient *bakcheion* of Athens published the minutes of its meeting at which new rules had been adopted to revive the association.[51] The new priest is Claudius Herodes, the great patron and sophist, consul in AD 143, who was to die in 179.[52] The collective name for the association is *Iobacchoi*. A dozen titles of office occur in the rules, none exactly matching the name of any of Agrippinilla's grades. There is to be a monthly meeting (*agora*), and others on

47. Sokolowski, *Lois sacrées des cités grecques*, 49.

48. Sokolowski, *Lois sacrées des cités grecques*, 181.

49. Vogliano, "La Grande Iscrizione Bacchica" and Cumont, "La grande inscription bacchique," discussed by McLean, "Agrippinilla Inscription."

50. Nappo, *Pompeii*, 152–57.

51. Sokolowski, *Lois sacrées des cités grecques*, 51; English translation Meyer, *Ancient Mysteries*, 96–9.

52. Ameling, *Herodes Atticus*.

festival days. Very detailed regulations are laid down with penalties against disorder on such occasions. But anyone who sues a member for assault in the public courts is also to be fined by the *Iobacchoi* (lines 91–5), while those who absent themselves from the *agora* called to deal with internal conflict are subjected to double the fine, and excluded until it is paid. The priest is to perform the customary *litourgiai*, including the libation for the bringing back of Bacchus. On that occasion, following the public-spirited innovation of his predecessor, he is to offer a eulogy of the god (*theologia*, line 115). Members are to mark events in their family and civil lives by libations. The treasurer is to be chosen for two years by secret ballot (*l*. 147), as with the election of new members (*l*. 35). Those who attend each other's funerals receive one jar of wine (*l*. 162). All this represents a determined effort (presumably amongst people already prominent) to create a self-regulating club, set apart a little from the civil community, and ostentatious in its display of cult-loyalty, promising members the privileges of a convivial social routine and a demise with honor. Pseudo-bucolic indulgence amongst the privileged is characteristic of the cult as practiced in later Roman times.[53]

The artists (*technitai*) of Dionysus formed themselves into a series of cult-groups across the Hellenistic world. They provided Athenian-style dramatic performances for many cities under royal patronage. From the time of Claudius Caesar they were organized through the "inter-city, ecumenical" synod with a central board in Rome that certified victors in the sacred contests for membership in their home *synodos*. This honor won them tax-privileges. By the third century membership could also be gained by undertaking a costly magistracy.[54] Diocletian tightened the rules, which applied also to the parallel organization of athletic victors (*Cod. Iust.* 10.54.1). The ecumenical synods acted as sovereign states, sending their own embassies to the cities. They were easily the most successful of the innumerable trade and professional associations that functioned under a patron deity, and unique in their international network, anticipating that of the *ekklēsiai*. Over 3,000 members are known by name, across 1,000 years.[55] But with their exclusive membership, imperial sponsorship, and strictly professional purpose they can hardly be classed as a cultic community.

---

53. According to Merkelbach, *Die Hirten des Dionysos*.

54. Frisch, *Zehn agonistische Papyri*.

55. Stephanis, *Dionysiakoi Technitai*, and there is extensive documentation (Poland, "Technitai"; Rouché, *Performers and Partisans*, 49–60, 223–37).

Sarapis and Isis[56]

Like Dionysus, Sarapis was in origin a god of the underworld, his name a merger of Osiris and Apis, at Memphis in Egypt. Promoted by the Ptolemies at Alexandria, he became the pathfinder for Isis through the Greek world. She even takes Sarapis as her consort,[57] becoming the dominant figure in Roman times, though Latin Serapis remains prominent in African provinces. The mortuary figure of jackal-headed Anubis was linked with the cult and also attracted particular attention in the Latin West. In their Hellenistic forms both Sarapis and Isis were celebrated as universal gods, accumulating functions that had been under other auspices.[58] The whole natural and social order is sustained by Isis, who actively promotes the best interests of all against both fate and fortune (so Apuleius, *Met.* 11.25). Plutarch, *Mor.* (*On Isis and Osiris*) 3.352c, saw her cult as leading to philosophic enquiry. Her rites contained *ēthikas . . . aitias*, nothing irrational, mythical, or superstitious (8.353e). There was no risk of innovation, for Isis blocked the evil Typhon from this (13.356b). Through *logos* Isis assumes all forms and ideas, being of ten thousand names (53.372e).[59]

From the second century there are literary tributes to Sarapis by Aelius Aristides (8.47–56 Dindorf) and to Isis by Apuleius (*Met.* 11).[60] The romance of Habrocomes and Anthia by Xenophon of Ephesus refers to the cult of Isis and has been construed as figuring their initiation into it.[61] In spite of the brilliant public ceremonial, its community structure remains unclarified. The *reformatio* of Lucius in Apuleius (11.27) is of course a literal reversion to his human form, but it leads to his initiation and total personal commitment to "this holy campaign" (*militia*, 11.15), including a public baptism surrounded by an "escort" (*cohors*, 11.23) of devotees. Yet no cause is being fought. Although Lucius was not rich, he had enough to pay the costs of admission.

---

56. For more on Sarapis and Isis see Takács, *Isis and Sarapis*.

57. Grandjean, *Une nouvelle arétalogie*, 17, line 17.

58. More than a dozen aretalogies and hymns are preserved in literary or documentary form: Grandjean, *Une nouvelle arétalogie*; Engelmann, *Die delische Sarapisaretalogie*, on the founding of the cult of Delos; Vanderlip, *Four Greek Hymns*; Zabkar, *Hymns to Isis*, including English translation and discussion of the main Greek and Latin texts, for which see also Horsley, *New Documents*, 1:10–21.

59. They have been collected by Bricault, *Myrionymi*. This Greek motif, unique to Isis, is confined to the flood of enthusiasm for her that runs from the time of Caligula to that of the Severi, and must have been organized, according to Bricault, "Isis Myrionyme."

60. Dindorf, *Aristides*.

61. Merkelbach, *Isis regina Zeus Sarapis*, against which see now O'Sullivan, *Xenophon of Ephesus*.

He planned to resume his profitable legal career, and on the strength of that was admitted at Rome to the ancient *collegium* of *pastophori* founded under Sulla, and to its quinquennial decurionate (11.30).

Nowhere in the epigraphic record is there decisive evidence for the development of Isiac cult-groups that go beyond the service of the cult itself.[62] In the early second-century "litany of Oxyrhynchus" (P.Oxy. 11.1380) all the sites at which Isis was worshiped are listed (fifty-five survive beyond Egypt itself), each with its distinctive titles of honor for her. Amongst her many general titles, presumably applicable anywhere, she is called "the one who supplies pleasures in the *synodoi*" (1.132). This should be taken to refer to the cult ceremonies at which a congregation was present. Apuleius provides vivid evidence of the joy on such occasions, solemn yet exhilarating. A fresco at Herculaneum shows some forty people aligned in two choirs as the priests perform the ritual.[63] Outside Delos there is not much evidence for the use of *synodos* for an association of priests. The Athenian Sarapiasts in 215/14 BC decree honors for various office-holders, including a *proeranistria*.[64] She is complimented for performing the sacrifices at the set times. The participation of women in the cult of Isis seems to vary greatly with time and place, never rising above 50 percent.[65] One may ask whether the *eranos* at Athens is not conceived as a primarily cultic body. Similarly with the *koinon* of *Isiastai eranistai* who confer honors in first-century Rhodes.[66] The *klisia* referred to by the Sarapiasts of second-century Thasos in their decree is to be taken as a cultic meal.[67] Invitations to the *klinē* of Sarapis are found amongst the papyri, in one case being issued in the name of Sarapis himself.[68]

At Tenos in the first century AD a dedication was made by a *symbiōsis philia*. It consists of five office-bearers headed by an Isiac *nauarchos* along

---

62. Over 1,000 inscriptions from outside Egypt were treated by Vidman, *Sylloge inscriptionum*. Some 3,150 epigraphically attested individuals were listed and classified by Mora, *Prosopografia Isiaca*. The organization of priestly grades has been studied by Baslez, "Une association isiaque"; *Recherches sur les conditions de pénétration*; and by Schönborn, *Die Pastophoren*. Vidman, *Isis und Sarapis*, presents a full analysis of the group terminology, and its dilemmas are treated by Koester, "Associations of the Egyptian Cult."

63. Merkelbach, *Isis regina Zeus Sarapis*, Abb. 72.

64. Vidman, *Sylloge inscriptionum*, no. 2.

65. For their distinctive dress, see Eingartner, *Isis und ihre Dienerinnen*.

66. Vidman, *Sylloge inscriptionum*, no. 177.

67. Vidman, *Sylloge inscriptionum*, no. 265, cf. 275, 291, 720, and 120.

68. Horsley, *New Documents*, 1:5–9.

with five "friends."[69] This seems like a classic association primarily concerned with its club life. The same goes for the *sodalicium vernarum colentes* (sic) *Isidem* of Valencia in the same period.[70] Slaves could hardly afford the expenses of full initiation and priesthood. On the other hand, the *Isiaci universi* who canvassed for votes on the wall opposite the temple of Isis at Pompeii will probably have been those in priestly grades.[71] There is no reason to think that uninitiated followers would use this name, or carry any weight in the election. In the third century at Ostia the worshipers of Serapis funded a *schola*,[72] while the *Isiaci* restored at their own cost a *margar(um)* (= *megaron*?).[73] These buildings imply community activities beyond those of the temple proper. Yet we have no direct evidence of ethical or theological training being attempted under the auspices of Isis. In spite of the intense emotional bonding created internationally by public rituals and private experience of the cult, the focus seems to be entirely on the ceremonial life, leaving little room for what we understand by a cultic community. Isis was for life at its best, but not for changing it.

Mithras[74]

Several cults brought to the West from Asia may have taken on Greek-type mystery practice. Most conspicuous was that of Cybele, the Mother of the gods (Magna Mater from Phrygia).[75] Her cult is the most frequently attested epigraphically amongst the 52 recorded at the Piraeus from the fifth to the first centuries BC.[76] Only a fifth of these can be seen to have had an associated cult-group, this being most common with her *orgeōnes* or *thiasōtai*. These groups come mostly from 222–174 BC, the same period which saw Magna Mater publicly introduced to Rome (204 BC). But only a single cult-group (*CIL* 6.494: *col(legii) culto(rum)*) stands out as no. 303 amongst the 449 artefacts and documents from Rome and Ostia recorded by M. J.

---

69. Vidman, *Sylloge inscriptionum*, no. 154.
70. Vidman, *Sylloge inscriptionum*, no. 762.
71. Vidman, *Sylloge inscriptionum*, nos. 487–9.
72. Vidman, *Sylloge inscriptionum*, no. 557, cf. 527 from Praeneste in AD 157.
73. Vidman, *Sylloge inscriptionum*, no. 560.
74. For more on Mithras see: Beard et al., *Religions of Rome*; Gordon, "Mithraism and Roman Society"; Kane, "Mithraic Cult Meal"; Liebeschuetz, "Expansion"; Thomas, "Magna Mater and Attis."
75. Roller, *In Search of God the Mother*.
76. Garland, *Piraeus*, 228–41.

Vermaseren.[77] Official celebrants of the cult are of course not uncommon, e.g., Vermaseren, *Corpus cultus Cybelae Attidisque*, 4.2 (*CIL* 10.3699) recording 87 *dendrophori* appointed at Cumae in AD 251.[78] One may suppose that a cult attractive of associations in its heyday in cosmopolitan Piraeus was confined at Rome largely to public ceremonial. With Mithras the position is very different in several ways.

At Arsameia on the Nymphaios in Commagene Mithras was featured in an enormous ritual system in honor of Mithradates I (ob. c. 70 BC). Twice a month in perpetuity the public feasting was to be open to all who met the challenging test of personal integrity.[79] Plutarch, *Pomp.* 24.5, says the rites of Mithras were first celebrated by the pirates (resettled by Pompeius in Cilicia after 67 BC?). But the extraordinary uniformity of the monuments from the Roman empire, their dating and distribution, all imply the creation of an independent cult at Rome itself late in the first century AD.[80] There must have been official goodwill, but there was no public or open ceremonial at all, and it attracted little attention at the literary level (*hairesis asēmotatē*): Origen, *Cels.* 6.22.

The typical Mithraeum, conceived as a cavern, was concealed from view, and furnished as a small dining-room. Its vaulted ceiling and the relief of Mithras slaying the bull represented an astrology of the descent and ascent of the soul. Only about twenty people could be present in it at the one time. It could hardly have been the scene of any full-blown sacrifice or festivities.[81] The period of greatest concentration is AD 150–250. Men from the army and public service are the typical initiates. There are seven grades of membership, none sacerdotal. *CIL* 14.286 from Portus is an album *sacrato[rum]* listing 27 names. *CIL* 11.5737 from Sentinum lists 37 *cultores*. The occasional references to a *collegium* or *sodalicium* need not refer to a Mithraic cult-group. The general assumption is that we are dealing with a series of tight-knit semi-professional fraternities that promoted imperial loyalty, neither cult nor community being their main concern.

Known only from monuments and documents of the second and third centuries AD, and sometimes coupled with that of Mithras, was the worship

---

77. Vermaseren, *Corpus cultus Cybelae Attidisque*, 3.303.
78. Vermaseren, *Corpus cultus Cybelae Attidisque*, 4.2.
79. Waldmann, *Die kommagenischen Kultreformen*.
80. Merkelbach, *Mithras*, 153–87; Jacobs, *Die Herkunft*.
81. Clauss, *Cultores Mithrae*, tallied 184 definite Mithraea, 673 Mithras reliefs, and 1,003 inscriptions from 480 sites, 19 of them in Rome. Of 997 attested individuals, 350 are from Rome and Italy, 102 from Rhine provinces, 423 from Danube provinces, and 122 from elsewhere in the empire.

of Jupiter of Doliche in Commagene.[82] It seems to have been unofficially fostered within the Roman army, yet extending into the frontier communities of the Rhine-Danube provinces, since women were included.[83] The distinction between *colitores, candidati, sacerdotes,* and *fratres,*[84] along with the small dining-rooms and the term *schola,*[85] suggest limited groups under instruction, but the lack of any surviving literary treatment leaves unclear whether they might be classified as cultic communities.[86]

Philosophical Movements[87]

It was in the philosophical schools of classical antiquity that one might have expected to meet one of the two main requirements for a cultic community. They offered a critique of the established patterns of life and thought, including theology, and thus opened the way to an alternative community.[88] But their students were mostly not bound into a collective effort to attain that, using their privileged philosophical training rather as an individual higher education that might enlarge their awareness of the world before inheriting their assured position in society.[89] Moreover, while like any ancient institution they sought divine patronage, the cult was not their driving force.

For cosmic and cultic wisdom alike, Greeks looked back especially to Orpheus. Orphic hymns and ritual texts were taken up by traveling diviners. There was a *bios Orphikos*, where one renounced animal sacrifice and the eating of meat.[90] The Derveni papyrus reveals a pre-Socratic Orphic practice of argumentative interpretation.[91] Initiation was central.[92] By late

82. Merlat, *Jupiter Dolichenus*.

83. Speidel, *Religion of Iuppiter Dolichenus*.

84. Hörig and Schwertheim, *Corpus Cultus Iovis Dolicheni*, no. 381 (*CIL* 6.406/30758).

85. Hörig and Schwertheim, *Corpus Cultus Iovis Dolicheni*, no. 409.

86. Beck, "Mithras Cult"; Beck, "Mysteries of Mithras"; Mitthof, "Der Vorstand der Kultgemeinden"; Clauss, *Roman Cult of Mithras*. Progression through the grades is documented by P.Berol. 21196: Brashear, *Mithraic Catechism*. The proposal of Dieterich, *Eine Mithrasliturgie*, to derive *PGM* 4.475–834 from the cult of Mithras, has not proved convincing more recently.

87. For more on philosophical movements see: Giversen, "Hermetic Communities?"; Wilken, "Collegia."

88. Mason, "Philosophiai."

89. Dorandi, "Organization and Structure."

90. Pl., *Leg.* 6, 782e; Guthrie, *Orpheus and Greek Religion*, 205, 254, 261.

91. Laks and Most, *Studies on the Derveni Papyrus*.

92. Graf, "Dionysian and Orphic Eschatology."

ON THIS ROCK I WILL BUILD MY COMMUNITY 73

antiquity the Neoplatonists counted Orphism as a primary source for theosophy. But there is no decisive evidence that the Orphic movement ever produced a cultic community.

Yet (under Orphic influence) the Pythagoreans set the pace.[93] Migrating from Samos to Croton, Pythagoras is credited with founding a socially active community there after 530 BC.[94] Nicomachus of Gerasa (c. AD 100) held that this very public movement went underground c. 450 BC after the political revolt against it (Iamblichus, *VP* 35, 252–53). Our understanding of it is conditioned by the introduction of Iamblichus (c. AD 300) to the *bios Pythagorikos*. The Pythagoreans of Croton were *koinobioi*, practicing *homodēmia* (*VP* 6, 29.32). These terms are not found earlier and may arise from a reaction to and retrojection across 800 years of the new ideals of Christian monasticism. The letters of the prominent Pythagorean women uphold a patriarchal order. The discovery (from the imperial period) of a *koine* paraphrase (P.Haun. 2, 13) from the Doric however confirms the continuing or revived appeal of Pythagorean ethics.[95] But it need not then have been much more than an intellectual fashion (Seneca, *Ep.* 108, 17–22).

The students of Plato or Aristotle met in the gymnasium of the Academy or Lyceum, open parks just outside Athens. Wilamowitz conjectured that they were constituted as *thiasoi* of the Muses, which he thought also to apply to the students of Epicurus in his Garden (though not to those of Zeno in the public Stoa).[96] There is however no adequate evidence that their schools needed to have any formal structure.[97] The four historic schools were granted salaried posts at Athens by Marcus Aurelius, but institutional continuity is not to be concluded from that:[98] *tot familiae philosophorum sine successore deficiunt* ("so many philosophers' households go defunct for lack of a successor," Seneca, *NQ* 7, 32, 2). St. Paul was interviewed only by Epicureans and Stoics (Acts 17:18). The Cynic origins of Stoicism no doubt worked against any formally structured community. A many-sided public intellectual program developed by Roman times without systematic organization.

But with the Epicureans there was from the beginning (Diogenes Laertius, 10.9–10) a collective commitment to a withdrawn and consciously alternative life.[99] Devotees sacrificed on the birthday of their god-like found-

---

93. Zhmud, *Wissenschaft, Philosophie und Religion*.
94. Burkert, "Craft Versus Sect."
95. Judge, "Woman's Behaviour."
96. Wilamowitz-Moellendorf, *Antigonos von Karystos*, 264–91.
97. Lynch, *Aristotle's School*, 108–27.
98. Lynch, *Aristotle's School*, 163–207.
99. Schmid, "Epicurus," 746–55.

er, carried around his image with them and displayed it in their bedrooms (Pliny the Elder, *Nat.* 35, 5). By his will there was a monthly *synodos* on the twentieth day (Diogenes Laertius 10.18). The *eikades* may be compared with the Christian *agapē*. Both movements developed their quasi-cult while repudiating en bloc the cultic ritual of the broader society. In both cases their moderate asceticism was mocked as a cloak for indulgent vice. At Herculaneum details have been found of the Epicurean organization and fees.[100] While public life was rejected, the Epicurean communities were open to all, including women.[101] The vast inscription of Diogenes of Oenoanda put Epicurean doctrines on permanent display.[102]

The school of Plotinus in the mid-third century AD also came close to constituting a philosophical community.[103] It did not moreover concentrate upon the training of students, but was open to all, while attracting both *zēlōtai* and *akroatai* from Rome's elite (Porphyry, *Plot.* 2). Plotinus himself resided in the house of the noble Gemina, where he offered solutions to other people's disputes, and accepted trusteeship of their children and estates on their death (9). The plan to revive (or create?) a city of philosophers (Platonopolis) in Campania under the patronage of Gallienus was blocked by political opponents (12). Plotinus sacrificed and entertained on the birthdays of Plato and Socrates (2), but rated his own *synousiai* ("conversations," 1.5.14) of more value than cultic ritual (10). But there is no evidence that the Neoplatonic school was institutionalized after his death.

There is only an indirect impression of any community structure for the gnostic movement,[104] criticized tenaciously by Plotinus (Porphyry, *Plot.* 16) and the Orthodox fathers alike, or for Hermetism.[105] Hermetic communities were proposed by Reitzenstein,[106] but rejected by Festugière.[107] In spite of their intellectual drive, no philosophical movement matched the dynamic bonding of cult to community which was to become historically formative with the Christians.[108]

100. Militello, *Memorie Epicuree* (P.Herc. 1418e, 310).
101. Frischer, *Sculpted Word*.
102. Smith, *Diogenes of Oinoanda*.
103. Goulet-Cazé, "L'école de Plotin."
104. Rudolph, *Gnosis*.
105. Fowden, *Egyptian Hermes*.
106. Reitzenstein, *Poimandres*, 248.
107. Festugière, *La révélation d'Hermes Trismégiste*, 1:82.
108. Dihle, "Ethik," 680.

Roman *Collegia*[109]

The twelve tables granted to the *sodales* in a *collegium* (*hetaeria*) the power to settle their own terms of agreement, just as Solon had allowed (*Digest* 47.22.4), provided no public law was broken. By a *lex Julia* and *senatus consultum* this was later limited to associations meeting only once a month to collect fees towards the burial of the subscribers. Such an association was created by the patron of the municipality of Lanuvium in AD 136, who published its rules in the temple of Antinous (*CIL* 14.2112). Burial was guaranteed to anyone who kept up the monthly payments. Non-servile subscribers took turns at funding six dinners in the year, on four anniversaries of the patronal family and those of Antinous and Diana. At these everyone had to stay in his prescribed place to avoid *seditio*. The magistrate (*quinquennalis*) offered incense and wine, receiving a double share of the distribution. If he acted without corruption (*integrē*) he would thereafter receive one and a half shares. To keep the peace, business questions could only be raised at the regular monthly meetings.

Such rules reflect a fear of political manipulation and embezzlement going back to the street fighting of Cicero's time. Trajan likewise banned the city of Nicomedia from creating a *collegium fabrum* for firefighting (Pliny the Younger, *Ep.* 10.34). The weekly meeting of the Christians was abandoned lest it also be construed as a political faction (*hetaeria*: 10.96). Even *eranoi* designed for self-help by the poor (*tenuiores*) were banned (10.93). Under Severus *religio* was allowed as a valid basis for meetings (*Digest* 27.22.1). The Christians apparently did not see themselves covered by that. All *collegia* will have offered sacrifice to a divine patron. Amongst the 300 cases noted by Waltzing where the cult is identified, over 40 different deities are found, the commonest (in order of frequency) being Hercules, Jupiter, Lares, Liber, Silvanus, Mithras, Mars, Isis, Diana, and Ceres. Most *collegia* were no doubt based on occupational or family bonds, and can hardly have sought to create any new community. The tightly structured rules and frequent commemorations (*ILS* 7211–365) show them to have been closely correlated with the ethos of public life. Mommsen considered that their planned conviviality would have led to group support for other social needs.[110] He was followed in this by Liebenam and Kornemann,[111] but Waltzing used his massive

---

109. For more on Roman *collegia* see: Ascough, "Translocal Relationships"; Ausbüttel, *Untersuchungen zu den Vereinen*; Fisher, "Roman Associations"; Kloppenborg and Wilson, *Voluntary Associations*; La Piana, "Foreign Groups"; Richardson, "Philo and Eusebius"; Safrai, "Communal Functions"; Van Nijf, *Civic World*.

110. Mommsen, *De Collegiis et Sodaliciis*, 91. Waltzing, *Étude historique*, 301.

111. Liebenam, *Zur Geschichte und Organisation*; Kornemann, "Collegium."

study to oppose it.[112] He noted that Trajan's acceptance of the special case made by Amisus in Bithynia shows that a particular Greek proposal ought not to be used to interpret the way Roman *collegia* functioned. De Robertis agreed that there was no evidence that they were social welfare institutions but took it as obvious that this must have been the case.[113] Kornemann's analogy from the more elaborate practice of military *collegia* was explored by Schulz-Falkenthal.[114] But the *collegia* were far too precisely structured to have developed a fuller community life of their own.

Ancient Near East: Egypt[115]

The possibility that a cult-group might take on a social welfare function does arise in Egypt. From the third-millennium national community that must have built the pyramid of fourth-dynasty Cheops to Pachomian monasticism's subjection of the individual to the whole there is a collectivist continuity, according to Lüddeckens.[116] Muszynski could identify no evidence prior to the twenty-sixth (Saite) dynasty of the sixth century BC, but did consider that there was a distinctively Egyptian type of *confrérie*, anticipating the *philoponoi* of Byzantine times. Préaux had also considered these bodies peculiar to Egypt, though using Greek terminology, in their contractual structure.[117]

The indigenous texts are reviewed by de Cenival.[118] P.dém.Lille 29 (de Cenival 3–10) is the annually renewable contract for the collective supply of sacrificial goods, with sanctions against default or misbehavior. Disputes are to be settled within the cult-group. Support is guaranteed for members unjustly imprisoned (but not for outsiders). P.Mich. 5.243, 6–9 specifies a fine for members of the group who do not come to the aid (*synepischeuein*) of someone seen to be in distress (*aēdia*) and join (*sylluein*) in its relief. The degree to which an *eranos* might function as a credit union (as the use of the Greek word implies) was considered by San Nicolò.[119]

---

112. Waltzing, *Étude historique*, 300–321; Waltzing, "Collegium," 356, 365; Waltzing, "Collegia," 2122–24.
113. De Robertis, *Storia delle corporazione*, 2:21–23.
114. Schulz-Falkenthal, "Gegenseiteigkeitshilfe und Unterstützungstätigkeit."
115. For more on Egypt see Wipszycka, "Les confréries."
116. Lüddeckens, "Gottesdienstliche Gemeinschaften."
117. Préaux, "À propos des associations."
118. De Cenival, *Les associations religieuses*.
119. San Nicolò, *Ägyptisches Vereinswesen*, 1:212–25; 2:105, 205–11.

This possibility was not taken up by Brashear.[120] It finds a parallel in the practice of *isophorion* identified by Rathbone, whereby the estate met the unpredictable liturgical burden of employees, recovering the cost from them on a more systematic basis.[121] This practice was no doubt superseded by the collective responsibility imposed upon occupational corporations when made hereditary after the reforms of Diocletian. The entrenched priestly structure of Egyptian temples probably also limited the development of any voluntary cultic community.[122]

Mesopotamia and Israel[123]

Archaeological and onomastic evidence for craftsmen occupying dedicated quarters since the third dynasty of Ur (mid-third millennium) was assessed by Mendelsohn.[124] In Palestine the evidence begins as early as the Hyksos period (mid-second millennium). Particular crafts (e.g., iron-working), along with ethnic or family ties, may have shaped the distinctive social practice of the Kenites, Rechabites, and (less probably) Nazirites. A cult-group of high-status drinkers, enjoying public recognition, is attested from late third-millennium Ebla and late second-millennium Ugarit. According to McLaughlin, it is referred to in Amos 6:7 and Jer 16:5, and may well identify also the revelers denounced in some other passages in the prophets.[125]

Uffenheimer argues (against Hölscher) that the prophetic tradition itself has ancient roots in the Hebrew phenomenon of collective ecstasy (Num 11:25).[126] The "school of the prophets" (1 Sam 19:18–24) was fostered to broaden the popular basis for the initiatives of Samuel. Ahab was confronted by 400 prophets under Zedekiah (1 Kgs 22:1–36). In Elisha's time the "sons of the prophets" formed a community that shared meals (2 Kgs 4:38–41) and even lived together (6:1). The rebuilding of Jerusalem under foreign protection created a new kind of cultic community, expressed in a limited assembly which committed itself to a stricter revival of the law (Neh 8:2), mixed marriages again being banned (13:25). This no doubt set the pattern for the sectarian zeal that was to seek the renewal of

120. Brashear, *Vereine im griechisch-römischen Ägypten*.

121. Rathbone, *Economic Rationalism*, 121–23, 133–34, 405–6.

122. Evans, *Social and Economic History*; Whitehorne, *Pagan Cults*.

123. For more on Mesopotamia and Israel see Frick, "Rechab, Rechabite."

124. Mendelsohn, "Gilds [sic] in Babylonia and Assyria," Mendelsohn, "Guilds in Ancient Palestine."

125. McLaughlin, *Marzēah in the Prophetic Literature*.

126. Uffenheimer, *Early Prophecy in Israel*, 271–75, 473–79; Hölscher, *Die Propheten*.

the Davidic kingdom by isolating the faithful remnant (foreshadowed in Ezek 11:13-25).[127]

Jewish Sects and Qumran[128]

The Maccabean revolt against Hellenization attracted the support of a *synagōgē* apparently calling themselves *Hasidim* ("saints," the *Hasidaioi* of 1 Macc 2:42; 7:13; 2 Macc 14:6). Their name perhaps echoed Ps 149:1. They may have been forerunners of the Pharisees and Essenes, whom Josephus identifies "at this time" as *haireseis* within Judaism (*A.J.* 13.171-2) along with the Sadducees (the last may have derived their name from the "sons of Zadok" of Ezek 48:11). The dating of such distinctions to such an early period has been confirmed by the recovery of the halakhic manifesto (unique at Qumran) "Some Works of the Law," 4QMMT.[129] The editors claim that three "groups" are distinguished in the letter: "we," "you," and "they," identified by Deines as those who were to become known respectively as Essenes, Sadducees, and Pharisees.[130]

Josephus distinguishes the three sects in terms of their views on philosophical questions. At the age of 16 (c. AD 54) he had undertaken the training provided by each of the three, and found it a burdensome experience (*Vita* 10-11). He calls the Essenes a *genos* practicing the same discipline as the Pythagoreans (*B.J.* 2.113; *A.J.* 15.371). Pliny calls them a *gens*, and assumes they have lived on the western shore of the Dead Sea for "thousands of ages" (*Nat.* 5.15.73). Philo, however, though he spoke of them as tens of thousands in number living in many towns, villages, and large crowded throngs (*homiloi*), says they cannot be called a *genos* since they are volunteers (*Hypoth. ap.* Eusebius, *Praep. ev.* 8.1.2). They arrange celebrations (*hetaireiai*) and shared meals (*syssitia*) on the basis of *thiasoi* (*Hypoth. ap.* Eusebius, *Praep. ev.* 8.1.5), which are also open houses (Philo, *Prob.* 85). But they offer no animal sacrifices (Philo, *Prob.*

---

127. Vogt, *Studie zur nachexilischen Gemeinde*, 157-60; Williamson, *Israel in the Books of Chronicles*, 132-40; Hogland, *Achaemenid Imperial Administration*, 241-47.

128. On Jewish sects and Qumran see: Beall, *Josephus' Description of the Essenes*; Cansdale, *Qumran*; Charlesworth and Knibb, "Community Organization"; Davies, *Damascus Covenant*; Haag, "Kult"; Koffmahn, "Die staatsrechtliche Stellung"; Kraabel, "Diaspora Synagogue"; Martinez, *People of the Dead Sea Scrolls*; Meyer and Sanders, *Jewish and Christian Self-definition*; Stegemann, *Die Essener*; Ulrich and Vanderkam, *Community*; Vermes and Goodman, *Essenes*.

129. Qimron and Strugnell, *Discoveries in the Judean Desert*.

130. Deines, "Pharisees." Note also Baumgarten, *Flourishing of Jewish Sects*; Stemberger, *Jewish Contemporaries of Jesus*.

75), concentrating upon ethical training through study of their inspired ancestral laws. This is done especially on the seventh day, which is *hiera*, in *hieroi topoi* called *synagōgai* (Philo, *Prob.* 80-81). Josephus notes the same feature. They approach their dining room *kathaper eis hagion ti temenos* ("as for some holy precinct," *B.J.* 2.119). Although they send offerings to the temple (in Jerusalem) they are excluded from it, and sacrifice separately (*A.J.* 18.19-20), which apparently refers to the sanctified dining. Josephus mentions a second order (*tagma*) of Essenes who even sanctify marriage (*B.J.* 2.160) which the main body had merely shunned. There is clearly here a conscious transfer of cult to life, creating what may plausibly be called a cultic community.[131] Baumgarten stresses the full-time commitment of the Essenes, who transferred to daily life ideals such as Greeks and Romans would have kept for Utopia while celebrating their dedicated fellowship only on a periodic basis (e.g., monthly).[132]

In spite of their later *haburoth* ("associations"), however, it is not clear that one should apply the term cult-group to first-century Pharisees (let alone the Sadducees)[133] or to the "fourth philosophy" noted by Josephus (*A.J.* 18.23), the Zealots (or Galileans). But Hengel stressed that all four combined political with religious interests.[134] This no doubt applies also to the Boethusians (Herodians?). Hegesippus, *ap.* Eusebius, *Hist. eccl.* 4.22.7, lists three other *haireseis*, the Hemerobaptists, Masbotheans (also baptist?),[135] and Samaritans, while a Jewish monastic sect across Lake Mareotis from Alexandria, the Therapeutae, somewhat resembling the Essenes, is described by (pseudo-?)Philo, *Contempl.* 11-40, 63-90. The presence there of female *therapeutrides* (88) led Richardson and Heuchan to propose that the Jewish temple at Leontopolis (in the Delta, c. 160 BC-AD 73) was also the site of a distinctive community.[136]

The "Qumran community" was alienated from the temple in Jerusalem. Instead they reached back to the ancient covenant, seeking its present renewal in the rituals of their common life, where abstinence for example symbolized sacrifice, and which in turn looked forward to the restoration of the temple after the ultimate victory of the righteous. The community is

---

131. Koffmahn, "Die staatsrechtliche Stellung," sees it as a "kleine Stadtordnung," but based on pre-exilic patterns and not on any Greek model.

132. Baumgarten, *Flourishing of Jewish Sects.*

133. Saldarini, *Pharisees, Scribes and Sadducees.*

134. Hengel, *Zealots.*

135. Thomas, "Baptistes," 1171.

136. Richardson and Heuchan, "Jewish Voluntary Associations."

formed to anticipate the cult.[137] The covenant is not "new," but it is now "eternal," and entered not by descent but by commitment. In this radical change it challenges the contemporary national cult with an alternative ideal, surely at the heart of what we must understand by cultic community.[138]

In its 200-year history the community collected in the Dead Sea Scrolls a variety of treatments of these themes which need not all be part of a unified system, or have come from the same source. "The Damascus Document" (CD, the "Zadokite fragments") is important for its historical retrospect, the "Rule of the Community" (1QS "The Manual of Discipline") for contemporary arrangements at Qumran, and the "Rule of the Congregation" (1QSa) for the ideal to come at the end, on which see Schiffman.[139] These and related texts (including 1QM, the "War Scroll", and 11QT, the "Temple Scroll") disclose an elaborately organized commune, enclosed and full-time, but not permanent, which cannot easily be identified from the literary sources—though an Essene link is often proposed. Talmon notes as unique (amongst other features) the identification of the *yahad* with the Bible as a "living" authority (as distinct from the closed rabbinic canon), still not textually crystallized, and open to imitation.[140] A solar (as distinct from lunar) calendar also marks Qumran off. The common usage of the times, however, is assumed as the source of many disciplinary and other routines of life by Weinfeld.[141] Yet the sacrifices, burial rules, and membership dues regular elsewhere are all absent, while Qumran offers uniquely the covenant blessings, moral and emotional pressure, and hymns of the biblical tradition. But because of its separation from wider society and focus on the *eschaton*, this cultic community lacks any concern (e.g.) for the poor.[142]

Synagogues[143]

As the name implies, synagogues must have begun as assemblies. Open-air meetings were held at the town gates (Deut 21:19; 1 Kgs 22:10; Prov 31:23).

137. Klinzing, *Die Umdeutung*; Ego et al., *Gemeinde ohne Tempel*.
138. See Christiansen, "Consciousness."
139. Schiffman, *Eschatological Community*.
140. Talmon, "Essential 'Community.'"
141. Weinfeld, *Organizational Pattern*.
142. Walker-Ramisch, "Graeco-Roman Voluntary Associations."
143. For more on synagogues, see Applebaum, "Organization"; Gutmann, "Origin"; Hengel, "Proseuche und Synagoge"; Horsley, "Synagogues"; Kasher, "Synagogues"; Kee, "Transformation"; Leon, *Jews*; Rajak, "Jewish Rights"; Rajak, "Jews and Christians"; Reynolds and Tannenbaum, *Jews and God-fearers*; Urman and Flesher, *Ancient*

Ezra's reading of the law took place in the square before the Water Gate (Neh 8:2). Since various kinds of business were handled this way and thus open to all, such an assembly can hardly constitute a cultic community, and especially since the sacrificial cult itself was confined to the temple in Jerusalem. The public reading of the law in other communities was held to go back to ancient times (Acts 15:21), perhaps to Josiah's purge of local cults after his reinstatement of it (2 Kgs 23:24). Alternatively, it could have arisen in the Babylonian captivity or after Ezra's restoration. But a common assumption now makes the synagogue a Pharisaic reaction to the Hellenization of the temple cult in the Maccabean era.[144] Lack of access to the temple may also explain why the earliest synagogues seem to have been formed abroad (especially in Egypt where the inscriptions document eight Ptolemaic *proseuchai*) or in Galilee. The first referred to in Jerusalem is the synagogue of the Freedmen (Acts 6:9), apparently formed amongst Hellenistic immigrants. This may also explain the synagogue built by Theodotus (*CIJ* 2.1404, often assumed to predate the fall of Jerusalem) "for reading law and teaching commandments." It contained "guest-rooms and water-supply to meet the needs of those from foreign parts."[145]

The first buildings explicitly referred to as synagogues are at Capernaum (Luke 7:5, endowed by a God-fearing centurion) and Corinth (Acts 18:7), next door to the house of Titius Justus, Paul's God-fearing host. Roman observers seem to have viewed the synagogues as cult centers. An epitome of Valerius Maximus 1.3.3 (based ultimately on a lost book of Livy) even speaks of the praetor of 139 BC destroying the "private altars" put up by Jews in public places in Rome.[146] Seneca[147] and Juvenal[148] also use sacral terminology of the Jewish community, although more concerned with its intellectual persuasiveness. The Jews are aware of the origin and meaning of their rite (*causas ritus sui*), says Seneca. Josephus on occasion uses *hieron* of synagogues, presumably accepting the Greek view of them as sanctuaries, and the Ptolemaic Jewish inscriptions sometimes refer to a *hagios topos*.[149]

The synagogue came into its own as a result of the destruction of Jewish national aspirations in three Roman wars (AD 70–135). The temple levy

---

Synagogues; Williams, "Structure."

144. Full discussion in Binder, *Into the Temple Courts*, 155–226, and Levine, *Ancient Synagogue*, 42–73.

145. For more on this, see Riesner, "Synagogues in Jerusalem," and Cotton et al., *Corpus Inscriptionum Iudaeae/Palaestinae*, vol. 1.1, no. 9.

146. Stern, *Greek and Latin Authors*, no. 147.

147. Stern, *Greek and Latin Authors*, 186, 189.

148. Stern, *Greek and Latin Authors*, 301.

149. Lifshitz, *Donateurs et fondateurs*, nos. 88–90.

that had once been sent to Jerusalem was applied by the Romans to the restoration of the temple of Jupiter Capitolinus. It presumably fell to the synagogue authorities to identify those liable to pay this tax (*CPJ* 2.160–229). In return Jews were exempted from liturgies and military service, which would have compromised their ban on idolatry. Philo had already distinguished the Jewish communities from Hellenic associations.[150] All Jews could by right of birth enjoy the privileges of their local synagogue. They had secured in defeat a subordinate form of national identity that was unparalleled and cannot readily be classified as a cultic community given its public status. Gentiles were free to attend.[151]

Romans already believed prior to AD 70 that they were being taken over by the Jews. Like them, laughs Horace, we poets will compel you to "join our crowd" (*Sat.* 1.4.143 *in hanc concedere turbam*). The "lifestyle" (*consuetudo*) of this "vicious race" (*gens sceleratissima*) has become so "influential" (*convaluit*) that it is accepted worldwide. *Victi victoribus leges dederunt* (Seneca on superstition, cited by Augustine, *Civ.* 6.11). The Acts of the Apostles features gentiles who attached themselves to the synagogues, "fearing God" yet often stopping short of circumcision (Acts 17:4, 12). It has been thought a tendentious fiction, designed to legitimize the breakaway churches they then formed. Levinskaya has however comprehensively demonstrated its plausibility.[152] She also confirms the close links with Judaism of those whose cult honored Theos Hypsistos (Acts 16:17).

The capacity of the synagogue to generate a body that can more obviously be treated as a cultic community is seen in the recently discovered inscription from Aphrodisias.[153] A *dekania* (decury?) was formed, originally of ten men, five with Hebrew names, two more called as well "proselyte," two with a Greek name identified as *theosebēs* ("God-fearer"), and one as *palatinos* ("official") and thus not likely to have been a Jew. They can hardly have been the statutory synagogue quorum, since the God-fearers are presumably not Jews either. Rather, it appears to be an association formed equally of those born to Judaism and those who have acquired an interest in it. The dean is a proselyte. Their objective is to "love learning" (as in Sirach, Prologue), to be "constant in blessing" and to "prevent grief." This inscription appears to have been added later to a much longer second-century list of what must be donors, divided into two groups (arranged in order of wealth?), one with 55 overwhelmingly Jewish names, the other with 52

150. Seland, "Philo and the Clubs."
151. Schiffman, *Who Was a Jew?*
152. Levinskaya, *Book of Acts.*
153. Judge, "Jews, Proselytes and God-fearers."

Greek names headed by nine (city) councilors. The latter group are explicitly classified as "God-fearers." The easiest interpretation is that there is a joint synagogue-city foundation for poor-relief from which a select cult-group of dedicated believers has arisen.

The Followers of Jesus[154]

The immediate followers of Jesus might have been taken for the school of a prophet or the disciples of a rabbi (Matt 9:14). But they were called at once to let go of the old order completely, tasting already that "beginning again" (*palingenesia*, Matt 19:28) in "the kingdom of the heavens," where even foreigners would sit at table with Abraham (Matt 8:11). Following Jesus had to be literal and total (Matt 19:27). He had no regular home-base, and was not the head of a household. But he indiscriminately accepted the hospitality of others, defending himself for eating and drinking when John (who baptized him) had fasted (Matt 11:19). Crowds of other people flocked to him, and there were secret disciples who could not face the cost of actually following (John 19:38). There was no security because there was no recognized model for such a movement, political yet pacifist, fundamentally challenging yet unstructured (Matt 23:8-12). The twelve may have symbolized the tribal structure of Israel (Matt 19:28), yet they were not chosen according to tribe. The seventy (Luke 10:1) hardly match either the seventy elders of Moses (Num 11:16) or the seventy-member Sanhedrin.[155] Since it looked to a momentous change, there was not even an appeal to the traditional motif of the remnant (Rom 9:27).[156] Jesus interacted closely with synagogues, Pharisees, Zealots, and the disciples of John, but conspicuously set aside the main preoccupations of each of them. Even the open practice of personal piety was to be avoided (Matt 6:1-6).[157]

Where possible ("always," John 18:20) Jesus taught in the temple as well as in synagogues, and the former was the focal point. The claim that he could pull down the temple of God (Matt 26:61) and in three days build another (Mark 14:58) was turned into a threat to change the customs which Moses had delivered (Acts 6:14). Rebuilding the temple became a key figure for Peter (1 Pet 2:5), Paul (1 Cor 3:9, 16-17; Eph 2:21), and

---

154. For more on the followers of Jesus see Brown, *Community*.

155. Some manuscripts mention seventy-two (rather than seventy) disciples at Luke 10:1.

156. Dahl, *Das Volk Gottes*, 161.

157. Further discussion in Hengel, *Charismatic Leader*; Theissen, *First Followers of Jesus*; Bolyki, *Jesu Tischgemeinschaften*.

others (Heb 3:6), transposed (like the image of the body) to the believing community. So vital was the idea that the routine verbal noun for the construction of a building was now (e.g., 1 Cor 14:12) also pressed into metaphorical service.[158] Yet the community being built was not called a temple, but *ekklēsia* (Matt 16:18). The adoption of this inadequate name (an assembly has no ongoing existence such as the building metaphor implies) was not explained. One must question the general assumption that it echoes the "*ekklēsia* in the wilderness" (Acts 7:38) under Moses, which also had no ongoing life. Moreover, the concept of a new *laos* of God (Rom 9:25; 1 Pet 2:10) is most elaborately developed without any use at all of the term *ekklēsia*. A more plausible trigger is the use of the word in the Psalms and Sirach, where it often seems to refer to those assembled to praise God in the temple (Ps 68:24-26; Sir 50:1-21).

To Greeks it may have seemed to echo the regular political *ekklēsia* of the Hellenistic citizen body (Acts 19:39-41) which had long been promoted as a sounding board of the royal or imperial will (cf. "my" *ekklēsia*, Matt 16:18). Paul's early identification of the *ekklēsia* as being "of God" (e.g., Gal 1:13) may then have been needed to guard the term against this ubiquitous ambiguity. Yet he is apparently already using *ekklēsia* for the community that persists beyond its periodic meeting. Such a meaning may explain the somewhat belated appearance of the term in Acts, in connection with the pooling of property amongst the community (5:11; cf. 8:3; 9:31). The dispersal of this community in turn perhaps gives rise to the plural use of *ekklēsia* by Paul for its geographically parallel replication (e.g., 1 Thess 2:14). The plurals in Psalms and Sirach by contrast represented the repetition of the same assembly in a chronological series. The remarkable NT expansion in the meaning of the word matches the implicit force of the dictum "I will build my *ekklēsia*" (Matt 16:18; cf. 18:17), looking no doubt also to the *panēgyris/ekklēsia* of the "heavenly Jerusalem" (Heb 12:22-23).[159]

Pauline and Other Communities[160]

After Pentecost the twelve apostles (led by Peter and John) baptized a rapidly growing *plēthos* of believers. Many priests joined them (Acts 6:7).

158. Vielhauer, *Oikodome*.

159. Further discussion in Dahl, *Das Volk Gottes*; Campbell, "Origin and Meaning"; McKelvey, *New Temple*; Berger, "Volksversammlung und Gemeinde Gottes."

160. For more on Pauline and other communities see the following: Arnold, *Colossian Syncretism*; Banks, *Paul's Idea of Community*; Blue, "Acts and the House Church"; Gülzow, "Soziale Gegebenheiten"; Hainz, *Ekklesia*; Hainz, "Koinonia bei Paulus"; Hills,

In the temple they praised God daily (cf. Luke 1:10), at home they shared their meals and goods, and in both places taught and preached Christ (Acts 2:42–47; 5:42), surely the very prototype of a cultic community. But the criticism of the temple cult by Stephen (Acts 7:48), a representative of the Greek-speaking diaspora believers, provoked a violent reaction. The latter were driven out, scattering across Judea, Samaria, and Galilee, and through the coastal cities to Phoenicia, Cyprus, and the metropolis of Antioch. Here many gentiles were won over, and dubbed *Christianoi* (Acts 11:26). The Latin suffix construes them as social activists. Famine relief was sent back to the *presbyteroi* in Jerusalem for distribution to the *adelphoi*. This international development was hardly expected, yet not wholly without precedent. Those who preached the baptism of John had also gone abroad (Acts 18:25; 19:3). There were Pharisaic missions (Matt 23:15). In AD 19 a noble Roman convert had been defrauded on the pretext of sending her donations back to Jerusalem (Josephus, *A.J.* 18.81–84).

In AD 44 John's brother James (the apostle) was executed and Peter arrested. Well before this, James the brother of Jesus was seen by Paul as counting with the apostles (Gal 1:19). From now (Acts 12:17) until his own execution in AD 62 the *hairesis* of the Nazarenes (Acts 24:5) under James maintained its standing in the temple with some support from the Pharisees (Acts 5:34; 15:5; 23:9). James however overturned the Pharisaic demand for the circumcision of gentile believers (Acts 15:5, 19). His judgment was sent to the converts in Syria and Cilicia under the authority of the apostles and elders and with the consent of the whole *ekklēsia* (Acts 15:22). Another letter from (presumably the same) James went to "the twelve tribes in the dispersion." It says nothing of any cultic or ritual obligation, being focused on the "complete law of liberty" (James 1:25). Pure *thrēskeia* consists in providing for the needs of orphans and widows (v. 27). The letter envisages a synagogue building (2:2) with proper seating for an equestrian patron, as well as an *ekklēsia* whose elders pray for the sick (5:14). The two institutions may have functioned in tandem: they need not be conflated. In Jerusalem James conscientiously guarded the temple bond (Acts 21:20–24). Hegesippus pictures him as a figure of high-priestly sanctity who could command the support of "all the tribes and the Gentiles as well" (*ap.* Eusebius, *Hist. eccl.* 2.23.4–18). His execution (at Sadducean initiative?) outraged many scrupulous admirers (the Pharisees? Josephus, *A.J.* 20.200–211). His brother

---

Common Life in the Early Church; Horrell, *Social Ethos of the Corinthian Correspondence*; Judge, *Social Pattern*; Judge, "Social Identity"; Klauck, *Herrenmahl und hellenistischer Kult*; Malherbe, *Social Aspects*; Meeks, *First Urban Christians*; Reicke, *Diakonie*; Reumann, "One Lord"; Sampley, *Pauline Partnership in Christ*; Wedderburn, "Paul and the Hellenistic Mystery Cults."

Jude looked back to the apostles (v. 17), attacking intellectual parasites who exploited the free meals (v. 12). Descendants of the brothers of Jesus outlived the destruction of the temple.[161]

The letter "to the Hebrews" was apparently written while the temple ritual was still in use (Heb 10:2, 11), but its main concern is to ensure that those who had abandoned the cult do not revert under pressure (10:32-9). They are to hold to the new covenant of Jeremiah, where the law is internalized (8:8-13). They have been enrolled in the *ekklēsia* of the heavenly Jerusalem (12:22-23), where they worship in the way that pleases God (v. 28). They have an "altar" from which those who worship in the (Mosaic) tent have "no right to eat" (13:10). Their sacrifice consists in praise to God, and the sharing of one's goods (vv. 15-16). Any conventional cult is thereby excluded.[162] The Gospel of Matthew was also written for a Jewish community alienated from its national tradition, and condemned for fraternizing with gentile believers. The kingdom of God will be taken away from Jerusalem, says Jesus (Matt 21:43), and given to an *ethnos* producing the fruits of it. The *ekklēsia* he will build (Matt 16:18) need not be large: two or three will suffice, but its authority is binding (Matt 18:15-20). The scribes and Pharisees are blind guides, who do not practice what they preach. They refuse to enter the kingdom of the heavens and lock others out, because they only care about appearances (Matt 23:1-39). Better to pray in secret, and fast in secret (Matt 6:1-13). "Something greater than the Temple is here" (Matt 12:6). The new *ekklēsia* will practice no public cult.[163]

There were soon networks of *ekklēsiai* also in the old-established Greek cities of Asia Minor, linked with Peter (whose first letter is addressed to the "migrants" in the North-Western provinces) or with John (whose revelation is sent to the seven *ekklēsiai* of the province of Asia). Both take cultic worship as a metaphor for the inward transformation of life. They are built into a spiritual house, a holy priesthood to offer spiritual sacrifices (1 Pet 2:5). Worship will no longer be centered on a sacred place, but must be offered "in spirit and in truth" (John 4:21-24). With the Pauline network we come close to the very process by which such communities were built up.

Paul's two earliest letters, Galatians and 1 Thessalonians, reveal the disputes through which the new communities were marked off from their Jewish and Greek forerunners respectively. In Galatians the dispute is over the obligations to Judaism of gentile believers. Paul passionately blames those spying on them (2:4), and the hypocrisy of Peter (2:13). They do not have to

---

161. Bauckham, *Jude and the Relatives of Jesus*; Painter, *Just James*.
162. De Silva, *Perseverance in Gratitude*.
163. Stanton, *Gospel for a New People*.

submit to the servile yoke of Sinai (4:25), but are called to freedom (5:1), a new foundation (6:15). Later Paul was to assert the advantage of Jews (Rom 3:1) over gentile believers, who were only grafted onto the old stock (Rom 11:17). There is no indication that a breach with the synagogues had yet occurred in Rome. Paul had not yet been there, and his letter is not sent to an *ekklēsia*. In 1 Thessalonians the dispute relates to social dependency (4:12). Some of the believers were giving up their trades (v. 11), presumably to be supported by the generosity of others. Paul himself could have enjoyed this, given the status his enterprise entitled him to, but he insisted on supporting himself (2:5–9). He had at first been protected by the hospitality of Jason, and other prominent people (Acts 17:4–5). Paul was writing from Corinth, where the social aspirations of his converts inspired serious animosity over his refusal (unlike the false apostles, 2 Cor 11:13) to accept the patronage offered, or to present himself in the style befitting an acknowledged authority. A different kind of community life was being promoted by Paul. These principled reversals of convention make it difficult to classify his *ekklēsiai* as Greek associations, which were meant to undergird the established order.

Heinrici argued that for similar reasons the *ekklēsia* could not have derived its form from the synagogue, but that the initial Roman tolerance of it implied a structural basis in the type of association derived by Foucart from the inscriptions, even though the Corinthian letters were preoccupied with the inner turmoil of their *ekklēsia*.[164] Hatch argued more extensively "that not only some but all the elements of the organization can be traced to external sources."[165] Although the common meals and close bonding may well have suggested or even reflected the practice of the clubs, the distinctiveness of the *ekklēsiai* is in various ways more conspicuous. Their purpose was fundamentally different: they were calling upon believers to build an altogether new community in anticipation of the coming kingdom. Their methods were didactic and argumentative, a kind of alternative education in the meaning and conduct of life. Their structure was not at first determined by any formal constitution, arising instead from the combination of charismatic initiative with authority delegated by the apostles. Their members were drawn from a wider social range than could easily be held in such close relations, linked together by the novel conception of various individual gifts contributed in mutual service to the common good. Finally, the *ekklēsiai*, though each complete in itself, formed an imitative

164. Heinrici, "Die Christengemeinde Korinths," 475–77, 479, 521.

165. Hatch, *Organization of the Early Christian Churches*, 26–39, 214. For analysis of the debate at the time, and of its renewal a century later, see Josaitis, *Edwin Hatch*; Kötting, "Die Alte Kirche"; Kloppenborg, "Edwin Hatch"; Schmeller, *Hierarchie und Egalität*, 9–24.

network that provided hospitality and financial support for members traveling across the empire and beyond.[166]

The *ekklēsiai* at first often gathered in private houses. Here they enjoyed social protection, and in return endorsed the household order. But they were not controlled by domestic authority, and their teaching sought to transform the spirit of domestic relationships from within. A similar ambivalence applied in their attitude to the public order. An essentially different manner of life was being created, that was to provide an alternative structure and a potential conflict of obligation in each dimension of the social order, whether *oikonomia, koinonia,* or *politeia*.[167]

The Pauline communities are also difficult to correlate with classical cult-groups. In Jerusalem Paul practiced the Jewish cult (Acts 24:14), but in his mission he transposed worship into a figure for the preaching of the gospel (Rom 1:9; 1 Cor 9:13-14). Believers were to practice a rational alternative to worship through self-sacrifice, that is by the transformation of their lifestyle and thinking.[168] But charismatic spontaneity and volubility must have shattered the procedural solemnity necessary to classical worship. The only explicit case of such a formal act of worship in a Pauline assembly is the *proskynēsis* of the hypothetical unbeliever of 1 Cor 14:25. As an *idiōtēs* ("outsider") nothing had indicated to him the presence of God until his conscience was convicted by the prophesying. There was no cult. It is only from the perspective of the fourth century (when the churches began to take up the sacral terms of the classical cults) that it is historically realistic to look back to the first for the development of Christian "worship." Likewise, one must guard against linking sacramental and other procedures too soon to possible classical models.

A similar circularity of argument is involved in the attempt to justify the application of the category "religion" to the New Testament churches. It presupposes the later transposition of the Latin term *religio* (scrupulosity, or "superstition" as the modern world sees it), making it in retrospect the honorific name for the whole complex of reconstructed belief and life that we now call "religion" (but which first-century Romans called *superstitio*).[169]

---

166. Judge, "Cultural Conformity" and "Appeal to Convention."

167. Further discussion in Hainz, *Ekklesia*; Kertelge, *Gemeinde und Amt*; Klauck, *Hausgemeinde und Hauskirche*; Hainz, *Koinonia*; Barton, "Communal Dimension"; Harrison, "Paul's House Churches"; Clarke, *Serve the Community of the Church*; Horrell, "'No Longer Jew or Greek.'"

168. Yet Thompson, "Romans 12:1-2," argues against those who hold that the meetings of the *ekklēsiai* could not have been construed as acts of worship; similarly, Peterson, "Worship of the New Community," 373-92.

169. This conceptual problem besets such notable projects as those of Smith

Second-century Community and Cult[170]

All three Roman writers of the early second century who comment on the Christians classify them as a *genus hominum* (Suetonius, *Nero* 16, 2) alienated from the rest (*odio humani generis*, Tacitus, *Ann.* 15.44.4) by social malpractice (*flagitia*, Tacitus, 2; Pliny the Younger, *Ep.* 10.96.2). The cause of this is a *superstitio* which is both novel and destructive (*nova et malefica*, Suetonius), of unrestrained depravity (*prava et immodica*, Pliny the Younger, *Ep.* 8) and deadly (*exitiabilis*, Tacitus, *Ann.* 3). Pliny discovered from those who recanted that all they had done was to meet before dawn, sing a hymn to Christ as though he were a god, and pledge themselves on oath (*sacramento*) not to commit any crime (Pliny had assumed the opposite since they had disbanded when he banned any *collegia* that might turn into action-groups). Later in the day they had taken a simple meal together. What proved they held to a dangerous *superstitio* however was not any of these details, but the commitment shown by two deaconesses under torture, presumably an unflinching testimony to their beliefs. Pliny refers to the mindlessness (*amentia*) of inflexible obstinacy (3–4) as itself requiring punishment. The offence was non-conformity. Later in the century Galen considered the indifference to death of some Christians and their lifelong celibacy to be truly philosophical. He did not however approve of the empirical (rather than logical) way of demonstrating truth in the school (*diatribe*) of Moses and Christ.[171]

His older contemporary, the philosopher Justin (Martyr), had been converted on this very principle: the prophets did not rely upon *apodeixis*, but were "witnesses to the truth above all demonstration" (*Dial.* 7). Paul had made the same point, rejecting logical persuasion for "the *apodeixis* of spiritual power" (1 Cor 2:4—the crucified Messiah?). This argument from historical testimony in turn provoked a novel critique of the gospel's historicity in the *alēthēs logos* of Celsus.[172] In Alexandria a philosophical school (*didaskaleion*, Eusebius, *Hist. eccl.* 5.10. l) sought intellectual reconciliation, conspicuously

---

(*Drudgery Divine*), of Betz ("Birth of Christianity as a Hellenistic religion"), and of Theissen (*Die Religion der ersten Christen*). The terminological artifice of Theissen's title is acknowledged: "Sie ebauten eine semiotische Kathedrale aus narrativen, rituellen und ethischen Materialen, eine Zeichen-*und* Lebenswelt" (385). This is why it would be confusing to classify the Pauline *ekklēsiai* as cultic communities. See further Judge, "Did the Churches Compete."

170. For more on second-century community and cult see Afanassieff, "L'assemblée"; Aune, *Cultic Setting*; Lampe, *From Paul to Valentinus*; MacMullen, *Christianizing*; Stockmeier, *Glaube und Religion*.

171. Walzer, *Galen on Jews and Christians*.

172. Andresen, *Logos und Nomos*.

in the writings of Clement, that went beyond the regular *catēchēsis* required for baptism.[173] Tertullian, moreover, rejected any partnership with the Academy (*De praesc. haeret.* 7), since the gospel had made further *curiositas* and *inquisitio* unnecessary. Philosophy only led on to heresy.

The term *secta* (with its politico-philosophical flavor) is however one that Tertullian accepts (*Apol.* 37.3). Yet Christians are not partisan, and should have been classified *inter licitas factiones* (38.1) since they are not interested in local politics but only in the universal *res publica* (38.3). As a *corpus* (39.1) their activity centers on collective pleas to God, which one may only share in if one passes the *censura* of the *litterae divinae* (39.2–4). The monthly payment is optional, and used not for feasting but for poor relief (39.5–6). Tertullian understands that it is because of their commitment (*superstitio*) that Christians are mocked as a *tertium genus* (*Ad nat.* 1.8.11, with commentary of Schneider).[174] But they are coterminous with all other *gentes*, filling every place and institution except only the temples (*Apol.* 37.4). That is the reason why, though claiming to be *dei secta* (39.6), they are not allowed to count as having a *religio* of their own (24.9). They do not yet qualify as a cultic community.

Abhorrence from idolatry and from the offering of sacrifice persisted, but ambiguity arises.[175] The prophetic denunciation is cited in the letter of Barnabas (2.4–5, 7–8), while the "new law" (*kainos nomos*) requires an offering indeed, but one not made by man: it is the broken heart (9–10). Fasting likewise must not go over to the law of "the others" (3.6), but the *laos* being prepared by the Lord will fast, as he demanded through Isaiah (58:4–10), in their acts of mercy towards the poor (Barn. 3.3). The old covenant was lost through idolatry (4.7–8), and now the temple has been destroyed (16.4). But we are a spiritual temple (16.10).

The Didache soon shows such principles being re-adjusted to allow for formal procedures. The hypocrites fast on the second and fifth days, so we must do it on the third and sixth (8.1). The Lord's prayer is to be recited thrice daily (8.3). Prophets are free to pray as they see fit (10.7), but there is a simple form of the Eucharist, already sanctified (9.5), and without prior confession of sins the "pure sacrifice" (Mal 1:11, 14, now linked with Matt 5:23–4) will be defiled (Did. 14.2). It is not clear in what respect this already conceives of the eucharistic celebration as a sacrifice.[176] A variety of

---

173. Scholten, "Die alexandrinische Katechetenschule."

174. Schneider, *Le premier livre Ad Nationes de Tertullien*, 187–90.

175. See Pesce, *ASE*, vols 18.1 and 19.1, "Il sacrificio nel Giudaismo e nel Cristianesimo" and "I cristiani e il sacrificio pagano e biblico" respectively.

176. See Niederwimmer, *Didache*, 196–99.

metaphorical applications of *thusia* is listed from second-century Christian authors by Ferguson.[177] Clement's first letter spoke of Jesus Christ as high priest of our *prosphorai* (36.1), while bishops have been "offering" the gifts in a holy manner (44.4). Justin (*Dial.* 41.3) takes the "pure offering" of the gentiles (Mal 1:11) as fulfilled in the eucharistic bread and cup. This is the "new oblation of the new covenant" according to Irenaeus (*Adv. haer.* 4.17.5). The sacrificial implications of it were to be emphatically spelled out in the third century by Cyprian (*Ep.* 63.14, 17; 67.3).

In a similar way the priestly terminology of the Septuagint was occasionally applied to the ministry in the *ekklēsiai*. In the Didache visiting prophets are not only given free rein with the eucharistic prayer, but are maintained as well from the first fruits "for they are your chief priests" (13.3). Polycrates of Ephesus (*ap.* Eusebius, *Hist. eccl.* 5.24.3) salutes the memory of the apostle John as the "priest wearing the ephod" (sc. the high priest, since he lay on the Lord's breast, John 21:20). Tertullian speaks of the irregular ordinations of those who entrust *sacerdotalia munera* to laymen (*De praesc. haeret.* 41), though he is alert to the way custom establishes rules that are not prescribed in Scripture (*De cor.* 3.4). Nevertheless, the biblical terminology for ministers prevailed and it was not until the fourth century that it became common to add hierarchical terms to it.[178]

From the classical side Lucian refers to the Christians as practicing a novel mystery cult (*teletē*) in which Peregrinus set himself up as *prophētēs kai thiasarchēs kai synagōgeus* through associating with their *hiereusin kai grammateusin* (*Peregr.* 11). Similarly, Celsus speaks of the disciples of Jesus as *thiasōtai*, a term Origen was to distance himself from (*Cels.* 2.70; 3.22-3). Yet Clement contrasts the *thiasos* of the *maenads* with the holy *choros* of the prophets (*Protr.* 1.2.2), and considers it better to become *thiasōtēs tou pantokratoros* than to choose demonic darkness (*Strom.* 4.8.68.4). A century later Eusebius was to make free use of the cultic imagery. Christ at the beginning instructs his *thiasōtai* (*Hist. eccl.* 1.3.12, 19), while in Constantine's day his *ekklēsiai* throughout the world constitute our *thiasos*. This is best taken as a stylistic device according to Bartelink.[179] For a review of the historical issue, see Colpe.[180] The ambiguities surrounding the classification of the unique character of second-century Christianity are treated by Lieu.[181]

177. Ferguson, *Encyclopedia of Early Christianity*, 818.
178. Kötting, "Die Aufnahme"; Dassmann, "Kirche."
179. Bartelink, "Thiasos and thiasōtēs."
180. Colpe, "Mysterienkult und Liturgie."
181. Lieu, "Forging of Christian Identity."

Third-century Community and Cult[182]

Far-reaching clarifications were attempted in the mid-third century, as the Roman state reached both its millennium and its military nadir. Origen belatedly produced a systematic reply to Celsus. The latter had opened his attack by recognizing how the Christians were bound together, more powerfully than by any oath, through their so-called *agape*. On this basis they formed compacts (*synthēkai*) in defiance of "the common law" (of civilized humankind). Against this Origen asserts "the law of truth" (*Cels.* 1.1). Just as it would be right to plot against a tyrant, so, in the case of the laws on images and godless polytheism, "it is not unreasonable to form compacts against the law for the sake of truth" (the earliest attested statement of such a principle). The Christians aim to save others by persuading them to break with a diabolical tyranny.

Decius, however, in 249 determined to restore Rome's fortunes through a traditional mass *supplicatio* to the gods. The force of such pledges lay in their spontaneity (Augustus, *Res gest. divi Aug.* 9.2). But now (for the first time) every word and action was to be rigidly prescribed and verified. Every man, woman, and child must personally have tasted the sacrifice and poured the libation. They must then submit to the special commissioners a written petition (*libellus*) to be countersigned with explicit testimony that they had been seen to do it. All must affirm that they had always sacrificed (an echo of the spontaneity principle?). The Christians construed it as an assault on "the law of truth" (there was never any question of exemption such as was secured to Jews by the tax system). Apart from the extant *libelli* the outcome is known from their intense reactions.[183] While many Christians submitted (*sacrificati*), or stopped short but induced the commissioners to sign anyway (*libellatici*), others publicly refused (*confessores*), in some cases being condemned to death (*martyres*), while many simply absconded, notably Cyprian and Dionysius.[184] Both were highly educated, wealthy adult converts, but episcopal leadership was challenged by the moral authority of confessors and martyrs. In Africa these issued thousands of petitions of reconciliation (*libelli pacis*, Cyprian, *Ep.* 20.2.2) for penitent *libellatici*, provoking a metaphorical civil war over the credentials of two rival systems of sacrifice (Cyrian, *De lapsis* 25). The organizational energy and international networks of the bishops match the claim of Origen (*Cels.* 1.7) that "almost the whole world has come to know the *kerygma* of Christians better than

182. For more on third-century community and cult see Judge, "Beginning of Religious History"; Stark, *Rise of Christianity*.

183. Selinger, *Mid-Third Century Persecutions*.

184. Clarke, "Two Mid-third Century Bishops."

the *placita* of philosophers." But more than academic truth was now at stake. The cultural solidarity of the empire as a whole was in jeopardy. For the first time the government switched its attention from personal loyalty to the structure of the Christian community in itself.

Valerian made no attempt to revive the Decian *libelli*. According to Dionysius (*ap*. Eusebius, *Hist. eccl.* 7.10.3) his *oikos* itself was a veritable *ekklēsia* of God, filled with *theosebeis*. In a clear shift towards the Christian sense of *religio* as a life commitment rather than a procedural one, he allowed (in 257) that there were those *qui Romanam religionem non colunt*, but they must perform the procedures all the same.[185] Recalcitrant *episcopi* and *presbyteri* were to be exiled and debarred from holding *conciliabula*, or going into the *coemeteria*. The report of Dionysius (*ap*. Eusebius, *Hist. eccl.* 7.11.3, 10, 11) coincides: no *synodoi* or *synagōgai*, no going into so-called *koimētēria*. The self-conscious use of the bizarre Christian sense of "dormitories" reveals the serious attention now being paid to the realities of the problem. Decius had tried to swamp it by reverting to a lost consensus, but Valerian will tackle it from the ground up. Nothing shocked classical ideals more profoundly than the celebration of the physical relics of death. The *ekklēsiai* had migrated far beyond the old *collegia funeraticia*. Cyprian (*Ep.* 67.6.2) condemns Martialis for using one, *exterarum gentium more*: they belong to foreign nations, while Cyprian stands with the new worldwide people, *cum omnibus omnino episcopis in toto mundo constitutis*. In Egypt, facing the exiled Dionysius, the governor attempted the first ethnic cleansing of Christians (Eusebius, *Hist. eccl.* 7.11.14). It failed. A year later (258) Valerian sharpened his analysis (Cyprian, *Ep.* 80.1.2): all clergy were to be executed immediately, and all men and women of Roman rank, including imperial freedmen, were to be stripped of their honors and estates. There are two drastic innovations here: the penalties are retrospective, recantation securing only one's basic citizenship; while confiscation strikes down the social welfare system of the *ekklēsiai*, maintained even from exile.[186] Such an intensive action against the churches was never attempted again. From 260 Valerian was a prisoner of war in Persia. His son Gallienus cancelled the program by edict.

When Dionysius and other surviving bishops sought its application to Egypt the rescript (translated by Eusebius, *Hist. eccl.* 7.13) focused upon the retrieval of *topoi thrēskeusimoi*. This unparalleled term may well have been retained in the Latin from the original Greek petition of the bishops. It discloses for the first time the existence of buildings dedicated to Christian use,

---

185. Heberlein, "Eine philologische Anmerkung."
186. Schwarte, "Die Christengesetze Valerians."

and thus requiring a new categorization. It also implies that they were not in private ownership (since bishops would not have been required for their retrieval), but that they were held by the bishops on behalf of the *corpus Christianorum*. Cyprian had already indicated how the *ekklēsia* gathered around its tribunal, the raised *pulpitum* (*Ep.* 38.2.1; 39.4.1; 5.2), from which the words of the gospel are read daily. A platform is needed where one must project one's voice across a throng of people, in a public assembly, the law courts, the theater, or when lecturing. It is not needed in a temple or for sacrificial cult. But Cyprian can see that analogy. If one gives in to heretics, he imagines, our *sacerdotes* might as well take away the Lord's *altare* and let the others install their images and idols with their *arae* in the sacred and revered *congestus* ("chancel"?) of our clergy (*Ep.* 59.18. l). The very horror of idolatrous cult is set up as a foil to ecclesiastical practice. *Altare* (cf. LXX *thusiastērion*) keeps its distance from the *arae* (cf. the *bōmos* of polytheistic sacrifice), which ought to stay outside anyway if they are for animal offerings.[187]

The synod that excommunicated Paul of Samosata in 268 complained of his theatrical showmanship on the *bēma* at ecclesiastical *synodoi*, enhanced by his use of a high throne and a *secretum*, or private sanctum (*ap.* Eusebius, *Hist. eccl.* 7.30.9). Paul refused to surrender the ecclesiastical *oikos* until Aurelian (on petition) assigned it to those nominated in writing by the Italian and Roman bishops "of the dogma" (*Hist. eccl.* 7.30.19). The need to determine ownership of the new buildings had led the bishops for the first time to an imperial ruling, which significantly enforced the Roman point of reference in church affairs. The same applied with the ecumenical synod of the Dionysiac artists.[188] The imperial government itself had long since smoothed away public debate: Aurelian is said to have reproached the senate with spinning out the argument as though they were meeting in a Christian *ekklēsia* and not in the temple of all the gods (*SHA* 26.20.5). The Neoplatonic critic Porphyry taunted the Christians with building very large *oikoi* so that they could pray together in them even though nothing stopped them praying in their own *oikiai*, since the Lord would hear them anywhere (*ap.* Macarius Magnes 4.21 = *fr.* 76 Harnack).[189] Writing of the huge influx of people into the *ekklēsiai* by the turn of the century, Eusebius calls their buildings *proseuktēria* ("prayer-halls"), and for the first time(?) uses the term *ekklēsiai* for the large-scale structures now being created (*Hist. eccl.* 8.1.5).[190] The decision of Aurelian in 270 had presumably given the churches at last corporate recognition in

---

187. Leclercq, "Autel."
188. Judge, "Ecumenical Synod."
189. Von Harnack, *Porphyrius*.
190. Richardson, "Architectural Transitions"; White, *Social Origins*.

Roman law. But their self-determined structure and ideology itself challenged the sovereignty of the Roman people.[191]

Fourth-century Community and Cult[192]

The destruction of buildings was a distinctive feature of Diocletian's campaign against the Christians, along with the burning of scriptures (Lactantius, *Mort.* 12.2; Eusebius, *Hist. eccl.* 8.2.1, 4). The term *ekklēsia* was presumably used for the buildings in the edict as it was even at village level in 304 (P.Oxy. 33.2673). When Galerius in 311 authorized rebuilding he called them *conventicula* (Lactantius, *Mort.* 34.4; *tous oikous en hois synēgonto*, Eusebius, *Hist. eccl.* 8.9). They were not seen as cult-sites, and Galerius allows the (non-cultic) respect (*observare, prosechein*) shown to the God of the Christians as distinct from the *cultum et religionem* (*thrēskeian*) one owed to the gods. (In the edict of Milan Constantine and Licinius were to make the same distinction, Lactantius, *Mort.* 48.3; Eusebius, *Hist. eccl.* 10.5.5.) Galerius knows to use the (non-cultic) *orare* (*iketeuein*) favored by Christians when he asks them to "plead" with their God for his safety (*salus, sōtēria*) and that of the *res publica* and of themselves (Lactantius, *Mort.* 34.5; Eusebius, *Hist. eccl.* 8.10). He would have known that this is precisely what Christians normally offered in defense when their loyalty was challenged. Their offence is elaborately explained at the beginning of the edict. It is not classified as the introduction of a *religio nova* (from abroad) based on "superstitious doctrines" as with the Manichaeans condemned in the edict of 302.[193] Instead the Christians are said to have abandoned the lifestyle (*secta, hairesis*) of their ancestors and arbitrarily to have made up laws for themselves to observe. The result was that *per diversa varios populos congregarent, en diaphorois diaphora plēthē synagein* (Lactantius, *Mort.* 34.2; Eusebius, *Hist. eccl.* 8.10). The Greek suggests that *per diversa* is not necessarily a geographical expression and that *varios* does not mean "various," in spite of recent translations. The correct sense of Eusebius was given by Valesius (prior to the recovery of Lactantius) in 1659: *in diversis sectis atque sententiis diversos cogerent coetus*.[194] Galerius objects to the Christians forming "divergent communities on deviant lines," splitting with their inherited

---

191. Ehrhardt, "Das Corpus Christi"; Saumagne, "Corpus Christianorum"; Herrmann, *Ecclesia in republica*; Brent, *Imperial Cult.*

192. For more on fourth-century community and cult see Lohse, *Askese und Mönchtum.*

193. Riccobono, *Fontes iuris romani antejustiniani*, 2:580–81.

194. De Valois (alias Valesius), "Eusebii Pamphili: Ecclesiasticæ Historiæ."

Roman culture. Deplorable though it was, he has decided to tolerate them on condition that they contribute in their own way to the common good. It is a calculated libertarian policy, to be overridden within a year of his own death. It differs from the biculturalism secured for the Jews by their tax, since the Christians were Romans. Their government has at last conceded Origen's point. One may lawfully pursue a higher truth than law itself.

The restoration of the buildings and return of exiles (many having been condemned to the mines) threatened to disrupt the lives of those who had taken over the properties of Christians. (Constantine and Licinius soon guaranteed compensation, Lactantius, *Mort.* 48.7-9; Eusebius, *Hist. eccl.* 10.5.9-11.) But at Antioch the administrator Theotecnus promoted instead a public petition for their exclusion from the city. Maximinus in 312 endorsed this as a model for other cities. Each received his rescript congratulating it on its pious adherence to the gods (Eusebius, *Hist. eccl.* 9.7.3-14, translated in person from the stele at Tyre). Latin fragments, notably from Colbasa, confirm the translation.[195] The formal *territorium* of each city was included, cutting off any quiet retreat into the local countryside. This apartheid policy was linked with the campaign, already launched by Theotecnus, to win back community support for the gods. *Hypomnemata* of Pilate discrediting Christ were publicly displayed in town and country, and set for memorization in primary school (Eusebius, *Hist. eccl.* 9.5.1-2), along with a scandalous exposure of what went on in the *kyriaka* ("Kirchen," "churches").

Maximinus built on this concern over their intellectual and moral drive, with its underlying theme of separate nationhood, a systematic answer to their organizational network. High-priests were appointed for each city and province, and given powers of arrest and the white uniform of public officials. They were required to offer daily sacrifices to all the gods, to confront Christians with their duty, and to hand over any recalcitrants to the magistrates (for expulsion?): Lactantius, *Mort.* 36.4-5; Eusebius, *Hist. eccl.* 9.4.2. By the following year (313), however, Maximinus denied that he had been responsible for any banishments, citing his refusal of the petitions from Nicomedia and other cities, and in effect reinstating the position of Galerius (Eusebius, *Hist. eccl.* 9.9a.1-12; 10.7-11). In the wake of these intractable problems came the decisive clarification of the legal status of the Christian community produced by Constantine in his agreement with Licinius at Milan in 313 (Lactantius, *Mort.* 48.7-9; Eusebius, *Hist. eccl.* 10.5.9-11). The Christians collectively constitute a *persona* or *prosōpon*, with corporate existence (*corpus* or *sōma*) in law. Both the concept and term

---

195. Chastagnol et al., *L'Année épigraphique*, 281, based on Mitchell, "Maximinus and the Christians in AD 312."

of legal as distinct from natural personhood are entirely absent from the greatest classifier amongst Roman jurists, Gaius, and the notion of a corporation acting in lieu of a person only gained currency in the legal science of the Middle Ages.[196] The "edict of Milan" however takes it for granted. But the repeated emphasis upon *corpus Christianorum* in our version (which Licinius issued at Nicomedia) implies that this latter concept was unfamiliar in the Greek East. The explanatory phrase, *id est ecclesiarum, non hominum singulorum*, was therefore taken by Ehrhardt as a gloss by Licinius himself.[197] It was moreover further processed by Eusebius in his translation, which fails to pick up *ecclesiarum*, though Ehrhardt thought it had only made its unusual appearance in official Latin for the benefit of the Greek provinces already familiar with the term. As for *corpus*, it had been applied to the churches a century earlier by Tertullian in Africa. It need not remain uncertain whether the gloss *id est corpori et conventiculis eorum* conceives *corpus* as a larger entity than *conventicula*, since *corpus* itself had already been defined in the earlier gloss as (plural) *ecclesiae*. Viewed this way one may take the policy of Constantine as an attempt to provide for these within the substructure of the national community, rather than adopting the more drastic final solutions of Galerius or Maximinus which faced up to the *tertium genus* theory as a serious threat to national solidarity.

For Eusebius, however, normalization fell far short of the truth of this moment. In his *ekklēsiastikē historia* (1.4), while admitting that Christians were a *neon ethnos*, he had stressed that their *theosebeia* was the most ancient, having been discovered by Abraham. His purpose then had been to trace the succession to orthodoxy within the principal *ekklēsiai*, much as though he were compiling the *philosophos historia* of a regular school. His history barely recognized the question of its bearing on that of the Roman world as a whole. But now he developed a 35-volume response to Porphyry's exposure of the intellectual and social inadequacy of the Christians. The time has come, he says (*Praep. Evang.* 1.5.10–12), to explain what may properly (*kyriōs*) be called Christianism (as distinct from Hellenism and Judaism), a new and authentic *theosophia*, accentuating by its name its innovatory character (*kainotomia*). Origen had already applied the Stoic idea of providence (*pronoia*) to history, and the overwhelming enthusiasm for the blossoming of Constantine's patronage swept Eusebius into a grand vision for the future.[198] As a broad movement of life and thought Eusebius has rightly seen that the

---

196. Schulz, *Classical Roman Law*, 71.
197. Ehrhardt, "Das Corpus Christi."
198. Kinzig, *Novitas Christiana*.

ekklēsiai have far outstripped the familiar conventions of local associations. But what can he say about cult?

Those outside our *thiasos* will still have a part in its benefits (*Hist. eccl.* 10.1.8). Our temples (*neōs*) are rising again to far greater splendor (2.1). One hymn of praise comes from all, with consecrated men performing the sacred rites (3.3). At the opening of the *neōs* in Tyre, Eusebius himself delivered the panegyric (*Hist. eccl.* 10.4.2–72). The imagery comes from the temple of Jerusalem, but its meaning is drawn from the New Testament. The priestly stole is the Holy Spirit (4.2), their praises come from the Psalms. Our kings have spat in the face of dead idols (4.16), acclaiming Christ as king of all by royal inscriptions in the city that rules the world. He has supplanted the violent customs of barbarous nations with mild and humane laws (4.18). He has set up throughout the earth a nation unheard of before (4.19). We are that living *naos* (he reverts to the *koine* form of the New Testament) into whose inmost sanctuary, the secrets of the rational soul, only the greatest High Priest of all may see (4.21–22). The rebuilding of the *basilica* is described, and interpreted in detail (4.55–69). The *thusiastērion* is where Jesus as great High Priest receives from all the sweet smell of incense and the bloodless, immaterial sacrifices they offer through prayers.

Constantine for his part took the shift to inner sanctity quite personally. He confides in Aelafius, imperial vicar of Africa, whom he knows also to be a *cultor* of the supreme God, that he fears the Divinity may be moved not only against the human race but against himself.[199] He will not be free of anxiety until he knows that everyone reveres the most sacred God with united observance in the due cult of the Catholic *religio* (or the most sacred Catholic law, as he had put it at the beginning). He is enraged (Eusebius, *Hist. eccl.* 10.5.21) that some should split off over the cult (*thrēskeia*) of the holy and heavenly power and over the Catholic cause (*hairesis*). The *corpus Christianorum* has quickly emerged, not as a secure component of the civil order, but as a totality whose coherence demands personal commitment from everyone. To the Catholic bishops (*CSEL* 26:208–10), whom the Lord has judged *dignos cultui suo*, he confides that there had been many things in him lacking in *iustitia*, which he had thought the supernal power could not see. But the Savior had had mercy on him. Christ's clemency however must have departed deservedly from those who will not obey the most sacred law. He knows this because they demand his judgment, when he awaits the judgment of Christ, while the judgment of the *sacerdotēs* should be received as though the Lord himself was sitting with them. But those unspeakable deceivers of *religio* will be sent to his court by the vicar of

---

199. Ziwsa, *CSEL*, 26:204–6.

Africa to contemplate there something worse than death. By such reasoning did the quest for mercy in the inner man convert the state itself into an instrument of cultic terror.[200]

By the middle of the fourth century Constantine's half-nephew, Julian, had privately turned his mind back to the classical cults. The bishop of Troy, Pegasius, showed him the local temple of Athena, closed now but carefully preserved. The bishop had kept the key (Julian, *Ep.* 79 Bidez and Cumont = *Ep.* 19 Wright). Coming to power in 361 as the last of Constantine's line, Julian committed himself to the reconstruction of Hellenism, consciously requiring the Greek cults to convert themselves into an adequate answer to the Galileans. We must add the practices that have done most to increase their atheism, *philanthrōpia* towards strangers, care for the tombs of the dead, and the contrived seriousness of life (*Ep.* 84 Bidez and Cumont = *Ep.* 22 Wright). Arsacius, as high-priest of Galatia, must compel his subordinates and their families to be committed (*spoudaioi*), they must avoid the theater and taverns, provide hostels for strangers and food for beggars, teach Hellenists to support public services, and insist on their own precedence over governing officials. In contrast with Maximinus, Julian expects that the Hellenic gods can be supported by activist cult-communities on the Christian model.[201] His own admirers knew how unreal it was, but Julian shares with Celsus and Porphyry an historically alert recognition of the social and intellectual force of the communities that were emptying the old cults of their value to ordinary people.

Ammianus Marcellinus, an admirer of Julian yet skeptical of his practice in such matters, himself failed as an historian to identify clearly the historic phenomenon of Christianization. It was taken for granted by him that the Christians shared in no way in the distinctives of the classical cults. The word *deus* does not arise in connection with them, and *numen* significantly only when Julian makes a pretense of addressing it at an Epiphany celebration (21.2.5). The virgins whom Sapor found *cultui divino sacratas* (18.10.4) were probably so described for their protection, *divinitas* (27.7.6) being in any case a preferred term amongst Christians. The deposition of Athanasius from his *sedes sacerdotalis* (15.7.9) likewise no doubt reflects the phrase used by Constantius. In spite of the favorite metaphors of Eusebius and others, Ammianus allows the Christians no *templum*, *delubrum*, or *fanum*, no *sacerdos*, no *sacra*, *caerimoniae*, *hostia*, or *ara*. All these belong exclusively to the gods. Similarly, *secta*, *doctrina*, and *theologus* belong elsewhere. But Ammianus self-consciously uses words that are in regular Christian usage

---

200. Judge, "Quest for Mercy."
201. Nicholson, "'Pagan Churches.'"

(even apologizing, as a Greek himself, for their origin): *ecclesia, synodus, episcopus, presbyter, diaconus, martyr, basilica*. For the phenomenon as a whole he couples the adjective *christianus* with *cultus, lex, religio,* and (a growing preference) with *ritus*. None of these four nouns is coupled in Ammianus with any other such adjective, none of them is used primarily in a cultic connection, and the case usage of the phrases differs strikingly from that of the same nouns in other connections. They indicate his broad sense of a committed practice he cannot define, and for which he has no word (*christianitas* is first attested in Cod. theod. 14.3.1 1 of 365). Ammianus is in strong reaction to it, however, often expressing that in military metaphors (e.g., 21.16.18). He carefully indicates why he dislikes synods and admires martyrs. He favors an uncontentious, ethically quietist, and tolerant Christianity, but cannot understand the turmoil stirred up by it, simply treating that as a vice. He knows how factionalized and brutal the Christians often are, but does not understand the doctrinal character of the disputes or their popular appeal. He is not aware of biblical authority, though familiar with its equivalent in classical and Egyptian culture, and only slightly conscious of the ecclesiastical welfare work, of monasticism, and of the influence of women. Thus, though familiar with the public impact of Christianity, Ammianus makes the typical historian's mistake of trying to explain its problems in terms of the general ones of the time. He would like to assimilate the socially positive aspects of Christianity, but is blind to the dogmatic sources of that. Yet in avoiding any terminological equation with the classical cults, and casting around for a different way of alluding to the phenomenon as a whole, like the good historian he is, he has indirectly registered the historical novelty (which we now call "religion") of beliefs about God creating an alternative culture. But he would have been puzzled to hear Eusebius presenting it figuratively as a cultic community.[202]

Like Galen two centuries before, Ammianus respected the philosophical commitment that led people to asceticism or to martyrdom. But he would surely have been appalled by the new institutional forms they were developing in his own day. Although the churches had been providing social support for female virginity and widowhood since New Testament times, it was not until the early fourth century that continent men first won social recognition, and a name. The word *monachos* is attested in this sense as early as 324.[203] It soon became a paradox to contemporary observers that the quest for singularity of life produced dramatic new types of collective action, horrific to the unbelieving and often confrontational with the

202. Judge, "Absence of Religion," reproduced as chapter 9 in the present volume.
203. Judge, "Earliest Attested Monk."

regular *ekklēsiai*. The combination of intense spiritual discipline with a radically differentiated lifestyle fully justifies bringing the new monasteries under the rubric "cultic community."[204] Even those not living coenobitically were preoccupied with human relations.[205] Driving it all was the Christian substitute for cultic ritual, the desire to practice the moral injunctions of Scripture to the fullest degree. There was however no more glorious public testimony to one's faith than to suffer execution for not renouncing it.[206] As Cyprian had found, the readiness to die conferred on the confessor a moral authority which challenged that of his bishop. To the revulsion of outsiders this trust was carried forward to the relics of the martyr, and to the burial site. In a total reversal of the classical instinct to shun a grave as polluting, the promise of life was now tied to the dead.[207] The relics, moreover, were moveable, and could be used to extend the privileged access to grace through the martyrs permanently into the future.[208] By such means the *ekklēsiai* could turn themselves into local sanctuaries with a divinely accredited patron, matching the old cults in community value. MacMullen speaks of a "seamless join of the old to the new."[209] Certainly the churches came to provide the cultic anchorage that was desired for the daily and seasonal round. But entrenched within it now was the corpus of texts that had driven their radical experiments in community reconstruction.

What Would It All Do for the World?[210]

The ruling fashion amongst ancient historians is to say that the conversion of Rome changed little or nothing, at least in the way life was experienced. All Ramsay MacMullen could find that was unique in the daily round was the sign of the cross. But that on its own points to something more profound than ritual. To the ancient critics the cross was a disgusting humiliation, making nonsense of any claim that Christ was divine. But to believers he already reigned from the cross. See the earliest narrative depiction of it on the British Museum ivory plaque of about AD 420.[211] It signaled an altogether different kind of rule, the rock, if you will, on which the new community was

204. Brakke, *Athanasius and the Politics of Asceticism*.
205. Gould, *Desert Fathers*.
206. Bowersock, *Martyrdom and Rome*.
207. Brown, *Cult of the Saints*.
208. Markus, "How on Earth."
209. MacMullen, *Christianity and Paganism*, 125.
210. For more on this see MacMullen, *Paganism in the Roman Empire*.
211. McGregor, *Seeing Salvation*, 123.

being built. It sidestepped all established order for this alternative society. In the meantime, the two had to live with each other, everyone having a stake in either. But in the end the new would supplant the old.

In late antiquity, in what seemed its hour of triumph, the social force of this was masked, as the *ekklēsiai* were drawn into the reassuring cultic comforts of the past. But at the least an alternative structure of thought was ensured. The perfect, stable, and permanent universe of classical thought was confronted by the proposition of a beginning and an end, and the discovery that things must progress. The massive dogmatic drive also kept open the potential for counter-cultic renewal. The doctrine of a truth higher than law had been formulated by Origen, and accepted reluctantly in practice by Galerius. Those who claim they were only acting under orders are no longer excused. The open society places moral responsibility on everyone. The onus of choice has made space for multiculturalism. But multiculturalism threatens the open society if it only locks us into our cultural past, protected from criticism. Australia does not have the excuse of an inherited ethnic mosaic. It falls to everyone to be open to a better choice, and to win a better understanding of how the world works.

7

Christian Innovation and its Contemporary Observers

How well did the historians, philosophers, and policy-makers of the empire understand the shift that was taking place in the conversion of Rome? This chapter argues that the historians failed to grasp how distinctive and significant were the Christian intellectual drive and social project—but the philosophers and policy-makers do seem to have understood the challenge these posed to traditional society. In three sections, the chapter surveys each of those groups: the way historians (Ammianus and Eusebius) framed the phenomenon, the way philosophers (especially Porphyry, Celsus, and Julian) opposed Christianity in support of Hellenism, and the attempts of policy-makers (Maximinus and Licinius) to counteract or exclude the Christians. First published in 1983 under the same title in Brian Croke and Alanna Emmett (now Nobbs), *History and Historians in Late Antiquity*, 13–29, this piece has since been reproduced in Judge, *Jerusalem and Athens*, 232–54, and appears here with one notable modification.[1]

What the Historians Could Not See

CAN THE QUESTION OF old and new in fourth-century historiography be related to that of the changes in the fourth-century world as a whole? In particular, what is the basic effect, in cultural terms, of the establishment of Christianity, and what does that have to do with the observations of Eusebius and Ammianus?

---

1. For this change, see n. 6 on page 105.

At the most obvious level, the struggle over Christianity centered on the relations between divine worship and the public life of the community. Both sides held that the welfare of the nation depended upon worshiping the right deity. Custom had traditionally supplied a simple answer to this problem. One's public duty was to respect the gods of one's ancestors. Insofar as Christianity restricted the choice to one God, it was introducing only a qualified novelty, for unitarian ideas were common, and the Christians accepted the traditionalist terms of the argument: "Our worship can be shown (historically) to be the oldest anyway." If this had been all there was to it, the fourth-century revolution would have been essentially a fortifying of the old order, as indeed many observers from both the classical and the Christian sides, both then and now, have held it to have been.

But insofar as Christian beliefs rested not on custom but on arguments about theology and about man's place in the world, it also came into conflict with the philosophical tradition of antiquity. At this level reconciliation was far less easy to secure. More important still for socio-cultural history is the fact that Christianity made a vastly more determined effort than other philosophical systems to remodel the ethical life (or at least the ideals) of the general community.

The almost total success of this effort points to a development probably without adequate parallel till then in human affairs. A conceptual system which claimed to explain and predict everything about human life was actually being put into some kind of general effect, contrary to the prevailing outlook. The ideas of an intellectual élite were being passed on to the whole community, and even imposed by the government as the new ordering principle of its life. We may thus locate the beginning of modern Western history in the fourth century. From this point governments and traditions compete with organized systems of thought for control of the community. The dualistic pattern which has imprinted itself on the character of Western social and cultural life has been established.[2]

The confusion of this development with a change in religion, shared as it was in the fourth century by writers from either side, prevented it being seen this way. Not that the religious change was a superficial element in the process historically. It was the familiarity of religious practice which provided the means by which the ideological re-ordering of the whole community was effected. Religion, however alien to Christianity, conferred social power upon it.

---

2. Dihle, "Antikes und Unantikes"; Judge, *Conversion of Rome*, reproduced as chapter 8 in the present volume.

Contemporary observers show their consciousness of the fact that a fundamental social change was at stake by speaking of the Christians as a separate nation. This was of course in itself a traditionalist device: nations are the entities which are entitled to have different customs. But since Christians had no national past or homeland, the conception of them as a nation also represents a provocative assessment of what was happening. The Christians had successfully created within the Roman world a range of social institutions on a national scale which were essentially at variance with the traditional pattern of life. The disruptive flourishing of monasticism and synods, for example, precisely in the face of the new establishment, suggests that in the last resort Constantine and Theodosius were the followers and not the makers of the basic split that was taking place in the structure of the civilized community.

Eusebius and Ammianus, being not simply honest men but historians, both suffer from the compulsion to limit their view of developments in their own day to what can be anticipated from the past. We are concerned with changes in historical method. But since one might have hoped that, if historians were capable of adapting their techniques at all, they might have done so in a way that would do more justice to what was actually happening, one may begin by posing that question.

(a) Ammianus

The historians would surely not have objected to the question, accepting as they did the principle of *to axiologon*, or concern for the things that were *"narratu ... digna,"* as Ammianus puts it (28.1.15).[3] Behind his frequently invoked principle of fidelity, there seems to lie a basic appeal to *veritas*, which he perhaps formulated in the lost Preface.[4] The concern for the ultimate truth of history may of course have led Ammianus, as it probably did Eunapius, deliberately to refrain from giving special attention to Christianity. (Or was there a digression devoted to that subject in the lost books?) But the basic desire to assimilate what is feared as novel comes through alike in the pained reproaches of Ammianus and in the outbursts of Eunapius.[5]

Like some of the Christian apologists of his day, Ammianus should have been happy enough to accept the identification of Christianity with religion in the Roman sense.[6] If the function of the gods is to protect the

3. Drexler, *Ammianstudien*, 3.
4. Sabbah, *La méthode d'Ammien Marcellin*, 19.
5. Sabbah, *La méthode d'Ammien Marcellin*, 55.
6. Editor's note: On the term "religion" in this connection, see now Judge, "Absence

civil order, why should anyone object to Rome's enjoying the patronage of a new and manifestly successful power in the heavens? Ammianus can even tolerate (or is it irony?) the murderous competition for succession to the see of Rome. Given the political and social rewards, including the generosity of rich matrons, it was explicable, within the traditional understanding of the place of religion in politics, that men should compete for such a prize (27.3.14). Certainly they would have been truly happy if they had preferred the more morally consistent restraint of provincial bishops (27.3.15). But Ammianus had less understanding of the argumentative confrontations over orthodoxy, which engulfed the court of Constantius and exhausted the public transport system with repeated synods. He could not see the importance of trying to persuade everyone else to one's own opinion. It was a mere battle of words, an old woman's superstition, compared with the simplicity of pure Christianity (21.16.18). Yet when you got them together, as Julian well knew, they were worse than wild beasts to each other, says Ammianus (22.5.4). The author of the *Historia Augusta* agreed. He makes Aurelian complain that the way the senators were going on one might have thought they were debating in a church (20.5).

Our historians are both touching the point and missing it at the same time. The kind of open contention that had once been possible in the senate was in fact now occurring in the churches. And because serious ideological struggles about the place of man in the world do tend to impose themselves upon public life, the churches were becoming a political arena.

Ammianus has fundamentally mistaken what is happening in spite of his reluctance to accept Christianity as a religion in the Roman sense. The same mistake of understanding had led to the failure of the persecutions. It was not just a matter of adapting the pantheon to a new manifestation of "the highest divinity."

What we are witnessing is the challenging of civilization for the first time by something which *we* now call a religion, that is, by a comprehensive set of beliefs on man and the world which is capable of determining the pattern of one's life even in contradiction of the established social order. The Western cultural tradition derives much of its vitality and argumentativeness from this phenomenon. Cantwell Smith has proposed that Manichaeism is historically the first example of a religion in this Western sense.[7] It would have been easier for us and for Ammianus if the peculiarly Roman term *religio* had never been taken over by Christianity in the fourth century.

---

of Religion," reproduced as chapter 9 in the present volume.

7. In a lecture at the XIVth International Congress of the International Association for the History of Religions, in Winnipeg on 21 August 1980, cf. Cantwell Smith, *Meaning*, 92–98.

Manichaeans and Christians alike, and their critics, had already formulated an agreed terminology which more adequately described the situation: they were a new race or nation, complete with gods and customs of their own, but paradoxically residing within no national boundaries. They cut across the existing pattern of political communities. Hence the bewildering climax of the persecutions. But the solution to them did not work either. The attempt to make Christianity into the religion of the Roman Empire broke down on the incompatibility of the phenomenon with religion in the existing sense. The truth was that Christianity was also incompatible with the state, so long as it retained within itself the seeds of all this trouble: the doctrine of a predetermined revelation of the truth about man and the demand that his life be conformed to it. Hence, in spite of the best efforts alike of Constantine and of Julian, such mind-bending fourth-century phenomena as synods and monasticism.

(b) Eusebius

In his *Ecclesiastical History* Eusebius is fully aware of being a pathfinder from a literary point of view, in that no other writer had previously collected the kind of material he proposes to bring forward (*Hist. eccl.* 1.1.3.4). But there is a double reason why his mind has not moved on to the possibility of using this opportunity to analyze the essential novelty of the great change he witnesses in his own day.

In the first place, although he could not deny that the race of Christians was new (νέον ὁμολογουμένως ἔθνος, *Hist. eccl.* 1.4.2), their way of life (ὁ βίος ... καὶ τῆς ἀγωγῆς ὁ τρόπος, 1.4.4) went back to creation, just as Jesus should not be thought of as novel merely because of the date of his incarnate *politeia* (*Hist. eccl.* 1.4.1). Mortley has recently argued that this by now familiar position was already worked out by Clement of Alexandria, who presented the Christians "as a lawful people under the quasi-kingly regime of Moses." Since Plato, of course, was only "Moses Atticizing", one could thus use history to represent the apparently novel race as the true heirs of the founder of the common culture of the Hellenizing world.[8]

Secondly, a major purpose of Eusebius in composing the *Hist. eccl.* was to insist that it was the same word of God which had guided the churches to his own day, in defiance of gnostic innovators (*Hist. eccl.* 1.1.1). It is no doubt his concern for orthodoxy that has led him to what has been hailed as a fundamental innovation in historiography, the extensive citation of

---

8. Mortley, "Past in Clement Alexandria."

primary documents.[9] Citation of texts had always been part of the business of proof, for example in law. The conversion of history into a technique of testing the truth in disputed cases is itself a mark of the invasion of classical culture as a whole by arguments about ultimate truth. Eusebius is probably at both levels practically unaware of the historical significance of what he was caught up in. But it was not lost on everyone at the time. Both the philosophical and the political critics of Christianity displayed some sense of the profound changes that threatened the social order of their day.

II. How the Philosophers Saw It

The collapse of the persecutions did not mean the end of the campaign against the churches. The basic objections had not been met by the political compromise, and there were other ways by which they could be pursued. Constantine hints several times at the skeptical observers whose criticisms he feared (Eusebius, *Hist. eccl.* 10.5.21 and *Vit. Const.* 2.60.2; Letter to Aelafius, *CSEL*, 26:204-6). At some stage, perhaps prior to Nicaea in 325, he had condemned the work of Porphyry, *Against the Christians*, to be burnt (Socrates, *Hist. eccl.* 1.9). Constantine proposes now to call the Arians "Porphyrians." Their books are also to be surrendered for burning, subject to the penalty of death. Eusebius was aware that the fifteen books of Porphyry had been written long before (about 270, in fact). But he seems not to have had to come to grips with them personally until the persecutions were over, which was after Porphyry had died (in 308). In his work *Against Hierocles* Eusebius thinks he is dealing with propaganda based on Celsus, but it is clear that the philosopher of the persecution had based his *Logos philalethes* on Porphyry. It was not long before Eusebius discovered the significance of the latter.[10] Jerome records (*Vir. ill.* 81) that he then produced twenty-five books against Porphyry. Apollinarius (*Vir. ill.* 104) was later to produce thirty.

In the second decade of the fourth century, the influx of new members into the churches led Eusebius to compose an elaborate introduction for them. The *Preparation for* and *Demonstration of the Gospel*. It was to deal in an orderly way with the whole range of intellectual difficulties which might

---

9. Momigliano, "Pagan and Christian Historiography," especially at 99, drawing attention (91) to Josephus as representing a similarly apologetic use of documents in history.

10. For the chronology I follow Sirinelli's introduction to the *Sources Chrétiennes* 1974 edition of Eusebius's *Preparation for the Gospel*. But it is now claimed that Eusebius had made extensive use of Porphyry's *Against the Christians* in the first edition of his *Chronicle* (*c.* 300 or even as early as 280): so Croke, "Era of Porphyry's Anti-Christian Polemic."

face the new believers. Therein Eusebius constantly refers to Porphyry, and at the very beginning of the *Preparation* it is from Porphyry that he draws the vivid summary of the objections of the Greeks (1.2.1–5).[11] "They say that we neither think like the Greeks nor act like foreigners. What then is it that is alien about us, and what is the novelty of our lifestyle?" The answer to this question is not that the Christians thought like Jews and lived like Greeks. Eusebius goes on to a series of questions which stress the unpardonable atrocity: the Christians have abandoned their national gods, to whom they are indebted for protection, and "by a mindless and unexamined act of faith" (1.2.4) adopted the universally condemned mythology of the Jews, who are the impious enemies of all peoples. But (and this is the heart of the objection) the Christians do not even apply themselves to the God of the Jews in the way their customs require, but follow a novel and solitary path of their own, respecting neither Greek nor Jewish ways (1.2.5).

(a) Porphyry

Did Porphyry go on to define or analyze this novelty? Probably not, for, with the characteristic conservatism of classical antiquity, he simply could not take seriously the possibility of an alternative way of life. Eusebius turns back on him his own catalogue of the methods of euthanasia amongst barbarian peoples (1.4.7). He claims that they have given up these atrocities solely on the strength of the teachings of Jesus as they have spread around the world. Eusebius thus admits the charges against "Christianism," and offers it as an alternative to Hellenism and Judaism, "its very name advertising its novelty" (1.5.12). But the rest of his *Preparation for the Gospel* is nevertheless not devoted to questions of social life, but to basic points in the doctrine of God. He endeavors to show up the weaknesses of polytheism together with its oracles and underlying fatalism (Books 1–6), and the superiority of Hebrew wisdom, which is in agreement with the best Platonic philosophy (Books 7–15). Of the 20 books of the *Demonstration of the Gospel*, the first 10, which alone are extant, deal with the reasons why Christians reject Moses and with the proofs of the divinity of Jesus from Hebrew prophecy. The lost books 11–20 probably continued this theme before finishing with the origins of the church. It is not impossible that Eusebius here attempted an assessment of the peculiar character of "Christianism," or he may have done it in the *Praeparatio* and *Demonstratio ecclesiastica*, to which Photius refers, if indeed these works are not simply the product of confusion on Photius's part.

11. Von Wilamowitz-Moellendorf, "Ein Bruchstück."

On the other hand, the fragments of Porphyry's work (mainly from the *Apocriticus* of Macarius Magnes, who was answering an early fourth-century critique of Christianity, assumed to have been a digest of Porphyry) confirm that the intellectual issues were paramount. The scale and seriousness of his attacks confirm the impression given by Eusebius. Porphyry was basically concerned with the "mindless and unexamined act of faith" upon which the peculiar life of the churches rested. He clearly recognized the power exercised over the minds of believers by the teaching of the Scriptures in church. He does not seem to have anticipated that religious sociology might want to find other explanations of the success of Christianity. Nevertheless, his criticisms frequently involve him in comments on contemporary church life, which show that he was an acute observer of what was going on there.[12]

Knowing the doctrines of Scripture as well as he did, Porphyry could see the inconsistency of Christians imitating the temples with large buildings of their own, even though they had no idols or sacrifices, and nothing prevented their praying at home, since the Lord would hear them anywhere (fr. 76). But he was also aware of the teaching activities that went on in the churches, for he understands the distinction between the catechumens and the "faithful" (fr. 26), who were fully initiated. He does not consider even bishops and presbyters fit to count among the "faithful" (fr. 95), since they did not live up to the gospel test of the grain of mustard seed (Matt 17:20). He also considers that Mark 16:17-18 would be a good test of fitness for the "priesthood" (he does not here use the Christian term), and especially of those competing for bishoprics (fr. 96). He knows that the churches uphold a "canon of truth" (fr. 38) handed down from Jesus, and is not impressed by the "tens of thousands" (fr. 36) who perished for it, which was pleasing neither to God nor to a reasonable man (fr. 64). Porphyry also recognizes the universal spread of the gospel (fr. 13), which only goes to show the falsity of the prediction in Matt 24:14, since the end has still not come.

But the most illuminating comments from the social point of view are perhaps those relating to the place of women and their property in the churches. In an earlier work, the *Philosophy from Oracles*, Porphyry had recognized the tenacity of Christian women (Augustine, *Civ.* 19.23).[13] A husband asked the oracle which god he should propitiate to retrieve his wife from Christianity. Apollo replied that it was easier to fly or write on water than recall to reason an impious and defiled woman—therefore leave

---

12. Yet Harnack's classification of a few fragments under this heading is arbitrary; the allusions may well have been only incidental to his main attack on Scripture: von Harnack, *Porphyrius*; Barnes, "Porphyry *Against the Christians*"; Benoît, "Le Contra Christianos de Porphyre."

13. Demarolle, "Les femmes chrétiennes."

her to her folly, for she mourns a dead god, condemned as he was by good judges and dishonorably executed in his prime. In *Against the Christians* (fr. 97), Porphyry alleged that women constituted their "senate" (so Jerome, who warns against the danger), dominating in the churches, and that the preference of the women "passed judgement on the priestly rank." The voting power of women was not seen as a sign of social progress, however. There was nothing surprising in Paul's having conquered the world (fr. 4). It was all done for profit. Men who were by origin peasants and paupers had used the familiar magic arts to induce "rich little women" to hand over their wealth. Porphyry took the saying about the camel and the eye of the needle (Matt 19:24) as a claim that the poor had privileged access to heaven (fr. 58). It was too immoral for him to credit it to Jesus. It must have been invented by certain paupers who coveted the property of the rich. Similarly, the challenge to the rich young ruler (Matt 19:21), which was to become the charter of monasticism, must have been invented by a distressed gentlewoman, like the ones Porphyry knew of, who had been persuaded to distribute all their property to the poor. The women had then started raising funds, abandoning their freedom for indecent begging, and adopting a pitiable appearance instead of happiness, and had moved into the houses of those who still had them. It was the ultimate outrage. Having given up their own property on the pretext of piety, they had been driven by want to covet that of others. Porphyry also knew of women committed to virginity who made a boast of it, claiming that they were filled with the Holy Spirit like "the one who had given birth to Jesus" (fr. 33). Porphyry's contempt for such women is clear. Did he fear the challenge their new way of life made to the accepted social order? Yet a generation later he was to write to his own wife against marriage and in favor of reducing one's material needs to the minimum. The ideals of the Christian women were probably closer to his own than he would have liked to admit.

The prevailing sarcasm of Porphyry's approach to Christianity probably prevented his making any rational appraisal of the contemporary social phenomenon. It also registers his concern at what he sensed as a form of religious mania. He had criticized the classical conception of the gods as well, and had given offence in that quarter. He was not concerned, as Celsus had been, with the national interest.

(b) Celsus

About the time of the "great persecution" there were published at least three philosophical critiques of Christianity. One was the digest of Porphyry to which Macarius Magnes later replied, of unknown authorship. The second author, likewise unidentified, wrote the three books "against the Christian name" which are referred to by Lactantius (*Div. inst.* 5.2). The latter regards him as a power-seeker and profiteer masquerading as philosopher, and holds that his work was written in ignorance of what it was he was attacking. The only hints as to its contents do not rise above the usual stereotype—Christianity was a superstition suited to old women; the world would be better off when everyone attended again to the cult of the gods.

The third author, also described by Lactantius (*Div. inst.* 5.2.12), can be safely identified with Hierocles, an experienced provincial governor who advised Diocletian on the opening of the persecution (*Mort.* 16.4). He went on to govern Egypt, and was a particularly provocative persecutor there. The two books of his *Logos philalethes*, addressed not "against," but "to" the Christians, are said by Lactantius to have concentrated on the inconsistencies of Scripture with such penetration that one might have thought he had once belonged to "our sect." He was especially hard on Peter and Paul, and the other apostles, who were common and uneducated men, and who were mostly fishermen (Lactantius adds that this lack of culture is a good assurance against their having been liars!). As for Jesus, he was the leader of a brigand army of 900 (a novelty in the tradition of polemics), and not to be compared for miracles with Apollonius of Tyana. Lactantius also tells us that the work contained the praises of "the highest God"—the same style Licinius was to use in the prayer he was given for his troops before their battle with Maximinus. Eusebius (*Contra Hieroclem* 1) claims that the work was a blatant plagiarism, taken from Celsus. He was at this stage no more able than Lactantius to recognize the hand of Porphyry behind the work.

It may be, however, that the shadow of Celsus lay more heavily over these debates than has been thought. As late as 335, when Eusebius delivered his speech "In Praise of Constantine" at the dedication of the Church of the Holy Sepulcher in Jerusalem, he still thought it important to come to grips with a number of the criticisms that had been first raised by Celsus.[14] It would perhaps be going too far to say that he was working from Celsus. But the similarity of the arguments that Eusebius faced is clear. The philosophical critique as he deals with it is inspired by two major sentiments. The first is a frustration with the fact that so many people should have been persuaded to accept a view of God that was intellectually untenable. It was quite arbitrary of the Christians to have singled out Jesus for divine honors when the world was rich in heroes, and polytheism corresponded well with the diversity of things. The incarnation was an impossible and unnecessary

---

14. Ehrhardt, "Eusebius and Celsus."

contamination of God's perfection, while the humiliation of Jesus on the cross proved that he could not have been divine anyway.

The second kind of argument to which Eusebius replies is inspired by concern over the social promiscuity of the Christian movement. In contrast with the universal judgment that one should associate with God what is best in life, the Christians deliberately cultivated the worst people. Jesus himself was of mean origin, and the disciples paltry. Yet this vulgar company, appearing only the day before yesterday, and in a backward corner of the empire, had had the impertinence to call in question hallowed national customs, and to address themselves without discrimination to people of any national tradition. This was a profanation of the state, stripping it of its divine sanctions. But in any case, the perverse judgment of the Christians had not been vindicated by their God in the passage of time. Andresen has argued that Celsus, in response to the novel development of a theology of history by Justin, had reacted uniquely amongst the critics of Christianity against the Greek tradition of understanding the cosmos in metaphysical categories.[15] But arguments from social and historical reality lack the security of the timeless. The remarkable shift of fortune which Eusebius had witnessed enabled him to convert the social deficiencies to which Celsus had appealed into trump cards. Celsus had mocked the Jews as frogs holding Sanhedrin round a pond, while the Christian worms held their *ekklēsia* in the dungheap, arguing about which of them was the worst sinner. God had larger things to think of. Plotinus, the teacher of Porphyry, though by no means hostile to Christians, would have agreed. It was absurd to call the least of men brothers and deny this name to the sun and the heavenly bodies. It was all a gross anthropomorphism, hopelessly overestimating the importance of man in the cosmos. But if the universe is stable, remarkable things still happen in the world of men. History might yet reveal the hand of God. In Eusebius's day the worms had suddenly turned, to rule the world.

(c) Julian

With Julian we meet at last a spokesman whose voice has not been stifled. We could hardly wish for a better qualified informant. Standing where he does, at the center of power, and at a time when the significance of the recent changes must have been apparent to anyone with an eye to see, and above all with his close personal involvement, he must have known the answers to our questions. Yet Julian is equally clearly an untypical if not

---

15. Andresen, *Logos und Nomos*.

unique participant. His acute sensitivities sharpen all the issues, but no doubt overstate them too.

Taking up the old complaint, he reproaches the Christians with "the spirit of apostasy" from the national religion (3.388).[16] The same idea had already been turned against him by his half-brother, Gallus (if the letter is genuine), in response to the rumor that he was thinking of abandoning the religion of his family (3.288). As the heirs of Constantine, their personal and national obligation now lay where Constantine's choice had fallen. In making his way back to Hellenism, however, Julian conceived of himself as called by Zeus and the other gods for the restoration of the true and truly ancient religion. He sets this out in a lengthy parable (2.130–48; cf. 3.12, 26, 148). At a critical point in his career he had prayed to the gods for a sign (2.282), and at other times received one apparently unsolicited (2.386; 3.4, 8). Julian's mind was highly alert to the need for guidance. Homer and Plato are bound to him personally, like amulets (3.98). He was no doubt familiar with the practice, documented by the many extracts from the Bible preserved on folded pieces of papyrus, whereby believers literally bound themselves to the words of God. The Bible had made a deep impression on Julian too. He alludes to passages of Scripture, expecting his non-Christian readers to understand the point (2.6, 36, 298, 304, 308). It was said that in his youth he had learnt it all by heart (Eunapius, *VS* 473).

The ancient religion, however, which he was determined to restore, or, as he called it, "Hellenism," could no longer be taken for granted. For all his intense conviction of its truth, Julian did not attempt to conceal from himself or anyone else the widespread disbelief and even disloyalty he faced. He defended himself with insults. "Dogs relieve themselves on the pillars in front of the schools and courts" (2.8). He admits the fact that the prefect of Egypt is openly ignoring his demand for the banishment of Athanasius (3.142). In the *Misopogon*, the satire on himself by which he reflects his frustration, he no doubt even exaggerates the degree to which the citizens of Antioch found his image and policies ridiculously outdated (2.470). But the omission of the city council to provide sacrifices for his visit to the temple of Zeus at Daphne, where it was left to the priest to find a goose from his private means (2.486), represents a tacit opposition to his wishes. He must have seen that it put a large question mark over the future. The temple of Apollo at Daphne had already been stripped for building materials (3.98).

But Julian was actively encouraging the development of a national community (*koinon*, 3.28) of the Hellenes, which could also claim its dedicated

---

16. These Julian references denote volume and page where the Greek text appears in W. C. Wright's Loeb edition.

patronesses (3.136). As the sole ruler of the Roman Empire, with the prospect of a long life ahead of him, he must have seemed to many a figure to be seriously reckoned with. He speaks of the unusual sight of crowded temple precincts, as people and magistrates hastened to applaud him and listen to his reproachful speeches (2.438). There were even bishops who kept their options open. Pegasius of Troy had all along been a secret admirer of the old gods, and was now free to take up a priesthood publicly (3.48–54). George, the Arian bishop of Alexandria, assassinated by the Christian mob, had possessed a good classical library which Julian had used in the past, and which he now hoped to rescue (2.74, 122). Even Basil, the future bishop of Caesarea and formerly a fellow-student of Julian's at Athens, received an invitation to court, with a public travel voucher into the bargain. Julian hoped for friendly academic debate (3.82).

Like his intellectual predecessors, and fortified in this no doubt by his Christian upbringing, Julian was fully conscious that the "madness of the Galileans" (3.122), by which they had introduced a novel "*kērygma*" and teaching (3.142) and inflicted a disease on the community (3.144), sprang from the study of Scripture. He recognized the passion for learning and argument that gripped the church at Alexandria, and the strong supply of teachers in it (3.150). But he also challenged the Galileans to put the matter to a proper educational test. Train a sample group of children in Scripture only, he proposed, and see whether they turn out any better than slaves (3.386). True to the philosophical ideal, Julian believes that knowledge is only possible for an élite. The Galileans were creating a false expectation amongst the people. For the same reason Julian objected to the Cynics taking seriously the opinions of common people (2.46). The churches, he rightly detected, had been tacitly relying upon the classical tradition to help them come to terms with educated society. But Jesus had only been known for 300 years, and his followers were really leeches, who sucked only the worst blood from the Jewish tradition to which they had attached themselves (3.376). He and the "fishermen-theologians" (3.188) had only been interested in the sinners, to whom Jesus immorally offered forgiveness (2.412), and in mean activities like curing cripples and blind paupers. You confined yourselves to backward peoples and places like this, Julian reminds them, because you never expected that "you would one day arrive at the position of power you now have" (3.376).

Yet in spite of his contempt for their vulgarity, Julian recognized that the attraction of the churches lay partly in their charitable work (2.302, 336; 3.68–70). He recognized the power of Jesus's command to "sell what you have and give to the poor," even though he could see that it made economic nonsense (3.430). He complained that the councilors of Antioch who neglected the sacrifices nevertheless allowed their wives to empty the cupboards to feed the poor—and to enjoy the reputation they won from it (2.490). The same women were allowed to "govern themselves" and have control over the bringing up of the children (2.472). Julian was enraged that Athanasius should have baptized "eminent Greek women" during his reign (2.142). Although he regarded the life of women as pitiable and emotionally unstable (2.64, 440), he knew their importance in the spread of the gospel (3.376). He also recognized the solidarity of the social classes created by Christian belief (2.474), in spite of the economic conflicts and exploitation in which the groups concerned were involved (2.502–12).

Features of church life new to his ear also took Julian's eye. He was by no means confined to the conventional objections to Christianity. The insubordination he faced in Alexandria and Antioch made clear to him the fact that the governing classes in such cities were now closely connected with the bishops. If his policies were frustrated, he could assume that the bishops and presbyters had been sitting in secret session with the local administration (3.46). When the people of Alexandria had tried to stop the dismantling of the temples, the prefect had turned his troops on them, "perhaps because he feared George more than Constantius" (3.62). The troubles at Alexandria and elsewhere made clear another novelty of the age, the state of civil war between rival Christian orthodoxies. Julian knows the technical terminology, and his sharp tongue does not spare the atrocities either of "heretics" (3.128) or of "clerics" (3.130). Neither Jesus nor Paul had authorized them to slaughter each other "because they did not mourn the dead body [of Jesus] in the same way" (3.376). Julian loved to depict Christianity as a cult of death. He was familiar with the fetishism of the cross (3.372), but above all his barbs were directed at the cult of the martyrs. He hinted that the Christians had turned out to be polytheists after all (3.374). Because the bones of the martyrs were kept there, he called the churches "tombs" (2.134, 484; 3.134). By seeking the inspiration of the dead in this way the churches were breaking the scriptural ban on sleeping among the tombs (3.416). "You have filled everything with tombs and monuments, but it is nowhere prescribed for you that you should abase yourselves before them and revere them" (3.414).

Apart from the petition of Isidore of Karanis (P.Col. 7.171), Julian is our earliest independent authority for monasticism. He admired asceticism as a philosopher. Marcus Aurelius "displayed a beauty beyond invention by the very fact that he kept himself uncared for and unadorned"; "His body shone with transparent light, most pure and clear, from lack of food" (2.371). Julian's chosen company of seven at Antioch pursued a kind of collective asceticism (2.466). The people of Antioch found his matted and lice-infested hair and beard revolting, together with his long nails and ink-stained hands (2.422–4). They objected to his sleeping alone (2.442). But he draws two vital distinctions. The Cynics did not go in for giving oracular advice, nor did they raise funds for the needy out of "mercy" as the Galileans called it. Here once more we find the two distinctive hallmarks of Christianity, this time explicitly identified for us by a peculiarly well-qualified disbeliever: the doctrine of revelation, and care for those in need.

Although Julian was heir to the military burden of the Roman Empire, and lost his life campaigning against the Persians, he was not seriously concerned with Christianity as a threat to national security, as had been the persecuting rulers. Religion was not for him in the first place a matter of the public interest. Julian was concerned for the intrinsic truth of "Hellenism," the recognition of which he believed to be central to the integrity of the classical tradition. His onslaught on Christianity set a style that was to find echoes amongst Greek writers of the old persuasion for a century or more. They immortalized their hero, and retreated into their academic preserves, prepared to sit out the siege indefinitely.[17] Julian's older contemporary, Libanius, the great rhetorician of Antioch, taught the generation of classicizing bishops that followed them. Yet he did not hesitate to take up Julian's criticisms of Christianity, as his speeches gave him opportunity. He was no campaigner, but the hypocrisy of the rabble-rousing monks, "the men clothed in black," especially incensed him. Eunapius, though, like Julian, a pupil of the Christian sophist, Prohaeresius, at Athens, spoke out in very similar terms. In his Lives of the Sophists he gave expression to his sense of the importance for Greek education of the élite succession of scholars. The rhetorician Themistius, however, who worked for both Constantius and Theodosius, attempted no direct criticism of Christianity. Reversing the attitude of Julian, he advocated a philosophical education that would make ethics popular, in the hope of creating a cultural bond between ruler and subject. He was content to praise Constantius, Julian, and Theodosius alike as philosophers. Such a spirit of compromise, which earned him the contempt of the intransigent sophists, secured the future of Hellenism more effectively than confrontation could ever have done. He showed the way to the Greek-Christian symbiosis of Byzantium.

17. For Libanius, see de Labriolle, *La Réaction païenne*, 429–33. For Eunapius, see Opelt, "Eunapios," and Ridley, "Eunapius and Zosimus." For Themistius, see Downey, "Themistius."

III. How the Policy-Makers Tried to Stop It

The philosophical critique of Christianity tells us how the movement was viewed within a limited circle of intellectuals. But their ongoing preoccupation with its illogicality and vulgarity, I believe, correctly identifies the mainspring: the beliefs of the Christians contradicted both the accepted ways of understanding the world and its hierarchy of social values. Beliefs and social action, moreover, were coupled together in a unique manner, with effects unknown before in classical antiquity. An alternative form of community life was being created, and had begun seriously to disorient those who valued the old city-based culture. The persecutions demonstrate the fact that this threat not only arose in the conceit of philosophers, but was taken to heart by government and public as well. The reasons are also clear. The concern was for national security, a fully traditional reaction.

But in the immediate aftermath of the "persecutions" we find a quite distinct kind of response at the public level, and one which is new to the classical tradition. If the Christians will not associate themselves in the proper way with the general community, they had better be excluded from it. The choice is now between full assimilation and apartheid. Coupled with this demand are attempts to generate a renewal of community support for the national cults. Their prestige had been injured by the capitulation of the government to the Christians. Now they are to be regenerated, but in a novel way. They will be reorganized so as to capture some of the sources of community strength and solidarity that had been effectively demonstrated in the organization of the churches.

(a) Maximinus

It is not clear who first thought of this method of treating the problem. As soon as the death of Galerius became known in May 311, Maximinus Daia moved to occupy Asia Minor. He had given effect to the edict of toleration by a rather more guarded circular issued to the governors of the East by his Praetorian Prefect, Sabinus (Eusebius, *Hist. eccl.* 9.1.3–6). Eusebius himself alludes (9.2) to a period of six months' respite for the churches. We may then imagine that the return of the exiles, and plans for the rebuilding of churches, would soon have created tension with those who had profited from their suppression.[18]

---

18. Moreover, Castritius has shown, in *Studien zu Maximinus Daia*, how the general economic interests of the cities were closely tied to the festivals and other commercial aspects of the public cults.

According to Lactantius (*Mort.* 36.3), Maximinus then arranged for deputations from the cities to seek from him a ban on the construction of meeting-places (*conventicula*) by the Christians. This was followed by the creation of high priests for each city. They were to be selected from the leading citizens, and were to sacrifice daily to all the gods. The existing priests of the various cults were to be subordinate to the high priest, and together they were to be responsible for preventing any meeting-places being built by Christians, and indeed for preventing their meeting at all.

The high priests of the various cities were grouped into provincial hierarchies, under a metropolitan. Eusebius stresses the novelty of these procedures (*Hist. eccl.* 9.7.1). The assimilation of the priesthoods to the pattern of civil authority parallels the development of such a pattern that had occurred amongst the churches. It represents a bid to upstage the Christians.

At Antioch the campaign was originated by Theotecnus, the city treasurer. He is presumably the imperial *curator civitatis*, which might support the assumption that the ultimate initiative came from above, though by this stage the post was usually filled from the local nobility. Like Epitynchanus, he was able to produce oracles to give himself credence (9.3).[19] They were presumably issued in the name of Zeus Philios, whose cult he managed. The cult-name is perhaps significant: the Christians are to be driven out in the name of the god of hospitality.

Eusebius says (*Hist. eccl.* 9.4.1) that the fashion of appealing to Maximinus for the exclusion of Christians spread from Antioch, and he stresses the selection of civil leaders as the new city and provincial high-priests (9.4.2). They had guards, and a military escort (8.14.9).

The campaign of Maximinus had also embraced public education. Fictitious "Acts of Pilate and Jesus" were devised (Eusebius, *Hist. eccl.* 9.5.1). They were to be officially displayed by means of inscriptions, and used as teaching material in schools, to be learnt by heart by the children. Maximinus also published in every city and place the revelations (extorted, according to Eusebius, by the military governor of Damascus) of public prostitutes on the indecencies which were performed in "the Lord's houses" (*Hist. eccl.* 9.5.2). Roman tradition was familiar with the public display of eulogistic treatments of history, but the convention had been to condemn the memories of the losers to oblivion. Now, however, the sense of ideological competition is apparent. The paradox of the deified criminal, which we know from the philosophers was a major source of offence in Christian doctrine, is to be dealt with openly, using even the elementary means of persuasion

---

19. For his inscription as "first high-priest, savior of his country, and legislator", found near Acmonia in Phrygia, see Grégoire, "Notes épigraphiques I."

available through the schools. Does this reflect an awareness of the influence of Christian doctrine on children? Their enemies were ahead of the churches in recognizing the uses of education for indoctrination. This must mark the beginning of what has become a major feature of Western civilization: the commitment of the state to a deliberate inculcation of its version of the truth, and conversion of education to this purpose. The ideologizing of society is then, by reaction, one of the most far-reaching consequences of the dogmatic drive of the churches.

(b) Licinius

Although Licinius is seen by Eusebius as the vindicator of the Christian cause over Maximinus, one may reasonably assume that the concerns of the cities upon which his campaign had rested remained the same, and that the new ruler would for political reasons at least be obliged to take them seriously.[20] As the tension built up towards his final conflict with Constantine (in 324), moreover, he must have found it prudent to cultivate anti-Christian opinion, given the strong personal commitment of Constantine to the churches. Eusebius says that he came to admire the anti-Christian policies of his predecessors in the East (*Hist. eccl.* 10.8.2). He began to "besiege" the Christians gradually, and without drawing too much attention to it (10.8.8). First, he removed all Christians from his household (10.8.9). He then excluded from service (although Eusebius uses the term "soldiers," this should probably be taken as a reference to the civil service) and downgraded those who would not sacrifice (10.8.10). Worse was to follow, but "must I recall all his deeds in detail?" asks Eusebius, "and the unlawful laws of that most lawless man?" (These remarks are important, in view of the claim that the *Hist. eccl.* does not justify our accepting the measures registered in the *Vit. Const.* as authentic.) There was a ban on taking food to prisoners or those in chains. No one was to be subject to the same suffering they sought to relieve (10.8.11). The emotional reaction of Eusebius (more extensive than indicated here) shows that Licinius had put his finger on a sensitive spot. Presumably he recognized the social influence established by the charitable practices of the Christians, and quietly cut the nerve of their ministry.

Eusebius then refers (without detail) to elimination of the most reputable bishops by having the governors lay traps for them. Unheard of means of death were employed (*Hist. eccl.* 10.8.14). The details given suggest only local atrocities on the part of the governors (10.8.17). Eusebius implies that the basis for the action was that the Christians were believed to be

---

20. That he did so is implied by Libanius, *Or.* 3.6 (in Foerster, *Libanii Opera*, 190).

praying for the victory of Constantine (10.8.16). In Amasia, and other cities of Pontus, some churches were demolished, others locked up (10.8.15). There would have been a general persecution had not Constantine's victory intervened (10.8.18–19).

Although Eusebius was clearly not very well informed at the time of his final revision of the history (soon after 324?), the *Life of Constantine* (even if genuine, published apparently only after Eusebius's death in 339?) provides striking additional details. The Eusebian authorship of this work has been seriously challenged on grounds of style and composition, which are rejected, with argument, by the latest editor.[21] He also dismisses, though without giving reasons, the objections brought against the details of the persecution in particular, which have been held to be a fabrication, based upon the attested policies of Theodosius against the heretics.[22] It is not possible here to debate this argument, but instead I propose to ask the question whether the details can be given a plausible explanation in relation to what Eusebius tells us in the *Hist. eccl.* of the policies of Licinius

But first, what of the documents in the *Vita Constantini*? The letter which is said to have been sent by Constantine to Eusebius himself and to all the other bishops on the repair and extension of neglected church buildings (*Vit. Const.* 2.46.1–3), although it refers to the restoration of freedom from "that dragon" (Licinius), nowhere suggests that any buildings had been destroyed, nor that there had been any confiscations. What has to be made good is the result of neglect, based partly on the fear of possible action against the churches.

Destruction of buildings is likewise not mentioned (though confiscation is) in the "complete provision" (*Vit. Const.* 2.41) for restoration of rights which Constantine made in an edict addressed "to the provincials of Palestine" (*Vit. Const.* 2.24–42), and which is said in one group of manuscripts to have been "the first letter sent after his victory over the tyrants by Constantine, Emperor (*basileus*) of the Romans, to those in the Eastern land." This is the edict of which "Eusebius" claims to have a personal signed copy. Its authenticity has been established by the identification of a fragment of it in P.Lond. 3.878. It directs that the following "cruel outrages and punishments" are to be reversed (26.2). On the personal front, the penalties specified are: exile beyond the frontiers (30.1); banishment to islands (31.1); condemnation to labor in mines or public works (32.1); loss of civil rank (32.2); loss of status in the government service (33); loss of social rank (34.1), with consequential condemnation to work in women's apartments or linen factories

21. Winkelmann, *Über das Leben*.
22. Cataudella, "La persecuzione," 48–83, 229–59.

(34.1) or reduction to the status of servant of the treasury (34.1); reduction to slavery (34.2). On the property front the penalties are: compulsory enrollment as councilor (which carried financial obligations) (30.1); confiscation of all property (30.2); confiscation of the deceased estates of martyrs (35.1) (next-of-kin are now to inherit or, in their absence, the churches); confiscation of church buildings, lands, and orchards (39); confiscation of martyrs' graves (40). In all these cases, restoration is required whether from individuals (37.1), who may have obtained the properties at auction (38), by purchase (41) or as gifts (41), or from the treasury (39).

It will be apparent that this list implies a far more extensive range of action than Eusebius had indicated in the *Hist. eccl.* It is hard to think that it was the result only of individual initiatives by the governors. That no particular prominence is given to the death penalty confirms the suspicion that in the *Hist. eccl.* Eusebius was making the most of it. On the other hand, the extensive range of status degradations and confiscations suggests a planned drive to reduce the wealth and social dignity of the church community. Two points not mentioned in the *Hist. eccl.* are particularly tell-tale. The compulsory enrollment of Christians as councilors presumably reverses the immunity granted to Catholic clergymen by Constantine in 313 (Eusebius, *Hist. eccl.* 10.7), and reinforced in 319 (*Cod. Theod.* 16.2.1, 2), though by 320 Constantine himself had had to stop the flight of propertied persons from their civil obligations by confining access to the clergy-posts to those too poor for council service (*Cod. Theod.* 16.2.3). Secondly, the confiscation of martyrs' graves presumably represents the same line of attack which had opened the campaign of Maximinus in 311. Thus although this catalogue does not and, being a list of individual penalties at law, could not substantiate the other measures attributed to Licinius in the *Vit. Const.*, its diversity, and the emphasis on the social effects of the policy, certainly justifies serious consideration of the others.

The first "law" attributed to Licinius (*Vit. Const.* 1.51.1) is a ban on the bishops meeting in synod, or even visiting each other for consultation. The author notes (51.2) that this is the only legitimate method by which ecclesiastical decisions are made. If this act is authentic, it is a well-calculated move to break down the extraordinary international nexus which had been created amongst the bishops, and to which Constantine had quickly learnt to subject himself for guidance in matters ecclesiastical. Even the reorganization of religion along provincial lines by Maximinus had not ventured to go so far. One can easily imagine how the tumultuous series of synods at Alexandria over Arianism may have given Licinius the excuse for a ban. Given the vast power which was shortly to be demonstrated by the councils, it could even be rated far-sighted. But quite apart from the threat of a state within the state, the socially disruptive factionalism in church life justified a curb on the politicking of bishops. It has been held that the purpose of the measure would have been to provoke the bishops into self-incriminating acts of retaliation.[23] In that case it would be amongst the "traps" alluded to in *Hist. eccl.* 10.8.4.

The second "law" (*Vit. Const.* 1.53.1) prevented women meeting for prayer with men, and excluded them from attendance at "instruction in virtue." The bishops were not to catechize women, but other women were to be selected to teach the women. Cataudella assumes that this represents a desire to prevent the kind of sexual scandals of which Maximinus had publicly accused the churches (*Hist. eccl.* 9.5.2), and that it must be unhistorical because the churches would not have found such a measure unwelcome in the circumstances assumed. But it is notable that in spite of gossip the Fathers of the church were generally inclined to justify the close associations they maintained with the patronesses who supplied them with funds and social prestige, while the orders of widows and virgins provided the backbone of the caring ministry of the churches. It might be sounder to suppose that the object of such a measure by Licinius would have been to break down this very effective system of social relations. One may also perhaps suspect in it an outworking of the contempt for the intellectual capacity of women which is a feature of the philosophical tradition, if not of the ecclesiastical one (Eusebius, *Praep. ev.* 1.4.14, 5.3). By making the women undertake the teaching of women, may not the hope have been that some of the impetus would be lost to the life of the churches through the intellectual degeneration which would follow on the notoriously productive female side?

One of the historically troublesome aspects of these extra measures attributed to Licinius in the *Vit. Const.* is their complete lack of attestation from other sources. It may be noted here, on the other hand, that a recently published papyrus documents a circle of women who ranked as "teachers" in the church (P.Strasb.Gr. 1900). The editor dates this text to later in the fourth century, and attributes it to heretical circles, who are known to have been willing to use women as teachers.[24] But the date should perhaps be reconsidered in the light of a possible *Sitz im Leben* during the campaign of Licinius.

A third measure requires church meetings to take place outside the city-gates in the open air (*Vit. Const.* 1.53.2). This is explicable in terms of the petitions to Maximinus requesting the exclusion of the Christians from the cities, while the denial of building rights may have been intended to

23. Feld, *Der Kaiser Licinius*.
24. Nagel, "Lettre chrétien sur papyrus."

cripple the charitable (or even indecent) activities which were associated with church buildings.

These three items are the major additions of the *Vit. Const.* to the account of the policies of Licinius given by Eusebius in the *Hist. eccl.* None of them is inconsistent with the picture presented there of a ruler gradually limiting the risks of a program he knew from experience could easily backfire. We know that Eusebius of Nicomedia retained the confidence of Licinius throughout, and that a relative of this bishop, the Praetorian Prefect Julius Julianus, was honored by Constantine with the consulship immediately after his defeat, and married into his family to become the grandfather of the Emperor Julian. It is clear therefore that Licinius had been following a policy of compromise rather than full confrontation. There is no reason to suppose that he was deliberately seeking a collision with Constantine: the pace was being set by the other side. But given the coming struggle he was bound to make the most of those who would not welcome the victory of the great patron of the churches. We should also not exclude the possibility that the main grievance of Licinius in ecclesiastical matters was with those who opposed Eusebius of Nicomedia as an Arian. Eusebius of Caesarea, however, has cast him as a total renegade, thus fully endorsing the propaganda of Constantine. Neither Eusebius nor any other author, composing the *Vit. Const.* from that point of view, would have been likely to invent such peculiar and unspectacular offences on Licinius's part as the three measures peculiar to the *Vit. Const.* The very difficulty of explaining them obliges the modern historian to consider more carefully the possibility that they are actual relics of the policy of Licinius. Any rhetorically capable writer in antiquity would have had far more sensational allegations ready to hand had he needed to invent them.

The difficulty of correlating the measures with other evidence for the history of the church in these times is a danger sign, of course. The innocent testimony of Isidore of Karanis (P.Col. 7.171) makes it quite certain that there was no serious constraint on church life in his corner of Egypt, and the same seems to have been the case with Alexandria. But we should remember that we do not know the chronology of the acts of Licinius. It is perfectly possible that a more detailed knowledge of the timing would enable us to fit in both the evidence for ecclesiastical freedom and the acts of repression. The same applies of course to the possibility that the policy was applied in different ways in different places. The *Vit. Const.* says that some of the measures were greeted with ridicule. We may imagine that they were only successful where there was public support, and administrators willing to gamble on a victory for Licinius. The situation everywhere must have been confused. From the city of Hermopolis Magna, in Egypt, we possess from about the year 320 the correspondence of a lawyer, Theophanes.[25] He was a cultivated man, with religious interests that are difficult to pin down, and had made a journey to Antioch to intervene in some questions of injustice arising from religious causes. Some editors have put him on the Christian side, others amongst their opponents. His sons say that they owe to their father an ability "to think little of those who think differently." Two correspondents address him as their "beloved brother", and another speaks of "the highest God" and yet another of "the grace of the Almighty God." But another correspondent again is certainly a "chief prophet" in the cult of Hermes Trismegistus. There may have been more realism in the attempt of Maximinus to affiliate all beliefs into one social structure of religion than church critics could allow. Licinius appears to have made a distinctive and more limited attempt to curb the social independence of the churches. Although not a Christian, and necessarily dependent upon the support of the classical gods in his conflict with Constantine (*Vit. Const.* 2.4; 2.5.2), he does not seem to have attempted to revive the city and provincial high-priesthoods of Maximinus. That, along with other more radical measures, was reserved for Julian.

IV. Who Saw Best What was Going On?

The conclusion then is this. Neither Eusebius nor Ammianus seems to have been in a position to see directly the basic nature of the changes going on.

Eusebius was too preoccupied with the need to demonstrate the maintenance of the orthodox succession against innovators to appreciate the ways in which the struggle over orthodoxy was itself shifting the center of power in the community out of the hands of the civil rulers. The official status accorded the churches, and their mass following, did not make it easier for Ammianus to see them as occupying an acceptable place within the old Roman pattern of religion. He failed to recognize the historical importance of things which repelled him, notably their argumentativeness, and assumed that it was an aberration rather than of the essence of Christianity. But the philosophers, and especially those who apparently had inside knowledge of the movement, Porphyry, Hierocles, and Julian, saw the need to cripple the intellectual drive of the churches by discrediting Scripture. They saw the new pattern of social alignments which it generated, and clearly sensed the threat to the very integrity of classical civilization. At the practical level, Maximinus and Licinius attempted to

---

25. Judge and Pickering, "Papyrus Documentation." Editor's note: See now also Matthews, *Journey of Theophanes*.

save the day by imposing a uniform religious structure on the community, and breaking down the institutions through which an alternative pattern of society was being built up within the Roman world.

History was not repeating itself. Insofar as fundamentally new arrangements for life were being introduced, especially in the West, classical historiography ceased to provide useful conventions for viewing it. The new ecclesiastical history failed to expand its horizons far enough to take in the full range of public life. Chronography provided a step in the right direction, towards a teleological explanation of man's progress through time, but its skeletal form left it also far short of the full analysis of the significance of the changes.

8

The Conversion of Rome

Ancient Sources of Modern Social Tensions

This chapter was first delivered as a lecture to the Macquarie University Convocation on April 14, 1978. It was published under the present title in 1980 by the Macquarie Ancient History Association, and reproduced (with the addition of the subheadings) in Judge, *Jerusalem and Athens*, 211–38. After a brief discussion of four papyri (transcribed and translated at the end of the chapter) illustrating the rise of Christianity through the third and fourth centuries, it turns to consider how and why the conversion of the empire took place—with particular discussion of the social realities of the early church, the way Christianity was perceived by historians, and the development of monasticism. This essay contends that it was the ideological commitment of the Christians that drove the social realities of Rome's conversion, and that the tensions this conversion produced are still inherent in the West. It was, in some sense, the end of ancient history and the beginning of the modern world.

THE CONVERSION OF ROME is told in miniature in four papyrus documents from the villages of Egypt.[1]

---

1. The texts and translations are reproduced in an appendix at the end of the chapter. For the literature on them see Judge and Pickering, "Papyrus Documentation." For full details of works referred to by the conventional papyrological sigla (P.Oxy., etc.) see Thomas and Pickering, *Papyrus Editions*. Editor's note: See now http://scriptorium.lib.duke.edu/ papyrus/texts/clist.html.

In the first (P.Oxy. 42.3035, published in 1974), an order is issued for the arrest of Petosorapis, son of Horus. Where we should expect the name of his occupation, he is described as *chresianos*. Since no other explanation of this term has been found, one may assume that he was known as a minister of the society which the general public (though not its members) had long come to speak of as "Christian." (The variant spelling may be explained as a phonetic one.) If so, this is not only the earliest dated papyrus evidence of the new faith (since the many earlier biblical papyri are not precisely dated), but presumably the earliest known reference to it in an official document surviving in contemporary form from anywhere in the empire (February 28, 256).[2] It is noteworthy that the order is addressed to the officials of a village, Mermertha. Both classical civilization and the life of the churches had been the exclusive property of the cities. But the papyri now begin to tell us the story of a profound cultural change. The churches are carrying urban institutions and ideas into the third world of ancient society, that of the peasantry whose unseen labor supported the parasitical glories of city life. We do not know why Petosorapis was to be arrested. There is no other action against Christians recorded for that year.[3] But it looks as if the official eye is already clearly focused on the new center of influence in the villages.

The second document (P.Oxy. 33.2673, published in 1968) was written for Aurelius Ammonius, son of Copreus, who calls himself "lector of the former church of the village of Chysis." This is the earliest dated reference (February 5, 304) in a papyrus document to the word *ekklēsia* (though a list of street wardens from Oxyrhynchus, P.Oxy. 1.43, which seems to refer to two churches, could be earlier). Apart from a business letter (P.Amh. 1.3a, written between 264 and 282), which refers to Maximus, the pope (*papas*) of Alexandria, and to a "lector" (who need not be an ecclesiastical one), it is also the earliest instance in the papyri of the use of an ecclesiastical title. It is interesting that we should begin to pick up this terminology first in civil documents. Papyrus letters of an earlier stage between believers preserve no trace of such institutional terms. Again, note the village location, and the substantial range of property which the government expects a church to possess (although this one at Chysis, further up river, had nothing that was on the list). Note also that the lector cannot write Greek. Presumably he had read out the Scriptures in church in Coptic, until it was broken up on

---

2. Judge and Pickering, "Biblical Papyri," give a complete list and analysis of the evidence.

3. I now think this implies too much. An order for arrest did not include the charge, which could have been an ordinary crime in this case, with *chresianos* being the official way of referring to the occupation of deacon or presbyter.

Diocletian's order. The government is well aware of the importance of the new institution, even in the most remote locality.

From only twenty years later (June 6, 324) comes the third document (P.Coll.Youtie 77, published in 1976), which shows the Constantinian establishment already in full effect.[4] Isidorus of Karanis is an impoverished but litigious farmer known to us from a voluminous archive running well back into the third century. Since this is the last of many such petitions from him, we may suppose the assault he reports was fatal. Nowhere else in his papers had any reference to Christianity been detected. But here at the very end it has unexpectedly surfaced in the form of a deacon and a monk. Antoninus is the earliest deacon known from the papyrus record. Isaac is the earliest monk so far referred to anywhere. Even in the vast ecclesiastical literature all the references to monasticism are from works written later, so that it has been possible in the past to doubt the tradition that attributed the adoption of the term *monachos* for ascetics to St. Antony, who is supposed to have started the fashion about 305. Our new papyrus, however, sharply alters the scene, for here is a monk who can be taken as much for granted as a deacon (and that in a document that will have to stand up in a court of law), without any need to specify further what such styles might mean. It is noteworthy that our earliest monk should appear neither in the cities, where the literary admirers of asceticism were concentrated, nor in the remote desert or monasteries into which the tradition projected its heroes, but in the petty world of village violence and poverty—in a fight over a single cow.

By the time of our fourth document, in the age of Constantius (P.Abinn. 55), deacons and presbyters, and their churches, have become prominent features of the papyrus documents of Egyptian village life. A presbyter from the Fayum could even call himself "pope" (P.Ross.-Georg. 2.28), like the great *papas* of Alexandria itself. The parish church for its part may now be referred to as the "catholic," or principal, church of the village, to distinguish it from subordinate or rival bodies. This petition of the deacon, Heron, illustrates the high status in their small world assumed by the servants of such a church. Abinnaeus was the regional military commander, guarding a fort against desert raiders who never came. All the trouble is internal. There has been something worse than the usual breakdown of village justice. Abinnaeus is appealed to by everyone as the local magnate who can make things work. His own power stems from personal visits to Constantinople, months away from the Fayum. But Aurelius Heron also has influential connections.

---

4. Though it should not have been, since this is still several months before the final overthrow of Licinius, who had in recent years been attempting to disestablish the churches again, without effect in the Fayûm obviously. For full discussion of this document, see Judge, "Earliest Use," reproduced as chapter 14 in this volume.

Unlike other petitioners, he is no humble suppliant. He begins with a sermonizing note to remind Abinnaeus of his responsibilities, and ends with a firm display of rank. The army and the church speak to each other on more or less equal terms. In a Meletian papyrus (P.Lond. 6.1914) of the previous decade we even see a military commander in Alexandria making public amends for atrocities committed by his troops against the visiting clergy. We are already on the threshold of the medieval order of power, and the civil authorities are seriously overshadowed. Unlike other petitioners, Heron does not even bother to ask Abinnaeus to ensure that the authorities see that justice is done. He calmly requests direct restitution from the military itself, "for I am a deacon of the catholic church." It is a symptom of the end for the thousand-year rule of republican humanism. We are watching it take place at a level in society that the Graeco-Roman city had ignored.

1. How Was Rome Converted?

But let me not deceive you. It will not be the thesis of this essay that the church emerged from below to conquer classical society as an "internal proletariat." This has long been the reigning orthodoxy, cultivated alike by ecclesiastical and Marxist historians, and summed up in Toynbee's very misleading phrase. It is just twenty years since I began in this city (Sydney) to propound an alternative view, which has since been taken up elsewhere and substantiated, so that in the latest analysis of the matter it has been called the "new consensus."[5] It goes like this. The New Testament communities were not a popular movement in the sense that they arose from below, and were led by simple, uneducated people. Certainly they had nothing much to do with the metropolitan elite of Rome, with which most of the extant literature is concerned. But equally they were entirely remote from the vast mass of people, who were buried on the land. In their Pauline form especially, the New Testament communities belong to the great Hellenistic cities, the intellectual centers of the Greek East, and spring from the highly argumentative activities of well-educated traveling experts. In the various centers they are promoted by the well-to-do leaders of the local Hellenistic-Jewish establishment. In that respect, from the social point of view, the gospel was not differently placed from other sets of ideas that were being propagated at the time.[6]

From the start, however, a striking new development appears. Regular associations of people were formed which consciously cut across several

5. Malherbe, *Social Aspects*, 31; Scroggs, "Sociological Interpretation."
6. Judge, "St Paul and Classical Society."

distinct grades of the social status system. The well-established patrons who promoted St. Paul and others were expected to draw their domestic servants and clients into a new order of relationships. This deliberate breaking of rank was imposed by St. Paul not only for what may be called ideological reasons (that is, his conception of the meaning of the crucifixion), but because of his own experience of status reversal downwards, which helped him give meaning to the paradox of the rejection of Christ. The social effects of the new order are as clear as they were unprecedented in classical society. For the first time argumentation about God, humanity, and the world, and about the grounds for human behavior in society, is being lifted bodily out of the cultural sanctuaries of philosophy, to which an elite system of education had confined it, and put to work in confrontation with the accepted social order. Such ideas had hitherto been insulated by the ranking system against any test of social practicality. But now a response is demanded in terms of the re-ordering of day-to-day social relations. The result is the incredibly rich and influential experience of the New Testament communities.[7]

In no sort of philosophically predetermined form, a whole new range of ideas on behavior is put into practice in a working experiment within the securely established Graeco-Roman order of society. Instead of the old status grades, bound up with nationality, culture, ownership, and gender, there was to be created a new body of relations between people "in Christ." Each would serve the others, on the strength of a fresh and individual endowment of the Spirit given to him for their good, and not for his own magnification. Paul envisaged a total liberation from the old order, but, paradoxically, not its immediate dissolution. It must even be sustained against premature collapse. It was the womb that must labor to give birth to the new world on the promised day. In the meantime, the new way of life would be practiced in the church. This paradox of now-but-not-yet reached an acute crisis with the conversion of Constantine. Was this the very dawning of the day, and was Christ now to rule the whole world through Caesar, or was the church merely to be sold out to the old order? So, on the one hand, Eusebius, and so, on the other, the Donatists and even, in a sense, their great antagonist, St. Augustine.

For the outside observer in the fourth century, like Ammianus, all that should have been involved was a change of religion. But the meetings which had first assembled in the wake of Paul's preaching would hardly have been recognized by their contemporaries as religious societies. Their main activity was not that of a cult in any recognizable classical sense. That would have demanded ritual, order, decorum—not to speak of a cult

7. Judge, "St Paul as a Radical Critic"; Banks, *Paul's Idea of Community*.

image and shrine. The churches were later to acquire such trappings, and to take over many of the functions of the classical cults. Religion provided the supernatural guarantees for the existing order. In a recently published second- or third-century papyrus (P.Oxy. 36.2782) a priest writes to instruct a priestess to go to the temple of Demeter in the village of Sinkepha "to perform the usual sacrifices on behalf of our lords the emperors (*autokratores*) and their victory and the rise of the Nile and the increase of the crops and the healthy balance of the climate." But by the fourth century we have a bishop, Serapion of Thmuis, writing to the monks to remind them that the Nile flood and the fertility of the land depended on their prayers.[8] Yet a stranger entering a meeting of Paul's followers would have thought he was in a dining club or a debating society.

More important for our question, they combined these two exercises, for what they debated was how their beliefs ought to affect their social relations, and they rapidly built up a corpus of authoritative writings to add to the Hebraic Scriptures with which it all began. Intellectual demands were multiplied by this process. Even though the churches transformed themselves into a religion, they still built firmly into their system the thoroughly un-religious activities from which they had taken their origin. The earliest minister in the papyri is a lector, not a priest. A recently published papyrus (P.Yale 1.3) contains a preacher's handbook from about the end of the third century, with excerpts from the Acts of the Apostles, heavily marked with lection signs, and other aids for delivery and exposition. The Scriptures were not only sacred books (as when excerpted for amulets), but sources of ideas for didactic use. Ammianus complained that Constantine spoiled what would have been a pure and straightforward religion by promoting the endless arguments of the bishops in their synods. Julian is said to have encouraged this to prevent them competing with his revival of classical religion—he knew from experience, says Ammianus (22.5.4), that when you got them in synods they were worse than wild beasts to each other. As Paul had soon discovered, it was not hard to turn the gifts of the Spirit to one's own ends. The author of the *Historia Augusta* makes Aurelian (20.5) complain to the senate that they are prolonging the debate as though they had met in a Christian church and not the temple of all the gods.

For an illustration of the way the new ideas worked out in a changed structure of social relations one may turn to a group of papyrus letters of the late third or early fourth century.[9] They are letters of recommendation,

8. *PG* 40.929.

9. Treu, "Christliche Empfehlungs-Schemabriefe"; Judge, "Earliest Use," 80–81, at 202–3 in the present volume.

to be taken from one group of believers to another when one was traveling. In one case the papyrus is clearly a form letter, prepared in advance, with the bearer's name written in subsequently. Security and hospitality when traveling had traditionally been the privilege of the powerful, who had relied upon a network of patronage and friendship, created by wealth. The letters of recommendation disclose the fact that these domestic advantages were now extended to the whole household of faith, who are accepted on trust, though complete strangers. They are sometimes designated "catechumens," with the stage of their instruction specified—"at the beginning of the gospel," or "up to Genesis," for example. An attractive picture of the freedom of movement which was opened up by the hospitality of fellow-believers is given by the diary of Egeria, written probably late in the fourth century.[10] This lady from Spain traveled all over the wilderness of the Middle East seeing the old sites of Bible times, and the latter-day sensation of the monks into the bargain. She even scaled Mt. Sinai. At every point she was met and looked after, and one may assume that the same service was provided for the many other devout tourists we hear of. The churches now disposed of funds on the scale that had only earlier been known in private hands, or those of the Caesars.

The new discipline not only created a source of social security for those unprotected by the power structure, but was used to curb the powerful as well. Only a year after the edict of Milan had ordered governors to restore confiscated properties to the churches, the synod of Arles resolved to supply those governors who were believers with ecclesiastical letters of communion, plus instructions to the bishops to exclude them from communion if they began to act contrary to church discipline.[11] A generation later Julian was to express his envy of the effectiveness of episcopal letters by attempting to institute their equivalent in his revived Hellenic religion.[12] The church network was not just a parallel to the civil hierarchy of power, however. Its ministers were not a professional caste, but were drawn from all ranks in society, and the call might come at any stage in life. The congregations assembled in the churches demonstrated on many occasions that they were more than willing to take these choices into their own hands.[13]

---

10. Translations are available by Wilkinson and Gingras (*ACW*, vol. 38).

11. Letter of the bishops in council at Arles to Pope Silvester, preserved in the dossier of documents on Donatism attached to the work of St. Optatus of Milevis, *CSEL*, 26:208.

12. Sozomen 5.16.3, Theodorus Anagnostes, *Historia ecclesiastica*, 135.

13. Eck, "Der Einfluss." For examples of election campaigns see Ammianus 27.3.12–13 and Sulpicius Severus, *Life of St Martin* 9.

The basic proposition I have to put is this. The conversion of Rome was effected through a combination of intellectual with social forces unprecedented in the classical experience. For the first time a powerful new set of ideas, such as would normally have been confined to the philosophical schools, was promoted systematically at other levels in the community. It is interesting that Themistius, one of the more guarded outside observers of this process, argued that philosophy itself should be made available at large to the people.[14] The novel organization of the churches was the product of this social extension of ideas. While in some respects it was built up within the established structure of the community (for example, in the fact that bishops were located in cities), it was potentially, and sometimes actually, in conflict with its civil counterpart (for example, in respect of the status ranking system of the public community). The fact that the gospel enshrined itself in cultic practices also lent vast social weight to the new arrangements. At the same time its intellectual vitality was far from being smothered. The canonization of Scripture, and the didactic and dogmatic drive that was built into church life, generated the perpetual debate that stunned refined observers in the classical tradition. Church writers for their part, in order to propagate their views, fully exploited the elaborate scholastic apparatus of exposition and interpretation that classical philosophy and literary science had built up. In this way they brought their new source of ideas into a working relationship with classical culture. By the end of the fourth century, even the most conservative scholars of the older tradition were quietly going over to, or going along with, the new outlook.[15]

2. The Problem for Intellectual Observers

The coupling together of the new ideas of the gospel with the social force represented by the church, which I am suggesting was the fulcrum for the conversion of Rome, is illustrated by the case of Marius Victorinus.[16] A Neoplatonist scholar and leading rhetorician of Rome, he was long feared by Christians for his cutting tongue. Eventually he confided that he had been won over, through privately studying the Scriptures. No one would believe it. But he duly presented himself for baptism in church, to be acclaimed there in a mass demonstration by the crowds. Augustine (*Conf.* 8.2 ff) celebrated this as an act of remarkable humiliation. He subsequently wrote the

---

14. Downey, "Themistius."

15. For the loss of heart in the old tradition in the West, see Cameron, "Paganism and Literature."

16. Hadot, *Marius Victorinus*.

earliest Latin commentary on St. Paul, practically incomprehensible according to Jerome (*Vir. ill.* 101): it was in advance of its times, being in principle much the same kind of commentary as a modern scholar might write. But he also knew how to speak plainly. He composed hymns setting out the gist of his new faith with extreme concision.

Hymns had always been part of the solemn worship of classical religion, but they were put to a striking new use in the fourth century as a vehicle for the expression and instruction of the crowds in the churches. Ambrose introduced them into his basilica at Milan.[17] A recently published Latin papyrus contains a very lively, popular hymn which takes you through the descent and life of Jesus under alphabetical headings, with a refrain for popular response.[18] A. D. Momigliano concluded a recent study on popular religion in late antiquity by pointing out that there was no such thing any more. The old distinction between the educated elite and the masses had been swept away. The same ideas and beliefs had come to preoccupy the minds of people at all levels of society.[19]

But in terms of practical behavior, had anything in the end been changed? When I once told A. H. M. Jones that I wanted to find out what difference it made to Rome to have been converted, he said he already knew the answer: None. Indeed, as his great work on the later Roman Empire subsequently made clear, he thought that Christian belief, if anything, led to a lowering of moral standards in the community. The grounds for such a view are obvious enough. The church established its ascendancy during a century in which Roman power, and the old tradition of civic humanism, was moving into dissolution, or at any rate transformation. Are we to see the conversion of Rome as a principal cause of these changes? Or was the church itself being converted into a residual form of the old civilization and helping to save the day, as Orosius was to argue?[20] It is clear that our subsequent cultural tradition presents an ill-reconciled mélange of Graeco-Roman and Judeo-Christian beliefs. And whether or not much difference was made to Rome in the fourth century, the mixture has generated very powerful effects in subsequent times.

But what did contemporaries think was happening to their civilization? And how did they explain the conversion of Rome? In spite of generations of both popular and scholarly criticism of the new way at earlier stages, and

17. Augustine, *Conf.* 9.7.15; Chr. Mohrmann, "La langue et le style"; Fontaine, "L'apport de la tradition."
18. Emmett (now Nobbs), "Fourth-Century Hymn" and "Subject of Psalmus Responsorius."
19. Momigliano, "Popular Religious Belief."
20. Lacroix, *Orose et ses idées.*

sporadic attempts to suppress it, there is no trace of any serious historical analysis from the outside of the great shift of allegiance in the fourth century. This must be attributed basically to the conservatism of historical convention, which did not admit such questions as topics of historical study. But one might at least have hoped for a digression in Ammianus, or a monograph. The only analytical study of contemporary problems is the anonymous treatise *De rebus bellicis*.[21] Amongst other things, it comes close to recognizing the mechanism of the inflation which flowed from Constantine's closing of the temples and the flooding of the market with their gold reserves. But the author was not working within the artificial limits of historical writing. Even the new style of ecclesiastical historiography, devised by Eusebius in the very decade of the Constantinian revolution, quickly imposed itself as an almost equally rigid convention. Being concerned with the records of episcopal succession, the preservation of the true faith, and so on, Eusebius was inspired to incorporate bodily into his work extracts from documents in their original wording. He thus became the founder of the modern historical practice of citing documentary evidence, the need for proof being born of dogma.[22] But his many imitators in late antiquity were so reluctant to adapt this excellent departure to fresh needs, that Sozomen, for example, felt obliged to apologize for dealing with the monks. They had first come into public notice just after the time Eusebius was writing, and thus ecclesiastical history had no rules for dealing with them.

Those who consider that the conversion of Rome changed nothing have the tacit but weighty support of Ammianus Marcellinus. The last great Roman historian, writing in the time of Theodosius, he lived through the crucial years of the establishment of Christendom. As a Greek who had taken up Latin studies, he possesses the broad and tolerant outlook, and the concern for Rome's future, that one might have expected to lead him to grapple with the question of changing beliefs. His mind was not closed by the prejudices of the metropolitan nobility around Symmachus, with whom he had no bond of sympathy. Yet he deliberately holds himself aloof from the question. It was not that he was unaware of the conflicts it caused. He admired Julian, but criticized his banning of Christian teachers in public schools. Ammianus condemned the luxury, ambition, and violence of papal politics in Rome, but paid tribute to the ascetic example of provincial bishops. It can be shown by such examples that he was not indifferent to the affairs of the church. But his concern was mainly with standards of public

---

21. Thompson, *Roman Reformer*.

22. Momigliano, "Pagan and Christian Historiography"; Grant, "Case against Eusebius"; Winkelmann, "Probleme der Zitate."

morality and order. We must either say that he did not see the full extent of what was happening (there is nothing on the monks, for example, and no attention to the intellectual drive of the church), or that he did not see it as of basic importance for Rome's future. He certainly never suggests that the Christians are the cause of Rome's troubles.[23]

This failure or refusal to take the matter seriously is shared with another Greek practitioner of Latin letters, the court poet Claudian, well enough at home with the new religion, but hardly a believer,[24] and with Ausonius, the Gallic gentleman-scholar, a nominal adherent for whom only the slightest demands arose from his belief, without touching in any way his thinking or social attitudes.[25] The Roman senatorial leader, Symmachus, was obliged by the lost cause he was fighting to refrain from any attempt at serious analysis of the triumphant policy. Absenting oneself from the altars of the Roman gods had become a matter of politics, he complained. He simply pleaded for tolerance.[26] The *Historia Augusta*, with its occasional jibes, is an even more irresponsible product of the vested interests of the old senatorial class.[27] Other writers of the time—Macrobius, Martianus Capella, even the historical epitomizers—utterly ignore the matter.[28] Only the poet Rutilius Claudius Namatianus, writing in 417, allows himself a couple of bitter outbursts, against monasticism.[29] There is no trace of the attempt to blame the Christians for the sack of Rome in 410, which provoked Augustine to begin his masterly treatise on the City of God. The proud champions of eternal Rome faced its end with eyes tight shut—or had their lips been sealed?[30]

The major Greek writers were more outspoken.[31] Only Themistius, the court orator of Constantinople, is an obvious trimmer.[32] Libanius, more independent in the Syrian metropolis of Antioch, made no attempt to conceal his disgust, especially at the monks.[33] His attitude was

23. Camus, *Ammien Marcellin*; Blockley, *Ammianus Marcellinus*.

24. Cameron, *Claudian*.

25. Chadwick, *Poetry and Letters*; Witke, *Numen litterarum*.

26. Barrow, *Prefect and Emperor*; Matthews, "Symmachus and the Oriental Cults."

27. Syme, *Ammianus and the Historia Augusta*, reviewed by Cameron; Syme, *Emperors and Biography*, reviewed by Graham.

28. Cameron, "Paganism and Literature"; Cameron and Cameron, "Christianity and Tradition"; Flamant, *Macrobe et le néoplatonisme*.

29. Doblhofer, *Rutilius Namatianus* shows that lines 439–48, 518–24, hardly represent a Christian criticism of monasticism, as has sometimes been thought.

30. Paschoud, *Roma Aeterna*.

31. de Labriolle, *La réaction paienne*.

32. Downey, "Themistius."

33. Libanius, *Or*. 2.32, 30.8; Petit, *Libanius*; Norman, *Autobiography*.

fully shared by Eunapius, one of the founders of Byzantine historiography, whose work survives in extracts only.[34] But there is nothing to suggest that he passed beyond contempt to serious criticism. The work of the imperial Julian is inspired by the same loathing. But since he alone enjoyed, briefly, a total freedom of action, his policies tell us plainly enough what he really thought was going wrong. One must remember, too, that as apostate from the new way, he was in a unique position amongst writers to get to the heart of the matter.[35]

Julian justified the ban on Christian teachers by appealing to the distinctively Christian principle of integrity. It was dishonest of them, and therefore bad for their pupils, to be teaching classical literature, full of the gods they denied. The evidence suggests that those outside the church—like Ammianus—could not see the point. But Julian had put his finger accurately upon a key link in the conversion of the Roman world—the exploitation of the intellectual tradition for Christian ends. The ban would also have social consequences for it would cut off Christian influence on the training of the educated classes—Julian always called Christians "Galileans" to emphasize their cultural inferiority. One of his own professors at Athens had been a Christian. Julian excused him from the ban, but Prohaeresius resigned anyway. So did Victorinus in Rome. The Christians took the point, and set to work to prepare for the church schools which Julian proposed they should now create. It was the first time the very modern question of ideology in education had raised its head.

Apart from the charges of hypocrisy, and of the immorality of the doctrine of forgiveness, Julian's main grievance against the "Galileans" was that they had introduced a sharp division between the sacred and the secular. Only Eusebius, in the first flush of Constantine's conversion, had ventured to proclaim the full integration of the imperial power into the kingdom of Christ on earth,[36] and Constantine himself was deeply conscious of his status as the unifier of all things and of the terrifying responsibilities he bore in this respect. He was infuriated by the fact that all the bishops wanted to do was argue, and dreaded that God might therefore take "some untoward step," as he ingenuously put it.[37] Clearly he did not know that blissful Jewish picture of the Heavenly Academy, where the

---

34. Opelt, "Eunapios"; Bartelink, "Eunape et le vocabulaire chrétien"; Ridley, "Eunapius and Zosimus."

35. Browning, *Emperor Julian*; Bowersock, *Julian the Apostate*.

36. Wallace-Hadrill, *Eusebius of Caesarea*.

37. Jones, *Constantine*; Dörries, *Das Selbstzeugnis*; Kraft, *Kaiser Konstantins religiöse Entwicklung*.

rabbis dispute points of law daily, with the Almighty as their teacher.[38] But Constantine's heirs entered heartily into the doctrinal debates, and effectively put an end to the Eusebian illusion.

Julian for his part, the last survivor of Constantine's house and the arch-antagonist of its ideals, determined to realize the dream in reverse form, by converting the traditional Hellenic cults into a religious organization of society modeled on church lines. They were to be brought under an episcopal hierarchy, and the priests were to officiate at set times in the temples so that the people could take part as a community. The intellectual and moral drive of the churches was also to be imposed on classical religion. Priests were to preach in the temples, and set an example of personal conduct, a requirement which flew in the face of religious tradition. The social contribution of the churches must be outclassed too. There were to be orphanages, hospitals, and homes founded, "so that we may take care of the unfortunate among our enemies, and not they of us." Even the detested monks must be countered by the foundation of monasteries and convents for the Hellenes. In all this Julian is showing how well, from his inside experience, he understood the social and intellectual dynamics of the movement he was determined to stop. But it is not obvious that anyone else ever saw the point so plainly.[39] Even before his premature death, it was clear from the amused skepticism of his own potential supporters that the classical way of life did not have it in its heart to accept such a revolution from within. Julian's deep belief in social commitment is another relic of his Christian upbringing. That was why he made it his habit, as he tells us, to insult the Cynics by calling them *apotaktitai*—a technical term used by the "Galileans" for those who withdrew from the world.[40]

---

38. Babylonian Talmud, B. Meṣ. 85b–6a, which may be too late for Constantine to have known it, though the idea has very ancient roots in the pre-exilic life of Israel, where altercation with the Lord was acceptable, prior to the stage when it was thought impious to dispute with God (for which information I thank Professor F. I. Andersen).

39. Porphyrius, who like Julian had once been close to church life, probably also saw it. His work, *Against the Christians*, survives only in fragments (see von Harnack, *Porphyrius*). I now believe that both Maximinus Daia and Licinius, in their successive last-ditch attempts to stop Constantine, put into practice counter-revolutionary reforms which anticipated Julian's, for which see LCL 29 (Julian, vol. 2), in Wright, *Works of the Emperor Julian*, 297–339 and LCL 157 (Julian, vol. 3), in Wright, *Works of the Emperor Julian*, 55–73.

40. Julian 224B, LCL 29 (Julian, vol. 2), in Wright, *Works of the Emperor Julian*, 123; Judge, "Earliest Use," 79, at 201–2 in the present volume.

3. Why the Problem has not Gone Away

Apart from Isidorus of Karanis, Julian is thus the earliest outsider to refer to monasticism. The universally bad reaction to the monks in the secular sources, and the not infrequent doubts about them amongst Christians, draw our attention to the fact that we have here an unexpected development that no one really knew how to handle.[41] We still do not know exactly how the fashion for retreat originated. Asceticism as a private discipline was admired in all traditions. In the second century Galen, the physician, even held that the practice of it showed that Christians were capable of philosophy. Monasticism was subsequently to draw much inspiration from classical sources. It has been shown that Athanasius's *Life of St Antony*, the orthodox charter of the movement, is modeled on a lost life of Pythagoras. Neoplatonists regretted their bodies as heartily as any hermit. Evagrius Ponticus, the first monk to set down the tradition of spirituality in writing, begins his book with the disarming claim, "The kingdom of heaven is apathy..."[42] It is pure Stoicism. But it was not such secure sentiments that gave rise to the reaction against the monks.

The key to the matter is that they repudiated the established social order in the most emphatic way possible, by abandoning all the familiar ties: public obligations, property, even family bonds. The hagiographic literature that sprang up in their wake glitters with spectacular renunciations. The fashion grew into a mass movement, that had to be curbed by law to hold the civil community together. It must be one of the most determined movements of self-alienation known to history. By the end of the century, the bishop of Oxyrhynchus could proudly claim, the city had gone into mass retreat, 10,000 monks and 20,000 virgins. They had swallowed up half the buildings in the town, quite apart from the ones who had taken to the desert. For the rich in particular, a long battle was needed to achieve the ideal. You could not just give away property, because the maintenance of civil services depended upon its being passed down in the family as was required by law. Nor could you just abandon your marriage, since a noble house was obliged by centuries of expectation to perpetuate itself. It took the younger Melania years to outwit the vested interests that stood in the way of her profession, including driving her husband to abstinence by provoking a near-fatal miscarriage through an exacting night of prayer and vigil. Even

---

41. See Judge, "Earliest Use" (ch. 14 below), for references to this and what follows. See also Gougaud, "Les critiques formulées"; Chitty, *Desert a City*; Rousseau, *Ascetics, Authority*.

42. Guillaumont and Guillaumont, *Evagre le Pontique*, 2:498.

her slaves refused to be freed, and rioted in the streets of Rome against this threat to their security, leading to many deaths.[43]

It is impossible to explain this drive to escape simply in social terms, although many social issues were caught up in it.[44] The Messalians, for example, tried to reform the public community along egalitarian lines. But people of every rank and circumstance followed the call to the desert. The monastic literature gives an overwhelmingly consistent answer to the question of the motive of the monks. Their aim was perfection, and they were responding directly to the challenge of Jesus when he had said to the rich young ruler (Matt 19:21), "If you would be perfect, go, sell what you possess and give it to the poor, and you will have treasure in heaven; and come, follow me." It is the most clear-cut case, however unexpected, of the capacity of the church to generate social—or anti-social—action by the direct exploitation of its primary sources of ideas. No one seems to have stopped to observe that Jesus himself had not gone so far, nor to reflect that following him might mean not cutting oneself off from other people, but giving oneself up for them. Literalism in interpreting the gospel also gave way in the face of Jesus's demand (Matt 6:16–18) that fasting should be done in secret, and that one should not be like the Pharisees, but anoint one's face so that no one would know you were fasting. The Didache (8.1) had solved that problem as early as the second century. Since the Pharisees did it on Tuesdays and Thursdays, the follower of Jesus simply had to do it on Wednesdays and Fridays. The great fourth-century fathers recognized that they had a real difficulty here, for the distinctive mark of fasting—dirty clothes—had become the glory of monasticism and all the more untouchable for the fact that it revolted polite sentiment on the classical side.[45] John Chrysostom came to the melancholy conclusion that Jesus could not have meant it literally, otherwise all the monks would be wrong, and even St. Augustine, that most ruthless searcher of the heart, who recognized that dirt too can be a form of pride, ducked the issue.[46] As for the left hand, which Jesus had said was not to know what

43. Gorce, *Vie de Sainte Mélanie*.

44. Nagel, *Die Motivierung*; Otto, *Die Antike im Umbruch*.

45. Jerome says, "Dirty clothes are the sign of a clean mind" (*Ep.* 125.7), but he had to insist that his nuns cut their hair, "lest they become covered with lice and encrusted dirt" (147.5). Antony (*Vit. Ant.* 47) wore a single garment (from 311?) to the end of his life (356?), never taking it off, nor washing. Theonas never washed after becoming bishop of Alexandria, except for one ceremonial ablution when touched by the shadow of a heretic (see text in Crum, "Texts Attributed to Peter of Alexandria," 393). But the rule of Pachomius gives instructions on the daily washing of their clothes by his monks.

46. John Chrysostom, *Homilies on Matthew* 20–21 (*PG* 57.287). Augustine, *Serm. Dom.* 2.12.40 (*PL* 34.1287) says it is pride "if one deliberately attracts people's attention by exceptional squalor and dirt," but refuses to accept that Jesus could literally have

the right hand was doing, some claimed that really meant you had to conceal your generosity from the unbeliever, or from your enemy, or from your wife—since she would have her mind on the household budget.

In this strange mixture of the literal and the figurative, of the call of Jesus and the age-old ideals of asceticism, lies the peculiar impulse of monasticism. At the personal level, it is the counterpart of Eusebius's attempt to set the emperor in relation to Christ in a unified and totally valid order, to build heaven on earth now. But in monasticism the social direction of the drive is reversed. Heaven is not to be built by renewing society from within, but by abandoning it altogether and finding heaven elsewhere. Athanasius said Antony had made the desert into a city, and Melania called the monastic life the citizenship of the angels. The desire for an ideologically coherent personal or public order of life is a distinctive hallmark of the fourth century, and one that has left its imprint on the Western tradition ever since. The church has long since settled for Augustine's much subtler conception of the coexistence of the two cities, and even monasticism seems at last to be relaxing its commitment to the externalization of perfection. But in the meantime, half the world has been engulfed by another attempt to give effect to absolute truth in the social order. Its roots may also lie in the fourth century, if it is true that the Hegelian structure which has shaped Marxist thought may be lined up with that of Proclus and the Neoplatonists, as Feuerbach observed.[47]

Monasticism demonstrates that in the last resort man does not live by forces that arise from the social system itself, inasmuch as the mind and will of man may still defy them. It also demonstrates the tenacious hold on man's mind exerted by the words of Scripture, however perverse one may think the effects of that to be. For these reasons I do not think we shall ever explain the conversion of Rome simply in terms of a social or political analysis of what happened, even though I have been stressing the social force which the new faith brought to bear through the organization of the churches and their assumption of a religious function in the community. But the engine that drove these changes along was the thinking and preaching and exposition of the great patristic writers. For sheer bulk their work

---

meant that one should wash one's face: it referred to inward joy. For what follows see 2.2.6–9 in the same work.

47. Feuerbach, *Principles*, 47; Löwith, *From Hegel to Nietzsche*, 39–40; Marx (*Capital*, 1:29), however, claims that his dialectic is the direct opposite of Hegel's; and Engels claimed that dialectic philosophy destroyed all theories of absolute truth, cf. Anderson, *Studies in Empirical Philosophy*, 295–96. I am grateful to Dr. J. Kilcullen for warning me of the complexities of the philosophical pedigree of this matter. For the broad historical comparison between two attempts to make the world conform to theory, see Otto, *Die Antike im Umbruch*, and Dihle, "Antikes und Unantikes."

outstrips that of what survives from classical antiquity, partly for the worst of reasons—they had the last word. But it was not just a confrontation. In recent decades an immense amount of detailed analysis has been carried out, tracing the intricate web of intellectual history in the fourth century, writer by writer. It is already clear that even with the most orthodox of the fathers, the pillars of catholic doctrine such as Athanasius, Ambrose, and Augustine, the involvement with the dominant Platonic philosophy of their day is very profound.[48] There is no general agreement as to whether they were simply "spoiling the Egyptians" and exploiting the cultural tradition for ends which remained uncontaminated by it, or whether the fourth century achieved a basic Hellenization of biblical ideas.

It is not surprising that we find this very difficult to sort out. In addition to its own intellectual products, the fourth century was responsible for establishing and handing down to us in their canonical form the twin corpora of classical and biblical literature. This very phenomenon of the preservation of already classic norms shows that they were not simply promoting a merger of cultural traditions. It is to this duality of our cultural sources that we owe the successive renaissances, reformations, and enlightenments that have generated the high intellectual productivity of the Western tradition. It is to the same feature that we owe the characteristic pattern of social tensions in our tradition. People have often debated the question of when the Roman empire may be said to have ended, with several attractive arguments pointing towards our own age, the twentieth century. Lest you think this professional imperialism on my part, let me turn the question around. When did the modern world begin? I have been putting before you the case for starting modern history in the fourth century. That was the first age in which the characteristic tensions of the West were drawn out. It was the first age in which serious conflicts of ideas impinged directly upon government and the social order.

From the classical side the main objections to Christian doctrine were as follows.[49] God's relation to the world was presented as too anthropocentric, so that man took priority over the natural order, and the direct revelation of God's mind to him took precedence over man's own reasoning based upon the study of nature. Greeks did not in the last resort see God as omnipotent, and man by consequence was in the Greek view firmly

---

48. Meijering, *Orthodoxy and Platonism*; Courcelle, *Recherches sur Saint Ambroise*; Madec, *Saint Ambroise et la philosophie*; Mandouze, *Augustin*. On the question in general see Von Ivánka, *Plato Christianus*; Meijering, "Wie platonisierten Christen?"; Dörries, "Zur Auseinandersetzung."

49. The propositions in this paragraph are based mainly on the evidence and analysis presented by Nestle, "Die Haupteinwände," and by Dihle, "Ethik."

bound into the order of nature as determined by fate. The Christians, they complained, profaned everything, by stripping both nature and government of its divine component. This destroyed the authority of the established order of things, and led to the unjust result of favoring the weak and sick in society rather than the good. The Christians for their part could charge that the Greeks debased both God and man to mere elements in the order of nature, and that their naturalistic system failed to explain the fundamental reality of evil. As for man, the lack of any adequate conception of the will or the conscience in Greek thought left him in the morally irresponsible position of a helpless victim of circumstance. The Christian view of the fallen nature of man and his need of redemption and divine endowment was the basis for the socially novel demand for humility and the subjection of each to the interests of the other.

You will recognize from these themes how tangled our Western tradition has become. It would be very unlikely that you could find anyone who is consistently heir to one or other side of the argument. I hear Catholic nuns strenuously advocating humanistic ideals of self-development, and humanists taking their stand on such distinctively Christian slogans as integrity and commitment. And so it was in late antiquity. It is not easy to say in individual cases how much is owed to Athens, and how much to Jerusalem. But historically it is this conflict built into our cultural tradition that has brought us to the argumentative, progressive, open societies of the West. And whichever side you think is right, before you press ahead to subject man and the social order once more to cosmic truth, remember the long and painful journey which has been necessary for church and community to disentangle themselves from the consequences of the conversion of Rome.

Appendix: Papyrus Documents of a Century of Change in the Villages of Egypt

1. P.Oxy. 42.3035, ed. Parsons: an order to arrest of February 28, 256, from Oxyrhynchus.

π(αρὰ) τοῦ πρυτάνεως
κωμάρχαις καὶ ἐπιστάταις εἰρήνης
κώμης Μερμέρθων. ἐξαυτῆς ἀνα-
πέμψατε Πετοσορᾶπιν Ὥρου χρησι-
5   ανόν, ἢ ὑμεῖς αὐτοὶ ἀνέλθατε.
(ἔτους) γ// Οὐαλεριανοῦ καὶ Γαλλιηνοῦ Σεβαστῶν
Φαμενὼθ γ̅

From the prytanis, to the comarchs and supervisors of the peace of the village of Mermertha. Send up immediately Petosorapis son of Horus, Christian (?), or else come up yourselves. Year 3 of Valerianus and Gallienus Augusti, Phamenoth 3.

2. P.Oxy. 33.2673, ed. Rea: a declaration of February 5, 304, preserved in triplicate from Oxyrhynchus.

ἐπὶ ὑπάτων τῶν κυρίων ἡμ[ῶν αὐτοκρατόρων]
Διοκλητιανοῦ τὸ ἔνατον καὶ Μαξ[ιμιανοῦ]
    τὸ η' Σεβαστῶν
Αὐρηλίοις Νείλῳ τῷ καὶ Ἀμμωνίῳ γυμ[( ) βουλ(ευτῇ)]
5   ἐνάρχῳ πρυτάνει καὶ Σαρμάτῃ καὶ Ματρίνῳ ἀμφ[οτέροις]
    γυμ( ) βουλ(ευταῖς) συνδίκοις τοῖς πᾶσι τῆς λαμ(πρᾶς) καὶ λαμ(προτάτης)
    Ὀξυρυγχιτῶν πόλεως (vac.)
    Αὐρήλιος Ἀμμώνιος Κοπρέως ἀναγνώστης τῆς ποτε ἐκ‹κ›λησίας κώμης Χύσεως
10 ἐπιθεμένων ὑμῶν ἐμοὶ ἀκολούθως
    τοῖς γραφ‹ε›ῖσι ὑπὸ Αὐρηλίου Ἀθανασίου ἐπιτρό-
    που πριουάτης ὡς ἐκ κελεύσεως τοῦ δια-
    σημ(οτάτου) μαγίστρου τῆς πριουάτης Νερατίου
    Ἀπολλωνί‹δ›ου περὶ τοῦ παραστῆσαι ἅπαντα
15 τὰ ‹ε›ἴδη τὰ [ἐ]ν τῇ αὐτῇ ποτε ἐκ‹κ›λησίᾳ καὶ ἐμοῦ
    προενεγ' καμένου μὴ ἔχειν τὴν ‹αὐτὴν› ἐκ‹κ›λη-
    σείαν μήτε χρυσὸν μήτε ἄσημον
    μήτε ἀργύριον μήτε ἐσθῆτα μήτε τετρά-
    ποδα μήτε ἀνδράποδα μήτε οἰκόπαιδα
20 μήτε ὑπάρχοντα μήτε ἀπὸ χαρισμάτων
    μηδ' αὖ ἀπὸ διαθηκῶν εἰ μὴ μόνην
    τὴν εὑ[ρε]τῖσαν χαλκῆ[ν] πύλην καὶ παραδο-
    τῖσαν τῷ λογιστῇ πρὸς τὸ κατενεγ' χθῆναι
    ἐπὶ τὴν λαμ(προτάτην) Ἀλεξάνδριαν ἀκολούθως τοῖς γρα-
25 φ‹ε›ῖσι ὑπὸ τοῦ διασημ(οτάτου) ἡμῶν ἡγεμόνος Κλωδίου
    Κο‹υ›λκιανοῦ καὶ ὀμνύω τὴν τῶν κυρίων ἡμῶν
    αὐτοκρατόρων Διοκλητιανοῦ καὶ Μαξιμιανοῦ Σεβασ(τῶν)
    καὶ Κωνσταντίου καὶ Μαξιμιανοῦ τῶν ἐπιφανεστάτων
    καισάρων τύχην ταῦθ' οὕτως ἔχειν καὶ μηδὲν διε-
30 ψεῦσθαι ἢ ἔνοχος εἴην τῷ θείῳ ὅρκῳ
    (ἔτους) κ' καὶ ιβ' τῶν κυρίων ἡμῶν Διοκλητιανοῦ καὶ Μαξιμανοῦ
    Σεβαστῶν καὶ Κωνσταντίου καὶ Μαξιμιανοῦ τῶν ἐπιφανεστάτων καισάρων
    Μεχεὶρ [ι'].
m.2 Αὐρήλιος Ἀμμώνιος ὤμοσα τὸν ὅρκον
35 ὡς (πρόκειται). Αὐρ(ήλιος) Σερῆνος ἔγρα(ψα) ὑ(πὲρ) αὐτοῦ μὴ
    εἰ(δότος) γρά(μματα).

In the consulship of our lords the *autokratores* (Lat. *imperatores*) Diocletian—for the ninth time—and Maximian—for the eighth time—the Augusti.

To Aurelius Neilus alias Ammonius (ex-?)gymnasiarch, senator, prytane in office, and to Aurelius Sarmates and Aurelius Matrinus, both (ex-?)gymnasiarchs, senators and syndics, all of the glorious and most glorious city of the Oxyrhynchites, Aurelius Ammonius, son of Copreus, lector of the former church of the village of Chysis.

Whereas you gave me orders in accordance with what was written by Aurelius Athanasius, *procurator rei privatae*, in virtue of a command of the most illustrious *magister rei privatae*, Neratius Apollonides, concerning the surrender of all the goods in the said former church and whereas I reported that the said church had neither gold nor silver nor money nor clothing[50] nor beasts nor slaves nor lands nor property either from grants or bequests, excepting only the bronze gate[51] which was found and delivered to the *logistes* to be carried down to the most glorious Alexandria in accordance with what was written by our most illustrious prefect Clodius Culcianus, I also swear by the genius of our lords the *autokratores* (Lat. *imperatores*) Diocletian and Maximian, the Augusti, and Constantius and Galerius, the most noble Caesars, that these things are so and that I have falsified nothing, or may I be liable to the divine oath.

In the 20th and 12th year of our lords Diocletian and Maximian, the Augusti and Constantius and Galerius, the most noble Caesars. Mecheir 10th.
(2nd hand) I, Aurelius Ammonius, swore the oath as aforesaid. I, Aurelius Serenus, wrote on his behalf because he does not know letters.

3. P.Coll.Youtie 2.77, ed. Lewis, modified by Bagnall in P.Col. 7.171: a petition of June 6(?), 324, from Karanis (Fayum).

Διοσκόρῳ Καίσωνι πραιπ(οσίτῳ) ε πάγου
παρὰ Ἰσιδώρου Πτολεμαίου ἀπὸ κώ(μης) Καρ[α]νίδος
τοῦ ὑμετέρου πάγου· τῶν θρεμμ[άτ]ων Παμού-
νεως καὶ Ἁρπάλου καταλυμηνα[μέ]νων ἦν

---

50. Though the Greek ἐσθῆτα is singular, Rea supplied "vestments(?)" as an interpretative gloss in his edition. *The Oxford Dictionary of the Christian Church* (Cross and Livingstone, at 1702) coyly allows that we have no trace of liturgical vestments until well after the fourth century (when the portraiture clearly shows bishops in civil clothing) though "we" assume there will have been special dress for officiants on the mosaic model (which they concede was a false train when previously assumed!).

51. The other two copies showed that πύλην (gate) in line 22 should have read ὕλην (material).

5 ἔχω σπορὰν καὶ μὴν καὶ τῆς β[οὸ]ς α[ὐτῶν] πάλιν
ἐν τῷ αὐτῷ τόπῳ καταβοσκηθείσης ὥστε ἀχρή-
σιμόν μοι τὴν γεωργίαν γενέσθαι, καὶ καταλαβο-
μένου μου τὴν βοῦν καὶ ἀνάγοντος αὐτὴν
ἐπὶ τῆς κώμης ἀπαντήσαντές μοι κατὰ τοὺς

10 ἀγροὺς μεγά‹λῳ› ῥοπάλῳ καὶ χαμιριφῇ ἐμὲ ποι-
ησάμενοι πληγαῖς κατέκοψαν καὶ τὴν βοῦν
ἀφείλαντο ὥσπερ καὶ αἱ περὶ ἐμὲ πληγαὶ
δηλοῦσιν, καὶ εἰ μὴ βοηθείας ἔτυχο(ν) ὑπὸ
τῶν παραγενομένων Ἀντωνίνου διάκο-

15 νος καὶ Ἰσὰκ μοναχοῦ τάχα ἂν τέλεόν
με ἀπώλεσαν. ὅθεν ἐπιδίδωμι τάδε
τὰ ἔνγραφα ἀξιῶν αὐτοὺς ἀχθῆναι ἐπὶ σοῦ
καὶ περὶ τῆς σπορᾶς καὶ περὶ τῆς ὕβρεως
τηρεῖσθαι ἐμοὶ καὶ τὸν λόγον ἐπὶ τοῦ

20 ἡγεμονικοῦ δικαστηρίου.....
τοῖς ἐσομένοις ὑπάτοις τὸ δ
Παῦνι ιβ

To Dioscorus Caeso, *praepositus* of the fifth *pagus*, from Isidorus son of Ptolemaeus of the village of Karanis in your *pagus*. The cattle of Pamounis and Harpalus damaged the planting which I have and what is more [their cow] grazed again in the same place so thoroughly that my husbandry has become useless. I caught the cow and was leading it up to the village when they met me in the fields with a big club, threw me to the ground, rained blows upon me and took away the cow—as indeed (the marks of) the blows all over me show—and if I had not chanced to obtain help from the deacon Antoninus and the monk Isaac, who happened by, they would quickly have finished me off completely. Therefore I submit this document, asking that they be brought before you to preserve my claim (to be heard) in the prefectural court ... both in the matter of the planting and in the matter of the assault.
The consuls-to-be for the fourth time, Payni 12.

4. P.Abinn. 55, ed. Bell et. al. = P.Lond. 2.412, ed. Kenyon: a petition of February 11, 351, from Fayum (Philadelphia?).

Φλαουίῳ Ἀβιν[ν]έῳ ἐξ ἀποπροτηκτώρων ἐπάρχῳ
εἴλης κάστρων Διονυσιάδος. παρὰ Αὐρηλίου
Ἥρωνο[ς] διάκω[ν]ος ἀπὸ κώμης Βερνικείδος τοῦ αὐτοῦ
νομοῦ χαίρειν. εἰ μὴ ὑπῆρχεν ἡμεῖν ἡ τῶν

5 νόμων ἀλήθεια πάλαι δ' ἂν ὑπὸ τῶν κακουργῶν
ἀναιλούμεθα. Εὔπορος τοίνυν υἱὸς Ἑρμεία
ἀπὸ κώμης Φιλαγρείδος τοῦ αὐτοῦ νομοῦ
ἐσύλησέν με ἔνδων τῆς οἰκείας, ἐπιβὰς
λῃστρεικῷ τρόπῳ, καὶ πᾶσαν τὴν ἐσθῆταν

10 συνελάβετο καὶ ε[ἰς] τὸ ἴδιον ἀνεστίλατω μέχρεις
δ[εῦ]ρω, δυναμ[έν]ου μου καὶ τ[ὰ]ς ἀποδίξει[ς ποι]εῖν
ὡς τούτου τήνδε τὴν κ[α]κουργίαν π[ε]ποιημένου.
διὼ ἀξ[ι]ῶ, πραιπόσιται κ[ύ]ριε, ἀπραγμώνος
ἃ ἀφήρπασέν μου [π]αρασχεθῆναί μο[ι]· διάκων γὰρ

15 τετ[ύ]χηκα τῆς κ[αθ]ολικῆς ἐκ«κ»[λ]ησίας. καὶ τούτου
τυχὼν εἰσαείν σοι εὐχαρειστήσω. διευτύχει.
[μετὰ τὴ]ν ὑπατείαν Φλ(αουίων) Σεργίου καὶ Νειγρεινιαν` οὖ'
τῶ[ν λαμπροτά]των, Μεχεὶρ ιζ.

To Flavius Abinnaeus, formerly one of the *protectores*, *praefectus alae* of the camp of Dionysias, from Aurelius Heron, deacon, of the village of Berenicis in the same nome, greeting. If we did not possess the truth of the laws we should long ago have been destroyed by evil-doers. Euporus then, son of Hermias, of the village of Philagris in the same nome, robbed me in my house, entering it in the manner of a robber, and seized all my clothing, and appropriated it to his own use until now, although I can demonstrate that it was he who perpetrated this outrage. Wherefore I ask, my lord *praepositus*, that what he robbed me of should be given to me without demur; for I am a deacon of the principal church. And obtaining this I shall owe you thanks forever. Farewell. After the consulship of Flavius Sergius and Nigrinianus the most illustrious, Mecheir 17.

9

The Absence of Religion, Even in Ammianus?

The basic argument of this chapter was first articulated when Judge was Visiting Professor of Classics and History at Berkeley in 1984.[1] The written version was not published until two decades later, appearing in 2004 under the present title in Treloar et al., *Making History for God*, 295–308. It was published again in Judge, *Jerusalem and Athens*, 264–75, and is reproduced here with minimal adaptation. The study attends to the way the fourth-century historian Ammianus Marcellinus perceived and described Christian practice from the outside. Reviewing the terminology Ammianus used, it seeks to illuminate what kind of movement Ammianus understood Christianity to be, given the Christian distinctives he observed (but failed to comprehend!) and the absence of our "religion" as a category in ancient thought.

THERE WAS NO UNDERSTANDING of "religion" in the ancient world of Greece and Rome. No such conception as we now hold existed then, no such classificatory component (as in "religion and society") or counterpart (as in "science and religion"), no particularizing use (as in "Roman religion"), no pluralizing use (as in "religions of the world").[2]

We merely retroject onto the Greeks and Romans something that has become necessary to our understanding of life, thus turning history into a

---

1. Since then several other relevant treatments have appeared: Hunt, "Christians and Christianity"; Neri, *Ammiano e il cristianesimo*; Rike, *Apex Omnium*. Alonso-Núñez, reviewing Neri, says: "it would have been worthwhile to have studied systematically Ammianus' attitude towards Christianity." Subsequent treatments include Matthews, *Roman Empire of Ammianus*, 424–51; Neri, "Ammianus' Definition of Christianity"; Barnes, *Ammianus Marcellinus*, 79–94 (see n. 7 below); Harrison, "Templum mundi totius."

2. Cantwell Smith, *Meaning and End of Religion*; Feil, *Religio*; Judge, "Beginning"; Harrison, *'Religion' and the Religions*.

hall of mirrors in which we contemplate ourselves under the illusion that we are looking at the Greeks and Romans. One can tell this by crossing out the word "religion" in any translation of any Greek or Latin text from prior to AD 200, and observing instead what the ancient writer actually said (sometimes nothing much at all, since at every turn English needs to cloak itself in abstracts in a way quite unnecessary in a highly inflected and thus more flexible language).

Our vocabulary of "religion" is not derived from the Greeks. They had no word for what we mean by it, and the odd words that prompt translators to say "religion," e.g., *eusebeia* (piety), *thrēskeia* (worship), have not passed into the abstract vocabulary of English. They were not part of the classificatory apparatus of Greek philosophy or education. By contrast, much of the terminology of our subject comes from Latin: "religion," "superstition," "piety," "cult," "sect," "rite," "doctrine," "creed," "faith," etc. None of the Latin originals of these terms is primarily or even mainly concerned with what we now call "religion." They reflect the take-over of the Latin language from the time of Tertullian (c. AD 200) for Christian purposes, and the transforming fusion of cultural traditions promoted by the Roman church in particular.

In AD 371 Valentinian, himself a Christian, instructed the senate that the ban on magical arts did not extend to the time-honored divinatory practice of the *haruspices* (*Cod. theod.* 9.16.9):

> I do not consider any rite permitted by our ancestors to be criminal. The laws issued by me at the beginning of my reign (*imperii*) are witness, whereby everyone was granted a free choice of practicing whatever (religion) his mind determined.

English "rite" here translates *religio* (which might well imply "ritual"), "practicing" translates *colendi* (implying more than "cult"), while I have added the brackets to "religion" to show that no such word at all appears (or was needed) in the Latin. But the eminent translator (A. H. M. Jones) has recognized that what Valentinian has in mind is what we now call "religion."[3] Its emergence in the fourth century has generated the principle of "free choice" (in contrast to inherited duty). Valentinian also understands that this was not simply "determined" in the mind, but developed there under influence: what he actually said was, "whatever his mind had drunk in" (*imbibisset*).

A contemporary of Valentinian and the last great Latin historian to stand outside this verbal tsunami, Ammianus Marcellinus (himself a Greek), coyly notes the fact that Christians were also transplanting Greek

---

3. Jones, *Later Roman Empire*, 1:150.

words into Latin. All are derived from the common vocabulary of secular life, without cultic significance: *ecclesia, synodus, basilica, episcopus, presbyter, diaconus, martyr*. He might well have added others, such as *monachus* or *coemeterium*. Ammianus sees no connection at all or even analogy between the sacral life of Greeks and Romans and the affairs of the Christians. The latter have no *deus*, no *templum, delubrum* or *fanum* ("shrine"), no *sacerdos*, no *sacra, caerimoniae, hostia* ("victim") or *ara* ("altar"). These all belong exclusively to the gods. Likewise, *secta, doctrina,* and *theologus* belong to philosophy or literature. But Christians do have their *religio, lex, cultus,* or *ritus,* none of which is a distinctively "religious" term.

The *Oxford Latin Dictionary* of 1982 (confined to authors writing before AD 200) shows the following senses (abbreviated) for *religio*:[4]

1. Taboo

2. Scruple

3. Impediment

4. + 5. Sanction

6. + 7. Awe

8. Ritual

9. Cult

10. Punctilio

One must ask the question: What more, if anything, does "religion" now mean? *The Macquarie Dictionary* (1981) offers:[5]

> 1. the quest for the values of the ideal life, involving three phases, the ideal, the practices for attaining the values of the ideal, and the theology or world view relating the quest to the environing universe. 2. a particular system in which the quest for the ideal life has been embodied: *the Christian religion*. 3. recognition on the part of man of a controlling superhuman power entitled to obedience, reverence, and worship. 4. the feeling or the spiritual attitude of those recognizing such a controlling power. 5. the manifestation of such feeling in conduct or life. 6. a point or matter of conscience, esp. when zealously or obsessively observed: *to make a religion of doing something.* 7. Obs.

4. Glare, *Oxford Latin Dictionary*, 1605–6. Editor's note: The *OLD* referenced here is the single-volume edition of 1982, but the definition in question was first published in 1980, at page 1605–6 in fascicle 7 of the 8-part series. See p. 41 above for the full list.

5. Delbridge, *Macquarie Dictionary*, 1486.

the practice of sacred rites or observances. 8. (pl.) *Obs.* religious rites. [ME, from L. *religio* fear of the gods, religious awe, sacredness, scrupulousness]

How does the *Macquarie* list differ from that of the *OLD*? The latter's overall motif is constraint (ranging from "bond" to "inhibition") but in the Macquarie list intellectual outreach is given primacy, tapering off in senses 6–8 to something like those of *OLD*, significantly now labeled "obsolete." The distinctives of a modern "religion" are that it has (a) an articulate view of the world as a whole, (b) a coherent set of rules for life, and (c) a communal identity that marks it off from other such complexes: "creed," "commitment," and "community"; or "belief," "behavior," and "belonging."

None of these items featured in the so-called "religion" of Graeco-Roman antiquity. One's daily sacrifice did not commit one to any doctrine or pattern of behavior, nor define any communal life other than the general one. Each of these concerns lay rather with philosophy. The most sharply defined case was that of the Epicureans. They were in practice "atheists," leaving the gods to the farthest reaches of the universe and forming inward-looking communities detached especially from *religio*. *Tantum religio potuit suadere malorum,* "So great was constraint's compulsive power for evil" (Lucretius 1.101). Other Romans contrasted *religio* with *superstitio*: *Religio deos colit, superstitio violat,* "Constraint cultivates the gods, credulity violates them" (Seneca, *De clementia* 2.5.1). Seneca was urging Nero to practice clemency, which is gentle and controlled (like *religio*), but not pity, for *misericordia* (like *superstitio*) is a vice of the weak mind that gives in to other people's problems. Roman authors consistently denounced the Christians for *superstitio*, because their behavior was "novel" and "dangerous" (Suetonius, *Nero* 16.2). By the fourth century the terms were inverted: the Christians claimed *religio* and denounced those loyal to their ancestral gods for *superstitio*.

There were innumerable gods, and (for philosophers) a singular deity that underlay them all like a Platonic idea. Gods manifested themselves in particular places and functions. Within such domains a sanctuary (*hieron, templum*) was marked out, within which some object (e.g., a statue) embodied the god, before whom sacrifice must be offered. This was done in every communal or public institution on every occasion, daily in every household, and for every human process or experience. The multiple phases of childbirth, for example, were protected each by its proper divinity. Everything must be maintained as it always had been. It was inconceivable that the gods would change anything. But constant care was needed lest you discontinued or overlooked their requirements.

The Christians rejected all the gods as demonic. They treated Christ of all people *quasi deo*, "as though he were a god" (Pliny the Younger, *Ep.* 10.96.8). Their intellectual premises were radically different from the naturalistic logic of the schools, turning instead on a reorientation of history towards the future. They set out to reconstruct community life, shocking everyone by the abandonment of ancestral practice. But from the third century they began to claim the sacral terminology of the classical cults, treating it by analogy (the sacrifice of praise), inspired by the typology of the classic Hebrew cult. Ammianus was apparently unaware of this subtle plundering of ideas. It secured for the churches the public solidarity their pioneering had once undermined. Only in the seventeenth century did it become possible to set "paganism," Judaism, Christianity, and Islam alongside each other as a series of "religions."[6]

Ammianus certainly did not see Christianity as a "religion." Not only did he not group it with the various cultic practices that upheld the civic order, such as modern historians of antiquity classify under this term, but neither did he anticipate the modern phenomenon to which we now apply it. That is, he did not conceive of "religion" as an alternative habit of thought and life, potentially critical of the civil order, and demarcating within that a particular community as a social whole in its own right.

Yet Ammianus lived through many of the complex developments that eventually brought about this historically fundamental shift. He might well have sensed the restructuring of society from a unitary to a bipolar form. He noticed and disliked some of the things about the Christians that marked this change. Yet he could not see it.

Eusebius could not see it either. An historian may not be the best-placed observer to understand and interpret the historical changes of his own day. The sharper insight lies with those who cross from the old to the new, or back again—with an Augustine, or a Julian—who have something to explain about themselves.[7]

Ammianus is noticing things he has observed, but not experienced. Yet the witness who is not aware that he does not understand offers a certain

---

6. Harrison, *'Religion' and the Religions*, 39, traces the series to Brerewood, *Enquiries* (1614). The plural had already appeared in Hooker, *Of the Lawes of Ecclesiasticall Politie*, 4:xi–2.

7. See Judge, "Christian Innovation," reproduced as chapter 7 in the present volume, for discussion of several fourth-century examples. Barnes, however, argues that Ammianus was indeed like Julian a renegade who had known it all from the inside but "closed his eyes" to engage in a "covert polemic": *Ammianus Marcellinus*, 79–94. Yet a renegade polemic, however covert, could hardly have resisted any exposure of the central place of Scripture in Christian life, or any desire to claim its social momentum for Hellenism, both prominent in Julian.

primary innocence, unaffected by the need to explain. Had Ammianus taken up the new term *Christianitas* he must already have accepted that he had something to justify. Instead, he tentatively adapts conventional language to the demands of the phenomenon that is concealed from his imagination. He is the good witness, not conscious of the key to what takes his eye.[8]

It is clear in particular that Ammianus did not associate the Christians with any divinity. Neither Christ nor God is named in connection with them. The term *deus* arises solely in relation to the traditional gods, or to Ammianus's central concept of the "sovereign will" or "power" (*summum numen*). This applies even where the speaker is a Christian (Constantius, 15.8.9–10). The Christians moreover practice no cult. All the terms distinctive of sacred buildings or ceremonies are exclusively used of the traditional cults. When *aedes* is used for a church (22.11.10) it is plural ("house"), not singular ("temple"). When a plural is required for the former the epithet *sacrae* is added (17.7.8; 27.9.10).

The only apparent exceptions to this at least prove the rule, but are probably to be brought under it anyway. The see of Alexandria is referred to as *sedes sacerdotalis* (15.7.9), but this perhaps adopts the "priestly" epithet applied to the bishop's chair by Constantius, whose *subscriptio* is referred to and would have been extant. Christian usage surely also explains the fact that Ammianus uses the plural *antistites* both for those who "preside over" the worship of gods (22.14.8, 23.6.24) and for bishops as a group (21.16.18, 22.5.3, 27.3.15, 29.5.15). The singular is once used for an anonymous bishop (20.7.7) and once for a named one (15.7.6). Individual bishops are otherwise identified by name and by the term *episcopus*. Christian Latin writers used *antistes* as a harmless equivalent of *episcopus*, and the variation in Ammianus need only be stylistic. Etymologically the word carries no sacral connotation, and was also used of the head of a philosophical school. For bishops it was the regular usage of the imperial chancellery.[9]

The virgins captured by Sapor are spoken of as "consecrated to divine service in the Christian way" (*Christiano ritu cultui divino sacratas*, 18.10.4), but this expression may be due to the assimilation of the virgins

---

8. *Christianitas* appears in *Cod. theod.* 14.3.11 (AD 365), where the *privilegium Christianitatis* is canceled in the case of those hoping to escape their duty as bakers. Marius Victorinus, in his commentaries on the Pauline epistles (post–362), begins to prefer *Christianitas* to the established loan-word *Christianismus* (also ignored by Ammianus). He understands how the term globalizes the distinctive Christian combination of behavior and insight: *lex tota . . . et totum mysterium Christianitatis* (*Comm. in Eph.* 1283A, in Locher, *Marii Victorini*, 190, cf. 1269C, 1272B).

9. Mohrmann, *Die altchristliche Sondersprache*, 108–9; Pighi, "Latinità cristiana"; Janssen, *Kultur und Sprache*.

in Ammianus's mind to the ancient Vestals.[10] Similarly the *ritus Christiani sacrarium* in which Hilarinus takes refuge (26.3.3) may have earned that cultic identity from the claim to sanctuary implied. *Divinitas* in 27.7.6 is sometimes taken as part of an interpolation (*id est divinitati acceptos*) since Ammianus has already given a careful explanation of the martyrs (22.11.10), but a monastic copyist would have offered a more adequate formula. Pighi takes the phrase as an echo of Cicero, *Rep.* 6.13 or Livy 1.19.5. In that case it is again hardly the Christian divinity that is in the mind of Ammianus. Alternatively, it may be an ironic echo of Christian eulogy.

Numen, the preferred term for the divinity in Ammianus, is twice used by him in connection with Christians, but on both occasions he means to claim them as worshipers of the true "power." Julian, secretly, a "worshipper of the gods" (21.2.4), observes the festival called Epiphany by the Christians, goes to "their *ekklēsia*" and "addresses the *numen*" (*numine orato*, 21.2.5), but not "their" *numen* (as in Rolfe's translation), in spite of the characteristically Christian term for prayer (*orare*, not *precari*).[11] Ammianus allows the "addressing" of the *numen* in a church because Julian is a true believer. Similarly, the lifestyle of some provincial bishops "commends them to the perpetual *numen* and its true worshippers as pure and reverent men" (27.3.15). The implication is that the metropolitan bishops who horrify Ammianus with their careerism are not acceptable to the divine power, whose true worshipers are not of course Christian.

What then does Ammianus think Christians are? The Latin formation of their name will have suggested a political faction or following. In so far as cult-groups had names they were not formed that way.[12] The Latin historical tradition does not treat *Christus* as the name of a god. The term *Christiani* had apparently been coined by Latin speakers in first-century Antioch in reaction to their contentious community behavior, *Christus* being construed as the faction leader. Fourth-century politics was still producing such loyalties: the tetrarchic forces of *Ioviani* and *Herculiani* (22.3.2, 25.6.2 etc.), and the *Constantiniani* (29.5.22). New Christian factions were also named this way, the *Damasiani* (*Collectio Avellana* 1.7),[13] or *Eunomiani* (*Cod. theod.* 16.5.8).

Ammianus clearly takes the name for granted. It calls for no explanation. That had been sufficiently dealt with by his predecessor, Tacitus (*Ann.* 15.44.2). No digression in the lost books need be posited in which he might

---

10. De Jonge, *Philological and Historical Commentary*, comm. ad loc.
11. Wagenvoort, "Orare, precari."
12. Judge, "Did the Churches Compete," 515.
13. Günther, *Epistulae Imperatorum*, 1.7

have explained the matter further. One may assume this from the absence of any back-reference in the extant books, such as one finds, e.g., for the tides of Britain (27.8.4) or the topography of Africa (29.5.18). His lack of consciousness of the problems he was failing to address may be sensed in the perfunctory note with which he concludes the brief digression on the different political styles of the metropolitan and provincial bishops—"this will be sufficient digression" (*hactenus deviasse sufficiet*, 27.3.15).[14]

Used as a noun, *Christianus* is normally plural, and points to collective action, just as when qualifying other nouns it defines a social whole. The *Christiani* assert their characteristic terminology (14.9.7; 21.2.5; 27.7.5). They act together in the community (22.5.3–4; 22.11.10; 22.13.2; 27.9.9). Teachers may be categorized as *Christiani* (25.4.20). When the noun is used of individuals, they are anonymous (31.12.9; 31.15.6). When named, Christians may be identified as such by their ecclesiastical rank. But no named individual is called *Christianus*, and of all the figures in Ammianus otherwise known to have been Christians, only Jovian is explicitly identified as such (25.10.15). In all of this Ammianus marks off the Christians from the general community, signaling his own sense of distance from them, and incomprehension.

But he also attempts to formulate the phenomenon more adequately, by coupling the adjective *Christianus* with four different nouns, *ritus*, *lex*, *cultus*, and *religio*. This is more than a matter of stylistic variation.[15] In that case we should have expected him to start with an agreed and common term (such as *Christianitas*). But this is the opposite process. Ammianus is looking for an effective term for something he does not adequately grasp, and which had no general name. But the four terms he experiments with have certain points in common. None of them (in particular neither *religio* nor *cultus*) is primarily used by Ammianus in connection with cultic practice. None of them is ever coupled by Ammianus with any other determinant parallel with *Christianus*.

Ritus Christianus is his increasingly preferred phrase. But his usage is grammatically and semantically rather unusual. Apart from 18.10.4 and 21.16.18, all his other nine instances are in the genitive case, rare earlier.[16] The genitive occurs otherwise in Ammianus only in 22.15.30 and 23.6.4. The word is normally found only in the ablative. This singularity of usage points

14. Emmett (now Nobbs), "Digressions," 42–53, conjectures that there were no digressions on lost "religious topics," the treatment of these being concentrated around the figure of Julian in the extant books.

15. Hagendahl, *Studia Ammianea*, 99–104, notes the scale of variation in Ammianus—28 alternative terms for dying, 35 for the dawn, etc.

16. 15.5.31; 22.10.7; 26.3.3; 27.3.13; 27.10.1; 28.6.27; 29.3.4; 29.5.15; 31.12.8.

to a particular value he tends to give the term in the Christian connection. It is anticipated in the Acts of the Scillitan Martyrs where the proconsul (of AD 180) reads his decree from its tablet:[17]

> that the rest, who admitted living in the Christian manner (*ritu Christiano se vivere*), should be executed, since they obstinately persisted though an opportunity of returning to Roman custom (*morem*) has been offered them.

Ritus thus hints at the alternative life-style of the Christians, contrasted with the Roman way of life. It is something more consciously constructive and comprehensive than "practice"—the Christian "movement" perhaps.

Christiana lex arises four times, more in the earlier books, and each time in the genitive case (15.7.6; 15.7.8; 20.7.7; 25.10.15). It is the forerunner of *ritus Christianus*, and helps to specify its meaning. The word is not otherwise used by Ammianus in the genitive, and never of traditional cult practice. Liberius (bishop of Rome) is *Christianae legis antistes* (15.7.6) "a superintendent of the Christian rule of life," a term favored by Christians themselves. Galletier compares *Cod. theod.* 16.2.5 (AD 323), *on eos, qui sanctissimae legi serviunt*, "those who serve the holiest rule of life," and 16.8.2 (330), *qui . . . in memorata secta degentes legi ipsi praesident*, (those Jews) "who live their lives in that cause and preside over its very rule of life."[18] The translation is justified, for Ammianus at least, by his tribute to Julian, whom a *lex quaedam vitae melioris* accompanied from his cradle to his last breath, "a kind of rule for a better life" (16.1.4).

Cultus Christianus (21.2.4) is the "Christian culture" to which Julian pretends to "cling" (*adhaerere*) lest anyone spot that he is secretly one of the *deorum cultores*. The "cultivation" (*cultus*) of the gods is mentioned half a dozen times, along with that of many other matters, agriculture, vesture, modesty, humanity, studies, the mind. Only with the Christians is it left unclear what is actually being cultivated.

Christiana religio (21.16.18) is the "Christian punctilio" or "commitment" which Ammianus finds "pure and simple" (*absolutam et simplicem*), as he has Constantius do for truth itself (14.10.13). It is only confused through the incessant argumentation fostered by the *superstitio* of Constantius. *Religio* in Ammianus, especially in the plural, mostly connotes the sanction of an oath, or scruple, and need not extend into what we call "religion." Valentinian is complimented for not taking sides (*medius stetit*) between "alternative commitments" (*religionum diversitates*, 30.9.5). Christian

17. Musurillo, *Acts of the Christian Martyrs*, 88.
18. Galletier and Fontaine, *Ammien Marcellin*, comm. ad loc.

writers use the term *diversitas* to indicate not a variety of interests but more particularly a "divergent" cause, as with a heresy. When Eupraxius speaks of *religio Christiana* cultivating the martyrs (27.7.6), he is highlighting the Christian "commitment" to that.

With each of these four terms, then, Ammianus is expanding the sense of the simple appellation *Christiani*. He instinctively seeks to express their character as a social movement. He knows that they are tenaciously opposed to the worship of the gods, and has no inclination at all to assimilate them to that. Although he lacks an adequate formulation of what he observes, there is a good deal of tell-tale detail that slips out in other comments.

Ammianus is familiar with the term *ecclesia* (21.2.5; 22.11.9; 22.13.2; 28.6.27), which, like *episcopus*, calls for no explanation. It refers to a building, each time in the singular, not an assembly. *Conventiculum* (15.5.31; 27.3.13) should, however, refer to that, since in the former case it occurs within the *regia*, so it seems, or even in the *aedicula* (though that could be an unrelated room), while in the latter it occurs within the *basilica Sicinini*. But in 28.4.29 it refers to a place of assembly.

Although *episcopus* is regularly used of named individuals, Ammianus twice uses *presbyter* for anonymous ones (29.3.4; 31.12.8), excusing the Greek word in the latter case by saying "this is what they call it" (*ut ipsi appellant*). Similarly, he had distanced himself from the title of a (named) *diaconus* (14.9.7), *ut appellant Christiani*. *Ephiphania* (21.2.5) is similarly excused; this is what the Christians "customarily call" (*dictitant*) their January holiday. But Ammianus refrains from asking why. By contrast there are two novel features of Christian practice that magnetize his attention. In either case he twice circles around the point, citing the distinctive usage, and allowing the context to supply a vivid impression of his reaction.

In his treatment of the intransigence of Liberius, Ammianus notes (15.6.7) that the "meeting" (*coetus*, a word also in use amongst Christians) which had deposed Athanasius, bishop of Alexandria, was called by them *synodus*. He repeats the comment in his obituary of Constantius when condemning him for the disruption caused by synods to the public transport system (21.16.18). The term had long since made its way into the Latin inscriptions of *collegia*, while the "ecumenical synod of Dionysiac artists" should have made it familiar throughout the empire.[19] Yet Ammianus surely used his (affected?) ignorance to express dislike. He shows no sense of the promising novelty of a representative and autonomous assembly that proved as difficult for Constantius to manage as were the popularly entrenched

---

19. Judge, "Ecumenical Synod," with the Latin ruling of the first tetrarchy addressed to the (combined) *synodus* of "xystics" and "thymelics" (*CPL* 241).

bishops individually. Instead he condemns him for taking the debate with such seriousness (*superstitione*, 21.16.18) as to promote discord, and at the same time (inconsistently?) condemns him for multiplying synods by trying to get the whole movement (*ritum*) to agree with him.

The *martyres* however seem to be more positively featured by Ammianus. In 363, after the lynching of George, bishop of Alexandria, his body was incinerated along with others to prevent a church being built for their relics (22.11.10). This used to happen with those who, having been tortured for their *religio* (commitment), met a "glorious" death with *intemerata fide* ("unsullied trust"). *Gloriosa* sounds Christian, but is also a favorite epithet with Ammianus, used explicitly of his own expected death in action at Amida in 355 (19.2.4). *Intemerata fides* likewise fits the Christians well, yet it echoes the ironic protestation of the Greek "deserter" who deceived the Trojans over the wooden horse (Vergil, *Aen.* 2.143). As with the second reference to the *martyres* (27.7.6) they are seen as a problem to be avoided. But Ammianus seems to admire their forthright commitment to their trust, unless one also takes the explanatory *id est divinitati acceptos* (noted above) as ironic.

It may well be then that Ammianus sees such dedication, as with that of the virgins captured by Sapor (18.10.4), as a feature of the *ritus Christianus*. But it is the submissive posture he approves. He is critical of Athanasius for raising himself above his *professio* (15.7.7) and trying to find out things that were extraneous (*externa*). Contrast the philosopher Maximus who did not divulge the oracle "out of respect for his *professio*" (21.1.42). In the case of George, who forgot it by stooping to become an informer (22.11.5), the obligation of one's *professio* is spelled out: it "only calls for justice and leniency" (*nihil nisi iustum suadet et lene*). The Christian *lex* also had a *propositum* ("purpose," 15.7.8), but Ammianus does not say what this might have been. In the case of Julian, his *propositum* was "to live correctly" (20.5.4), while that of the citizens of Rome was "peace and quiet" (*quies*, 27.9.9).

Ammianus surely wished for as much from the Christians. Its improbability is reflected in his (unconscious?) penchant for talking about them in terms of an administrative or military command structure. This need not have been pejorative with a writer consciously at home in such matters, and Christians themselves were not averse from militancy, as a metaphor. But Ammianus expressly condemns Constantius for "feeding (their disagreements) with battles over words" (*aluit concertatione verborum*, 21.16.18). This is more than metaphorical. It led to the "hamstringing" (*succideret nervos*) of the transport service, with "squads" (*catervis*) of bishops "shuttling back and forth" (*ultro citroque discurrentibus*, the language of the battlefield).

The synod "discharged (Athanasius) from the commission he held" (*removit a sacramento quod obtinebat*, 15.7.7). George was subsequently "appointed" (*ordinatus*, 22.11.4). Ammianus need not have known that "sacrament" and "ordination" already had their particular Christian use. Athanasius had been "in command" (*praesidebat*) over the Christian *lex* (15.7.8), but Liberius was "of higher rank" (*auctoritate . . . potiore*, 15.7.10). These were confronted by the rival champions. Julian had long since secretly "deserted" (*desciverat*, 21.2.4) from the *cultus Christianus*. Plato had challenged Jupiter in fullness of speech, having "seen action" (*militavit*, 22.16.22) "in glorious wisdom."

Other phenomena are noticed without any discernible explanation being suggested. Hostility to the temple cult (22.5.1; 22.11.7–9; 22.13.2) was presumably clarified when Ammianus had dealt with Constantine. The same may apply to the use of tombs as sanctuaries (22.11.10; 27.7.5); but their Christian identity is not always noted (18.7.7; 19.3.1; 22.12.18). The power of popular opinion (15.7.10; 22.5.3–4; 22.11.10) is perhaps not peculiar to the Christians. The political independence of bishops surely is (15.7.6, 9–10; 22.11.3–11; 27.3.12–15); yet there is no reference to its legislative sanction (e.g., *Cod. theod.* 16.2.12 of September 23, 355, exempting bishops from the civil courts). The drive for orthodoxy is noted (21.2.4, 21.16.18, 22.5.3–4, 30.9.5); yet its confused politicization over Athanasius (15.7.6–10) is missed. Churches are seen as refuges (15.5.31[?], 26.3.3); their meetings expose the community to attack (27.10.1–2, 28.6.27); they supply anonymous mediators in war (20.7.7–9, 29.5.15, 31.12.8–9, 31.15.6).[20]

An uncontentious, ethically quietist, and tolerant movement would have the approval of Ammianus; he does not understand either the intellectual or the social turmoil stirred up by the Christians, and simply treats that as a vice. The life-style of the "provincial *antistites*" (27.3.15) which commended them to the "perpetual *numen*" consisted in "a slender diet" (*tenuitas edendi*), "drinking in a most sparing way" (*potandique parcissime*), cheap clothes, and eyes fixed on the ground. Those who preferred urban ostentation, with the regal life-style of the Roman see, funded by generous matrons, may as well fight for it (27.3.14). "They get their money" (*mercedem*, Matt 6:2), he might well have added, for Ammianus goes on, it has been suggested, to echo the beatitudes:[21] "They would be truly blessed" (*beati re vera*) if they copied the provincial bishops.

---

20. An implicit renewal of the old charge of disloyalty, according to Angliviel de la Beaumelle, "Remarques sur l'attitude," 15–23.

21. Pighi, "Latinità Cristiana," 53.

As well as disliking the opulence of Damasus and Ursinus, riding in state, and dressing "elegantly" (*circumspecte*, 27.3.14), or the serious "religiosity" (*superstitio*, 21.16.18) of Constantius, Ammianus repeatedly blames "Christians" (sc. their leaders) for violent factionalism and personal brutality. It was their "disputes" (*iurgia*, 27.9.9) which stirred up mass factionalism (21.16.18; 22.5.3; 22.11.10; 27.3.12); Ammianus is equally disgusted by the circus factions (28.4.29–30). But with Christians there is a particularly horrible side: they turn on their own kind. Julian had learned from experience that most of them are more "fatal" (*ferales*, 22.4.5) to each other than wild beasts are to humankind. The adjective is otherwise used of the fatal "outrages" (*ausa*) of informers (15.7.1; 22.11.5) and of a treason-trial torturer (19.12.8). The Alexandrians turned on Bishop George because they had too often suffered from his viper's fangs (22.11.3).

What Ammianus misunderstands in all this is the way it is driven by doctrinal controversy, and the Christian need for dogmatic orthodoxy, as in the disputes over Athanasius (15.7.8) and George (22.11.5). He cannot see how this sharpens popular loyalty (15.7.10) and intolerance (22.11.8). He misses the dogmatic principle behind Julian's action against Christian teachers (22.10.7), and consequently misunderstands the point of Julian's transferring to the Christians the jibe of Marcus Aurelius against the Jews (22.5.4–5).

Behind it all lies the apparent unawareness of Ammianus in the face of the two most profoundly innovative features of the movement: the systematic passing down to the popular level of the demand for dogmatic rectitude, and the new kinds of social activism driven by that. Ammianus knew of the importance of theological learning and of sacred books in both classical (14.11.25–26; 21.1.8) and Egyptian (22.16.20) culture, but these were of course élite traditions seeking and causing no social turmoil. The didactic use of the biblical literature was intended to transform the people's life. Ammianus seems wholly unconscious of the social welfare programs that enraged his hero, Julian, unless they are implied by the "offerings" (*oblationes*, 27.3.14) of the Roman matrons. He is equally unaware of the passion for an angelic life, even though monasticism was currently horrifying other classical observers, unless that is acknowledged in the episode of the virgins (18.10.4) or his admiration for abstemious bishops (27.3.15).

Overall Ammianus is well aware of the impact of the Christians on public life. He attempts to grasp it by correlating its problems (civil disruption, personal hostility) with the general predicament of the community. He would like to isolate and assimilate such good aspects as he saw (truth and modesty). But he misses the dogmatic sources of it all. Yet in tacitly avoiding any confusion of terms with the province of the gods and their cult, and casting around for a way of conceiving the movement as a social whole, he indirectly registers the historical novelty ("religion," in the modern sense) of beliefs about God creating an alternative culture.

10

Did the "Flood of Words" Change Nothing?

This chapter is a review of Ramsay MacMullen's *Christianity and Paganism in the Fourth to Eighth Centuries* (New Haven, CT: Yale University Press, 1997). A shortened version was published in *JRH* 23.2 (1999) 240–41. The full text appeared in Judge, *Engaging Rome and Jerusalem*, 61–64, under the present title and with introduction and footnotes supplied by the editor (Piggin). The present version retains that title as well as the full text and notes (both lightly adapted). After setting MacMullen's volume in the context of his previous scholarship, the review outlines the arguments made in each of the book's four parts. In response, it suggests two significant and related flaws in MacMullen's outlook: the treatment of Christianity and "paganism" under the rubric of "religion" and a lack of appreciation for the cultural and theoretical transformations that were to follow from the Christian worldview.

FOR THIRTY-FIVE YEARS NOW Ramsay MacMullen has been leading us back and forth across the no-man's-land of later antiquity. He skillfully gathers the scraps of evidence that tell of the experience of ordinary people in baffling times. It began in 1963 with *Soldier and Civilian in the Later Roman Empire*, deliberately focused on the third and fourth centuries to span the great divide traditionally marked between them.

With *Paganism in the Roman Empire* (1981) MacMullen portrayed "the whole resilient, living fabric of belief" during the two centuries leading up to the first public church council, Nicaea (AD 325).[1] He sought "to sponge out of the picture . . . those false outlines and colors that have been painted in" by Christian triumphalism, looking for someone else to

---

1. MacMullen, *Paganism*, 130.

re-work that aspect of it, "but not too fast."[2] In the event he quickly stepped into the gap himself with *Christianizing the Roman Empire (A.D. 100–400)* (1984), "the growth of the church as seen from the outside."[3] It is "actually hard to imagine" how anyone could have known much about the life of the churches.[4] But three million converts had been shocked into it, even before Constantine.[5] The majority, however, silently persisted in the old ways long after he had added official inducement.[6] This puzzle provides the topic for MacMullen's present book.

Christianity and Paganism insists that much less was changed than the bishops required. "A spongy mass of tolerance and tradition" absorbed "the tremendous will of the one God" (2). "Even the stupidest plowboy would know better than to discard all the divine aid of his tradition in exchange for what someone tried to prove in no more than the breath of words" (9). Moreover, it is the flood of words (from this epoch everything preserved is Christian, except Zosimus) that has misrepresented "the true proportions of religious history" (3). MacMullen develops his theme in four revisionist movements, each embracing the whole span.

The first is "Persecution." Given the "deficiencies" of Christianity, conversions "could only be made through intimidation" (151). More positive explanations are explicitly rejected. The churches did not offer more to women and slaves (7n13, *pace* Brown and Chadwick).[7] The preaching was not intelligible to all (10n27, *pace* Cameron).[8] Instead, Christianity was imposed by an elite that had abandoned a "nobler" culture for a more vulgar one (10). Their aggressive and exclusive demands were clouded by a "fog of dark disapproval" and a "mist of love—for each other" (13). They confronted "the rich, complicated faith of the persecuted" pagans (19) through "the wielding of power on behalf of co-religionists (22), and the rising curve of "judicial savagery" (31). Two and a half centuries after Constantine, "Justinian was still engaged in the war upon dissent" (151). "The extremes of conceivable pressure were brought to bear" (72).

2. MacMullen, *Paganism*, xiii.
3. MacMullen, *Christianizing the Roman Empire*, vii.
4. MacMullen, *Christianizing the Roman Empire*, 104.
5. MacMullen, *Christianizing the Roman Empire*, 110.
6. MacMullen, *Christianizing the Roman Empire*, 118.
7. See Brown, *Cult of the Saints*, 46: " Women had been [a] blank on the map of the Classical city . . By contrast the Christian church, from an early time, had encouraged women to take on a public role, in their own right." For Chadwick, see McManners, *Oxford Illustrated History*, 69: "the egalitarianism by which aristocrats and their slaves shared in one and the same eucharist is extraordinary."
8. Cameron, *Christianity and the Rhetoric of Empire*, e.g., 8, 36, 39.

Next comes "The Cost to the Persecuted." The pressure could only be slowly intensified, since the bishops worked "from the top down" (73) and there was no "organized missionary effort" (33). They were attacking "demons," but for others it was the whole annual cycle of their lives that was at stake, particularly the cheerful celebrations, starting with the gift-giving and all-night street parties of the New Year (36). They were expected to give up "the remarkable diversity of cult-centered arts, activities, and psychological rewards, in the traditional forms" (152). Crowded processions, with flowers, were highlights of the year. The sacrificial system fed directly into public feasting and drinking. The temples had been fairgrounds, providing shelter and relief for many who were destitute or handicapped, as Libanius noted (45). Community dancing and singing were part of it. Especially for the eight or nine tenths of the population living remote from cities it was not going to be easy to strip life of the customary pleasures that sweetened it (153). "The old religion suited most people very well" (69).

With "Superstition" MacMullen takes up a topic he (along with Momigliano) had earlier identified as the key to the late antique transformation. What caused the collapse of the rationalist tradition of high culture, as still flourishing in the times of Pliny, Plutarch, and Plotinus (76–78)? Why did Porphyry and Iamblichus, the immediate successors of Plotinus in the late third century, cease to "restrain their resort to the divine in explaining experience" (85)? This shift preceded the recognition of Christianity. It must have been caused by the swamping of the governing elite by small-town clerks and soldiers promoted from the ranks (83). Under Diocletian the high-level bureaucracy had exploded to 30–35,000 from the 300 of Caracalla's day (seventy years earlier). A similar proliferation followed in the number of bishops, "new people with their old ideas getting into positions from which they could be heard" (87). So the long, but select succession in philosophy sank beneath the tide of superstition.

Finally, under "Assimilation," we are shown the "wonderfully dynamic phase in church history" in which the people refused to abandon the "smiles of paganism" for "the downturned mouth, the sorrowing, gabled eyebrows of Byzantine and medieval piety" (154). There was a "seamless join of the old to the new," and "the flow from non-Christian into Christian usage was thus unbroken" (125), "all but the cross a part of pagan tradition" (157).

Admirers of MacMullen's genial combinations may yet wonder how he would link the ploughboy's happy supernaturalism with the grim repression that came as its mentality took control of the world. Life at the bottom had no doubt been more than dancing in the streets anyway. As for the wordy bishops, there must surely be more to be said. The long twilight of ancient science, trapped in its own non-empirical logic, was not induced by them. It was, by contrast, their dogmatism, reducing the cosmos to an artifact, that eventually dissolved the illusory music of the spheres, opening the world at last to a truly empirical science, testing things rather than proving them logically. History too was to be transformed. The sorrowing gaze is the mark of moralism, the new answerability of man, which treats people as far more than superficial types, their own self-consciousness itself becoming the battleground of life. Hence (indirectly) the need for documentation in history, and the preoccupation of modern culture with the personal struggle.

Ramsay MacMullen has been reading in Augustine the ancient sources of this modern revolution. His present book in effect offers us one reason why it was delayed—submerged in the church's perpetuation of the old culture. But if Augustine's congregation could not follow his sermons, his many correspondents in positions of power understood him well, and the collapse of political authority should have opened the way for his ideas more quickly to reconstruct the world. Ramsay MacMullen's nostalgia and horror of dogma have masked a more profound historical puzzle than the one he has generously illuminated.

The reason for this is clear. He can only see Christianity in terms of "religion" (though he is alert to the ambiguities of that word), with "paganism" as its counterpart. Certainly the bishops were seized by this polarity, and in the end compromised with it as MacMullen demonstrates. But their overwhelming intellectual enterprise, from which he recoils, had little or nothing to do with what we mean by "religion" in the ancient world (the customary sanctification of the daily round). It was basically the opposite of that: a sustained and calculated subversion of the classical understanding of the world, rejecting fundamental principles of philosophy, psychology, education, and politics, creating as a result an alternative community structure—a "religion" in the modern sense (for the first time). May we hope for another book on this?

11

Destroying the Gods

Larry W. Hurtado's book *Destroyer of the Gods: Early Christian Distinctiveness in the Roman World* condenses many insights from Hurtado's Edinburgh research program into a single volume. This chapter, first published (without the present title) in *Ancient History: Resources for Teachers* 46 (2016), is a review of that volume. The review comments appreciatively on Hurtado's treatment of four distinctive aspects of early Christianity: its theological character, its non-ethnic identity, its literary culture, and its social standards. Hurtado was a research partner of the Ancient History program at Macquarie University, and won British funds to host Macquarie's input in Edinburgh. Hurtado passed away in November 2019 while the present volume was in preparation.

LARRY W. HURTADO's *DESTROYER of the Gods* has won the 2017 award of the American Publishers Association for the field of Archaeology and Ancient History.

Looking back across his own specialized works arising from his former professorial field (New Testament Language, Literature, and Theology), as noted below, our generous but cautious Edinburgh colleague reviews the outcome for a more general readership. He begins with what non-Christians at the time thought they saw.[1] Most ancient commentators were seriously disconcerted, itself a mark of the distinctiveness of the problem, which led to "social, and then political, opposition."[2] For the second-century philosopher of history, Celsus, it was "a social phenomenon fraught with danger." But in that case we need an adequate treatment of "what made early converts think it worth . . . the considerable social costs."

1. Hurtado, *Destroyer*, 15–36.
2. Hurtado, *Destroyer*, 35.

The first crux is theological: "A New Kind of Faith."[3] Paul "did not change religion."[4] We face "a novel movement within the Jewish tradition."[5] It has a "distinctive 'dyadic' pattern in which the one God and Jesus were central." This however represents "a new kind of what we would call 'religion' . . . that proved revolutionary in what 'religion' came to mean thereafter." The inverted commas for "religion" (to which a whole segment had been devoted) are the author's own:[6] they point to the classic historian's dilemma. We are aware of the consequences of what happened, while trying to do justice to the uncomprehending experience of those who lived through it all. It would have been clearer simply to have used the concepts that were applicable at the time. Hurtado cites in this matter Brent Nongbri, *Before Religion: A History of a Modern Concept*, but has consciously pulled back from my own solution.[7] For Jews at least the belief and practice that arose around Jesus was "categorically without precedent."[8] See Hurtado's earlier works, *One God, One Lord: Early Christian Devotion and Ancient Jewish Monotheism* and (to launch a new series of memorial lectures at Ben Gurion University in Israel) *How on Earth did Jesus become a God?*.

This leads to "A Different Identity."[9] In "the ancient Roman setting" one's identity was basically ethnic or national. "Indeed . . . it might well be anachronistic to try to separate what we moderns call "religion" from what we call "ethnicity" or "culture" . . . "religion" as a separate sphere of life is very much a modern notion, foreign to the ancient world."[10] Another "new deity," Dea Roma, had indeed arisen from local initiatives.[11] But it was translocal and transethnic, not displacing local gods.[12] This also applies to what Hurtado calls "Voluntary Religion":[13] Mithras and Isis, for example, attracted widespread support, as did some philosophical traditions, but it was not exclusive. "In no way did it comprise a fundamental change in how you understood your religious identity."[14] The new "Christian religious identity,"

3. Hurtado, *Destroyer*, 37–76.
4. Hurtado, *Destroyer*, 204n3.
5. Hurtado, *Destroyer*, 76.
6. Hurtado, *Destroyer*, 38–44.
7. Hurtado, *Destroyer*, 213n5; 43 with 215n17.
8. Hurtado, *Destroyer*, 74.
9. Hurtado, *Destroyer*, 77–104.
10. Hurtado, *Destroyer*, 79.
11. Hurtado, *Destroyer*, 80.
12. Hurtado, *Destroyer*, 82.
13. Hurtado, *Destroyer*, 82–87.
14. Hurtado, *Destroyer*, 87.

however, "cut across ethnic lines."[15] The term *ekklēsia* in effect is a claim for Jews and gentiles to constitute "God's special people."[16] The language of "people," "nation," and "race" was an early "part of the self-descriptive vocabulary" of Christians.[17] I might have added that this is matched by our earliest outsider's formulations: their "tribe" (Greek *phylon*, Josephus, *Ant.* 18.63, from c. AD 94), or "human type" (Latin *genus hominum*, Suetonius, *Nero* 16.2, from c. AD 122). None of the first three Latin commentators even noticed the connection with Judaism.

Next comes "A 'Bookish' Religion," following *The Earliest Christian Artifacts: Manuscripts and Christian Origins*.[18] "'Textuality' was central."[19] If we assume that "the majority of people were functionally illiterate," the free citation of Scripture, even in letters addressed to largely gentile communities, implies efficient public reading.[20] Easily managed copies must have been available. Unlike Roman-era copies of literary texts, the early biblical ones are more marked by elementary punctuation and spacing, for the use of readers in "Christian corporate worship."[21] This last phrase, normative now with US Protestant churches, would of course have shocked St. Paul. Not only does he not mention formal reading in church as one of the gifts of the Spirit, but the only "worship" he endorses is the "reasonable service" of a transformed mind (Rom 12:1–2). Indeed, we may compare the authoritative/critical use of traditional teaching in a philosophical school.[22] "Early Christianity was phenomenally prolific and varied in literary output."[23] The gospels moreover are unique in genre, attracting imitative expansion.[24] The production and circulation of ancient texts however implies much painstaking labor. The development of the utilitarian codex ("book") form seems to have been favored particularly for the supply of Scripture, in contrast with the prestige of the classic roll ("volume") required for high literature in both Judaism and Hellenism.[25] The contraction of the "sacred names" in writing Scriptural texts is a purely visual symbol of the new faith (retaining the inflection helped you

---

15. Hurtado, *Destroyer*, 90.
16. Hurtado, *Destroyer*, 99.
17. Hurtado, *Destroyer*, 101.
18. Hurtado, *Destroyer*, 105–41.
19. Hurtado, *Destroyer*, 141.
20. Hurtado, *Destroyer*, 108.
21. Hurtado, *Destroyer*, 109.
22. Hurtado, *Destroyer*, 111.
23. Hurtado, *Destroyer*, 119.
24. Hurtado, *Destroyer*, 123.
25. Hurtado, *Destroyer*, 135.

read the words of course in full). Thus art perhaps begins subtly to sidestep the Mosaic ban on any "graven image."[26]

Finally, in "A New Way to Live," we find that "early Christianity represented a distinctive kind of social effort to reshape behavior."[27] It was not simply a matter of "Give no offence to Jews or to Greeks," for Paul adds a third test: "or to the church of God" (1 Cor 10:31). In matters like the rejection of unwanted offspring, or of blood sports in the arena, the church intensified existing scruples. But while he may appear to reflect the classic male orientation of sexual relations Paul is in reality rejecting that.[28] The strict monogamy always assumed for wives is now demanded of husbands too. The commitment is entirely reciprocal. Each is to serve the need of the other. Moreover the church as a whole is required to discipline unchastity.[29] "This alone represented a major shift in comparison to the attitudes of the larger Roman world."[30] Cultivating adolescent minors in an erotic partnership had been idealized. But second-century manuals of church discipline turned it upside down into "child abuse."[31] Contemporary philosophers at best advised restraint for the ethical honor of the male. The household codes of the churches are distinctive in that they directly instruct men, women, children, bond and free, in equal terms, in a "discourse situation" or "group social setting" where all are present to hear their respective commitments to each other.[32]

Hurtado's *Destroyer* is rich in details of recent opinion on these matters, with much cautious qualification of his own conclusions. He cites the assertion of J. B. Rives that Christian expansion was "a development that ultimately entailed the fundamental transformation" of the Graeco-Roman world.[33] Yet Hurtado writes as though it might even be thought "triumphalist" to observe the beginnings of different modern values in the sources of which he is a professional expert. His restraint is all the more persuasive. Its accessible style will make it valuable reading at any level of education.

---

26. Hurtado, *Destroyer*, 141.
27. Hurtado, *Destroyer*, 143–81; citation at 172.
28. Hurtado, *Destroyer*, 156.
29. Hurtado, *Destroyer*, 161.
30. Hurtado, *Destroyer*, 165.
31. Hurtado, *Destroyer*, 168.
32. Hurtado, *Destroyer*, 180.
33. Hurtado, *Destroyer*, 226.

12

Why No Church Schools in Antiquity?

The ancient church did not, in general, provide formal or institutional "Christian" education for its children. This chapter treats attitudes and practice regarding education (both in civil and church life) that produced such a result. In doing so it first outlines the general education system before turning to consider the Christian outlook in three successive periods: the New Testament era, the period of (often intellectual) conflict in the second and third centuries, and the period from Constantine and after as Christendom became established. The study was written for the 1967 Syllabus for the Certificate in Christian Education, a correspondence course sponsored by the Australian Teachers' Christian Fellowship. It was subsequently published under the present title with an introductory note from the editor (Stuart Piggin) in Judge, *Engaging Rome and Jerusalem*, 253–64. Beyond the removal of the editorial introduction, the present reproduction differs only slightly from the text presented in *Engaging Rome and Jerusalem*.

Introduction

IF WE TAKE CHRISTIAN EDUCATION in the sense of the formal schooling of children in particular, the example set by the churches of the first five centuries AD is almost entirely negative. Far from taking any systematic steps in the matter, they deliberately maintained a policy of inaction which they themselves recognized as possibly suicidal. Modern students of the subject must therefore not only ask themselves the reasons for the primitive attitude, and whether they may not include principles which still apply today, but why it was that in fact the churches flourished on such a paradoxical policy.

Throughout the Graeco-Roman Mediterranean there had been established by the first century AD a remarkably uniform and static system of education that was correctly understood to be fundamental to the classical civilization. It consisted of three stages: elementary schooling (reading, writing, and arithmetic), grammar school (mainly for classical literature) and rhetoric (the higher literacy essential for all public and professional careers). At every stage of this process, which dominated the formative years of childhood and adolescence, the material for study was, from the Christian point of view, pernicious. The first words a child wrote were the names of the old gods and of mythical figures, often monsters of immorality; the grammar school elaborately inculcated the traditional values enshrined in the poets; on the verge of adult life the son of Christian parents was drilled by his rhetorician in the specious pros and cons of a set of hypothetical court cases thoroughly unsavory in their subject matter. All this was freely admitted by the church fathers to be "poison" to the mind. But there was no attempt to change it, nor anything but extreme surprise at the rare suggestion that change was possible. The fathers concentrated instead upon providing the antidote through domestic and church training.

The school system, although standardized and to an increasing extent sponsored by the local public authorities, was certainly not closed to development in the interest of Christian education. The teaching profession was not exclusive, and was indeed of almost menial social status. Yet instead of Christians taking their place in it with a view to reform, as they might easily have done, the practice of teaching was generally frowned upon by church authorities for the very reason that it involved leading children into error. It was bad enough that children had to pass through the schools, without Christians actually running them.

The position is not to be explained in terms of the relations between the churches and the secular power, for it remains essentially the same in spite of revolutionary changes in that field. In the first period of this study (the first century) the churches scarcely came within the cognizance of the public authorities at all. During the second (the second and third centuries) they existed in a state of tension with the government, and were subject to occasional attacks. But in the third period (the fourth and fifth centuries) the churches were in a position to dictate public policy to a large extent, yet there is still no sign of a desire to reform the educational system. If anything, the churches begin to feel some responsibility for maintaining traditional education. Finally, with the collapse of the old order of society, it was the monasteries that preserved classical literature through the Middle Ages.

The unwillingness of the churches to interfere with the process of formal education in spite of its dangers is no doubt a mark of the degree to which their own life was based technically upon the traditional training. The languages in which the Scriptures were used (Greek and Latin), and the great intellectual demands they imposed, made a classical education as valuable for the study of Christian doctrine as it was for the pursuit of the classical philosophies, with which the new way may well be compared. These tended to become complete systems of life and thought, to which one was converted, and they challenged the truth of other systems, and indeed of certain values of the educational process, as drastically as did Christianity. But, like it, they naturally took for granted that one started within the classical tradition.

The Jews, on the other hand, increasingly drew back from the extensive cultural assimilation with the Greeks which prevailed in the first century AD, developing their own system of schools based upon the Bible, Mishnah, and Talmud. Extirpated from their national homeland with a ferocity far greater than any practiced on the Christians, they withdrew into the shelter of an exclusive culture of their own, and thus found themselves committed to the ghetto. The Christians instead adopted an uneasy compromise with the older order, until they made it their own. Outside the Graeco-Roman world the preaching of the gospel itself created new traditions of civilization. Since there was no sacred language, the necessary literacy was provided in the vernacular. Here the churches, as in modern missions, became pioneers of formal education, and the creators of national literatures upon a religious basis. Thus were the Coptic and Syriac languages, long submerged by the Greek then universal to cultivated people in the Levant, raised to literary status, while in the north the conversion of the Germans and later of the Slavs had a similar effect upon their languages. New Christian civilizations were built upon Christian systems of education. But where Greek and Latin were used there was no Christian education in the formal sense: instead, the churches provided in effect a special training for adults which supplemented and corrected their formal education.

I. The Period of the New Testament Churches

(a) Did the churches draw upon educated people?

In spite of Paul's writing down of the Corinthians' "wisdom" (l Cor 1:26–30) and his own disclaimer (2:13) of professional methods of teaching, the Corinthian letters are in fact full of evidence that the church at Corinth was dominated by well-educated and intellectually fastidious people. It was not their ignorance so much as their pretensions to knowledge that caused Paul trouble. This general impression can be substantiated by a study of the actual individuals whose names are known in connection with the New Testament churches with which Paul was concerned. About half of them (more than forty) can be shown to belong to the class of prosperous city householders who provided the premises and social sponsorship for the church meetings. They were people amongst whom a full classical education was taken for granted. Other members of the churches may have been drawn from less well-educated circles, but there is little trace of them. Those in slavery would no doubt be servants in the great houses which sheltered the churches, and might themselves be well-educated people, since much secretarial, financial, and literary work was done by slaves trained in the house for the purpose.

The other half of those who are known by name are occupied directly with the mission work of Paul. He himself appears as a figure of some intellectual magnitude in the Hellenistic cities, attracting friends and rivals at the highest social levels. It is clear that he was judged even among his followers by professional rhetorical standards, although since he was trained at Jerusalem he may not have had the complete Hellenic education himself. Yet he and his many assistants were engaged in an enterprise that made considerable academic and rhetorical demands. Starting with the highly literate circle of the synagogues and their Hellenic admirers, they were setting up societies where study, exposition, and argument had a large part to play. Certainly the churches were not an academic elite, like the philosophical schools. But neither were they simply a popular religious movement. Drawing upon a wide cross-section of urban society, they represent in one sense a movement for adult education, bringing those already trained in the Hellenic way under the discipline of the Lord (Heb 12:5).

(b) Why is education not discussed in the New Testament?

Although various other social institutions (e.g., slavery, the family, the state) are brought under review from the point of view of the gospel, education in the formal sense is nowhere discussed in the New Testament. It would be a mistake, however, to set this fact up against the conclusion of the last paragraph, as though it was not necessary to be educated in order to be a Christian. It is rather a matter of taking for granted what was the common childhood experience. The widespread use of metaphors from education to describe the new way of life confirms that it rested upon this basis, and that the old and new ways of life were two consecutive levels of experience, not creating any direct problems for each other. It is noteworthy that in the lists of qualifications for office in the pastoral epistles there is no stress upon education: the normal education is again taken for granted.

(c) How were children educated in the first churches?

Since there is no New Testament evidence on the subject, and since the notion of church schools does not occur in the subsequent centuries, we must assume that New Testament parents simply provided the normal classical education for their children. This would mean sending them out to a teacher in the case of poorer people, or, in the case of the wealthier houses which we take to have been the basis of the first churches, using domestic servants as teachers.

Did they receive any specifically religious education? It had been a condition of the covenant with Abraham (as well as the means by which it was perpetuated) that parents teach their children the way of the Lord. In the case of the churches the gospel tradition was handed down through special ministries in church. Did this take the place of parental duty in the case of children? It is apparent from the fact that children (along with parents, servants, and other social groups) are separately addressed in the epistles that they were present at the meetings. But apart from this there is no sign of any special provision for them. The parallel case of women is suggestive. They were also present, but not allowed to teach, nor to ask questions. They had to ask their husbands at home, and the older women were expected to train the younger ones, presumably also in private. The particular case of widows strengthens the point: the church was not to be called on to help with their maintenance unless it was impossible for the family to fulfill its responsibility. All of this implies that the church would not have provided even religious training for the children of its members.

Timothy was given Scriptural training by his mother and grandmother (his father was a Greek), as Jewish practice required, and Paul lays upon fathers the duty of bringing up their children in the discipline and instruction of the Lord. He also warns them of some unspecified practice which might frustrate their children. There is perhaps an echo here of contemporary disputes on the role of punishment. Jesus had spoken in extreme terms of those who caused children to sin, and insisted that the disciples admit children who were brought to him. The father's care for his children serves as a figure of God's training of men, and of the apostle's care for his converts. Successful management of children is a prerequisite for office in the church. These various strands of evidence go to show that while the churches as such took up no corporate responsibility for the religious training of children, the individual members were expected to prepare their children at home in the knowledge of the Lord, at the same time as they were attending church, and receiving their formal education in the usual way.

2. The Churches in Conflict with Society

The two centuries which followed the apostolic age produced a far greater volume of Christian writings, which substantially confirms the picture that must be drawn, largely by inference, from the scantier evidences of the New Testament. It was a period during which the churches were involved in a growing conflict with the rest of the community, breaking out occasionally into violence and official action against them. The second century was an age of comfortable refinement during which Christians, for reasons which are not clear, were mostly viewed with strong distaste. In the third century the Roman world entered an age of troubles, compounded of economic problems and horrifying invasions from beyond the frontiers. Religious feelings intensified, and totalitarian governments attempted to impose ideological unity to hold civilization together. In the course of these changes, as the churches steadily gained converts, there developed a great academic debate over the truth and intellectual respectability of the new way.

Among the charges most frequently raised against Christianity was that it was a barbarous novelty. In a classicizing society nothing was so damning as to be new. The Christians could hardly deny the novelty of Christ, but they did their best to provide some longer perspectives by stressing the antiquity of the Old Testament and finding anticipations of the New Testament in classical Greek literature. But the constant reference to Scripture only accentuated the other fault, that of barbarity. Neither the New Testament nor the Septuagint version of the Old Testament was written in anything like classical Greek. They were therefore thoroughly repugnant to the literary taste of all educated people. When it is considered that this included many Christians as well as their critics, the fact that the churches took no steps to avoid the educational system which posed such problems becomes all the more remarkable. Instead the scholars of the church took up the weapons of classical rhetoric to defend their new belief.

The letter of Clement of Rome, the first of the apostolic fathers, as the earliest group of post-New Testament writers are known, to the Corinthians (AD 96) already shows a much more accomplished use of formal rhetorical training than the work of any New Testament writer. When we come to those who addressed themselves not to fellow Christians, but to their critics, the identification with classical standards is naturally very complete. Justin Martyr, the greatest of the early apologists, who addressed two works to the Caesar Antoninus Pius (AD 138-61) as well as another (the *Dialogue with Trypho*) to Jews, practiced as a professional philosopher. After trying in turn the disciplines of the Stoic, Peripatetic, Pythagorean, and Platonic schools he was converted to Christianity and taught the new philosophy at Rome. Thereafter there was a positive fashion, evidenced by the funerary monuments, for presenting the Christian scholar in the pose of classical philosopher.

In Alexandria, the greatest if not the oldest center of Hellenic learning, the scene during the first century of brutal riots between Jews and Greeks but also of the synthesizing work of the Jewish Platonist, Philo, there was formed during the last part of the second century what appears to have been a regular Christian educational institution, the so-called catechetical school. This is not to be confused with, though it no doubt developed from, the ordinary instruction of catechumens which was presumably part of the ministry in every congregation. Catechumenal instruction was the standard grounding in doctrine given to candidates for baptism. The catechetical school, however, was an institute for advanced studies conducted under the auspices of a notable Christian scholar, and concentrating upon theology. It was not a theological college in the sense of training men for the ministry (this was nowhere provided for in an institutional way), but a seat of learning for its own sake, associated with a center of university studies. It has been supposed that every university city acquired such a school, but the evidence is only adequate for the cases of Alexandria and its great Eastern rivals, Caesarea in Palestine, with Antioch and Edessa in Syria. In each case the fame of the school rested upon an individual scholar, and only in Alexandria was there sufficient continuity from one scholar to his successor, and sufficient episcopal recognition, for us to speak of it as a formal institution of Christian education.

Even so the importance of the Alexandrian school lies not in the institution, but in the personal achievement of its two greatest heads, Clement (AD 200-203) and Origen (203-230). It was the special accomplishment of the polymath Clement to establish a harmonious relationship between Christian belief and the body of classical philosophy, while Origen both elaborated Christian doctrine itself into a system of theology comparable with the great philosophies and provided in his allegorical method of exegesis an attractive approach to bridging the classical tradition and the Bible. Although the orthodoxy of their Platonizing method was open to question, they left the Greek churches a body of learning of the greatest intellectual respectability.

While Greek Egypt thus produced a new level of Christian erudition, Roman Africa to the West was establishing an equally literate but more practical and polemical tradition of Christian writing in Latin. While the Greek fathers were philosophers, the Latins were by profession rhetoricians. For them the literary poverty of the Bible, only recently translated into Latin, was an even worse problem than it was for the Greeks. At the end of the second century the lawyer Minucius Felix produced a dialogue, the *Octavius*, a work of conscious elegance, designed to present a reasonable case for belief to the educated Roman. Another African lawyer, Tertullian, at the same time commenced his massive output of controversial work which brilliantly established the Latin language as a new ecclesiastical weapon. Later in the third century followed the work of three more great African controversialists, all of whom practiced as rhetoricians: Cyprian, Arnobius, and Lactantius.

Thus in the two centuries after the apostles, leading scholars in the churches fought a battle for the intellectual recognition of the faith. Their triumph is proof of the literary and philosophical vitality that new ideas could yet bring to the classical way of life, for there was no sign of any desire to break more fundamentally with the traditional system of education at its formal levels. The right of an educated man to believe the gospel was vindicated from the top.

3. The Establishment of Christendom

After Constantine's victory (AD 312) and the official recognition of the new religion,[1] the now abundant resources of ecclesiastical scholarship were turned largely to the doctrinal controversies involved in the definition of orthodoxy. The question of the use of the classical schooling was less likely than ever to become a problem. But in the year 362 a remarkable attack was made on the integrity of the Christian use of the schools. The young Caesar Julian, revolting against the religion of the murderous house of Constantine, of which he was the last survivor, debarred Christians from teaching classical literature. His reason was the dishonesty implicit in their profession, when they privately scorned the ideas enshrined in what they taught in school. Instead he challenged them to go to the churches of the "Galileans," as he contemptuously called them, and expound Matthew and Luke instead.

---

1. Editor's note: Since composing the present chapter in its original form, Judge has moved away from the terminology of "the new religion," and indeed from the category of "religion" as a relevant aid for understanding early Christianity. On this see Judge, "Absence of Religion," reproduced as chapter 9 in the present volume.

This was the first public declaration that education should be on a religious basis. It is remarkable that it should have come from the anti-Christian side, and reflects the conversion of classicism itself into a religious cause in reaction to the triumph of Christianity. It is not hard to imagine that had Julian lived his policy would soon have resulted in a dual system of education. As it was, he died within the year of the decree, but not before two enterprising Christian teachers had set their hand to the task and produced the Scriptures in a form suitable for educational use. In the plan of the two Apollinares (they were father and son, of the same name) each section of the Bible would have to play the part of some form of classical literature, so that the Gospels were rewritten as Platonic dialogues, and so on.[2]

In the aftermath of this brief upheaval, three great scholars of the Greek churches of the East gave their minds to the problem, from the Christian point of view, of the proper use of classical studies. Basil, Bishop of Caesarea in Cappadocia, addressed to his nephews a treatise *To Young Men on the Advantages of Greek Literature*. This was no very positive approach, but a demonstration that one might derive from the classics certain impressions that were a suitable preparation for later initiation into the full body of Christian doctrine. It is essentially a conscientious effort, by one who had himself had a very thorough classical education, to show that schoolboys need not be corrupted by their work, but the onus is left fully upon parents and the teachers in church (the latter in second place) to see that they are trained in Christian belief.

Gregory of Nyssa, the younger brother of Basil, and like him a great Cappadocian bishop, seems to have received his formal education itself within the family. In addition to a work *On the Life of Moses* in which he allegorically applies Moses's attitude to the spoils of Egypt to the problem Basil had discussed (Moses's basket is a figure of the classical education in which the Christian child is reared for greater ends), he produced an important work *On Christian Education* itself. He was perhaps the first to express the process by which one is born anew and formed on the model of Christ as an educational one. It is known that in the monasteries, which Basil had introduced to Cappadocia, for the first time education was being provided for poorer children, perhaps on a directly religious basis. The possibility of a distinctively Christian system of education may be seen in these developments.

Meanwhile something similar was happening in Syria, where the leading Christian scholar was John Chrysostom. In an early work *Against the*

---

2. The first attested case of a primary school teacher using biblical texts is that of Protogenes in Egypt in 374 (Theodoret, *Hist. eccl.* 4.15.3–14.

Detractors of the Monastic Life he actually proposed that young men might be more soundly brought up in a monastery than in the traditional schools. It appears that a public scandal had been caused when certain young men of the city had gone off to join the monks, and that John was anxious to seize the occasion to criticize the moral pitfalls of the common educational system. In a much later work, *On Vainglory or the Right Way for Parents to Bring up their Children*, he withdrew his impulsive approval of the monastic experiment, and while not relaxing his anxiety about the moral risks of education, returns to the standard Christian position with an attractively practical account of how parents can instill Bible knowledge into their children at home. This is justly famous for its simile of the child's mind as a city with its five gates (the senses of taste, hearing, sight, smell, touch).

While the Eastern scholars discussed the duties of parental training in relation to public education, two great Western divines set down important principles on the ecclesiastical side of education. Jerome, the Roman biblical scholar, has left two letters (107 and 128) in which he guides the parents of two little girls, Paula and Pacatula, in the best way of preparing them for the life of virginity to which they have been dedicated. He admits that such a task is a formidable one in the city, and wishes he could prepare them instead in the nunnery which he had founded at Jerusalem. For this reason it is obviously best to regard his extremely rigorous personal rules and entirely biblical study material as evidence for monastic training rather than as a model for the normal education of Christian children.

The African bishop Augustine included in his vast output of academic work a very considerable amount of educational theorizing, centered similarly upon ecclesiastical needs. His most important works in the field were *On the Catechization of the Uninitiated*, *On the Teacher* and *On Christian Instruction*. In spite of the fact that this all represents a formidable program for theological training in relation to other disciplines, the more remarkable feature is that so masterful a figure as Augustine still made no attempt to implement it in a formal institution. It remains as a great body of private guidance for those preparing themselves for ecclesiastical service.

In the course of the fifth century Western Europe and Africa were overrun by the Germanic migrations and direct Roman rule collapsed. With it went much of the old standard of living, including the classical educational system. Bishops extended the practice of preparing men for the ministry personally into a new system of schools to make up educational deficiencies in their candidates, and by AD 529 it was obligatory even upon each parish to conduct a school to ensure a supply of educated persons for the services of the church. Scholarship in the higher sense found its refuge in the monasteries. But in the East, where Roman power remained unbroken, the monasteries retained their somewhat revolutionary character, and at the Council of Chalcedon in AD 451 the training of children for secular occupations in monasteries was banned, thus terminating the experiments foreshadowed in Chrysostom's time (c. 347–407) in favor of the traditional system of education.

13

What Makes a Philosophical School?

This chapter takes as its starting-point two inscriptions from Bithynia, created in honor of "philosophers." It attends to the details of those texts, asking whether they might constitute evidence of a formal philosophical "school" with a venue, an organized community, and legal status as an association. It does so by considering traces of philosophers or philosophical schools in the papyri and inscriptions, thereby providing a neat and effective overview of the (lack of) documentary evidence for such schools in antiquity. The original text of this piece, published in *New Documents*, vol. 10 (2012), is expanded here to address the "pluralisation of philosophy" across the second and third centuries, as well as today.

Bursa   Marble Bases   II

Ed.pr. - Mendel, "Catalogue," nos. 407 and 409; Şahin, "Ein Stein aus Hadrianoi," 257–58; Schwertheim, *Inschriften von Hadrianoi und Hadrianeia* (= *I.Hadrianoi*), 43–44, nos. 51–52; Corsten, *Die Inschriften von Prusa ad Olympum* (= *I.Prusa Olymp.*), 34–36, nos. 17–18.[1]

---

1. The text provided in *New Documents Illustrating Early Christianity: Greek and Other Inscriptions and Papyri Published 1988–1992*, edited by S. R. Llewelyn et al., Grand Rapids: Eerdmans, 2012, contained several small errors which have been corrected here.

17

(vac.) Ἀγαθῆι (vac.) τύχηι·	(vac.) For good (vac.) fortune.
κατὰ δόγμα τῆς βουλῆς	By resolution of the council
καὶ τοῦ δήμοθ Π. Ἀβιάνι-	and people (honoring) P. Aviani-
ον Βαλέριον Λυσιμά-	us Valerius Lysima-
5 χου υἱὸν φιλόσοφον	chus's son, philosopher,
τὸν φιλόπολιν ♠ T. ♠	the city's friend; T.
Ἀβιάνιος Ἀρριανὸς	Avianius Arrianus
⁑ τὸν φίλον. ⁑	(honors) (his) friend.

18

(vac.) Ἀγαθῆι τύχηι· (vac.)	(vac.) For good fortune. (vac.)
T. Ἀουιάνιον Βᾶσσον	(Honoring) T. Avianius Bassus
Πολύαινον στωϊκὸν φ[ι]-	Polyaenus, Stoic phi-
λόσοφον ♠ Ἀουιάνιος ‘α-	losopher. Avianius A-
5 πολλώνιος φιλόσοφος	pollonius, philosopher,
κατὰ τὸ δόγμα τῆς πό-	by resolution of the ci-
λεως τῆς Ἀδριανῶν	ty of (the) Hadrianoi
τῶν πρὸς τῶι Ὀλυ[μπωι]	facing (Mt) Olympus
τὸν ἑαυτοῦ φί[λον]	(for) his personal friend
10 [ἐκ τ]ῶν ἰδίων [ἀνέστη]-	from his own (means) [erect]-
(vac.) σεν. (vac.)	(vac.) ed (this.) (vac.)

Given the authorization of 18 by resolution of the city of the Hadrianoi, Schwertheim (following Şahin) had taken both inscriptions into *I.Hadrianoi*.[2] But since they have been preserved with a group including *I.Prusa Olymp.* 13, which contains reference to a Bithyniarch, Corsten took both 17 and 18 as coming from Prusa (the fact that both had in a later age been built there into the "Castle Gate," Hisar kapısı, does not of course itself settle the matter).[3] Hadrianoi lies in Mysia, some 50 kilometers south-southwest across the Rhyndacus, with the boundary between Bithynia and the Roman province of Asia running along the intervening Mt. Olympus. On the public life of Bithynia in particular we have not only the speeches of Dio Chrysostom but the letters of Pliny from his governorship, so that its cultural scene in general may be assessed.[4]

2. Şahin, "Ein Stein aus Hadrianoi," 258; Schwertheim, *Die Inschriften von Hadrianoi*, no. 52.

3. Corsten, *Die Inschriften von Prusa*, 3.

4. Bekker-Nielsen, *Urban Life*; Harris, "Bithynia"; Stephan, *Honoratioren, Griechen, Polisbürger*.

Corsten might well have added that specifying the city's actual name (the Hadrianoi) may itself imply that 18 was not designed for display there (whereas the identity of the city in 17 was taken for granted). He suggests that Apollonius may have been a citizen of the Hadrianoi who nevertheless belonged to "the school of philosophers" in Prusa, while the honorand, Polyaenus, was a citizen of Prusa who had perhaps undertaken office in Hadrianoi or had otherwise come forward there as a benefactor. Yet since Apollonius was paying for 18 anyway, we should still need to ask why the Hadrianoi was mentioned at all: was public initiative required to validate (or enhance) the honor?

In the *Lexicon of Greek Personal Names* Corsten lists Apollonius and Polyaenus (no. 18) under Prusa (or, in brackets, Hadrianoi), but Arrianus and Lysimachus (no. 17) simply under Prusa.[5] One must indeed allow the possibility that the two documents do not belong together geographically; or, given the coincidence of content, that they all come from Hadrianoi (a suggestion of Şahin). Schwertheim identified the stone of 18 as an altar, not a base, while the disposition of the texts on the two stones varies.

Their juxtaposition has nevertheless led Corsten to classify the four (or five?) individuals mentioned as "a school of philosophers," fortified by their all being members of the same Roman *gens* (Avianii are not otherwise attested in either of the cities concerned, nor in the more extensively documented and indexed Ephesus, Philippi, or Thessalonica, but several are recorded in the inscriptions of Rome itself). He takes the explicit definition of the relationships by the two dedicators as "friendship" to refer to the formal constitution of the "school" as a lawful association, and assumes that its philosophical commitment was to Stoicism, since Polyaenus is so identified.

It is not uncommon for an individual to be identified in the documents as *philosophos*, not necessarily because of the famous stereotype.[6] In Ephesus the philosophers so named are not specified as part of the regular training system. By contrast the sophists and their *paideutai* ("pupils") enjoy privileges determined by the proconsul himself (*I.Eph.* 216, line 8). The *mathētai* ("students") request a public tribute for their *sophistes*, Soteros (*I.Eph.* 1548). A triumviral edict grants exemptions to "the *paideutai* and the *sophistai* or the *iatroi*"; i.e., medical practitioners (*I.Eph.* 4101, line 10).

---

5. Corsten, *Lexicon*, vol. VA.

6. Zanker, *Mask of Socrates*, cf. Pliny the Younger, *Ep.* 1.10.5–7. For a range of epigraphic philosophers see Tod, "Sidelights on Greek Philosophers"; Robert and Robert, "Bulletin Épigraphique," 513–16; Habicht, "Zu den Inschriften"; Barnes, "Ancient Philosophers." The last also treats Christians seen as philosophers, as does Stroumsa, *Barbarian Philosophy*; cf. Horsley, *New Documents*, 4:257–58 on the singular "philosopher-nun" of *I.Nikaia* 1.550). For the Papyri see Pruneti, "Il termine φιλόσοφος."

For the interaction between philosophy and the community in general see André, Bowersock, Hahn, and Manning.[7]

Inspired by the Jew who leases a "hall" (*exedra*) and basement from two "nuns" (*monachai apotaktikai*, P.Oxy. 3203), Horsley contests the common translation of *scholē* (Acts 19:9) as "lecture-hall" as though it were an enclosed chamber.[8] Rather, it suggests a more public meeting-point. "Paul embarks on his daily discussions and debate with others who have their own philosophies and *modus vivendi* . . . a group of people to whom addresses were given during their leisure hours." Tyrannus may well have been the benefactor who had embellished the venue. The rhetoric of Acts 19:10 gives the impression of easy accessibility.

It is indeed the case that *scholē* ("leisure") retains its primary sense (cf. Latin *otium*), of the condition under which philosophy may best be practiced.[9] As with *I.Prusa Olymp.* 17–18, it is not usually part of the Greek text at all when we choose to speak of a philosophical "school" (the meanings we have now assigned to the inherited word impose themselves even when the original is not present, cf. the similar problem we face with the term "religion"). Note the difficulty in clarifying the physical arrangements even for the most famous school of all, the Academy.[10] The Pompeian mosaic (frontispiece to Goulet's *Dictionnaire*, cf. Billot) imaginatively displays the leisurely and casual setting; contrast the formality of the Ostia grave relief where a schoolteacher is presented as an idealized philosopher, yet emphatically formal, as the wooden codices and writing desks of the pupils make clear.[11]

In the Latin inscriptions of Rome the term *schola* or *scola* appears already to indicate a purpose-built structure. The inscriptions of Ephesus (though not of Prusa or Hadrianoi) record by contrast the provision of *exedrae*, essentially the semi-circular open face of an existing building, suitable for public gathering.[12] Stertinius Orpex was responsible for one set into a wall of the stadium (*I.Eph.* 2113). A monument to T. Flavius Sophron, *libertus Augusti*, was set up on the right side of an *exedra* "as you entered" (*I.Eph.* 2261, line 4). Another, under Domitian, connected *stoa* and *agora* with its array of statues (*I.Eph.* 3005). Seating (*symphelia*, Lat. *subsellia*) was provided in the one connected with the *stoa* and its walls (*I.Eph.* 3065).

---

7. André, "Les écoles philosophiques," Bowersock, "Philosophy in the Second Sophistic"; Hahn, *Der Philosoph und die Gesellschaft*; Manning, "School Philosophy."

8. Horsley, *New Documents*, 1:129–30.

9. Reydams-Schils, *Roman Stoics*, 99–113.

10. Billot, "Académie," esp. 783 for the later stages.

11. Zanker, *Mask of Socrates*, 261, fig. 140.

12. Nielsen, "Exedra," 5:261–62.

Using the modern senses of the term "school" it is therefore not at all obvious that we should think of a particular building dedicated to philosophical discussion between teachers and students. Nor is it much more plausible to envisage a "school" in the sense of a likeminded community of specialists sustained by a shared social life. In particular there is a shortage of documentary or other evidence to support the specific proposal of Corsten that the people named in 17 and 18 were members enrolled in a *Verein* (sc. a formal association in law). Nor does the reference (at 35, lines 35) to *I.Prusa Olymp.* 24 secure the point since those creating that monument are explicitly *hetairoi* (line 2, "companions," sc. enrolled members) in a *koinon* (line 8, the generic term covering the several more explicit categories of Greek formal "association.")[13] Our inscriptions lack any comparable indication—contrast cases such as the cultic groups of Dionysius at Philadelphia or of Agrippinilla at Torre Nova.[14] Both of these also appear to have been based on a family network, but show very elaborate structural rules. Philosophy however might also be passed on in a family as with *IG*, vol. 10, 2.1.145, *ll.* 6–9, Sosibius *philosophos*, son of Sosibius the *philosophos*.

Across the whole millennium of the Greek philosophical "schools," in the grander sense of an intellectual tradition sustained through many generations, it is rare to find clear evidence of any ongoing formal structure.[15] Those who come closest to it, and then only in particular instances, are the Pythagoreans and Epicureans.[16] We may set aside of course the classic establishments of Athens and Alexandria.[17]

It is unusual in the inscriptions to find a *philosophos* identified by his dogmatic position as our Polyaenus is (18, lines 3–4). Stoicism in this period seems to have often been taken for granted, with the philosopher typically ranging across several fields, so to name one a Stoic implies a more consistent position.[18] From Ephesus we have an Alexandrian "eclectic" (*I.Eph.* 789), while the city's benefactor Heraclides, priest of Artemis, is honored for his "scholarly power" (*tēn en tō mathēmati dynamin, I.Eph.* 683 A, line 5), which implies a profession as philosopher. Two others are identified as Platonic: *I.Eph.* 3901, 4340. From Rome there are Stoics attested in *CIL* 6.9784, 9785, and an Epicurean in *CIL* 6.37813.

13. Judge, "On This Rock," 621–24, at 58–63 in the present volume.
14. Judge, "On This Rock," 624 and 627–28 respectively, at 62–63 and 66 in the present volume.
15. Dorandi, "Organization."
16. Judge, "On this Rock," 633–36, at 72–74 in the present volume.
17. Watts, "Academic Life."
18. Dillon, *Musonius Rufus*; Gill, "School"; Strange and Zupko, *Stoicism*.

In the Greek cities of Asia Minor it is clear that philosophers also enjoyed public recognition, hence the many tributes to individuals identified as such. Yet without more explicit evidence (e.g., *I.Eph.* 616, a *philosophos* honored for several no doubt costly appointments) it is better to see them as independent gurus, distinguished from and no doubt often critical of the practitioners of rhetorical persuasion, mastery of whose arts was a necessity for public leadership in the city, a strenuous training hardly suggestive of *scholē*. The sophists thus had a formal stake in public education,[19] whereas the philosophical "schools" dogmatically maintained the freedom of their leisurely intellectual discussions.[20] But of course by the second century in particular such a master as Dio Chrysostom of Prusa shows how one might seriously embrace both of these functions at different times in one's life.[21]

The venerable city of Prusa ("Bursa"), home-base of Dio, had been a Bithynian royal seat 400 years earlier, though the latter 200 years had perhaps been somewhat neglected under Roman control.[22] But the pluralized name of "Hadrianoi" referred to a tribal nation with the hunting grounds we know attracted Hadrian, and who were thus perhaps elevated by him to Greek city status. Likewise several already existing cities were newly entitled "Hadrianopolis," presumably during his grand tours of the civilized East in AD 124 or 131.

Spanning the Aegean as leader of Rome, Hadrian created an international cultural Panhellenion, of which he was to become the divinized hero.[23] His chosen successor, T. Aurelius Antoninus ("Pius"), however, was more concerned with the Western empire. The once eminent Wilhelm Weber spoke of Antoninus as proconsul of Asia being "thrust into the microcosm of Asia Minor with its competing jealousies and no less its new panhellenic movement."[24] But Hadrian had already obliged Antoninus to adopt, as his own successor, the young Marcus Aurelius. Finally, under Caracalla's "*constitutio Antoniniana*" of AD 212, all free subjects of the empire were to be registered as Roman citizens in the "*gens Aurelia.*"[25]

Beyond the metropolitan centers, the epitaph of Aberkios from Phrygian Hierapolis showed the freedom with which Christians might

19. Winter, *Philo and Paul*.

20. Haake, *Der Philosoph in der Stadt*; Haake, "Philosopher and Priest"; Herman, *Ritualised Friendship*.

21. Jones, *Culture and Society*; Jones, *Roman World*; Stanton, "Sophists and Philosophers"; Swain, *Hellenism and Empire*.

22. Pliny the Younger, *Ep.* 10.23.

23. Spawforth, "Panhellenion, Attic."

24. Weber, "Antonines," 328.

25. Honoré, "Constitution, Antonine."

then publicly allude to their beliefs.[26] The various other such epigraphic indicators from outback Anatolia have now been comprehensively analyzed by McKechnie.[27]

Marcus Aurelius had enlarged the scope and sense of Greek philosophy itself in two dimensions that foreshadowed the great intellectual engagements of late antiquity.[28] In political terms he lifted his horizon above that of his own city (Rome) to a citizenship of all the world. In personal terms he concentrated his thinking in Greek (not intended for publication?) upon the serenity of his own internal self-acceptance. The emotional tragedy of the Christians, however, repelled him.[29]

Visiting Athens in 175 Marcus endowed the city (for the first time) with separate philosophical chairs in the four great disciplines of Plato, Aristotle, the Stoics, and the Epicureans. This in effect formalized the Greek doctrinal position, opening the range of thought "for all humanity" (Cassius Dio, epitome of book 72), yet provoking also no doubt other ways of understanding reality? Across the Oriental provinces he often left the "marks" of his own philosophy, and during the winter of 175/6 in Alexandria he treated himself as a public philosopher on every occasion.[30] The "scriptural school" of Pantaenus, influenced by the Stoics (Eusebius, *Hist. eccl.* 5.10–11), may well have had Christian predecessors already teaching there.

In late antique Platonism there has been discerned a shift towards concern for one's personal identity.[31] A European conference has explored the epistemological tension that developed in the later Roman empire, calling it the "pluralization of philosophy."[32] Following his "Barbarian Philosophy" Stroumsa (from the Hebrew University of Jerusalem) has now delivered his "Scriptural Universe."[33] From "the Pacific rim" a conference drawing upon ancient world studies now compares Plato and Confucius on "Cultivating the Good Life."[34]

For the concurrent 2016 conference of the Shanghai Academy of the Social Sciences on "Bible and the Values" there was presented my own scenario

26. Kearsley, "Epitaph of Aberkios."
27. McKechnie, *Christianizing Asia Minor.*
28. Stanton, "Marcus Aurelius" and "Cosmopolitan Ideas."
29. Marcus Aurelius, *To himself* 11.3.2.
30. *Scriptores Historiae Augustae*, "Marcus Antoninus" 25.3.
31. Dodds, *Pagan and Christian in an Age of Anxiety*; Mortley, "Plotinus."
32. "Konkurrenz von Schulen"—see Riedweg, *Philosophia in der Konkurrenz von Schulen.*
33. Storumsa, *Barbarian Philosophy* and *Scriptural Universe.*
34. Lai et al., *Cultivating the Good Life.*

of "The Secular Jerusalem of the West."[35] It argues that the modern developmental universe, the opening of the social order to individual vocation, and our plea for personal compassion, all flow from the revelatory worldview of Jerusalem rather than from the rationally predetermined universe of the Athenian schools. The intellectual encounter was indeed being observed in late antiquity, but more in philosophical terms. The modern breakthrough had to wait until priority was given to the reality of historical experience.

35. Judge, "Secular Jerusalem."

14

The "First Monk" and the Origin of Monasticism

This chapter first appeared as Judge, "The Earliest Use of *monachos* for "Monk" (P.Coll.Youtie 77) and the Origins of Monasticism," *JAC* 20 (1977) 72–89. An adaptation was previously printed in Judge, *Jerusalem and Athens*, 156–77; the present version differs only in minor details from that publication. The study focuses upon the development of various forms of monastic life and the terminology used for them—a focus prompted by the publication (now more than four decades ago) of a papyrus featuring the earliest use of the Greek term *monachos* (whence comes the English "monk") with reference to a monk. After discussing that papyrus and the person depicted therein, the study turns to figures such as Athanasius and Jerome, and especially to the papyrus record (both public documents and the archives of various ascetics) to consider what kinds of asceticism were known in what eras and how they came to bear the title of *monachos*. It concludes with a series of tentative hypotheses for critical consideration by others.

THE NEWLY PUBLISHED PETITION of Aurelius Isidorus of Karanis, dated to June 6(?), 324, cites a *monachos*, Isaac (along with a *diakōn*, Antoninus) as having rescued him from death by assault.[1] This is the earliest reference so far

---

1. Hanson, *Collectanea Papyrologica*, 2.77, with this particular papyrus edited by N. Lewis. The text has been re-edited by R. S. Bagnall, appearing (with a few modifications) as P.Col. 7.171. On the key term, Bagnall informs me that both editors agree that "there is no doubt that the reading is correct." I have found no other title or proper name that can be reconciled with the photograph kindly lent by Columbia University. Editor's note: Digital photographs are now publicly available online—see http://papyri.info/ddbdp/p.col;7;171/images.

known to the "monk" as a recognized figure in society. The fact that it should appear in a secular document, especially one of such early date, has an important bearing on the question of the origins of monasticism.[2] In particular, it is a signpost of a quite unexpected kind on the way to discovering how the style *monachos* came to be applied to ascetics, and what it meant.[3]

Isidorus has given us little more than the name and title of Isaac to help us envisage what our first "monk" was like. Yet he was eloquent on his own affairs, leaving us a long trail of petitions amongst his voluminous business records.[4]

In no other document of the archive has any reference to Christianity been established, though it has been suggested that the name Johannes implies a former Christian or Jewish family that had lapsed.[5] The bareness of this record makes the matter-of-fact appearance of a deacon and a monk at the very last all the more striking. Antoninus is the earliest of a number of deacons who are mentioned in or who initiate formal documents of public life in the villages of Egypt during the generation which runs down to the middle of the century.[6] Taken together they show that deacons were active

---

2. Judge and Pickering, "Papyrus Documentation," 22, lists no other certain secular reference which can be dated before mid-century. Julian refers to *apotaktitai* in 362 (224 B = *Or.* 7.18 Bidez). The other attacks on the monks by him (288 B = *Ep.* 89 Bidez) and Libanius (*Or.* 2.32, 30.8 Förster) do not mention their name, but *monachos* is used (with the scholar's conventional apology for the neologism) in that of Eunapius (*VS* 6.11.6 [472]), written after 396. There are references to monks in imperial mandates of 370 or 373, where refugees from curial duties are spoken of who (*Cod. theod.* 12.1.63) *cum coetibus monazonton congregantur*, and of 390 (*Cod. theod.* 16.3.1), where *monachi* are to be compelled to live in *deserta loca*. Rutilius Claudius Namatianus, writing in 417, introduces the term *monachi* as the self-appointed "Greek" name of the detested hermits (*Red.* 1.441).

3. For historical survey see Heussi, *Der Ursprung* and Lohse, *Askese und Mönchtum*. For word usage, see Morard, "Monachos, moine."

4. The 146 documents in Boak and Youtie, *Archive of Aurelius Isidorus*, go back as far as 267, become much more frequent from late in the third century, and run down to 324. There are 21 petitions in this collection, and P.Merton 2.92 (31 May 324) and our text (a week later) are the last. The beating was perhaps fatal.

5. This judgement of Boak and Youtie (*Archive of Aurelius Isidorus*, 377–78n2) is based upon the fact that Johannes ("certainly descended from a Jewish or Christian family") was a former or present gymnasiarch, a post they consider virtually incompatible with the Jewish faith at this stage (304) and "unusual" in one of Christian faith. Against this should be weighed the evidence summarized by Judge and Pickering, "Papyrus Documentation," 69, though none of that is decisive. Boak and and Youtie (315n3) think that Polion son of Peter is a Christian on account of his father's name, and the name, Paul, used of several people in the archive, has been mentioned in the same connection by van Haelst, "Les sources papyrologiques," 498.

6. Judge and Pickering, "Papyrus Documentation," 66. But could *diakon* have been a monastic title?

and prominent figures in village affairs. Antoninus is the only instance in this group where the deacon is mentioned by another person who can be assumed not to be a member of the church. That he can be cited in this way by an outsider appealing to the *praepositus pagi* confirms the local effectiveness of the Constantinian establishment. His rank adds weight to the petition, and his evidence will be available to support the plea.

P.Col. inv. 187 = Collectanea Papyrologica 2.77

Text and translation of N. Lewis, modified by R. S. Bagnall in P.Col. 7.171. Image and transcription now available online.[7]

Διοσκόρῳ Καίσωνι πραιπ(οσίτῳ) ε πάγου
παρὰ Ἰσιδώρου Πτολεμαίου ἀπὸ κώ(μης) Καρ[α]νίδος
τοῦ ὑμετέρου πάγου· τῶν θρεμμ[άτ]ων Παμού-
νεως καὶ Ἁρπάλου καταλυμηνα[μέ]νων ἣν

5   ἔχω σπορὰν καὶ μὴν καὶ τῆς β[οὸ]ς α[ὐτῶν] παλιν
ἐν τῷ αὐτῷ τόπῳ καταβοσκηθείσης ὥστε ἀχρή-
σιμόν μοι τὴν γεωργίαν γενέσθαι, καὶ καταλαβο-
μένου μου τὴν βοῦν καὶ ἀνάγοντος αὐτὴν
ἐπὶ τῆς κώμης ἀπαντήσαντές μοι κατὰ τοὺς

10 ἀγροὺς μεγά<λῳ> ῥοπάλῳ καὶ χαμιριφῇ ἐμὲ ποι-
ησάμενοι πληγαῖς κατέκοψαν καὶ τὴν βοῦν
ἀφείλαντο ὥσπερ καὶ αἱ περὶ ἐμὲ πληγαὶ
δηλοῦσιν, καὶ εἰ μὴ βοηθείας ἔτυχο(ν) ὑπὸ
τῶν παραγενομένων Ἀντωνίνου διάκο-

15 νος καὶ Ἰσὰκ μοναχοῦ τάχα ἂν τέλεόν
με ἀπώλεσαν. ὅθεν ἐπιδίδωμι τάδε
τὰ ἔγγραφα ἀξιῶν αὐτοὺς ἀχθῆναι ἐπὶ σοῦ
καὶ περὶ τῆς σπορᾶς καὶ περὶ τῆς ὕβρεως
τηρεῖσθαι ἐμοὶ καὶ τὸν λόγον ἐπὶ τοῦ

20 ἡγεμονικοῦ δικαστηρίου.....
τοῖς ἐσομένοις ὑπάτοις τὸ δ
Παῦνι ιβ

---

[7]. http://www.papyri.info/ddbdp/p.coll.youtie;2;77. URL correct as of October 2019.

> To Dioscorus Caeso, *praepositus* of the fifth *pagus*, from Isidorus son of Ptolemaeus of the village of Karanis in your *pagus*. The cattle of Pamounis and Harpalus damaged the planting which I have and what is more [their cow] grazed again in the same place so thoroughly that my husbandry has become useless. I caught the cow and was leading it up to the village when they met me in the fields with a big club, threw me to the ground, rained blows upon me and took away the cow—as indeed (the marks of) the blows all over me show—and if I had not chanced to obtain help from the deacon Antoninus and the monk Isaac, who happened by, they would quickly have finished me off completely. Therefore I submit this document, asking that they be brought before you to preserve my claim (to be heard) in the prefectural court ... both in the matter of the planting and in the matter of the assault.
> The consuls-to-be for the fourth time, Payni 12.

Similar considerations apply to the monk, Isaac, whose position, from Isidorus's point of view, parallels that of Antoninus. It is taken for granted that he can be identified by the public authorities. He is no remote hermit. On the other hand, his association with the deacon suggests that he is in some way church-related, and not a monk from a coenobitic monastery. Since no further details are given, it can be assumed that he belongs to the village of Karanis. The citing of his style in a civil document implies that it offered Isidorus a familiar and respectable security. It is the purpose of the present discussion to try to place this irreducibly solid and domestic figure who has suddenly appeared in the very dream-land of monasticism's heroic age.

But what did he actually do? Did he join in the fight? Or did his mere appearance work the trick? And if the latter, is he already on the way to becoming that "holy man" of the village, whose patronage has been shown to be such a universal resort in the Syrian villages of a later time?[8] There is nothing to suggest this last possibility, and a good deal against it. For one thing, the deacon is named first, so that no special appeal to the monk is implied, but if anything the opposite. One might imagine that a supernatural deliverance would have advanced the cause of Isidorus; but the absence of any hint as to how the help was applied leaves us only the likelihood of a routine encounter. Even a serious struggle is ruled out by such considerations. Since only two assailants are named, and only one club, it is next to certain that there were no more; Isidorus's case does not stand to gain by under-reporting the scale of the assault on him. My guess is that when the numbers changed from 2:1 to 2:3 the incident was over. Since the others made off with the cow, Isidorus still came out seriously the worse for the encounter. Isaac had proved a friend in need, but no wonder-worker.

8. Brown, *Cult of the Saints*.

The first instance of *monachos* in an ecclesiastical writer is found in the commentary on the Psalms by Eusebius of Caesarea, written, it seems, early in the last decade of his life, which began in 330:[9]

τὸ γοῦν πρῶτον τάγμα τῶν ἐν Χριστῷ προκοπτόντων τὸ τῶν μοναχῶν τυγχάνει.

Eusebius is reflecting on the significance of the four different Greek versions of Ps 67:6 he has before him, of which that of Symmachus, the second-century Ebionite, read *monachoi*. On the strength of this word, Eusebius appears to take the verse to refer to the monks (with whom he expects his readers to be familiar?) and uses the alternative translations to spell out different aspects of monasticism. "Giving the *monachoi* a home" was God's first and greatest provision for humankind, because they are the "front rank" of those "advancing in Christ." By the same token they are "rare" (*spanioi*). This explains why Aquila in his version called them *monogeneis*, likening them to the "only-begotten" Son of God, while the Septuagint translation *monotropoi* draws attention to the fact that they do not chop and change, but hold to the "one way" that leads to the pinnacle of virtue. The "fifth edition" called them *monozōnoi*. This word shows that they were *monēreis* and "girded up on their own" (καθ' ἑαυτοὺς ἀνεζωσμένους).

Reitzenstein, writing before the publication of the archive of Apa Paieous (see below), was able to assume that the term *monachoi* was not

---

9. *PG* 23.689 B. For the date, see Moreau, "Eusebius von Caesarea," 1064. The full comment (689 A–D): Κατοικίζει, φησί, μονοτρόπους ἐν οἴκῳ. Κατὰ δὲ τὸν Σύμμαχον, δίδωσιν οἰκεῖν μοναχοῖς οἰκίαν· καὶ κατὰ τὸν Ἀκύλαν, καθίζει μονογενεῖς οἴκονδε· κατὰ δὲ τὴν πέμπτην ἔκδοσιν, κατοικίζει μονοζώνους ἐν οἴκῳ. Καὶ τοῦτ᾽ ἦν τὸ πρῶτον αὐτοῦ κατόρθωμα· ὃ δὴ καὶ μέγιστον τῶν αὐτοῦ κατορθωμάτων τῷ τῶν ἀνθρώπων δεδώρηται γένει. Τὸ γοῦν πρῶτον τάγμα τῶν ἐν Χριστῷ προκοπτόντων τὸ τῶν μοναχῶν τυγχάνει. Σπάνιοι δέ εἰσιν οὗτοι· διὸ κατὰ τὸν Ἀκύλαν μονογενεῖς ὠνομάσθησαν ἀφωμοιωμένοι τῷ μονογενεῖ Υἱῷ τοῦ Θεοῦ. Κατὰ δὲ τοὺς Ἑβδομήκοντα μονότροποι τυγχάνουσιν, ἀλλ᾽ οὐ πολύτροποι, οὐδὲ ἄλλοτε ἄλλως τὸν ἑαυτῶν μεταβάλλοντες τρόπον, ἕνα δὲ μόνον κατορθοῦντες, τὸν εἰς ἄκρον ἥκοντα ἀρετῆς. Μονοζώνους δὲ αὐτοὺς ἡ πέμπτη ἔκδοσις ὠνόμασεν, ὡς ἂν μονήρεις καὶ καθ᾽ ἑαυτοὺς ἀνεζωσμένους. Τοιοῦτοι δὲ πάντες εἰσὶν οἱ τὸν μονήρη καὶ ἁγνὸν κατορθοῦντες βίον, ὧν πρῶτοι γεγόνασιν οἱ τοῦ Σωτῆρος ἡμῶν μαθηταί, οἷς εἴρητο· Μὴ κτήσησθε χρυσόν, μηδὲ ἄργυρον εἰς τὰς ζώνας ὑμῶν, μὴ πήραν εἰς ὁδόν, μηδὲ ὑποδήματα, μηδὲ ῥαβδόν. Ἐν γὰρ τῷ λέγειν μὴ δεῖν κτήσασθαι χρυσὸν μηδὲ ἄργυρον εἰς τὰς ζώνας ἀνεζωσμένους αὐτοὺς εἰσάγει. Οὕτω δὲ καὶ πᾶσιν ἡμῖν ὁ Ἀπόστολος παρακελεύεται λέγων· στῆτε οὖν περιζωσάμενοι τὴν ὀσφὺν ὑμῶν ἐν ἀληθείᾳ. Καὶ οἱ τὸ Πάσχα δὲ ἐσίοντες ἐκελεύοντο τὰς ὀσφῦς ἔχειν περιεζωσμένας. Τοῦτο δὴ οὖν πρῶτον κατορθοῖ τοῖς ἐν δυσμαῖς οἰκοῦσιν ἐπιδημήσας ὁ θεσπιζόμενος. Ἀπὸ γὰρ τῶν προλεχθέντων ὀρφανῶν καὶ τῶν δηλωθεισῶν χηρῶν ἀφορίσας, ἐξαίρετον καὶ τιμιώτατον ἑαυτῷ τάγμα τὸ τῶν μονοτρόπων κατοικίζει αὐτοὺς ἐν οἴκῳ, δηλαδὴ ἐν τῇ Ἐκκλησίᾳ αὐτοῦ, παραμένειν καὶ κατοικεῖν ἐν αὐτῇ καταξιῶν αὐτούς.

in use for "monks" before the middle of the fourth century.[10] He held the passage in Eusebius to be corrupt in any case, and emended it by filling a lacuna after *spanioi*. But his main argument for there being no reference to "monks" here was that, when summing up the discussion, Eusebius picks up again the idea of a *tagma* but applies it to the *monotropoi*, thus showing that neither of the terms had any particular force for him. But Eusebius only does this because he is expounding the Septuagint text and needs to pick up its terminology again before passing on to the next phrase. Other patristic commentators interpret the *monotropoi* entirely in terms of personal morality, without referring to the alternative version of Symmachus.[11] But the retention of *tagma* ("rank" or "order" in society) by Eusebius, linked as it is with a reminder of the orders of widows and orphans referred to in the previous verse of the Psalm, clearly implies an organized body of people. The new papyrus must put the matter virtually beyond doubt, since if the *monachoi* were already a public institution in Egypt by 324, and even the first coenobitic monasteries were under way in Palestine by 330, Eusebius and his audience are already in a position where they are only too likely to take the word as a reference to monks.

But what does Eusebius mean by calling them *monēreis*? Morard, who holds that the historical function of the word *monachos* must have been to carry forward into Greek and Coptic usage a Semitic ideal of life that centered on celibacy (Heb. *yāḥîd*, Syr. *iḥîḏāyā*), believes (in this detail following Reitzenstein) that it is possible to show that *monēreis* specifically refers to sexual continence.[12] She is supported by the fact that, immediately after saying that they are "girded up on their own", Eusebius identifies them as all those who "lead a solitary and chaste life" (μονήρη καὶ ἁγνὸν κατορθοῦντες βίον). There can be little doubt that this is a reference to continence (though whether *monērēs* on its own would convey this sense is another matter), nor would one expect a treatment of monasticism without that feature of it being brought out.

The chief preoccupation of Eusebius is, however, surely with a different, if related, feature. He is concerned with their homelessness and lack of means

10. Reitzenstein, *Des Athanasius Werk*, 8, 47, 60, 61.

11. E.g., Athanasius, *PG* 27.293, Cyril of Alexandria, *PG* 69.1145, Theodoret of Cyrrhus, *PG* 80.1485, though Morard, "Monachos, moine," 352–53, thinks the comments of "Athanasius" can be harmonized with those of Eusebius. Jerome, *PL* 26.1013, uses the word *monachi* in his commentary, but defines it in a way (*in quibus non cohabitat peccatum*) which shows he does not have monks as a social rank in mind, but all those of moral purity. Rufinus, *PL* 21.912, ignores the monks.

12. Morard, "Monachos, moine," 381; Reitzenstein, *Des Athanasius Werk*, 61. For the Syrian background see Vööbus, *History of Asceticism*.

of support. The first example, he says, of those who chose the "solitary and chaste life" was that of the disciples, whom Jesus had commanded not to carry gold or silver in their belts (*zōnai*)—which shows how one can speak of them as "girded up on their own" (thus explaining the *monozōnoi* of the "fifth edition"), suggests Eusebius. I take this to mean that he is invoking the saying about the money-less belts to interpret the *monozōnoi* as those who abandon their normal means of support. This, he goes on to say, is why they are favored first after the widows and orphans of the preceding verse, and "given a house to dwell in", which is the subject of Ps 67:7. This house, Eusebius then explains, is the church. In all of this (quite lengthy) flight of "exegesis," Eusebius makes no attempt to draw out celibacy as the guiding principle of monasticism. He is concerned to use the various renderings to show that *monachoi* are "single-minded" in their social situation, and thus in need of a home provided by God. But even if I have misunderstood this point, and Eusebius does mean us to understand the *monachoi* essentially as celibates, that does not settle the crucial historical question.

Could it really have been the phenomenon of continence that had suddenly led to the recognition of a new rank of persons in (or out of) society, shortly before the time at which Eusebius was writing? As Morard shows, there was a deep-seated tradition of this kind in Jewish circles, going back at least to Qumran, and the ideal of *enkrateia* has roots also in the Graeco-Roman culture.[13] More especially, for at least two centuries now, celibacy had been a feature of church life, celebrated by many of the fathers, and attracting the admiration even of an outsider in Galen.[14] It is no doubt the case that *monachos* in Symmachus did pick up this ideal.[15] But in spite of the outstanding qualifications of Eusebius as a historical archivist, in expounding the psalm-translators he is making no attempt to use them as sources in the history of ideas. He seems simply to be assuming that they function as authoritative guides to the meaning of the ancient Hebrew texts for an ecclesiastical institution of his own day.

People's habits, ideas or traditions require a name (and thus indicate a social status) when they have to be marked off from those of other people, or when others react to them when they need to be organized in some way. This

---

13. Morard, "Monachos, moine," 354–57; Chadwick, "Enkrateia," 343–65; Meredith, "Asceticism, Christian and Greek."

14. Koch, *Quellen zur Geschichte*; on Galen see Walzer, "Galenos," 783.

15. The word is also used by Theodotion at Ps 67:7, and by Symmachus at Gen 2:18. Aquila uses it at Gen 2:18; 22:2; Ps 21:21; 24:16; 34:17; and (in a verbal form) 85:11. The full range of alternative translations for each of these passages is set out by Morard, "Monachos, moine," 348. They are discussed by Adam, "Grundbegriffe des Mönchtums."

happened very early with the "virgins" and "widows," but down to the fourth century the fathers heap their praises on the male equivalents without finding any need to create a name for such people. And all along, if Morard's theory is correct, the word *monachos* was sitting there, with the required meaning ready-made, waiting to be used.[16] The belated need to have a status name for male ascetics (whatever the name in itself might "mean" in terms of its historical origins or the sense given to it by a particular writer at an earlier stage) is not therefore likely to have arisen from the fact of celibacy itself—there was nothing new about that. It will have been caused by some other, novel feature of their affairs. The *Ecclesiastical History* of Eusebius is surely a good pointer to how recently this had occurred. It went through four revisions (between 312 and 325, according to Schwartz), as Eusebius tried to keep pace with the rapidly changing affairs of the church in his own day.[17] But he still had not had any occasion to apply a special term to the ascetics.

Whatever the history of its origin in Egypt, there can be little doubt that the success of the term *monachos* as the universally accepted name for monks is due to the propaganda of Athanasius and Jerome. Athanasius had tried to mobilize the monks against Arian infiltrators, as an epigraphic copy of his letter to them makes clear. They are addressed as follows:[18]

[Ἀθ]ανάσιος τοῖς ἀπ[ανταχοῦ ὁ-]

[ρθ]οδόξοις μοναχο[ῖς τοῖς τὸν μ-]

[ον]ήρη βίον ἀσκοῦσ[ι καὶ ἐν πίστ-]

[ει] Χ(ριστο)ῦ ἱδρυμένοις, ἀ[γαπητοῖς καὶ]

[πο]θεινοτάτοις [ἀδελφοῖς ἐν κυρ-]

[ίῳ] χαίρειν.

---

16. A study of the circumlocutions that helped them do without it would be an instructive contribution to the discussion of the origins of monasticism. E.g., *masculus continens*, Ps.Cyprian, *De singularitate clericorum* 19 (*CSEL*, vol. 3.3).

17. For the dates, Quasten, *Patrology* 3:315, with Moreau, "Eusebius von Caesarea," 1072. Eusebius speaks of asceticism either as the "apostolic" or as the "philosophic" life (Reitzenstein, *Des Athanasius Werk*, 54–59). Eusebius, *Hist. eccl.* 2.17 shows no awareness of any contemporary monasticism of a residential kind.

18. SB 5.8698, lines 4–9. Full epigraphic text in Crum and White, *Monastery of Epiphanius at Thebes* 2, no. 585. The letter may have been composed during the period (355–361) which Athanasius spent with the monks. Cf. *PG* 25.692 A. The epigraphic fragments confirm the superiority of the Old Latin version over the Greek text preferred by Migne, *PG* 26.1185–88. The phrase containing *monachos* is unique to the epigraphic copy, dated IV by SB (Lefebvre) but VI–VII by van Haelst (*Catalogue*, no. 625).

This defines monasticism both in terms of personal discipline ("practicing the solitary—or single—life") and of domestic arrangements ("residing in the faith of Christ"). I judge this to be stating in effect that monks are ascetics whose "single life" (whether in relation to marriage or in some more general moral sense) has expressed itself in a change of residence, so that they depend directly upon Christ (presumably as anchorites or in a coenobitic monastery) rather than upon the ordinary pattern of domestic and civil life. One must note also the clear implication that the monks need to be claimed for orthodoxy.

Athanasius was a confidant of Antony, the great hermit, and inherited one of his two sheepskins—his only legacy—on his death, c. 356. Shortly afterwards (? 357) he brought out his "Life" of Antony, with a view to promoting him as a champion of orthodoxy, and thus binding a now powerful social force to the right cause. He recognizes that there is a longer tradition of the single-minded life (Antony himself took up the ascetic way c. 271, and the old hermit he followed had already done twenty years). But he reserved the term *monachos* precisely for the point at which the practice became the center of public excitement and began to constitute a social movement. This occurred about 305, when Antony broke out of his twenty-year self-imprisonment (καθ' ἑαυτὸν ἀσκούμενος—surely not a reference to celibacy) in the ruined fort (or fountain-house), and began to challenge others to take up the call:[19]

> ἔπεισε πολλοὺς αἱρήσασθαι τὸν μονήρη βίον, καὶ οὕτω λοιπὸν γέγονε καὶ ἐν τοῖς ὄρεσι μοναστήρια, καὶ ἡ ἔρημος ἐπολίσθη ὑπὸ μοναχῶν, ἐξελθόντων ἀπὸ τῶν ἰδίων καὶ ἀπογραψαμένων τὴν ἐν τοῖς οὐρανοῖς πολιτείαν.

It is to be noted here that the "solitary life" is not presented at all in terms of celibacy (although everyone would know that was part of it), but rather as "the abandonment of one's own" and "enrolment in the citizenship that is in heaven." It is an expressly socio-political notion, or indeed geopolitical, which dares even to conceive of the desert (the home of demons) as a *polis*.[20]

---

19. Athanasius, *Vit. Ant.* 14 (*PG* 26.835–976). The other sheepskin of Antony went to Serapion, bishop of Thmuis, who in writing to the monks (and not about them, as Athanasius was), at some time later than the *vita*, addresses them by the still much more common name of *monazontes* (*PG* 40.925–41).

20. On the literary structure and sources of the *vita*, see Reitzenstein, *Des Athanasius Werk*, who demonstrates the effects of a (lost) life of Pythagoras on aspects of the work, Dörries, *Die Vita Antonii als Geschichtsquelle*, who shows by a comparison of the 38 apophthegms of Antony with the *vita* that the historical teaching and lifestyle of Antony differed in important ways from that presented by Athanasius, who

THE "FIRST MONK" AND THE ORIGIN OF MONASTICISM

In view of our new papyrus monk, one should note that the center of these activities of Antony was a day's walk from Karanis. The only detailed episode attributed to this time is that in which Antony was preserved from the crocodiles, when he had to cross the Arsinoite canal "because he needed to inspect the brothers" (*Vit. Ant.* 15: χρεία δὲ ἦν ἡ τῶν ἀδελφῶν ἐπίσκεψις). This is meant to imply that Antony took responsibility for other monks in the Arsinoite nome, to which Karanis belonged. There is no reason why our Isaac should not have been one of them, but it is important to note the difference between his pattern of life and that favored by Antony.[21]

In about 313 Antony abandoned the hornets' nest he had stirred up in the settled heartland of Egypt, and set off across the desert to spend his remaining 43 years as the complete hermit in a distant mountain retreat. By about 320, Pachomius was to take up the task of bringing order to the rapidly growing numbers who remained closer to home, by setting up the first coenobitic monastery. In the deserted village of Tabennisi the voice had said to him:[22]

παράμεινον ὧδε καὶ ποίησον μοναστήριον· ἐλεύσονται γὰρ πολλοὶ πρός σε, γενέσθαι μοναχοί.

By the time of Jerome, it was unthinkable that a monk could be anything but a hermit or a coenobitic, two types which had in common not only celibacy, but the determination to detach oneself as completely as possible from the ordinary social pattern of the community. The only meaning available to

---

had axes of his own to grind (e. g., Antony as champion of orthodoxy, the submission of monks to the hierarchy). In particular, Apophthegm 23 (Dörries *Die Vita Antonii als Geschichtsquelle*, 156) shows that Antony recognized a superior tradition of ascetic fathers before his own day. But none of this prevents us from allowing that Athanasius could be right in putting the origins of public interest in the movement in the first decade of the century, and in applying the term *monachos* first at that stage. In the incident in *Vit. Ant.* 46, where Antony and his brother-monks tried to appear in court to support the martyrs (c. 310), Athanasius has the judge pronounce against the presence of the monks. It is a fair assumption that in his view the word *monachos* was properly applied only to this publicly recognized profession, though he does not explicitly say what he understood the word to mean, or whether he thought it had had any prior currency. For dates and a narrative reconstruction of the movement, see Chitty, *Desert a City*.

21. An Isaac replaces Macarius (who is elsewhere given as a leading disciple of Antony) in the sixth-century Syriac version of the letter of Serapion of Thmuis written on Antony's death in 356 to his disciples (and otherwise lost except for a later Armenian version). Draguet, "Une lettre," 12n1. But our Isaac had certainly not followed Antony into the desert, at least before 324.

22. *Vita Prima S. Pachomii* 12, in Halkin, *Sancti Pachomii vitae Graecae*. On the terminology of the Pachomian monastery, see Ruppert, *Das pachomianische Mönchtum*, 60–84. On the dependence of Pachomius upon anchoritic ideals, see Bacht, *Antonius und Pachomius*.

monachos in Latin was "solitary" in the social sense; there was next to nothing left of the "single-minded" ethical ideal to which the Greek term had alluded in its pre-monastic life.[23] Jerome furiously repudiates a third type of monk, which seems in fact to be none other than that of our *monachos* of Karanis, living still within his village, and participating actively in its civil and church affairs. According to Jerome, such monks live in small household communities. They are quarrelsome, profiteering, over-dressed, and abuse their church connections, and, if words could kill, Jerome would gladly be rid of them (35: *his igitur quasi quibusdam pestibus exterminatis*). The root of his objection is clear: they will not submit themselves to orders:[24]

> Tria sunt in Aegypto genera monachorum: coenobium, quod illi sauhes gentili lingua vocant, nos 'in commune viventes' possumus appellare; anachoretae, qui soli habitant per deserta et ab eo, quod procul ab hominibus recesserint, nuncupantur; tertium genus est quod dicunt remnuoth, deterrimum atque neglectum et quod in nostra provincia aut solum aut primum est. hi bini vel terni nec multo plures simul habitant suo arbitratu ac dicione viventes et de eo, quod laboraverint, in medium partes conferunt, ut habeant alimenta communia. Habitant autem quam plurimum in urbibus et castellis, et, quasi ars sit sancta, non vita, quidquid vendiderint, maioris est pretii. Inter hos saepe sunt iurgia, quia suo viventes cibo non patiuntur se alicui esse subiectos. Apud hos affectata sunt omnia : laxae manicae, caligae follicantes, vestis grossior, crebra suspiria, visitatio virginum, detractio clericorum, et si quando festior dies venerit, saturantur ad vomitum.

23. So the linguists, but see my remark at note 11 above on Jerome's commentary on Ps 67:7. The earliest attested use of *monachus* is in the anonymous translation of the *Vita Antonii*, dated to about 370, though *monasterium* was only introduced in that of Evagrius of Antioch. The former is edited by Bartelink, *Vita di Antonio*. The *vita* was translated by 360 according to Lorenz, "Die Anfänge." Jerome's earliest dateable use of *monachus* is from 374 (*Ep*. 3, to Rufinus). On the history of the two words in fourth-century usage, see Lorié, *Spiritual Terminology*, 24–34, 43–51; Lienhard, *Paulinus of Nola*, 60–69. Jerome comes closer than Athanasius (who simply implies it) to claiming that the name *monachus* was devised by or for Antony, when he states that Amathas and Macarius, the two disciples, maintained that Antony's forerunner Paul *principem istius rei fuisse, non nominis* (*Vita S. Pauli primi eremitae* 1 [*PL* 23.18]). The meaning of "solitary" is established by Jer. *Ep*. (*CSEL* 54) 58.5 *monachus, id est solus*, 14.6 *interpretare vocabulum monachi, hoc est nomen tuum quid facis in turba, qui solus es*? That the Greek term came to be understood in the same way is shown by the epigram of a cynical observer of about 400, Palladas (Cameron, "Palladas and Christian Polemic," 29): Εἰ μοναχοί, τί τοσοίδε; τοσοίδε δὲ πῶς πάλι μοῦνοι; ὦ πλῆθυς μοναχῶν ψευσαμένη μονάδα. (*Anth. pal*. 11.384).

24. Jerome, *Ep*. 22.34 (*CSEL* 54).

These strictures of Jerome are matched in virulence by those of Julian, when he denounces the Cynics by likening them to the ones the "impious Galileans" call *apotaktitai*.[25] They make small sacrifices, he says, only to get their hands on everything else, and enjoy special attention and flattery into the bargain:

τούτων οἱ πλείους μικρὰ προέμενοι πολλὰ πάνυ, μᾶλλον δὲ τὰ πάντα πανταχόθεν ξυγκομίζουσι, καὶ προσκτῶνται τὸ τιμᾶσθαι καὶ δορυφορεῖσθαι καὶ θεραπεύεσθαι.

Now Julian is writing this in 362, but he claims it has long been his practice to use the term *apotaktitai* as a nickname for Cynics. Since we know that the idea behind this word has a distinctively Christian history (derived from the use of the verb in Luke 14:33) there can be little doubt that Julian is correctly preserving from his Christian upbringing the name of a distinct order in the churches which attracted attention by its collective practice of renunciation.[26] Epiphanius, who had been for thirty years from c. 335 head of a monastery in Judea, writing c. 376 (*PG* 41.1040 C), uses the name as the self-chosen style of an heretical sect in Phrygia, Pamphylia, and Cilicia, whose principal name for themselves was *apostolikoi*. But there is frequent reference to their place in orthodox church life in the diary of Egeria, which may have been written in Jerusalem as early as 381–384. What she knows in her Western homeland as *monachi* she found sub-divided in the East into *ascites* (who are clearly hermits), *monazontes* and *aputactitae*. Her *aputactitae* cannot be easily distinguished from the *monazontes*, and both appear to constitute a recognized rank in the activities of the church. *Aputactitae* may include both men and women (23.3; 23.6; 39.3), as is also the case with *monachi*. The *aputactitae* are especially noted for fasting (28.3, 41), and, with the *monachi*, they come together in Jerusalem to celebrate the Encaenia from Mesopotamia, Syria, Egypt, and the Thebaid, as well as from other (less monastic) regions (49.1).[27]

Lambert held that this intermediate form of monasticism flourished in the other eastern provinces (where Julian would have met it), but that in Egypt the majority of the monks took to the desert, carrying the adjective *apotaktikos* with them as a general badge of their profession. It is true that

---

25. 224 B = *Or.* 7.18 Bidez. Libanius, *Or.* 30.8, also deals with this type of monk, while Julian, *Ep.* 89b and Libanius, *Or.* 2.32 condemn hermits.

26. Rothenhäusler and Oppenheim, "Apotaxis."

27. Morard, "Monachos, moine," 403–6; Lambert, "Apotactites et Apotaxamènes," 2604–26, esp. 2607, 2614. Wilkinson, *Egeria's Travels*, 35, does not accept the identification with Jerome's *remnuoth*. Gingras, *Egeria*, 15, allows 394 as the earliest date, but prefers 404 or 417.

the desert veterans largely monopolize the pious literature of the fourth century. They became a magnet for tourists, especially from the West, and inspired countless imitators in the indecently hospitable climates abroad. But in Egypt huge numbers of apotactics withdrew within the shelter of their own towns and villages. They are Jerome's *remnuoth* and Egeria's *aputactitae*. True, Rufinus tells us in the Prologue to his History of the Monks (*PL* 21.389-90) that while there were some in the suburban areas and others in the countryside, there were more scattered through the desert, and they were the ones of quality. But when he visited Oxyrhynchus he found more monasteries than houses in the city, with monks occupying public buildings and abandoned temples as well. The bishop told him the town had 10,000 monks and 20,000 virgins (*PL* 21.408-9). Far from abandoning the city, the retreat seems to have swallowed it up. These statements by writers later in the fourth century, when the fashion was at its height, do not of course settle the question of how it all began. But a slender trail of papyrus evidence may help us to work our way back.

There survives a number of personal letters in which there is thought to be reference to a community of a more intimate kind than the church itself. Usually this suggestion arises because the letters speak of a group of "beloved brothers" associated with the writer or recipient, and in a number of cases the bearer is recommended formally from one group to the other.[28] In this collection of letters, Naldini has assigned the following cases, in each of which the presence of such groups has been suggested, to the late third or early fourth century:[29]

P.Alex. 29	(Naldini 19)	a recommendation
SB 10.10255	(Naldini 20)	a form letter for recommending catechumens, with the name entered later
P.Gron. 17	(Naldini 24)	a complaint about behavior not befitting "the habit we wear," ἡμῶν τῶι προσχήματι [ὃ ἀμ]φιπερικείμεθα
P.Gron. 18	(Naldini 25)	a complaint, referring to the *papas*, from the Arsinoite nome

---

28. Treu, "Christliche Empfehlungs-Schemabriefe auf Papyrus," deals with Naldini no. 19, 20, 28, 29, 50 and 94, together with P.Oxy. 36.2785, and is responsible for the revised reading of the last text, which is followed below. He appears to take the letters as being from congregations (*Gemeinden*) rather than from more restricted groups, and refers to Julian's attempt to imitate "episcopal" letters of recommendation (Sozomen, *Hist. eccl.* 5.16.3, Theod. Anag. 135).

29. Naldini, *Il Cristianesimo in Egitto*.

THE "FIRST MONK" AND THE ORIGIN OF MONASTICISM 203

PSI 3.208	(Naldini 28)	a recommendation
PSI 9.1041	(Naldini 29)	a recommendation of catechumens
PSI 15.1492	(Naldini 30)	not between "brothers", but written by Sotas, author of the preceding two, to a "son" who may donate land to the *topos*, κατὰ τὸ πα̣λ[αιὸν] ἔθος

It has been proposed by van Haelst that all of these letters should be dated on paleographical and stylistic grounds to the latter third of the third century rather than to the fourth, and he associates with them the following cases, which Naldini had dated, in the first case III–IV, and otherwise to the fourth century:[30]

P.Got. 11	(Naldini 23)	asking help for women being taken before a magistrate
P.Oxy. 31.2603	(Naldini 47)	a recommendation, asking for the travelers to be received, although not catechumens, and for the addressee to write to "the others" so that they may be received in each *topos*
P.Oxy. 8.1162	(Naldini 50)	a recommendation from a *presbyteros* to his fellow *presbyteroi* and *diakonoi* in each *topos*
P.Iand. 100	(Naldini 87)	a report to two "fathers" on the sale of goods, greeting all the "brothers" in the *monasterion*
SB 5.7629	(Naldini 94)	a recommendation to the "beloved brothers" in each *topos*
P.Oxy. 12.1574	(not in Naldini)	January 15, 324, sending a jar of wine to "the brothers" (but nothing else that suggests Christian belief)

To these two lists must now be added:

P.Oxy. 36.2785	(not in Naldini)	a recommendation of a "sister" and a catechumen to the *papas*, Sotas, and his "brothers," from a group of *presbyteroi*

---

30. Van Haelst, "Les sources papyrologiques," 498–99.

It will be apparent that, apart from P.Iand. 100 (which Naldini dates to the second half of the fourth century), nothing about the terminology suggests that these letters might have had anything to do with the type of coenobitic monastery established by Pachomius. It is however clear that there is an institution called the *topos*, and that "by long-standing custom" (PSI 15.1492) it accepts gifts of land. The members seem to express their status in their clothes (P.Gron. 17). It is also clear that the main business of these letters is to do with church life; the groups seem to be especially responsible for catechumens. One could envisage their being apotactic communities, especially if these may be supposed to have been supporting agencies in church life, providing disciplinary training for catechumens and hospitality for them in the community houses. But the fact that two of the letters are passed between ministers of the churches (P.Oxy. 8.1162, 36.2785) does not fit this picture. The *topoi* may simply be the churches themselves.

There are certain public documents of Egypt, however, from the middle of the fourth century, which may be held to establish the presence of apotactics with a recognized rank in the civil community, though the first instance is rather doubtful:

P.Amh. 2.142	(Judge and Pickering 28)	a farmer, Aurelius Germanus, petitions to the *praeses*, c. 340–45; his enemies despised his *apragmosynē* and his *schēma* (the text breaks off here)

This is quite likely to be just the common plea of innocence in such cases, though the presence of the word *schēma* does not form part of the usual formula. It is hard to imagine how a working farmer could claim his garb as a status symbol, though it was distinctive enough in town. An edict of Caracalla (P.Giss. 40, col. 2, line 28) makes the point that the "appearance and dress" (*schēma*) of rural Egyptians made them unsuited to city life. P.Gron. 17, noted above, shows that in church circles there was a costume (*proschēma*) to which respect was due. But in a public document Germanus would surely have needed to indicate the status claimed for his dress if it was to have any effect, and, failing better evidence, it is probably safer to leave *schēma* here as a reference to his way of life rather than to his "habit."

P.Würzb. 16	(Judge and Pickering 37)	October 10, 349: a deacon gives surety for a village *presbyteros*, the document being written by Agathon, *apota]ktikos*, whose father had been a *prytanis* at Arsinoe[31]

Subject only to no serious alternative restoration being proposed, one may safely take this as a reference to the church rank of *apotaktikos*, since the deacon's position is clear, if not that of the *presbyteros* (does he hold a civil or ecclesiastical post?). The *apotaktikos* in this instance is using the social status of his father to add weight to his ecclesiastical dignity.

P.Flor. 1.71, line 722	(Judge and Pickering 22)	Macarius, *apotaktikos*, is registered as a landholder in an official list of Hermopolis

Macarius is one of a small minority of landholders who are identified by status (along with other church figures and priests of other religions). The implication of this case is that the renunciation made by *apotaktikoi* did not prevent their holding land. Jerome presents the *remnuoth* as engaged in gainful labor and residing in a community house. PSI 15.1492 shows that it was customary for the *topos* to accept gifts of land.

Later in the century, the position is illuminated by two further civil documents:

P.Lips. 28	(not in Judge and Pickering)	December 31, 381: a widowed (?) woman at Hermopolis entrusts her orphaned grandson, Paesis, to his uncle Silvanus, *apotaktikos*, to be his son (by *adrogatio*) and heir to his property (*pragmata*)
P.Oxy. 44.3203	(not in Judge and Pickering)	June/July, 400: lease of one ground-floor *topos* (an *exedra*) together with a vault in the basement, furnished, by Jose, *Ioudaios*, from two natural sisters, Theodora and Tauris, *monachai apotaktikai*

The nature of the *pragmata* which the ten-year-old Paesis will inherit from Silvanus is not specified, nor is there any reference to other heirs, but the adoption illustrates the degree to which an *apotaktikos* might retain family ties, though presumably living apart (the grandmother was perhaps

---

31. When first published, the present paper identified the deacon as a "deacon of the catholic church"—an error by dittography from Judge and Pickering, "Papyrus Documentation," 36.

to have the actual care of the boy). Theodora and Tauris are the only women in the cases reviewed to whom the terms *monachos* and *apotaktikos* are applied, and provide the only instance of the direct association of the two styles (though Egeria brings them together, in a way that is not at all clear). Presumably the *apotaktikai* of Oxyrhynchus are a sub-class of *monachai*. The two sisters will have been amongst the "20,000" *virgines* whom Rufinus heard to have been established in houses there at this time. Is their *topos* simply a residential suite for themselves, or does their reference to the ground-floor room as an *exedra* imply that a larger number of people were to use it? Later in the document it is referred to as a *symposion*.

Before one advances too far on such slender evidence, however, one must note another papyrus letter where the rank of *apotaktikos* might seem at first sight better related to one of Jerome's other types of monk:

P.Herm.Rees 9   (Naldini 84)   Apa Johannes is addressed as *apotaktikos* in a request for prayer

In P.Herm.Rees 7 (Naldini, *Il Cristianesimo in Egitto*, 82) a different request is addressed to Johannes as *anachoretes*, a title he takes to himself in 10 (Naldini, *Il Cristianesimo in Egitto*, 85), while a third correspondent, in a typically anxious plea for help, P.Herm.Rees 8 (Naldini, *Il Cristianesimo in Egitto*, 83), does not specify his status, but greets also "all the brothers laboring with" him. Johannes is not therefore a solitary anchorite, nor does he live far away from the action—the correspondent who calls him *anachoretes* (7) is seeking his intervention in high places to have himself exempted from military service (he has already had to surrender his children for debt, and is ill). Johannes's own letter (10), badly broken though it is, shows that he was involved with others in a civil court case, and is appealing for the help of a patron. Another *anachoretes*, Sabinus of PSI 13.1342 (Naldini, *Il Cristianesimo in Egitto*, 86), received an official demand from the *sitologoi* for tax payments in respect of a tradesman, for whom he must have been answerable in some way. In spite of his title of *anachoretes*, therefore, Apa Johannes may not have been so far removed from the position of Jerome's worldly *remnuoth*, and the addressing of him as *apotaktikos* may be a better index of his position in the civil community.[32]

32. Morard, "Monachos, moine," 407–10; Henne, "Documents et travaux." *Anachoresis* was the time-honored remedy of hard-pressed Egyptians—flight from responsibility by total disappearance, but modified by the Christian ideal of *apotaxis*, a withdrawal for moral reasons, which paradoxically made the anchorite a powerful source of help in social disasters. Van Haelst, "Les sources papyrologiques," 500, thinks one could date these letters to the first half of the fourth century, though the earlier editors had

THE "FIRST MONK" AND THE ORIGIN OF MONASTICISM 207

One may contrast his situation with that of another intercessor known to us from the mid-fourth century:

| P.Lond. 6.1925 | (Judge and Pickering 13) | Apa Papnutius is addressed as *anachoretes* in a request for prayer. |

There are six other letters in his archive (P.Lond. 6.1923–24, 1926–29) in which no title is extant.[33] In 1925 *anachoretes* is written on the verso, followed by a damaged address which appears to say that he can be found at the "monks' station," *monē monachōn*. Yet there is no other indication that he is caught up in community affairs. Papnutius seems the very model of the "holy man" of Egypt, as we know him from the hagiographical sources—as remote from the world as he is from his (high-class?) correspondents, who pour out urgent pleas for his prayers without stopping to explain their troubles. Only in the case of Valeria (1926) do we have details—she has a desperate problem with her breathing, but trusts in the revelations vouchsafed to *askountes kai thrēskeuontes* Papnutius is also spoken of as an athlete, pursuing a glorious and holy *politeia* of his own, in which he has renounced the world (1927, lines 31, 37, 39). Here surely is the true anchorite, and no mere *apotaktikos*.[34]

Similar questions of classification arise with the very substantial body of evidence contained in the Meletian archive, of which the first two and most important of the texts are dated to 334 and 335(?) respectively:

| P.Lond. 6.1913–22 | (Judge and Pickering 12) | Correspondence of Apa Paieous, *presbyteros*, *homologetes*, and (?) *monachos* |

In the first letter, Pageus (= Paieous?) reports to the *proestōtes monēs monachōn* at Hathor that he has been called to Constantine's council at Caesarea, and formally confirms the arrangements he has made for a deputy to take his place as head of the community of monks at his village of Hipponon.[35] The "monks' station at Hathor" is described as being "in

---

preferred the second half.

33. Editor's note: The name "Papnutius" was spelled in other papyri from this archive as "Paphnutius," with reference to the same individual.

34. For the social power of the anchorite, see Serapion of Thmuis, letter to the disciples of Antony (Draguet, "Une letter"), sec. 17, 22, and p. 23, and letter to the monks (*PG* 40.929 A–B), where the fertility of the land, and especially the flooding of the Nile, is attributed to their prayers.

35. On the identity of Pageus and Paieous see Holl, "Die Bedeutung," 293. The identity of the two leaders does not affect the case I put for seeing two monasteries where

the eastern desert of the Upper Cynopolite nome." It could be an enclosed monastery of the Pachomian type. But it has collective leadership, to judge from the plural *proestōtes*, and Pageus is answerable in some way to it for the affairs of his own group. They are also *monachoi* and belong to a *monē* (line 9) but are hardly constituted on the Pachomian model, since the constitutional assembly described takes place "in the presence of" Patabeis, the *presbyteros* of Hipponon, Papnutius the deacon from Paminpesla, Proous the "former (or original?) monk," and "of many others" (text here heavily restored). Pageus is himself a *presbyteros*, and responsible for the full administration of the *monē*, including the appointment of *oikonomoi* (l. 14). The assembly has been called to approve the nomination of his own natural brother to take his place while he is away at Caesarea.[36] There is an undertaking that no innovations will be made without reference to the *proestōtes*. Since Hipponon is in the Heracleopolite nome, it seems to me likely that its community is a different one from that at Hathor, although ultimately subordinate to its "patrons." Whatever the arrangements in the desert at Hathor, the daughter house at Hipponon is closely integrated with the local church community, and is in some sense under the superintendence of its ministers as well. It is an apotactic monastery.

The second letter (1914) in this archive is the famous report to Paieous on the mistreatment of the Meletian visitors to Alexandria by Athanasius, whose party had the use of the imperial troops. The writer calls the victims "brothers," while in citing the restrictions placed on them he indicates that they were referred to by the Athanasian party as "the monks of the Meletians." This confirms the implication of the later propaganda of Athanasius: the claim of orthodoxy upon the monks needed to be asserted precisely because that title was firmly established (from the beginning?) in the wrong hands. The violent abuse of the Meletian monks in Alexandria also makes one wonder what kind of "solitaries" they were—certainly not ones in full retreat from society.

The rest of the archive consists of more private letters addressed to Paieous, who now (1920) emerges as a *homologētēs*, one of the heroes of the Meletian resistance in the persecutions. Five letters are in Greek (1915–1919), two in Achmimic (1920–1921) and one in "Middle Egyptian" (1922).

Holl (and Bell?) appear to assume only one. If they are right, one has to explain why the assembly had to be reported at all, and why Patabeis should have been called *presbyteros* of Hipponon when he was at Hathor. But 1920 is addressed to Paieous at Hathor and greets a "Patabeit" with him, as does 1914. In any case a series of monasteries is implied in 1970.

36. Rousseau, "Blood-relationships," discusses a number of other exceptions to the rule that monks cut off natural bonds.

The evidence they supply for Paieous's style of life is conflicting. He receives pleas for money from a debtor whose children had been taken into slavery (1915–1916). A desperate renegade asks him to use his influence to reconcile him with his monastery, by writing "around the houses," *kata monēn* (1917). He receives gifts, and requests for prayer (1918, 1921); traffic in food both ways is referred to (1920, 1922) and the two different correspondents claim a *lebitōn* or tunic (the word is carried over into the Coptic), in one case (1920) made according to a pattern they had agreed upon. The same letter includes greetings to women and children.

What kind of a monk then is Paieous, if he is one at all? Certainly not a withdrawn anchorite, although he enjoys a reputation as intercessor. But he corresponds more to Apa Johannes than to Apa Papnutius: he is an influential political and community leader, as both Constantine and Athanasius recognized. In his own village he is both *presbyteros* and in charge of the church monastery. He is perhaps a member of the college of "patrons" which seems to take ultimate responsibility for a series of "stations" of Meletian monks. No wonder Athanasius and Jerome had to work so hard to make clear what a proper monk was!

Who then first earned the style *monachos*? Athanasius and Jerome agree in implying (though I do not think they actually say so) that it was the special property of Antony and his kind, and is correctly applied to them from the point at which they began to mark themselves off openly from the community at large (c. 305). It then passed to the organized form of *anachoresis* in the monasteries of Pachomius. But in that case, it seems to me highly unlikely that the ascetics who had long found their place privately within church life, but without breaking with the civil community, would have either wanted the name, or been likely to win it as a bonus. The total withdrawal of the others must have seemed a kind of censure on them (as Jerome certainly thinks it is) and their reaction would surely have been to coin a rival name for themselves to defend their time-honored practice against the sensational innovation.

But Isaac of Karanis proves that they had an established hold on the name, taken for granted in public life, in the very wake of the new developments. Must one not therefore conclude that it was first devised for them (because of some new turn in their affairs), and only later (by a spiraling competition in mortification?) carried forward to the more drastic types, so that it could eventually be half-denied to the original bearers by Athanasius and Jerome?

If this calculation is sound, we must then posit an event, or change of fashion, different from and prior to the creation of either eremitism (in its Antonian form) or coenobitism, but perhaps close in time to them, and part of a swift series of developments that led on to them. The apotactic movement (as later attested) meets this requirement. It represents the point at which the men at last followed the pattern long set for virgins and widows, and set up houses of their own in town, in which the life of personal renunciation and service in the church would be practiced.

Thus although they broke visibly with their ordinary domestic ties, they retained a place in society, and so required a name. They ranked as an order in the church (the *tagma* of Eusebius, to whom God gave a home in the church) and we should therefore expect them to pass on their church name for formal use by the community in speaking of them, as happened with other church titles. This name was *apotaktikoi* in Egypt, or *apotaktitai* further north. The Coptic-speaking people called them *remnuoth*, at least to start with.[37] Where then did the name *monachos* come from? My guess is that it was a popular nick-name for *apotaktikoi*, arising perhaps from some distinctive feature of their "withdrawal."

The word *monachos* is an adjective with a regular place in Greek thought, notably in Plotinus.[38] It is also found in the documentary papyri in two practical connections.[39] It denotes the original or top copy when documents are being multiplied. It also has a usage in relation to clothing, possibly to denote a single as opposed to a double thickness of cloth. This raises the possibility that the term was popularly applied to the *apotaktikoi* because they had not only changed their residence but adopted a distinctive style of dress. We know that the assumption of the monk's habit quickly became the point at which emotionally and ceremonially the commitment was made.[40] We also know that the form of dress was carefully prescribed

---

37. For its meaning ("people who live alone" or "cell-dwellers"?) see Reitzenstein, *Des Athanasius Werk*, 45. The fact that it gained no currency in Coptic Christian literature (which took over *monachos* and *anachoretes*) led him to suppose that it must have had a pre-Christian meaning.

38. Morard, "Monachos, moine," 336–40.

39. Morard, "Monachos, moine," 341–46.

40. Tertullian (*Virg.* 10) regretted that there was no distinctive garb for male ascetics in his day. For the first decades of the fourth century there are retrospective allusions: Hilarion, immediately upon seeing Antony, took up residence with him (Jerome, *Vit. Hil.* 3 [PL 23.31 A]) *mutato pristino habitu*; Antony confined himself to a single garment for the rest of his life (*Vit. Ant.* 47); Palaemon invested Pachomius (*Vita Sancti Pachomii* 7 [PL 73.233]). The rule of Pachomius 16 (PG 40.949) provided that ἐάν τις προσέλθῃ τῇ μονῇ, θέλων γενέσθαι ἀποτακτικός . . . ἐνδύσουσιν αὐτὸν τὸ σχῆμα τὸ ἀποτακτικόν, which Jerome rendered (*Vit. Hil.* 49 [PL 23.73]) *habitus monachorum*. Cf. P.Gron. 17, P.Amh. 2.142, discussed above. The invention of monastic dress (in the Thebaid?) was attributed to Patermutius (PG 65.448 D). For a full collection of evidence see Oppenheim, *Das Mönchskleid*, and for the symbolic use of dress for social rank, Kolb, "Zur Statussymbolik im antiken Rom."

(e.g., the tunic had to be sleeveless).[41] The dirty, or black, clothes of the monks were the physical features most singled out in secular denunciations of them.[42] The critical question here would be whether the *lebitōn*, or other characteristic garment, was in fact very unusual, or whether the particular form was being specified simply because it was the most ordinary.[43]

A new line of attack on the subject was opened up by the publication of the Coptic Gospel of Thomas ("The Secret Sayings of Jesus") discovered at Nag Hammadi.[44] A key ideal of this work is that of human "singularity." It does not matter for the present argument what the correct definition of this is (Klijn, for example, has argued that it refers to the winning back of the true human unity of primal Adam, through the overcoming of sexual differentiation). Two Coptic terms occur in this connection, but in three of the sayings the Greek loan-word *monachos* is found (16, 49, 75).

At least three literary origins have been proposed for the Gospel: (a) an original composition in Coptic; (b) a translation from a Syriac original; (c) a translation from a Greek version of a Syriac original. This last possibility is supported by the correspondence between the Gospel and the Oxyrhynchus Greek fragments (P.Oxy. 1.654, 655) and, assuming it is the most plausible, our attention is directed (as with Symmachus) to the meaning of *monachos* in a second-century Greek work of Semitic inspiration. The Oxyrhynchus fragments just fail to survive for any of the three places at which *monachos* is used in the Coptic. But it is most likely that the loan-word would have been carried forward because it occurred only in those three sayings, and

41. Rule of Pachomius," in Boon, *Pachomiana Latina*, 2: *vestimentum, id est tunicam lineam absque manicis quam lebitonarium vocant*. The Greek *lebitōn* is found in the Coptic letters P.Lond. 6.1920, 1922, discussed above (where Bell translates it "cloak"), and possibly in P.Oxy. 14.1683 (Naldini, *Il Cristianesimo in Egitto*, 65). The *lebitōn* appears to have been a particular form of *kolobion* (PG 34.1138 A).

42. Eunapius, *VS* 6.11.7; 7.3.5 (472, 476), and other secular allusions referred to in note 3 above. Jerome also attacked the blackshirts (*Ep.* 22.28), yet made a fetish of dirt himself: *Ep.* 38.5 *nos, quia serica veste non utimur, monachi iudicamur*; 125.7 *sordidae vestes candidae mentis indicia sint*; *PL* 30.346 D *pallor et sordes tuae gemmae sint*. "Rule of Pachomius" (Boon, *Pachomiana Latina*, 67, 70), however, paid great attention to the washing of the *lebitōn*.

43. Note the important difference in this respect between the formulation of the "Rule of Pachomius" in the edition of Boon, *Pachomiana Latina*, praef. 4: *duo lebitonaria, quod genus absque manicis Aegyptii vestimenti est*, and the version given in *PL* 23.66: *duo lebitonaria, quod Aegyptiis monachis genus vestimenti est sine manicis*. The Coptic tunics preserved from the Fayum have "sleeves closed tightly at the wrists," Boucher, *History of Costume*, 101.

44. Morard, "Monachos, moine," 362–77. Out of the extensive discussion note especially Harl, "À propos des logia de Jésus"; Klijn, "'Single One'"; Adam, "Der Monachos-Gedanke"; Quispel, "L'évangile selon Thomas"; Quispel, *Makarius*; Ménard, *L'évangile selon Thomas*.

was either not open to being represented by a further variation of the Coptic terminology for one-ness, or was known to have a particular value in the Greek (no doubt as representing the Syriac *iḥîḏāyā*).

For reasons given earlier in this discussion, I do not consider it historically plausible that in second-century church circles the word could have signified the kind of socially identified figure to which it was applied in the monasticism of the fourth century. But, whatever the literary origin of the Coptic work, we must recognize the possibility that the Greek loan-word was adopted by the Coptic author (whether from a prior work, or from current usage in the first two cases above) because at the time he was writing he knew that *monachos* was the name of a recognized social type in Egypt. In that case the meaning of the word in the Gospel of Thomas could be that of "monk," provided that the dating of the Coptic composition fell later than the time at which that sense became current in Egypt.

The Nag Hammadi codex was most probably written early in the second half of the fourth century, and I suppose one should say on general grounds that a Coptic collection of Gospel sayings is not likely to have been prepared earlier than about AD 300. One must next ask whether it is likely that a gnostic scholar would have fancied taking over the loan-word *monachos* if he knew that it meant one of the "front rank" of those "advancing in Christ" in the churches. Conversely, the question arises as to whether Athanasius would have been eager to secure the word to orthodoxy if he knew that it already had a safe place in gnostic lore (cornering it from the Meletians would be a much less risky gambit).

The former question becomes the more acute the further on into the fourth century one brings the date of the gnostic composition of the Gospel of Thomas, while the latter is eased by a later date. If it could be placed within the first two decades of the century, a time of acute disorientation, before the councils and rival champions of doctrinal purity began to clear the theological air, and establish new party-lines, and while the monastic movement itself was still taking shape, we might simply envisage that the new style caught on quickly in unrelated circles. It was after all likely to appeal to the hearts of those of all persuasions who regretted their sexuality, and sought to alienate themselves from society. This is more easy to imagine if it was not a doctrinal term at all (as *apotaktikos* was) but simply a catchy style arising from some incidental popular reaction to the movement that had sprung up. It then lay with the passage of time and ecclesiastical propaganda to see who could assert a title to the word when the very great and paradoxical reverse-influence of the monks on society became apparent.

Isaac of Karanis is thus left as the first landfall in a sea of speculation. In the hope that a critical reaction, and the better knowledge that others

THE "FIRST MONK" AND THE ORIGIN OF MONASTICISM 213

can bring to bear, will extend our new foothold, I sum up the discussion in a series of hypotheses. It must be stressed that they are not seen by me as conclusions.

a. Late in the third or early fourth century, the long tradition of male asceticism in the churches adopted for the first time a social form, matching the arrangements long before made for virgins and widows: the men became a *tagma* in the church (Eusebius).

b. Its socially distinctive features were a change of residence, from ordinary domestic circumstances to a community house (Jerome), and of dress (P.Gron. 17).

c. The community called themselves "brothers," but their church name was *apotaktikoi* (Egeria's and Julian's *apotaktitai*) which passed into official currency in the community at large (P.Flor.71).

d. The general public responded with a new name, *monachos*, which would have picked up a feature that caught the popular eye (the "solitary" lifestyle, or a detail of dress?).

e. The concealed eremitic tradition which Antony had inherited impinged on the new movement, with the result that many went over to a total withdrawal from the civil community, taking the new names with them, and resurrecting the old Egyptian style of *anachoretes* as well.

f. The Pachomian monasteries provided for coenobitic life, but at the new level of social detachment that had come in.

g. P.Coll.Youtie 77 demonstrates that by 324 *monachos* was a recognized public style for the original apotactic type of ascetic, ranking alongside the ministers of the church.

h. In the early 330s Eusebius shows that *monachoi* was then also a recognized name in church circles for the apotactic *tagma*.

i. In the 330s, the Meletian archive (P.Lond. 6.1913–22) applies *monachoi* to the members of "stations" that are still apotactic in being closely church-related, but overshadowed by the coenobitic discipline of Pachomian type, and the revered anchoritic individual.

j. About the middle of the century, the archive of Apa Papnutius (P.Lond. 6.1923–29) illustrates the sway exercised over people's minds by a total recluse, while that of Apa Johannes (P.Herm.Rees 7–10) shows one still closely involved in the public community—a mixture of *anachoretes* and *apotaktikos*, as his correspondents indicate.

k. From the time of Antony's death in 356, Athanasius and others run a literary campaign to vindicate the pure types of monasticism for orthodoxy, while the contempt of churchmen (Jerome) and secular critics (Julian and Libanius) alike demonstrates how the original apotactic form continued to flourish in the churches.

l. At the end of the century, P.Oxy. 44.3203 confirms that apotactics are an urban category of monks, and that the two terms can now be used of women as well as men, in both respects supporting the implications of Egeria's account.[45]

---

45. Supplementary note: P.Berl.inv. 13897 (Naldini, *Il Cristianesimo in Egitto*, 36) and P.Oxy. 14.1774 (Naldini, *Il Cristianesimo in Egitto*, 37) document an early fourth-century community of women. For another type of urban church-related association, the *philoponoi*, see Wipszycka, "Les confréries." See also Barison, "Ricerche sui monasteri," which provides a systematic catalogue from the beginning.

15

The Impact of Paul's Gospel on Ancient Society

This chapter was first published in 2000 in Bolt and Thompson's volume in honor of Peter T. O'Brien, *The Gospel to the Nations* (at pages 297–308), and has subsequently been reproduced in Judge, *Jerusalem and Athens*, 58–68. It appears here with only minor editorial changes. The discussion is framed around two Pauline concepts which have impacted the modern world: the "inner man" which undergirds modern psychologizing, and the "one new man" (the church built up in Christ), from which springs the modern toleration of social autonomy or an alternative community. After sketching these legacies, Judge notes the cultural significance of Paul for later antiquity before asking how those two Pauline notions may have affected the development of Christian monasticism and of Christian martyrdom respectively.

THIS TITLE (OFFERED TO ME by the editors of *The Gospel to the Nations*) was bound to tempt a footloose student of history onto very tricky ground. Our honorand himself has warned that Paul gave no direct instructions covering what we mean by "impact." The new life of the churches was indeed revolutionary. But it was designed for fulfillment when the existing "society" reached the end of its time. In this life it "remains hidden."[1]

I know that this should not trouble an ancient historian. The reigning fashion is to insist that the conversion of Rome changed nothing of social consequence.[2] If so, we may as well say the question evaporates. Paul con-

1. O'Brien, "Church," 117. Paul's "social theory of organisation" has been described as "truly novel and innovative. As a transition strategy, the pattern is emergent rather than imposed": Marshall, "Enigmatic Apostle," 174.

2. MacMullen, "What Difference Did Christianity Make?" 341: "non-Christian

verted the world all right, but since he was not looking for any particular changes in it, we need not bother looking for them either. Yet we know that our own world, the modern one, certainly bears the most profound imprint of biblical thought.[3] We may, then, at least ask why that had not happened already in antiquity, or (if it had) why people have not noticed it.

A further problem in looking for "impact" is how to distinguish the impress of Paul from that of the New Testament as a whole. And if one were to go only for Pauline distinctives, one might well end up only with marginal issues rather than central ones. I propose therefore to treat as Pauline such positions as I judge basic to his thinking, even though they may be shared in one way or another with comparable positions in the Gospels or other writings. But they will be concepts that he decisively develops, and which are terminologically identifiable as his.

I propose to find a way around the main impasse by taking both key terms in the broadest sense. By "gospel" I shall mean the whole body of Paul's teaching (generated presumably from the gospel in its strict sense). By "society" I shall mean not only the fabric of social relations but the formative ideas or conventions behind them which we might ordinarily refer to as "culture." The question being taken this way (and allowing for my further caveat above), I then start with the following proposition: in the modern world the impact of Pauline teaching on our culture may be recognized most clearly at two focal points.

I. The "Inner Man" and the "One New Man" in Modern Society

The first is our preoccupation with the "inner man" (Rom 7:22; Eph 3:16).[4] In classical culture interest was concentrated upon the individual and his fate, seen in relation to external events. So in Greek tragedy the drama typically centers upon the inability of even the well-meaning to spot the point in time. Their zeal then slips over into the fateful arrogance (*hybris*) that provokes doom (*nemesis*). Or in Stoic (and much other) ethical thinking the aim is to guard one's own integrity unshaken by the emotional shocks

---

moral history runs parallel to Christian. Or the two are one."

3. Judge, "Biblical Shape."

4. The use of this translation is out of favor with publishers, but if I say "inner being" or "inner self" I lose the strong sense, created by the use of *anthrōpos* ("man"), that the inner self is the definitive person. I also destroy the verbal concurrence with my second focal point, the "one new man," where *anthrōpos* would have to be translated "humanity," wiping out the strikingly personal character of the Greek concept here also. Both "men" are embodied "in Christ" (Eph 2:13; 3:17). Chamblin, "Psychology."

of contact with others. Pity (if it lacks moderation, Alcinous, *Didaskalikos*, 32.4) is as much a vice of the soul as cruelty. The cardinal virtues are generally properties of character: courage (*arete*, "enterprise"), prudence (*phronesis*), self-control (*sophrosyne*). Such qualities are not featured in biblical culture, which focuses rather on constructive responses to others: trust (*pistis*), hope (*elpis*), and care (*agape*). Justice (*dikaiosyne*), the fourth cardinal virtue, is, however, in Greek inscriptions to be seen in social action, though it is not featured from that perspective in biblical culture, where it means righteousness (in God's sight).[5] In Pauline thought it is credited to the believer "without works" (Rom 4:6). In broad terms one may say that in the Hellenic tradition the problems of life centered upon keeping one's balance, and preserving the good one possessed. Education would train one successfully in this.[6]

It was Paul who most dramatically shattered such self-assurance. Not only did he see the cosmos as itself corrupted from without ("sin entered," Rom 5:12, a notion unthinkable when the cosmos was by definition complete, perfect and unchanging), but the evil had enslaved even his own will (Rom 7:14–25). The drama is no longer one of adjustment to fate within a closed system. Its limits explode at the cosmic level, while a microcosm of conflict is exposed within one's own heart.

The distant source of this apocalypse is clear: The Serpent in the Garden, and the demand of the Shema for total commitment of one's inmost being (Deut 6:5, "You shall love the Lord your God with all your heart, and with all your soul, and with all your might"). A phrase similar to Paul's "inner man" is found in both Plato (*Rep.* 9.589A) and Plotinus (*Enn.* 1.1.10) for the self-mastery of reason. But the Pauline scenario reaches out, from indwelling sin (Rom 7:20) to the liberating Spirit of life (8:2). Transformed by the renewal of our mind (12:2), we take the body for the temple of the Holy Spirit (1 Cor 6:19), as we are daily renewed within (2 Cor 4:16), a new creation (5:17).

Paul's searching of his own heart is, for his time, unparalleled in its candor. It was pursued even more ruthlessly by Augustine.[7] The

---

5. *Dikaiosyne* stands for fair dealing in the market-place, inscribed on weights and deified by magistrates: Robert, *Documents de l'Asie Mineure méridionale*, 25–29.

6. Many in antiquity, like Suetonius and Tacitus, appear to have thought character was fixed from birth: Lindsay, "Characterisation," 301; Gill, "Question of Character Development"; Swain, "Character Change in Plutarch."

7. Grossi, "Anthropology," 45: "Augustine . . . who definitively disjoined anthropology from cosmology, for whom man interrogates himself directly to find out who he is and filters the whole of the reality he encounters, not excluding God, through himself."

self-disclosure we now expect in autobiography was not a feature of ancient culture, which concentrated on self-display.[8] Ancient romances waited on their happy ending with all the breathlessness of a soap opera. But modern novels and films are engrossed with our deeper dilemmas of motivation and morality. We look to them for a kind of psychological autobiography. The fact that the modern novel (as its name implies, an innovation) emerged in the period between the hey-days of the Puritans and of the Methodists may tell the tale. It is the cultural imprint, surely, of Paul's inner quest.[9] Similarly, our ideas of individual vocation and gifts are the cultural legacy of Paul's doctrine of the Spirit.

The second focal point of Pauline teaching that has profoundly marked modern culture is his concept of the "one new man" (Eph 2:15). This is his answer to the polarization of Jew and gentile. The "one new man" is not, however, a new type of individual. The "one body" of the cross (2:16) reconciles the two, who are now "of joint body" (*syssōma*, 3:6). The neologism seeks to imply an organic unity that is in fact social. This has already been made clear by the repeated use of metaphors from the civil order. Previously excluded from the "commonwealth" of Israel as "foreigners" to the covenants (2:12), the gentiles have exchanged their status of "resident aliens" for that of "joint citizens with the saints," and thus "members of God's household" (2:19). The figure then shifts again, to one forged for this very purpose. The whole "construction" (*oikodomē*, elsewhere often ineffectively translated as "edification," which itself arises from the Latin term for "building") "grows" into a "sacred shrine in the Lord" (2:21). As a metaphor, *oikodomē* seems to have been another innovation of Paul's. It is a favorite way of his expressing the social reconstruction for which the new "assemblies" meet. Everything is to serve that end (1 Cor 14:26).[10]

It is not clear to me how far Paul expected this to work out in practice, given the continuing synagogue assemblies from which the churches arose. But I have no doubt that the social autonomy asserted in the name of the "one new man" is the historic source of what we now call the "open society." The right to an alternative lifestyle, grudgingly tolerated by "national values," has been won, with painful slowness, from the blood of the martyrs.

---

8. Misch, *History of Autobiography*. On the psychology of the phenomenon, see Hutch, *Meaning of Lives*.

9. Watt, *Rise of the Novel*. For the view that fairy tales were driven out of English popular culture by the Puritans and other intellectual moralists, and that "novels . . . are an alternative to Methodism," see Hunter, *Before Novels*, 143, 134. On the ancient romances see Tatum, *Search*.

10. Barclay, "One New Man," making the point that "new" (*kainos*) connotes not repetition but radical innovation.

Rejection of status consciousness (*prosopolempsia*, a term first attested in Rom 2:11) no doubt springs from the same source.

II. Paul in Later Antiquity

Fragments of all the Pauline letters (except those to Timothy) survive from Egypt prior to Constantine's taking control there. The earliest papyri happen to be from the letters to Titus and Philemon. The survival rate for the subsequent parts of the New Testament, and for the Gospels of Matthew and John, is stronger. From the early fourth century comes a writing exercise based on the opening of Romans. From the end of it there is a bilingual text of Ephesians (Greek and Latin), and an alphabetic acrostic in verse using Pauline terms and themes.[11] This papyrus record shows the Pauline corpus in active use.[12]

The apocryphal Acts of Paul (and Thecla), a second-century romance that also filled in the missing correspondence between Paul and the Corinthians, was probably more popular still.[13] In the year 307, however, the bishop of Thmuis in Egypt, Phileas, was interrogated by the prefect, Culcianus, on the facts about Paul. Two Greek papyrus transcripts of the trial have been published.[14] The governor needed to persuade the bishop, a wealthy community leader, to offer the public sacrifices. The governor himself seems quite familiar with the weak points in the bishop's position, or had been briefed by a well-informed consultant. Several of the gambits use detailed knowledge of Paul to catch the bishop out.

Culcianus asks whether Paul had not sacrificed (alluding perhaps to Acts 21:26). Phileas denies it. Later, on the resurrection of the body, Culcianus asks whether Paul had not rejected it (switching him with those he complains of in 1 Cor 15:12?). Phileas flatly denies this too. "Then who did deny it?" "I'm not telling you," retorts Phileas. After another change of tack, Culcianus asks whether Paul was not a persecutor (as indeed the latter affirms in 1 Cor 15:9, Gal 1:13, Phil 3:6). Another flat denial (is Phileas losing his grip?). Culcianus presses home the advantage: Was Paul untrained (*idiōtēs*, the very word he cites against himself at 2 Cor 11:6)? Was he not a Syrian, and

11. P.Oxy. 2.209 (Romans); PSI 13.1306 (Ephesians); P.Bodmer 47 (acrostic, published by Carlini and Bandini, "P.Bodmer XLVII").

12. For the use of Scripture in church and community see Kaczynski, *Das Wort Gottes*.

13. Details of the extant papyri and translations in Schneemelcher, *New Testament Apocrypha*, vol. 2; discussion in Bremmer, *Apocryphal Acts of Paul and Thecla*.

14. Pietersma, *Acts of Phileas*; Latin text and translation available in Musurillo, *Acts of the Christian Martyrs*.

did he not lecture in Aramaic? "No," says Phileas, "He was a Hebrew. But he also lectured in Greek, and was of the highest distinction, excelling everyone." They argue about whether Paul was superior to Plato (Phileas offers to teach Paul to Culcianus). "He was more profound than any man. He convinced all the philosophers." Later Culcianus comes back for a last attempt. "Was Paul God?" "No," answers Phileas. "Who was he then?" Phileas replies: "He was a man like ourselves, but the Spirit of God was in him; and so he performed signs and wonders and acts of virtue in the Spirit."

The key part assigned to Paul in this cross-questioning demonstrates that he had become far more than a romantic hero. His identity, intellectual standing, and integrity are critical to the bishop's resistance. As the champion of orthodoxy, the government has to be able to undercut him. It may not always have been so clear.

For the earliest generations after the New Testament period Paul has been called "the thorn in the flesh" of the churches.[15] Some of the most popular writings stood outside his influence. This is conspicuously true of the Shepherd of Hermas, which rivals Paul's letters in its frequency of papyrus remains. The Didache, Epistle of Barnabas and the apologists draw largely upon material from non-Pauline sources. They sought antiquity. Only Marcion is a thoroughgoing Paulinist.[16] Some of the gnostic traditions took Paul up, especially in his romantic dress. They understood 1 Cor 15:46–48 to justify their doctrine of three types of men with fixed natures. Not for nothing did Tertullian call him "the apostle of the heretics."[17]

With Irenaeus, Clement of Alexandria, Tertullian, and Origen, spanning the second half of the second century and the first of the third, Paul comes into his own as a major authority.[18] But his establishment, and the need to prove the self-consistency of Scripture, have blunted the response to some of his more challenging insights.[19] It could not be admitted, for example, that his soul-searching was an authentic account of his own experience, since he must have been perfect, the model for imitation, as he had imitated Christ, a point he himself had made (1 Cor 11:1). For Origen he was already "divine." So his problems had only been assumed for our instruction.[20]

15. Dassmann, *Der Stachel im Fleisch*; Lindemann, "Der Apostel Paulus."

16. Hoffmann, *Marcion*.

17. Wiles, *Divine Apostle*, 29–30, 18 (citing Tertullian, *Adv. Marc.* 3.5.4); Pagels, *The Gnostic Paul*.

18. Noormann, *Irenäus als Paulusinterpret*.

19. Mitchell, "Variable and Many-sided Man."

20. Patristic citations of Scripture across the first three centuries are tabulated in *Biblia patristica*, which extends to seven volumes plus a supplement on Philo, and the data therein have now been made available through the online "Biblindex" database at

Neither the "inner man" nor the "one new man," so far as I have seen, attracted particular attention from commentators during the first four centuries.[21] Not, at any rate, for their potential social impact. Symptomatic of this is the case of Marius Victorinus.[22] He was ideally placed to answer our question. Professor of Rhetoric at Rome in the time of Julian, he resigned his chair after the ban on Christian teachers (362). We possess quite extensive literary works of his, both as a believer and from the time before his conversion, which happened slowly while he was already a famous man. His baptism was a public sensation, according to Augustine (*Conf.* 8.2). He must have been fully conscious of the cultural significance of what was happening to him and to his age. Yet his Pauline commentaries stick closely to the text.[23] He amplifies it into a copious paraphrase, aiming to spell out the nuances of Paul's thought strictly in Pauline terms. There is no symbolic interpretation such as others had used to escape the hard word. Yet he sometimes misses the point. Observers of our contemporary wave of Bible translators will recognize the problem. One slips too easily into one's own ideas.

Commenting on the "one new man" (Eph 2:16) Victorinus says (trans. M. J. Edwards, note 21 above):

> Their souls have thus been reconciled to the eternal and the spiritual, to all things above. The Savior, through the Spirit, indeed the Holy Spirit, descended into souls. He thereby joined what had been separated, spiritual things and souls, so as to make the souls themselves spiritual. He has established them in himself, as he says, "in a new person." What is this new person? The spiritual person, as distinguished from the old person, who was soul struggling against flesh.

Whatever one may think of this as an interpretation of Pauline anthropology (and the English translator has syncopated it somewhat towards the end), it appears completely to miss the point that Paul is talking about the uniting of Jew and gentile in the "one new man," a social and not a

---

http://www.biblindex.mom.fr. It emerges from these tallies that in all periods 1 Corinthians is cited much more often than Romans (except in the case of Origen), though the letters are of similar length, and far more often than the somewhat shorter 2 Corinthians, Ephesians always more often than Galatians, and Colossians than Philippians, two pairs also of similar length.

21. Patristic commentaries are catalogued, together with the homilies, in Sieben, *Kirchenväterhomilien*. Extracts from the commentators, in translation, are given in the new series Ancient Christian Commentary on Scripture (edited by T. C. Oden). For evaluation, see Wiles, *Divine Apostle*, and Young, *Biblical Exegesis*.

22. Hadot, *Marius Victorinus*.

23. Locher, *Marii Victorini Afri Commentarii*; Souter, *Earliest Latin Commentaries*.

psychological aim. Nor can one say it is a temporary diversion on the part of Victorinus. When he comes in 2:19 to "fellow-citizens with the saints" he defines the latter as "the apostles, prophets and all who formerly experienced God or spoke divinely through the Spirit dwelling within them." Yet in 2:17 he had recognized that "those who are near" are "obviously Jews."

In addition to the vast corpus of patristic homilists and commentators, there were being circulated at the time substantial critiques of Scripture. Most of these (e.g., Celsus, Porphyry, and others that are anonymous) are preserved only by citation in the refutations that its defenders published.[24] Of those that survive in their own right, the most instructive for our purposes are the works of Julian. As the last heir of the house of Constantine, he had been brought up on Scripture, though secretly rejecting it. On coming to power, he set out to reinvigorate the classical cults on the model of the churches. This illusion baffled his supporters, and the reforms would have perished through irrelevance anyway had his premature death not canceled the question.[25] The central preoccupation of both critics and defenders of Scripture is with its alleged inconsistencies.

Since my assignment, however, concerns "impact on society," I will take the two most spectacular public manifestations of the Gospel, allowing them as possible outworkings of the two Pauline focal points I have named. They are monasticism (for the "inner man") and martyrdom (for the "one new man").

III. The "Inner Man" and the *Monachoi*

The earliest classical author to take a better than negative notice of "the school (*diatribe*) of Moses and Christ" was the medical polymath Galen, in the second century. He saw what we call monasticism and martyrdom as the two things Christians sometimes do that align them with true philosophers. We all see for ourselves, he says, that they despise death, and that they shun sex out of a kind of modesty. There are women and men among them who have avoided intercourse throughout their lives. There are also those so far advanced in self-discipline and dedicated study that they yield nothing to true philosophers.[26]

---

24. The critiques are reproduced with translations in the order of the biblical books in Rinaldi, *Biblia Gentium*. Celsus can be largely reconstructed from the response of Origen: Borrett, "Celsus."

25. Smith, *Julian's Gods*, is more reserved on these issues.

26. This fragment, preserved in Arabic, is reproduced in Latin in Boer, *Scriptorum paganorum*. In general, see Wilken, *Christians*.

By the fourth century the practice of celibacy had institutionalized itself in the person of the monk (*monachos*, "solitary" or "single-minded"). The term is first attested in this sense in a civil petition of 324.[27] Commenting on 1 Cor 7:25 and 1 Tim 4:1, an anonymous critic later asked, "How is it that certain people boast of their virginity as if it were some great thing, and say that they are filled with the Holy Ghost similarly to her who was the mother of Jesus?" (*BG* 708). In the churches too there were those who judged that the Pauline option had been upstaged by monasticism. We have polemical works by Jerome defending the new discipline against Helvidius (AD 383), Jovinian (AD 393), and Vigilantius (AD 406). In the meantime, an influential literature was developing around it, inspired by Athanasius's idealizing *Life of Antonius*, and the latter's published letters.[28]

Asceticism was not itself a distinctive of the Christian tradition.[29] But a Christian practice of "spirituality" made use of it.[30] At the social level, however, fourth-century monasticism produced reactions of horror or contempt. Julian (himself admired for his asceticism) accused the monks of exploiting their sacrifices for gain like the Cynics (LCL 27, Julian, 2:122). Their retreat to the desert came from misanthropy (LCL 29, Julian, 2:296).

Libanius, who revered Julian's memory, called them pale, tomb-living enemies of the gods (*Or.* 62.10). They pack themselves into caves, moderate only in dress (*Or.* 2.32). The black elephants attack the temples, concealing gluttony under artificial pallor, artisans aping philosophy (*Or.* 30.8–31).

In the meantime, the Christian Roman government strove to regulate the new craze. Legislation in 370 accused men of taking to the desert to escape civil duties (*Cod. theod.* 12.1.63). In 390, however, the monks were obliged to stay in their desert (16.3.1, revoked two years later, 16.3.2). In 390, bishops who admitted tonsured women to the altars were deposed (16.2.27). In 398 bishops were made responsible if monks in their territory gave sanctuary against the law (9.40.16).[31]

The historian Eunapius (fr. 55) complains that the Goths of Alaric had their own tribe of so-called monks, for admission to which one needed only sweep around in dirty cloaks and tunics, and to be evil and plausible. Those who destroyed the Serapeum at Alexandria in 389, he says, were human pigs, who needed only black clothes and public squalor to achieve tyranny,

27. Judge, "Earliest Attested Monk." See more fully chapter 14 above.
28. Brakke, *Athanasius and the Politics of Asceticism*; Rubenson, *Letters of St Antony*.
29. Wimbush, *Ascetic Behaviour*.
30. Ladner, *Idea of Reform*, entirely devoted to reform of the "inner man." For a theological "deepening" see Williams, *Wound of Knowledge*.
31. For a complete catalogue of legislation relating to Christian practice or ideals, see Joannou, *La législation impériale*, 311–476.

chaining the human race to the dishonest slave-cult of the martyrs (*Lives of the Sophists* 6.11.6). The poet Palladas quipped, "How can you be solitaries when you go around in crowds?" (*Anth. pal.* 11.384). Writing of the year 403, the historian Zosimus asserts that the monks were taking over most of the land, impoverishing everyone (*Historia Nova* 5.23.4).

Can we call this the impact of Paul's problems with the "inner man"? He would surely have joined the lost voices of those who condemned it. Yet the quest of Antony for a radical victory over the enemy within must owe something to his insights. Should the "inner man" have been locked away again?

IV. The "One New Man" and the *Martyres*

From the official viewpoint, the "one new man" was a non-starter. Though many Romans were interested in Judaism, going over to it was disgraceful. All the more, to have tried to create a new (potentially universal) citizenship would have seemed superfluous. Rome was already well on the way in practice to achieving that much herself. In the event, the Jews were to be violently suppressed in their main homelands in the late first and early second centuries. But their traditional autonomy of lifestyle was respected, and secured by a place in the tax system. In spite of the fashionable assumption in New Testament studies that the demarcation between Jews and Christians proceeded only by slow and mixed stages, and was not inescapable, the Romans seem never to have seriously linked the two. No one, Roman, Jew or Christian, across two and a half centuries of baffling repression, appears to have thought of the obvious: let the Christians go their own way and tax them too for the privilege. The whole point was that the Christians owed national loyalty to their own Roman or Greek culture, their birthright, and the law of their fathers. The Christians rejected this. They obeyed a higher law, and for ancestry appealed to Abraham.[32]

On one thing the Romans and the Christians readily agreed. They were treating themselves as a separate nation, a "third race," as Tertullian put it, between Jews and Romans.[33] In terms of political philosophy the matter was formulated for the Christians by Origen (*Cels.* 1.1): "It is not wrong to form associations against the law for the sake of truth." This is the first time in recorded history that the right to self-determination was defined. Would Paul have shrunk from this as the outcome of his "one new man"? I think not.

32. Judge, "Judaism and the Rise of Christianity."
33. Harnack, *Mission*, especially 2:vii, 2:240–65, and 2:266–78.

But the price was high. Paul understood the cost of witnessing. He had seen Stephen pay it. He paid it himself, no doubt.[34] The Romans could accommodate the perverse will to die, within limits.[35] There came the point, however, where it was, for the government, self-defeating. It risked the neglect of the very gods it was supposed to appease. In his edict of toleration of 311, the dying Galerius, a monster to the Christians, reiterated the unchanging complaint against them. They were creating deviant communities on divergent principles (Lactantius, *Mort.* 34.2: *per diversa varios populos congregarent*). But the time had come when they should at least pray (*orare*, the distinctive Christian term) to their own God for their own safety, and for his. The wall came down. Rome accepted the Christian principle of self-determination.

Three generations later, it was still unclear to Ammianus Marcellinus what the nature of the Christian community was.[36] Ammianus is the last great historian of Rome, the heir of Tacitus. He toyed with various terms: *ritus christianus, christiana lex, cultus christianus, christiana religio*. He has no parallel for such an adjective with any of these nouns, and none of them in his usage relates primarily to what we call "religion" in antiquity. He is casting about for a way of formulating the cultural phenomenon as a whole. His older contemporary, Marius Victorinus, had already adopted the neologism, *christianitas*.

Ammianus coyly accepts, with apologies to his Latin readers, several Greek terms now making their way back into Latin (he is himself a Greek!): *presbyter, diaconus, synodus, martyr*. The latter two are very public phenomena which he carefully explains. He also habitually assimilates the episcopal system to a military command structure. He accepts the professionalism of the Christian calling, and the dedication of virgins and martyrs. He likes the uncontentious, ethically quietist and tolerant elements. He recognizes the drive for orthodoxy, the political independence of bishops, the solidarity of the communities. He recoils from factionalism, brutality, pomp, and superstition as he saw it already in the churches.

Yet many crucial aspects escape him. He does not see the connection between doctrinal commitment and political troubles. He does not see the biblical sources of dogmatic controversy. He seems unaware of the influence

---

34. Tajra, *Martyrdom of St Paul*.

35. Bowersock, *Martyrdom and Rome*.

36. The following remarks are based upon my own reading of Ammianus—see Judge, "Christian Innovation" and "Absence of Religion," reproduced as chapters 7 and 9 respectively in the present volume. Recent studies include Barnes, *Ammianus Marcellinus*; Matthews, *Roman Empire*; Rike, *Apex Omnium*; Hunt, "Christians and Christianity"; Neri, *Ammiano e il cristianesimo*.

of women in the churches, of the charitable enterprise, even of monasticism (apart from the virgins). But he fully grasps the impact upon public life of the phenomenon he cannot either clearly perceive or define. He wants to isolate its positive behavior and assimilate that to the general good. In both his uncertainty and his intentions he is registering, as an instinctively responsible student, the historical novelty of beliefs about God creating an alternative culture, which is what we now mean by "religion."

Paul may not exactly have intended this for his "one new man," but it holds within it still the keys to the higher destiny he had in mind. The social impact has been profound, but mostly very long delayed.[37] However difficult it may be to trace historical cause and effect, one need have no doubt that in the long run a dominant source of cultural transformation in the West (and now worldwide) has been the churches' repeatedly seeking a fresh start from Scripture.[38]

---

37. According to Kinzig, *Novitas christiana*, reviewed by Wilken, Christianity did, probably, create the idea of cultural progress.

38. In Dr. Peter O'Brien we salute a master of that fine art, especially now in his searching commentary on the letter to the Ephesians.

16

Athena, the Unknown God of the Churches

This overview was first published (under the present title) in Judge, *Engaging Rome and Jerusalem*, 65–68. Prior to that, however, it was originally provided for an address delivered in 2001 to a meeting of ISCAST—the Institute for the Study of Christianity in an Age of Science and Technology—in Brisbane, Australia. It notes Graeco-Roman concepts of cult, theology, science, and ethics in order to ask how some of those concepts have been received (or challenged) in the history of the Roman and modern worlds. Given the context for which this piece was first developed, it has a particular focus on the interface of "science" and "religion."

"Science" and "religion" were, for most people in antiquity, not antithetical. *Theologia* was an element of science, since the gods were part of the material totality (though far removed from human interests, according to Epicurus). Only scientists (that is, "philosophers") held creed-like axioms. Creeds were not needed for the cult of the gods. The hated vulgarization of Christian dogma opened theology (and thus philosophy and science) to everyone, embedding belief and morality in ritualized worship. But the explosive results for science were delayed for 1,300 years because the churches also tied themselves to Aristotelian naturalism.

The classical "cult-group" (e.g., the synod of Highest Zeus) is a small self-governing men's club offering specific benefits, from drinking to funerals.[1] Their rules focus on curbing turmoil. The Pauline churches also had drinking problems, but were much more open (e.g., mixed membership) and dedicated to the reconstruction of social relationships through studied interaction. Unlike the Hellenistic clubs, they offered training for a new life.

---

1. Nock, *Essays on Religion*, 1:416. See now the texts collected in Ascough et al., *Associations*.

The Christian self-classification (*ekklēsia*) inescapably paralleled the public "assembly" of the civil body. Our word "church" loses this telling concurrence. But Luther translated it by *Gemeinde*, and every German place still embraces two modes of "community," civil and ecclesiastical.

The term "religion" also confuses the issue. Our concept of a series of religions dates only from 1614.[2] *Religio* meant the scrupulous practice of inherited rites (though often not understood). But when we speak of ancient "religions" we retroject our modern concept of religion as commitment to life-changing beliefs (which may set us apart from our tradition). Romans called this *superstitio*, and what they called *religio* we now call "superstition." The modern concept of "religion" comes from Christianization. Ancient cult was not meant to reform belief or life, but to anchor the status quo in ritual.

Theology and ethics belonged to philosophy. Over the first three centuries the churches rejected cult outright (as idolatrous) but came to terms with the cardinal virtues, *arete* (courage), prudence, self-control, and justice. They were the qualities of character by which philosophers had fortified the soul against passion (the shocks of contact with others). Paul's "things that abide," however, are not self-protective, but positive responses to others: *pistis* (trust), *elpis* (hope), and *agape* (care).

The late first-century letter of Ammonius to Apollonius (P.Oxy. 42.3057) reveals an ethical counselor cautioning his patron against the risk of troubles amongst his circle. It would give "others" occasion against them. He urges *homonoia* ("oneness of mind") and *philallelia* ("mutual attraction"). This has led to the proposal that it is a Christian letter (and, if so, the earliest recovered from Egyptian papyri). The sentiments (though not the words) may remind one of Paul. But in his greeting and farewell Ammonius again offers no echo of biblical phraseology, such as might have been expected if that was his guiding light. By contrast, his delicate feeling for status (which Paul had scornfully rejected) seems central to the bond.

The apologists, however, leaned more towards the classical ideals, as we do now. *Arete* is written into our prayers as the new means of grace ("courage to believe," "courage to embrace forgiveness," etc.). Secular ethicists turn even the Pauline outreach itself into self-protection ("taking care of yourself is a form of kindness," "fidelity . . . is about being faithful to yourself and your needs"). Yet the whole community now admires compassion (once a vice of the soul, like cruelty), and commitment.

In 362 Julian took over the empire and debarred Christians from teaching in the classical schools. Since they did not accept the gods of

---

2. Harrison, *'Religion' and the Religions*, 39.

Homer, they could not conscientiously teach from the classics. Instead, they should start their own schools and teach from the Bible. Julian knew it well (he was the last of Constantine's house). He also knew that biblical Greek was educationally impossible (it was too "common"). Apollinarius set out to paraphrase it all into the classical styles. Marius Victorinus left his chair of rhetoric at Rome to write philosophical theology, and commentaries on Paul. But the bishop of Troy, Pegasius, sided with Julian. Eight years before, when the latter's change of heart was not yet public, Pegasius had shown him the local temple of Athena, closed now but carefully preserved. The bishop had kept the key.[3]

But the long custody of classical culture by the churches did not in the end lock away the new view of the world. When symbolism was finally abandoned as the key to Scripture, and it was taken at face value, the perfect and eternal cosmos of Aristotle was opened to the test of experiment, history to documentary proof, and public life challenged by dissent.

In the twenty-first century the churches are still often left nourishing a conservative social and intellectual culture and its unknown god (Athena!). Science is presented by the media as their enemy. But modern science (the empirical as distinct from logical testing of fact) is itself the product of the biblical doctrine of creation. (It is not merely ironic that contemporary cosmology also posits a beginning and an end, in contrast with the perpetual circularity of Greek logic.) Yet church life tends to foster a harmonious fatalism that is the hangover from Paul's Stoic peers, while environmentalism absorbs man back into a static, naturalistic cosmos that has no proper conceptual basis in the evolutionary science spawned out of Genesis.

---

3. Julian, *Ep.* 19.

Bibliography

Adam, A. "Der Monachos-Gedanke innerhalb der Spiritualität der alten Kirche." In *Glaube, Geist, Geschichte: Festschrift E. Benz zum 60. Geburtstage am 17. November 1967*, edited by G. Muller and W. Zeller, 259–65. Leiden: Brill, 1967.

———. "Grundbegriffe des Mönchtums in sprachlicher Sicht." *ZKG* 64 (1953–1954) 209–39.

Adams, J. duQ. *The Populus of Augustine and Jerome: A Study in the Patristic Sense of Community*. New Haven, CT: Yale University Press, 1971.

Afanassieff, N. "L'Assemblée eucharistique unique dans l'Église ancienne." *Kleronomia* 6 (1974) 1–36.

Alfaric, P. *Origines sociales du Christianisme*. Paris: Publications de l'Union rationaliste, 1959.

Alföldy, Geza. *Römische Sozialgeschichte*. Wiesbaden: Steiner, 1975.

Allenbach, J., et al., eds. *Biblia patristica: index des citations et allusions bibliques dans la litterature patristique*. 7 vols plus supplement. Paris: Centre National de la Recherche Scientifique, 1975–2000.

Alonso-Núñez, J. M. Review of *Ammiano e il cristianesimo*, by V. Neri. *CR* 37 (1987) 103–4.

Ameling, W. *Herodes Atticus*. Hildesheim: Olms, 1983.

Anderson, J. *Studies in Empirical Philosophy*. Sydney: Angus & Robertson, 1962.

André, J.-M. "Les écoles philosophiques aux deux premiers siècles de l'Empire." *ANRW* II 36 (1987) 5–77.

Andresen, C. *Die Kirchen der alten Christenheit*. Stuttgart: Kohlhammer, 1971.

———. *Logos und Nomos: die Polemik des Kelsos wider das Christentum*. Berlin: De Gruyter, 1955.

Angliviel de la Beaumelle, L. "Remarques sur l'attitude d'Ammien Marcellin à l'égard du christianisme." In *Mélanges d'histoire ancienne offerts à William Seston*, 15–23. Paris: Boccard, 1974.

Applebaum, S. "The Organization of the Jewish Communities in the Diaspora." In *The Jewish People in the First Century: Historical Geography, Political History, Social, Cultural and Religious Life and Institutions*, edited by S. Safrai and M. Stern with D. Flusser and W. C. van Unnik, 1:464–503. Assen: Van Gorcum, 1974.

Arnaoutoglou, I. *Forms and Legal Aspects of Religious Associations in Ancient Athens*. PhD diss., University of Glasgow, 1993.

Arnold, C. B. *The Colossian Syncretism: The Interface between Christianity and Folk Belief*. Tübingen: Mohr Siebeck, 1995.

Ascough, R. S. "Translocal Relationships Among Voluntary Associations and Early Christianity." *JECS* 5 (1997) 223–41.
Ascough, R. S., et al. *Associations in the Greco-Roman World: A Sourcebook.* Waco, TX: Baylor University Press, 2012.
Aune, D. E. *The Cultic Setting of Realized Eschatology in Early Christianity.* Leiden: Brill, 1972.
Ausbüttel, F. M. *Untersuchungen zu den Vereinen im Westen des römischen Reiches.* Kallmünz: Lassleben, 1982.
Bachmann, M. "Zur Rezeptions-und Traditionsgeschichte des paulinischen Ausdrucks ἔργα νόμου: Notizen im Blick auf Verhaltensregeln im frühen Christentum als einer 'Gruppenreligion.'" In *Gruppenreligionen im römischen Reich*, edited by J. Rüpke, 69–86. Tübingen: Mohr Siebeck, 2007.
Bacht, H. *Antonius und Pachomius: von der Anachorese zum Cönobitentum.* Rome: Herder, 1956.
Banks, R. *Paul's Idea of Community: The Early House Churches in their Historical Setting.* 2nd ed. Peabody, MA: Hendrickson, 1994.
Barclay, W. "The One New Man." In *Unity and Diversity in New Testament Theology. Essays in Honor of George E. Ladd*, edited by R. A. Guelich, 73–81. Grand Rapids: Eerdmans, 1978.
Barison, P. "Ricerche sui monasteri dell'Egitto bizantino ed arabo secondo i documenti dei papiri greci." *Aeg* 18 (1938) 29–148.
Barnes, J. "Ancient Philosophers." In *Philosophy and Power in the Graeco-Roman World: Essays in Honour of Miriam Griffin*, edited by G. Clark and T. Rajak, 293–306. Oxford: Oxford University Press, 2002.
Barnes, T. D. *Ammianus Marcellinus and the Representation of Historical Reality.* London: Cornell University Press, 1998.
———. "Porphyry *Against the Christians*: Date and the Attribution of Fragments." *The Journal of Theological Studies* 24 (1973) 424–442.
———. *Tertullian: A Historical and Literary Study.* Oxford: Clarendon Press, 1971.
Barrow, R. H. *Prefect and Emperor: The "Relationes" of Symmachus, A.D. 384.* Oxford: Clarendon, 1973.
Bartelink, G. J. M. "Eunape et le vocabulaire chrétien." *VC* 23 (1969) 293–303.
———. "*Thiasos* et *thiasōtēs* chez les auteurs chrétiens." *OCP* 45 (1979) 267–78.
———. *Vita di Antonio.* Verona: Mondadori, 1974.
Barton, S. C. "The Communal Dimension of Earliest Christianity: A Critical Survey of the Field." *JTS* 43 (1992) 399–427.
Barton, S. C., and G. H. R. Horsley. "A Hellenistic Cult Group and the New Testament Churches." *JAC* 24 (1981) 7–41.
Baslez, M.-F. *Recherches sur les conditions de pénétration et de diffusion des religions orientales à Délos.* Paris: École normale supérieure de jeunes filles, 1977.
———. "Une association isiaque: les Mélanéphores" *CdE* 50 (1975) 297–303.
Bauckham, R. *Jude and the Relatives of Jesus in the Early Church.* Edinburgh: T. & T. Clark, 1990.
Baumgarten, A. *The Flourishing of Jewish Sects in the Maccabean Era: An Interpretation.* Leiden: Brill, 1997.
———. "Graeco-Roman Voluntary Associations and Ancient Jewish Sects." In *Jews in a Graeco-Roman World*, edited by M. Goodman, 93–111. Oxford: Oxford University Press, 1998.

Beall, T. S. *Josephus' Description of the Essenes Illustrated by the Dead Sea Scrolls.* Cambridge: Cambridge University Press, 1988.
Beard, M., J. North, and S. Price, eds. *Religions of Rome.* 2 vols. Cambridge: Cambridge University Press, 1998.
Beck, R. "The Mithras Cult as Association." *SR* 21 (1992) 3–13.
———. "The Mysteries of Mithras: A New Account of their Genesis." *JRS* 88 (1998) 115–28.
Bekker-Nielsen, T. *Urban Life and Local Politics in Roman Bithynia. The Small World of Dion Chrysostomos.* Aarhus: Aarhus University Press, 2008.
Benoît, A. "Le Contra christianos de Porphyre: où en est la collecte des fragments?" In *Paganisme, Judaïsme, Christianisme: Influences et affrontements dans le monde antique, Mélanges offerts à Marcel Simon,* 261–75. Paris: Boccard, 1978.
Berger, K. "Volksversammlung und Gemeinde Gottes. Zu den Anfängen der christlichen Verwendung von 'ekklesia.'" *ZTK* 73 (1976) 167–207.
Betz, H. D. "The Birth of Christianity as a Hellenistic Religion." *JR* 74 (1994) 1–25.
———. *Der Apostel Paulus und die sokratische Tradition.* Tübingen: Mohr Siebeck, 1972.
Bianchi, U., and Vermaseren, M. J. *La soteriologia dei culti orientali nell' impero romano.* Leiden: Brill, 1982.
Bidez, I., and F. Cumont. *Imp. Caesaris Flavii Claudii Juliani: Epistulae, Leges, Poematia, Fragmenta Varia.* Paris: Belles Lettres, 1922.
Bilde, P. "The Meaning of Roman Mithraism." In *Rethinking Religion: Studies in the Hellenistic Process,* edited by J. Podemann Sørensen, 31–47. Copenhagen: Museum Tusculanum Press, 1989.
Billot, F. "Académie (topographie et archéologie)." In *Dictionnaire des philosophes antiques,* edited by R. Goulet, 1:693–789. Paris: Centre national de la recherche scientifique, 1989.
Binder, D. D. *Into the Temple Courts the Place of the Synagogues in the Second Temple Period.* Atlanta: Society of Biblical Literature, 1999.
Blockley, R. C. *Ammianus Marcellinus: A Study of his Historiography and Political Thought.* Brussels: Latomus, 1975.
Blue, B. B. "Acts and the House Church." In *The Book of Acts in Its Graeco-Roman Setting,* edited by D. W. J. Gill and C. Gempf, 119–222. Grand Rapids: Eerdmans, 1994.
Boak, A. E. R., and H. C. Youtie. *The Archive of Aurelius Isidorus in the Egyptian Museum, Cairo, and the University of Michigan.* Ann Arbor: University of Michigan Press, 1960.
Boer, W. den. *Scriptorum paganorum I-IV saec. de Christianis testimonia.* Leiden: Brill, 1948.
Bolkestein, H. *Wohltätigkeit und Armenpflege im vorchristlichen Altertum: Ein Beitrag zum Problem "Moral und Gesellschaft."* Utrecht: Oosthoek, 1939.
Bolyki, J. *Jesu Tischgemeinschaften.* Tübingen: Mohr Siebeck 1998.
Bookidis, N. "Ritual Dining in the Sanctuary of Demeter and Kore at Corinth: Some Questions." In *Sympotica: A Symposium on the Symposion,* edited by O. Murray, 86–94. Oxford: Oxford University Press, 1990.
Boon, A. *Pachomiana latina. Règle et épîtres de s. Pachôme, épître de s. Théodore et 'Liber' de s. Orsiesius.* Leuven: Bureaux de la Revue, 1932.

Borrett, M. "Celsus: A Pagan Perspective on Scripture." In *The Bible in Greek Christian Antiquity*, edited by P. M. Blowers, 259-88. Notre Dame: University of Notre Dame Press, 1997.

Boucher, F. *A History of Costume in the West*. London: Thames & Hudson, 1967.

Bowersock, G. *Julian the Apostate*. Cambridge, MA: Harvard University Press, 1978.

———. *Martyrdom and Rome*. Cambridge: Cambridge University Press, 1995.

———. "Philosophy in the Second Sophistic." In *Philosophy and Power in the Graeco-Roman World: Essays in Honour of Miriam Griffin*, edited by G. Clark and T. Rajak, 157-70. Oxford: Oxford University Press, 2002.

Boyce, M. *Textual Sources for the Study of Zoroastrianism*. Manchester: Manchester University Press, 1984.

Brakke, D. *Athanasius and the Politics of Asceticism*. Oxford: Clarendon, 1995.

Brashear, W. M. *A Mithraic Catechism from Egypt: (P.Berol. 21196)*. Vienna: Holzhausens, 1992.

———. *Vereine im griechisch-römischen Ägypten*. Konstanz: Universitätsverlag Konstanz, 1993.

Bremmer, J. *The Apocryphal Acts of Paul and Thecla*. Kampen: Kok Pharos, 1996.

Brent, A. *The Imperial Cult and the Development of Church Order: Concepts and Images of Authority in Paganism and Early Christianity Before the Age of Cyprian*. Leiden: Brill, 1999.

Brerewood, E. *Enquiries Touching the Diversity of Languages and Religions through the Cheife Parts of the World*. London: John Bill, 1614.

Bricault, L. "Isis Myrionyme." In *Hommages à Jean Leclant: Études Isiaques*, edited by C. M. Berger et al., 3:67-86. Cairo: Institut français d'archéologie orientale, 1994.

———. *Myrionymi: Les épiclèses grecques et latines d'Isis, de Sarapis et d'Anubis*. Berlin: De Gruyter, 1996.

Brown, P. R. L. "Arnaldo Dante Momigliano, 1908-1987." *Proceedings of the British Academy* 74 (1988) 405-42.

———. *The Body and Society: Men, Women, and Sexual Renunciation in Early Christianity*. New York: Columbia University Press, 1988.

———. *The Cult of the Saints: its Rise and Function in Latin Christianity*. Chicago: Chicago University Press, 1981.

———. *The Making of Late Antiquity*. Cambridge, MA: Harvard University Press, 1978.

———. "The Rise and Function of the Holy Man in Late Antiquity." *JRS* 61 (1971) 80-101.

———. *The World of Late Antiquity: AD 150-750*. London: Thames and Hudson, 1971.

Brown, R. E. *The Community of the Beloved Disciple*. New York: Paulist, 1979.

Browning, R. *The Emperor Julian*. London: Weidenfeld and Nicolson, 1975.

Burkert, W. *Ancient Mystery Cults*. Cambridge, MA: Harvard University Press, 1987.

———. "Craft Versus Sect: The Problem of Orphics and Pythagoreans." In *Jewish and Christian Self-Definition: Self-Definition in the Greco-Roman World*, edited by B. Meyer and E. P. Sanders, 1-22. Philadelphia: Fortress, 1982.

Cameron, Alan. *Claudian: Poetry and Propaganda at the Court of Honorius*. Oxford: Clarendon, 1970.

———. "Paganism and Literature in Late Fourth Century Rome." In *Christianisme et formes littéraires de l'Antiquité tardive en Occident*, edited by M. Fuhrmann, 1-30. Geneva: Fondation Hardt, 1977.

———. "Palladas and Christian Polemic." *JRS* 55 (1965) 17-30.

---. Review of *Ammianus and the Historia Augusta*, by R. Syme. *JRS* 61 (1971) 255–67.

Cameron, Averil. *Christianity and the Rhetoric of Empire: The Development of Christian Discourse*. Berkeley: University of California Press, 1991.

Cameron, A., and A. Cameron. "Christianity and Tradition in the Historiography of the Late Empire." *CQ* 14 (1964) 316–28.

Campbell, J. Y. "The Origin and Meaning of the Christian Use of the Word *ekklesia*." *JTS* 49 (1948) 130–142.

Camus, P.-M. *Ammien Marcellin: témoin des courants culturels et religieux à la fin du IVe siècle*. Paris: Belles Lettres, 1967.

Cancik, H. "Haus, Schule, Gemeinde: Zur Organisation von 'fremder Religion' in Rom (1– 3.Jh.n.Chr.)." In *Gruppenreligionen im römischen Reich*, edited by J. Rüpke, 31–48. Tübingen: Mohr Siebeck, 2007.

---. "The History of Culture, Religion, and Institutions in Ancient Historiography: Philological Observations concerning Luke's History." *JBL* 116 (1997) 673–95.

---. "Wahrnehmung, Vermeidung, Entheiligung, Aneignung: Fremde Religionen bei Tertullian, im Talmud (AZ) und bei Eusebius." In *Texte als Medium und Reflexion von Religion im römischen Reich*, edited by D. Elm von der Osten et al., 227–32.

Cancik, H., and J. Rüpke, eds. *Römische Reichsreligion und Provinzialreligion*. Tübingen: Mohr Siebeck, 1997.

Cansdale, L. *Qumran and the Essenes. A Re-Evaluation of the Evidence*. Tübingen: Mohr Siebeck, 1997.

Cantwell Smith, W. *The Meaning and End of Religion: a New Approach to the Religious Traditions of Mankind*. New York: Macmillan, 1962.

Carleton Paget, J. "Jewish Proselytism at the Time of Christian Origins: Chimera or Reality?" *JSNT* 62 (1996) 65–103.

Carlini, A., and M. Bandini. "P. Bodmer XLVII: un acrostico alfabetico tra Susanna–Daniele e Tucidide." *MH* 48 (1991) 158–68.

Case, S. J. *The Social Origins of Christianity*. Chicago: University of Chicago, 1923.

Castritius, H. *Studien zu Maximinus Daia*. Kallmünz: Lassleben, 1969.

Cataudella, M. "La persecuzione di Licinio e l'autenticità della Vita Constantini." *Athenaeum* 48 (1970) 48–83, 229–59.

Chadwick, H. "Enkrateia." *RAC* 5 (1962) 343–65.

---. *Origen: Contra Celsum*. Cambridge: Cambridge University Press, 1953.

Chadwick, N. K. *Poetry and Letters in Early Christian Gaul*. London: Bowes & Bowes, 1955.

Chamblin, J. K. "Psychology." In *Dictionary of Paul and his Letters*, edited by G. F. Hawthorne et al., 765–75. Downers Grove, IL: Intervarsity, 1993.

Charlesworth, J. H., and M. A. Knibb. "Community Organization." In *Encyclopedia of the Dead Sea Scrolls*, edited by L. H. Sciffman and J. C. VanderKam, 133–40. New York: Oxford University Press, 2000.

Chastagnol, A., et al., eds. *L'Année épigraphique* 1988 (1991) 281–82.

Chitty, D. J. *The Desert a City: An Introduction to the Study of Egyptian and Palestinian Monasticism Under the Christian Empire*. Oxford: Blackwell, 1966.

Christiansen, E.J. "The Consciousness of Belonging to God's Covenant and What it Entails According to the Damascus Document and the Community Rule." In *Qumran Between the Old and New Testaments*, edited by F. H. Cryer and T. L. Thompson, 69–97. Sheffield: Sheffield Academic, 1998.

Clarke, A. D. *Serve the Community of the Church: Christians as Leaders and Ministers.* Grand Rapids: Eerdmans, 2000.

Clarke, G. W. "Two Mid-third Century Bishops: Cyprian of Carthage and Dionysius of Alexandria." In *Ancient History in a Modern University: Early Christianity, Late Antiquity, and Beyond*, edited by T. W. Hillard, R. A. Kearsley, C. E. V. Nixon, and A. M. Nobbs, 317–28. Grand Rapids: Eerdmans, 1998.

Claude, D. *Adel, Kirche und Königtum im Westgotenreich.* Sigmaringen: Jan Thorbecke Verlag, 1971.

Clauss, M. *Cultores Mithrae: die Anhängerschaft des Mithras-Kultes.* Stuttgart: Steiner, 1992.

———. *The Roman Cult of Mithras: The God and His Mysteries.* New York: Routledge, 2000.

Cole, S.G. "The Mysteries at Samothrace during the Roman Period." *ANRW* II 18 (1989) 1564–98.

———. *Theoi Megaloi: The Cult of the Great Gods at Samothrace.* Leiden: Brill, 1984.

Colpe, C. "Mysterienkult und Liturgie: Zum Vergleich heidnischer Rituale und christlicher Sakramente." In *Spätantike und Christentum: Beiträge zur Religions- und Geistesgeschichte der griechisch-römischen Kultur und Zivilisation der Kaiserzeit*, edited by C. Colpe, L. Honnefelder and M. Lutz-Bachmann, 203–28. Berlin: Akademie Verlag, 1992.

Corsten, T. *Die Inschriften von Prusa ad Olympum.* 2 vols. Bonn: Habelt, 1991–1993.

———, ed. *A Lexicon of Greek Personal Names.* Vol. VA. Coastal Asia Minor: Pontos to Ionia. Oxford: Clarendon, 2010.

Cotter, W. "The Collegia and Roman Law: State Restrictions on Voluntary Associations 64 BCE-200 CE." In *Voluntary Associations in the Graeco-Roman World*, edited by J. S. Kloppenborg and S. G. Wilson, 74–89. London: Routledge, 1996.

Cotton, H. M., et al., eds. *Corpus Inscriptionum Iudaeae/Palaestinae: A Multi-Lingual Corpus of the Inscriptions from Alexander to Muhammad, volume 1: Jerusalem.* Berlin: De Gruyter, 2010.

Countryman, L. W. *The Rich Christian in the Church of the Early Empire: Contradictions and Accommodations.* New York: Mellen, 1980.

Courcelle, P. *Recherches sur Saint Ambroise.* Paris: Études Augustiniennes, 1973.

Creed, J. L. *Lactantius: De mortibus persecutorum.* Oxford: Clarendon, 1984.

Croke, B. "The Era of Porphyry's Anti-Christian Polemic." *JRH* 13 (1984) 1–14.

Cross, F. L., and E. A. Livingstone, eds. *The Oxford Dictionary of the Christian Church.* Rev. 3rd ed. Oxford: Oxford University Press, 2005.

Crum, W. E. "Texts Attributed to Peter of Alexandria." *JTS* 4 (1903) 387–97.

Crum, W. E., and H. G. Evelyn-White. *The Monastery of Epiphanius at Thebes.* New York: Arno, 1973.

Cumont, F. "La grande inscription bacchique du Metropolitan Museum, II. Commentaire religieux de l'inscription." *AJA* 37 (1933) 232–67.

Dagron, G. *Naissance d'une capitale: Constantinople et ses institutions de 330 à 451.* Paris: Presses Universitaires de France, 1974.

Dahl, N. A. *Das Volk Gottes: Eine Untersuchung zum Kirchenbewusstsein des Urchristentums.* Darmstadt: Wissenschaftliche Buchgesellschaft, 1963.

Dassmann, E. *Der Stachel im Fleisch: Paulus in der frühchristlichen literatur bis Irenäus.* Münster: Aschendorff, 1979.

———. "Kirche, geistliches Amt und Gemeindeverständnis zwischen antikem Erbe und christlichen Impulsen." In *Spätantike und Christentum: Beiträge zur Religions- und Geistesgeschichte der griechisch-römischen Kultur und Zivilisation der Kaiserzeit*, edited by C. Colpe, L. Honnefelder and M. Lutz-Bachmann, 249–69. Berlin: Akademie Verlag, 1992.

Davies, P. R. *The Damascus Covenant: An Interpretation of the "Damascus Document."* Sheffield: PUB, 1983.

Davies, J. P. *Rome's Religious History: Livy, Tacitus, and Ammianus on their Gods*. Cambridge: Cambridge University Press, 2004.

Davies, S. L. *The Revolt of the Widows: The Social World of the Apocryphal Acts*. Carbondale: Southern Illinois University Press, 1980.

De Cazanove, O. *L'association dionysiaque dans les sociétés anciennes: Actes de la Table ronde organisée par l'École Française de Rome (Rome 24–25 mai 1984)*. Rome: Ecole française de Rome, 1986.

De Cenival, F. *Les associations religieuses en Égypte d'après les documents démotiques*. Cairo: Institut français d'archéologie orientale, 1972.

De Coulanges, Fustel. *La cité antique: Étude sur le culte, le droit, les institutions de la Grèce et de Rome*. Paris: Hachette, 1908.

De Jonge, P. *Philological and Historical Commentary on Ammianus Marcellinus XVIII*. Groningen: Bouma, 1980.

De Labriolle, P. *La Réaction païenne: Étude sur la polémique antichrétienne du 1er au VIe siècle*. Paris: L'artisan du livre, 1934.

De Robertis, F. M. *Storia delle corporazioni e del regime associativo nel mondo romano*. 2 vols. Bari: Adriatica, 1971.

De Ste Croix, G. E. M. *The Class Struggle in the Ancient Greek World: From the Archaic Age to the Arab Conquests*. Ithaca: Cornell University Press, 1981.

De Valois, H. "Eusebii Pamphili: Ecclesiasticæ Historiæ." In *Patrologiae Cursus Completus: Series Græca*, edited by J.-P. Migne, 20:10–44. Paris: Petit-Montrouge, 1857.

Deines, R. "The Pharisees." In *Justification and Variegated Nomism: The Complexities of Second Temple Judaism*, edited by D. A. Carson et al., 443–504. Tübingen: Mohr Siebeck, 2001.

Deissmann, A. *Das Urchristentum und die unteren Schichten*. Göttingen: Vandenhoeck & Ruprecht, 1908.

———. *Licht vom Osten: Das Neue Testament und die neudeckten Texte der hellenistisch-römischen Welt*. Tübingen: J. C. B. Mohr, 1908.

Delbridge, A., ed. *The Macquarie Dictionary*. St. Leonards, NSW: Macquarie Library, 1981.

Demarolle, J.-M. "Les femmes chrétiennes vues par Porphyre." *JAC* 13 (1970) 42–47.

deSilva, D. A. *Perseverance in Gratitude: A Socio-Rhetorical Commentary on the Epistle to the Hebrews*. Grand Rapids: Eerdmans, 2000.

Diesner, H.-J. *Studien zur Gesellschaftslehre und sozialen Haltung Augustins*. Halle: Niemeyer, 1954.

Dieterich, A. *Eine Mithrasliturgie*. 3rd ed. Leipzig: Teubner, 1923.

Dihle, A. "Antikes und Unantikes in der früchristlichen Staatstheorie." In *Assimilation et résistance à la culture gréco-romaine dans le monde ancien. Travaux du VIe Congrès International d'Etudes Classiques (Madrid, Septembre 1974)*, edited by D. M. Pippidi, 323–32. Bucharest: Editura Academiei, 1976.

———. "Ethik." *RAC* 6 (1964) 646–797.
———. *Der Kanon der zwei Tugenden*. Cologne: Westdeutscher Verlag, 1968.
Dillon, J. T. *Musonius Rufus and Education in The Good Life: A Model of Teaching and Living Virtue*. Dallas: University Press of America, 2004.
Dindorf, W. *Aristides*. Hildesheim: Olms, 1964.
Doblhofer, E., ed. *Rutilius Namatianus: De reditu suo siue iter Gallicum*. Heidelberg: Winter, 1972.
Dodds, E. R. *Pagan and Christian in an Age of Anxiety: Some Aspects of Religious Experience from Marcus Aurelius to Constantine*. Cambridge: Cambridge University Press, 1965.
Dorandi, T. "Organization and Structure of the Philosophical Schools." In *The Cambridge History of Hellenistic Philosophy*, edited by K. Algra et al., 55–62. Cambridge: Cambridge University Press, 1999.
Dörries, H. *Das Selbstzeugnis Kaiser Konstantins*. Göttingen: Vandenhoeck & Ruprecht, 1964.
———. *Die Vita Antonii als Geschichtsquelle*. Göttingen: Vandenhoeck & Ruprecht, 1949.
———. "Zur Auseinandersetzung zwischen Platonismus und Christentum." In *Platonica Minora*, 454–523. Munich: Fink, 1976.
Downey, G. "Themistius and the Defense of Hellenism in the Fourth Century." *HTR* 50 (1957) 259–74.
Draguet, R. "Une lettre de Sérapion de Thmuis." *Mus* 64 (1951) 1–25.
Drexler, H. *Ammianstudien*. Hildesheim: Olms, 1974.
Duchrow, U. *Christenheit und Weltverantwortung: Traditionsgeschichte und systematische Struktur der Zweireichelehre*. Stuttgart: Klett, 1970.
Dunn, J. D. G. "Boundary Markers in Early Christianity." In *Gruppenreligionen im römischen Reich*, edited by J. Rüpke, 49–68. Tübingen: Mohr Siebeck, 2007.
Eck, W. "Der Einfluss der konstantinischen Wende auf die Auswahl der Bischöfe im 4. und 5. Jahrhundert." *Chiron* 8 (1978) 561–85.
Ego, B., et al., eds. *Gemeinde ohne Tempel: zur Substituierung und Transformation des Jerusalemer Tempels und seines Kults im alten Testament, antiken Judentum und frühen Christentum*. Tübingen: Mohr Siebeck, 1999.
Ehrhardt, A. "Das Corpus Christi und die Korporationen im spätrömischen Recht." *Romanistische Abteilung* 70 (1953) 299–347 and 71 (1954) 25–40.
Ehrhardt, C. T. H. R. "Eusebius and Celsus." *JAC* 22 (1979) 40–49.
Eingartner, J. *Isis und ihre Dienerinnen in der Kunst der römischen Kaiserzeit*. Leiden: Brill, 1991.
Elliott, J. H. *A Home for the Homeless: A Sociological Exegesis of 1 Peter, its Situation and Strategy*. Philadelphia: Fortress, 1981.
Emmett, A. M. "The Digressions in the Lost Books of Ammianus Marcellinus." In *History and Historians in Late Antiquity*, edited by B. Croke and A. Emmett, 42–53. Sydney: Pergamon, 1983.
———. "A Fourth-Century Hymn to the Virgin Mary?" In *New Documents Illustrating Early Christianity: A Review of Greek Inscriptions and Papyri Published in 1977*, edited by G. H. R. Horsley, 141–46. North Ryde: The Ancient History Documentary Research Centre, 1982.
———. "The Subject of Psalmus Responsorius: P. Barc. 149b–153." *Museum Philologum Londiniense* 2 (1977) 99–108.

Engelmann, H. *Die delische Sarapisaretalogie*. Meisenheim: Hain, 1964.
Evans, J. A. S. *A Social and Economic History of an Egyptian Temple in the Greco-Roman Period*. New Haven, CT: Yale University Press, 1961.
Feeney, D. C. *Literature and Religion at Rome: Cultures, Contexts, and Beliefs*. Cambridge: Cambridge University Press, 1998.
Feil, E. *Religio: die Geschichte eines neuzeitlichen Grundbegriffs vom Frühchristentum bis zur Reformation*. 2 vols. Göttingen: Vandenhoeck & Ruprecht, 1986–1997.
Feld, H. *Der Kaiser Licinius*. PhD diss., Universität Saarbrücken, 1960.
Ferguson, E., ed. *Encyclopedia of Early Christianity*. London: St. James, 1990.
Ferguson, W. S. "The Attic Orgeones." *HTR* 37 (1944) 61–140.
Festugiére, A. J. *Antioche paienne et chrétienne: Libanius, Chrysostome et les moines de Syrie*. Paris: de Boccard, 1959.
———. *La révélation d' Hermes Trismégiste: L'astrologie et les sciences occultes*. Paris: Belles Lettres, 1989.
Feuerbach, L. *Principles of the Philosophy of the Future*. New York; Indianapolis: Bobbs-Merrill, 1966.
Filson, F. V. "The Significance of the Early House Churches." *JBL* 58 (1939) 105–12.
Finley, M. *The Ancient Economy*. Berkeley: University of California Press, 1973.
Fisher, N. R. E. "Greek Associations, Symposia, and Clubs." In *Civilization of the Ancient Mediterranean: Greece and Rome*, edited by M. Grant and R. Kitzinger, 2:1167–97. New York: Scribner's, 1988.
———. "Roman Associations, Dinner Parties, and Clubs." In *Civilization of the Ancient Mediterranean: Greece and Rome*, edited by M. Grant and R. Kitzinger, 2:1199–1225. New York: Scribner's, 1988.
Flamant, J. *Macrobe et le néoplatonisme latin, à la fin du 4e siècle*. Leiden: Brill, 1979.
Foerster, R. *Libanii Opera*. Leipzig: Teubner, 1903.
Fontaine, J. "L'apport de la tradition poétique romaine à la formation de l'hymnodie latine chrétienne." *Revue des études latines* 52 (1974) 318–55.
Foucart, P. *Des associations religieuses chez les Grecs, thiases, éranes, orgéons*. Paris: Chez Klincksieck, 1873.
Fowden, G. *The Egyptian Hermes: A Historical Approach to the Late Pagan Mind*. Cambridge: Cambridge University Press, 1986.
Fredouille, J.-C. *Tertullien et la conversion de la culture antique*. Paris: Études Augustiniennes, 1972.
Frend, W. H. C. *The Donatist Church: A Movement of Protest in Roman North Africa*. Oxford: Clarendon, 1952.
Freyburger-Galland, M.-L. "Les associations religieuses." In *Sectes religieuses en Grèce et à Rome dans l'antiquité païenne*, edited by M.-L. Freyburger-Galland et al., 61–74. Paris: Belles Lettres, 1986.
Freyne, S. *Galilee: From Alexander the Great to Hadrian, 323 B.C.E. to 135 C.E.: A Study of Second Temple Judaism*. Edinburgh: T. & T. Clark, 1980.
Frick, F. S. "Rechab, Rechabite." In *Anchor Bible Dictionary*, edited by David Noel Freedman, 5:630–32. New York: Doubleday, 1992.
Frisch, P. *Zehn agonistische Papyri*. Opladen: Westdeutscher Verlag, 1986.
Frischer, B. *The Sculpted Word: Epicureanism and Philosophical Recruitment in Ancient Greece*. Berkeley: University of California Press, 1982.
Gagé, J. *Les classes sociales dans l'Empire romain*. Paris: Payot, 1964.

Gager, John G. *Kingdom and Community: The Social World of Early Christianity.* Englewood Cliffs, NJ: Prentice-Hall, 1975.
———. "Shall We Marry Our Enemies? Sociology and the New Testament." *Int* 36 (1982) 256–65.
Galletier, É., and J. Fontaine. *Ammien Marcellin: Histoire.* 6 vols. Paris: Belles Lettres, 1968–99.
Garland, R. *The Piraeus: From the Fifth to the First Century BC.* Ithaca, NY: Cornell University Press, 1987.
Garnsey, P. *Social Status and Legal Privilege in the Roman Empire.* Oxford: Clarendon, 1970.
Gaudemet, J. *L'Église dans l'Empire romain (IVe—Ve siècles).* Paris: Sirey, 1958.
Gill, C. "The Question of Character Development: Plutarch and Tacitus." *CQ* 33 (1983) 469–87.
———. "The School in the Roman Imperial Period." In *The Cambridge Companion to the Stoics,* edited by B. Inwood, 33–58. Cambridge: Cambridge University Press, 2003.
Gingras, G. E. *Egeria: Diary of a Pilgrimage.* Ancient Christian Writers 38. New York: Newman, 1970.
Giversen, Soren. "Hermetic Communities?" In *Rethinking Religion: Studies in the Hellenistic Process,* edited by J. Podemann Sørensen, 49–54. Copenhagen: Museum Tusculanum, 1989.
Glare, P. G. W. *Oxford Latin Dictionary.* 8 vols. Oxford: Oxford University Press, 1968–1982.
Goodman, M. "Jewish Proselytising in the First Century." In *Jews among Pagans and Christians in the Roman Empire,* edited by J. Lieu et al., 53–78. London: Routledge, 1992.
———. "Nerva, the Fiscus Judaicus and Jewish Identity." *JRS* 79 (1989) 40–44.
Gorce, D. *Vie de Sainte Mélanie.* Paris: Éditions du Cerf, 1962.
Gordon, R. L. "Mithraism and Roman Society: Social Factors in the Explanation of Religious Change in the Roman Empire." *Religion* 2 (1972) 92–121.
Gougaud, L. "Les critiques formulées contre les premiers moines d'occident." *Revue Mabillon* 24 (1934) 145–63.
Gould, G. *The Desert Fathers on Monastic Community.* Oxford: Clarendon, 1993.
Goulet-Cazé, M.-O. "L'école de Plotin." In *Porphyre. La vie de Plotin,* edited by L. Brisson et al., 1:231–57. Paris: Vrin, 1982.
Graf, F. "Dionysian and Orphic Eschatology." In *Masks of Dionysus,* edited by T. Carpenter and C. Faraone, 239–58. Ithaca: Cornell University Press, 1993.
Graham, A. Review of *Emperors and Biography,* by R. Syme. *JRS* 63 (1973) 259–60.
Grandjean, Yves. *Une nouvelle arétalogie d'Isis à Maronée.* Leiden: Brill, 1975.
Grant, F. C. *The Economic Background of the Gospels.* London: Oxford University Press, 1926.
Grant, R. M. *Augustus to Constantine: The Rise and Triumph of Christianity in the Roman World.* New York: Harper and Row, 1970.
———. "The Case Against Eusebius: Or, Did the Father of the Church History Write History." *STPatr* 12 (1975) 413–21.
———. *Early Christianity and Society: Seven Studies.* New York: Harper and Row, 1977.

BIBLIOGRAPHY

———. *The Social Setting of Second-Century Christianity*. In *Jewish and Christian Self-Definition: The Shaping of Christianity in the Second and Third Centuries*, edited by E. P. Sanders, 16–29. Philadelphia: Fortress, 1980.

Grégoire, H. "Notes épigraphiques I: La religion de Maximin Daia." *Byzantion* 8 (1933) 49–56.

Grimm, B. *Unterschungen zur sozialen Stellung der frühen Christen in der römischen Gesellschaft*. PhD diss., Munich, 1975.

Grossi, V. "Anthropology." In *Encyclopedia of the Early Church*, edited by A. di Berardino, 45. New York: Oxford University Press, 1992.

Gruen, E. S. "The Bacchanalian Affair." In *Studies in Greek Culture and Roman Policy*, 34–78. Leiden: Brill, 1990.

———. *Studies in Greek Culture and Roman Policy*. Leiden: Brill, 1990.

Guillaumont, A., and C. Guillaumont. *Evagre le Pontique: Traité pratique, ou le moine*, Volume 2. Paris: Éditions du Cerf, 1971.

Gülzow, H. *Christentum und Sklaverei, in den ersten drei Jahrhunderten*. Bonn: Habelt, 1969.

———. "Soziale Gegebenheiten der altkirchlichen Mission." In *Die Alte Kirche*, edited by H. Fröhnes and U. W. Knorr, 189–226. Munich: Kaiser Verlag, 1974.

Günther, O. *Epistolae Imperatorum Pontificum Aliorum Inde ab a. CCCLXVII usque DLIII datae Avellana Quae Dicitur Collectio*. Corpus Scriptorum Ecclesiasticorum Latinorum 35. Vienna: Tempsky, 1895.

Guthrie, W. K. C. *Orpheus and Greek Religion: A Study of the Orphic Movement*. London: Methuen, 1935.

Gutmann, J. "The Origin of the Synagogue." In *The Synagogue: Studies in Origins, Archaeology and Architecture*, edited by J. Gutmann, 72–76. New York: Ktav, 1975.

Haag, H. "Kult, Liturgie und Gemeindeleben in Qumran." *Archiv für Liturgiewissenschaft* 17 (1976) 222–39.

Haake, M. *Der Philosoph in der Stadt: Untersuchungen zur öffentlichen Rede über Philosophen und Philosophie in der hellenistischen Poleis*. Munich: Beck, 2007.

———. "Philosopher and Priest: The Image of the Intellectual and the Social Practice of the Elites in the Eastern Roman Empire (First–Third Centuries AD)." In *Practitioners of the Divine: Greek Priests and Religious Officials from Homer to Heliodorus*, edited by B. Dignas and K. Trampedach, 145–65. Cambridge, MA: Harvard University Press, 2008.

Habicht, C. "Zu den Inschriften, in denen Philosophen genannt sind." In *Die Inschriften des Asklepieions*, 162. Berlin: De Gruyter, 1969.

Hadot, P. *Marius Victorinus: recherches sur sa vie et ses œuvres*. Paris: Études Augustiniennes, 1971.

Hagendahl, H. *Studia Ammianea*. Uppsala: Appelsbergs, 1921.

Hahn, J. *Der Philosoph und die Gesellschaft: Selbstverständnis, öffentliches Auftreten und populäre Erwartungen in der hohen Kaiserzeit*. Stuttgart: Steiner, 1989.

Hainz, J. *Ekklesia: Strukturen paulinischer Gemeindetheologie und Gemeindeordnung*. Regensburg: Pustet, 1972.

———. "Koinonia bei Paulus." In *Religious Propaganda and Missionary Competition in the New Testament World: Essays Honoring Dieter Georgi*, edited by L. Bormann et al., 375–91. Leiden: Brill, 1994.

———. *Koinonia: "Kirche" als Gemeinschaft bei Paulus*. Regensburg: Pustet, 1982.

Halkin, F. *Sancti Pachomii vitae Graecae*. Brussels: Société des Bollandistes, 1932.

Hammond, M. *City-State and World-State in Greek and Roman Political Theory until Augustus*. Cambridge, MA: Harvard University Press, 1951.
Hands, A. R. *Charities and Social Aid in Greece and Rome*. Ithaca: Cornell University Press, 1968.
Hanson, A. E. *Collectanea Papyrologica: Texts Published in Honor of H.C. Youtie*. 2 vols. Bonn: Habelt, 1976.
Harl, M. "À propos des Logia de Jésus: le sens du mot μοναχός." *REG* 73 (1960) 464–74.
Harris, B. F. "Bithynia: Roman Sovereignty and the Survival of Hellenism." *ANRW* II 7 (1980) 857–901.
Harrison, J. R. "Paul's House Churches and the Cultic Association." *RTR* 58 (1999) 31–47.
Harrison, P. *The Bible, Protestantism, and the Rise of Natural Science*. Cambridge: Cambridge University Press, 1998.
———. *'Religion' and the Religions in the English Enlightenment*. Cambridge: Cambridge University Press, 2010.
Harrison, T. E. H. "Templum mundi totius: Ammianus and a religious ideal of Rome." In *The Late Roman World and its Historian: Interpreting Ammianus Marcellinus*, edited by E. D. Hunt and J. W. Drijvers, 178–90. London: Routledge, 1999.
Hatch, E. *The Organization of the Early Christian Churches: Eight Lectures Delivered before the University of Oxford, in the Year 1880, on the Foundation of the Late Rev. John Bampton, M.A., Canon of Salisbury*. London: Rivington's, 1881.
Heberlein, F. "Eine philologische Anmerkung zu "Romanas caerimonias recognoscere" (Acta Cypriani 1)." In *Festschrift für Paul Klopsch*, edited by U. Kindermann et al., 83–100. Göppingen: Kümmerle, 1988.
Heinrici, G. "Die Christengemeinde Korinths und die religiösen genossenschaften der Griechen." *ZWT* 19 (1876) 465–525.
Hengel, M. *The Charismatic Leader and His Followers*. Edinburgh: T. & T. Clark, 1981.
———. *Die Zeloten: Untersuchungen zur Jüdischen Freiheitsbewegung in der Zeit von Herodes I. bis 70 n. Chr.* Leiden: Brill, 1961.
———. *Eigentum und Reichtum in der frühen Kirche: Aspekte einer frühchristlichen Sozialgeschichte*. Stuttgart: Calwer, 1973.
———. *Judentum und Hellenismus; Studien zu ihrer Begegnung unter besonderer Berücksichtigung Palästinas bis zur Mitte des 2. Jh. v. Chr.* WUNT 10. Tübingen: J. C. B. Mohr, 1969.
———. "Proseuche und Synagoge: Jüdische Gemeinde, Gotteshaus und Gottesdienst in der Diaspora und in Palästina." In *Tradition und Glaube: Das frühe Christentum in Seiner Umwelt. Festgabe für Karl Georg Kuhn zum 65. Geburtstag*, edited by G. Jeremias and H. Stegemann, 157–84. Göttingen: Vandenhoeck & Ruprecht, 1971.
———. *The Zealots: Investigations into the Jewish Freedom Movement in the Period from Herod 1 until 70 A.D*. Edinburgh: T. & T. Clark, 1989.
Henne, H. "Documents et travaux sur l'anachoresis." In *Akten des VIII. internationalen Papyrologenkongresses Wien 1955*, edited by H. Gerstinger, 58–66. Vienna: Rohrer, 1956.
Henrichs, A. "Dionysus." In *The Oxford Classical Dictionary*, edited by S. Hornblower and A. Spawforth, 479–82. Oxford: Oxford University Press, 1996.
Herman, G. *Ritualised Friendship and the Greek City*. Cambridge: Cambridge University Press 1987.

Herrmann, E. *Ecclesia in republica: die Entwicklung der Kirche von pseudostaatlicher zu staatlich inkorporierter Existenz.* Frankfurt am Main: Lang, 1980.
Heussi, K. *Der Ursprung des Mönchtums.* Tübingen: J. C. B. Mohr, 1936.
Hills, J. V. *Common Life in the Early Church: Essays Honoring Graydon F. Snyder.* Harrisburg, PA: Trinity, 1998.
Hock, R. F. *The Social Context of Paul's Ministry: Tentmaking and Apostleship.* Philadelphia: Fortress, 1980.
Hoffmann, R. J. *Marcion: On the Restitution of Christianity: An Essay on the Development of Radical Paulinist Theology in the Second Century.* Chico, CA: Scholars, 1984.
Hogland, K. G. *Achaemenid Imperial Administration in Syria-Palestine and the Missions of Ezra and Nehemiah.* Atlanta: Scholars, 1992.
Holl, K. "Die Bedeutung der neuveröfftentlichen melitianischen Urkunden für die Kirchengeschichte." In *Gesammelte Aufsätze zur Kirchengeschichte: Der Osten,* 283-97. Darmstadt: Wissenschaftliche Buchgesellschaft, 1964.
Holmberg, B. *Paul and Power: The Structure of Authority in the Primitive Church as Reflected in the Pauline Epistles.* Philadelphia: Fortress, 1980.
Hölscher, G. *Die Propheten: Untersuchungen zur Religionsgeschichte Israels.* Leipzig: Hinrichs, 1914.
Honoré, T. "Constitution, Antonine." In *The Oxford Classical Dictionary,* edited by S. Hornblower and A. Spawforth, 368. Oxford: Oxford University Press, 1996.
Hooker, R. *Of the Lawes of Ecclesiasticall Politie, Volume 4.* London: John Windet, 1594.
Hörig, M., and E. Schwertheim. *Corpus Cultus Iovis Dolicheni.* Leiden: Brill, 1987.
Hornus, J.-M. *Evangile et Labarum. Étude sur l'attitude du christianisme primitif devant les problèmes de l'état, de la guerre et de la violence.* Geneva: Labor & Fides, 1960.
Horrell, D. G. "'No Longer Jew or Greek': Paul's corporate Christology and the Construction of Christian Community." In *Christology, Controversy and Community,* edited by D. G. Horrell and C. M. Tuckett, 321-44. Leiden: Brill, 2000.
———. *The Social Ethos of the Corinthian Correspondence: Interests and Ideology From 1 Corinthians to 1 Clement.* Edinburgh, T. & T. Clark, 1996.
Horsley, G. H. R. *New Documents Illustrating Early Christianity: A Review of the Greek Inscriptions and Papyri Published in 1976.* North Ryde: The Ancient History Documentary Research Centre, 1981.
Horsley, R. A. "Synagogues in Galilee and the Gospels." In *Evolution of the Synagogue: Problems and Progress,* edited by H. C. Kee and L. H. Cohick, 46-69. Harrisburg, PA: Trinity, 1999.
Hunt, E. D. "Christians and Christianity in Ammianus Marcellinus." *CQ* 35 (1985) 186-200.
Hunter, J. P. *Before Novels: The Cultural Contexts of Eighteenth-Century English Fiction.* New York: Norton, 1990.
Hurtado, L. W. *Destroyer of the Gods: Early Christian Distinctiveness in the Roman World.* Waco, TX: Baylor University Press, 2016.
Hutch, R. A. *The Meaning of Lives: Biography, Autobiography, and the Spiritual Quest.* London: Cassell, 1997.
Isichei, E. A. *Political Thinking: Some Christian Interpretations of the Roman Empire from Tertullian to Salvian.* Christchurch, NZ: University of Canterbury, 1964.
Jacobs, B. *Die Herkunft und Entstehung der römischen Mithrasmysterien: Überlegungen zur Rolle des Stifters und zu den astronomischen Hintergründen der Kultlegende.* Konstanz: Universitätsverlag Konstanz, 1999.

Janssen, H. *Kultur und Sprache: zur Geschichte der alten Kirche im Spiegel der Sprachentwicklung: von Tertullian bis Cyprian.* Nijmegen: Dekker & van de Vegt, 1938.

Jeremias, J. *Jerusalem zur Zeit Jesu: eine kulturgeschichtliche Untersuchung zur neutestamentlichen Zeitgeschichte.* Leipzig: E. Pfeiffer, 1923.

Joannou, P.-P. *La législation impériale et la christianisation de l'Empire Romain (311–476).* Rome: Pontificium Institutum Orientalium Studiorum, 1972.

Jones, A. H. M. *Constantine and the Conversion of Europe.* London: Hodder & Stoughton, 1948.

———. *The Greek City of Alexander to Justinian.* Oxford: Clarendon, 1940.

———. *The Later Roman Empire 284–602: A Social, Economic, and Administrative Survey.* 3 vols. Oxford: Blackwell, 1964.

Jones, C. P. *Culture and Society in Lucian.* Cambridge, MA: Harvard University Press, 1986.

———. *The Roman World of Dio Chrysostom.* Cambridge, MA: Harvard University Press, 1978.

Josaitis, N. F. *Edwin Hatch and Early Church Order.* Gembloux: J. Duculot, 1971.

Judge, E. A. "The Absence of Religion, Even in Ammianus?" In *Making History for God*, edited by G. R. Treloar and R. D. Linder, 295–308. Sydney: Centre for the Study of Australian Christianity/Robert Menzies College, 2004. Reproduced in Judge, *Jerusalem and Athens*, 264–75 and as chapter 9 of the present volume.

———. "*Antike und Christentum*: Some Recent Work from Cologne." *Prudentia* 5 (1973) 1–13. Reproduced in Judge, *Jerusalem and Athens*, 69–79.

———. "The Appeal to Convention in Paul." In *The New Testament in its First Century Setting: Essays on Context and Background in Honour of B. W. Winter on His 65th Birthday*, edited by P. J. Williams et al., 178–89. Grand Rapids: Eerdmans, 2004. Reproduced in Judge, *The First Christians*, 684–92.

———. "Athena, the Unknown God of the Churches." Paper presented to the Institute for the Study of Christianity in an Age of Science, Brisbane, April 26, 2001. Published in Judge, *Engaging Rome and Jerusalem*, 65–68 and as chapter 16 of the present volume.

———. "The Beginning of Religious History." *JRH* 15 (1989) 394–412. Reproduced in Judge, *Jerusalem and Athens*, 11–31.

———. "The Biblical Shape of Modern Culture." *Kategoria* 3 (199) 9–30. Reproduced in Judge, *First Christians*, 717–32 and in Judge, *Paul and the Conflict of Cultures*, 143–58.

———. "Christian Education in the Early Church." *Syllabus for the Certificate in Christian Education* (1967) 1–8. Reproduced as "Why No Church Schools in Antiquity? Christian Education in the Early Church" in Judge, *Engaging Rome and Jerusalem*, 253–64, and as chapter 12 of the present volume.

———. "Christian Innovation and its Contemporary Observers." In *History and Historians in Late Antiquity*, edited by B. Croke and A. Emmett, 13–29. Sydney: Pergamon, 1983. Reproduced in Judge, *Jerusalem and Athens*, 232–54 and as chapter 7 of the present volume.

———. *Christliche Gruppen in nichtchristlicher Gesellschaft: die Sozialstruktur christlicher Gruppen im ersten Jahrhundert.* Wuppertal: Brockhaus, 1964. Reproduced in Judge, *The First Christians*, 464–525.

———. *The Conversion of Rome: Ancient Sources of Modern Social Tensions.* North Ryde: Macquarie Ancient History Association, 1980. Reproduced in Judge, *Jerusalem and Athens*, 211–38 and as chapter 8 of the present volume.

———. "Cultural Conformity and Innovation in Paul: Some Clues from Contemporary Documents." *TynBul* 35 (1984) 3–24. Reproduced in Judge, *Social Distinctives*, 157–74.

———. "Did the Churches Compete with Cult-groups?" In *Early Christianity and Classical Culture: Comparative Studies in Honor of Abraham J. Malherbe*, edited by J. T. Fitzgerald et al., 501–24. Leiden: Brill, 2003. Reproduced in Judge, *The First Christians*, 597–618.

———. "Did the 'Flood of Words' Change Nothing?" in Judge, *Engaging Rome and Jerusalem: Historical Essays for Our Time*, 61–64. North Melbourne: Australian Scholarly, 2014.

———. "Diversity Versus the Body Corporate." *St. Mark's Review* 225 (2013) 8–15. Reproduced as chapter 1 of the present volume.

———. "The Earliest Attested Monk." In *New Documents Illustrating Early Christianity: A Review of Greek Inscriptions and Papyri Published in 1976*, edited by G. H. R. Horsley, 141–46. North Ryde: The Ancient History Documentary Research Centre, 1981.

———. "The Earliest Use of *monachos* for "Monk" (P.Coll.Youtie 77) and the Origins of Monasticism." *JAC* 20 (1977) 72–89. Reproduced in Judge, *Jerusalem and Athens*, 156–77, and as chapter 14 of the present volume.

———. "The Ecumenical Synod of Dionysiac Artists." In *New Documents Illustrating Early Christianity: A Review of the Greek Inscriptions and Papyri Published in 1986–87*, edited by S. R. Llewelyn, 67–68. Grand Rapids: Eerdmans, 2002. Reproduced in Judge, *Jerusalem and Athens*, 137–39.

———. *Engaging Rome and Jerusalem: Historical Essays for Our Time.* Edited by S. Piggin. North Melbourne: Australian Scholarly, 2014.

———. *The First Christians in the Roman World: Augustan and New Testament Essays.* Edited by J. R. Harrison. Tübingen: Mohr Siebeck, 2008.

———. "Gesellschaft und Christentum III: Neues Testament und Gesellschaft und Christentum IV: Alte Kirche." *TRE* 12 (1984) 764–73. Reproduced as chapter 2 of the present volume.

———. "Group Religions in the Roman Empire." In Judge, *Jerusalem and Athens*, 32–43. Tübingen: Mohr Siebeck, 2010.

———. "The Impact of Paul's Gospel on Ancient Society." In *The Gospel to the Nations: Perspectives on Paul's Mission in Honour of P. T. O'Brien*, 297–308. Leicester: Inter-Varsity Press, 2000. Reproduced in Judge, *Jerusalem and Athens*, 58–68, and as chapter 15 of the present volume.

———. *Jerusalem and Athens: Cultural Transformation in Late Antiquity.* Edited by A. Nobbs. Tübingen: Mohr Siebeck, 2010.

———. "Jews, Proselytes and God-fearers Club Together." In *New Documents Illustrating Early Christianity: A Review of the Greek Inscriptions and Papyri Published in 1986–87*, edited by S. R. Llewelyn, 73–80. Grand Rapids: Eerdmans, 2002. Reproduced in Judge, *Jerusalem and Athens*, 121–29.

———. "Judaism and the Rise of Christianity: A Roman Perspective." *TynBul* 45 (1994) 355–68. Reproduced in Judge, *The First Christians*, 431–41.

———. "Kultgemeinde, (Kultverein)." *RAC* 22 (2007) 393–438.

———. "On This Rock I Will Build My *ekkle*[set macron over e]*sia*: Counter-cultic Springs of Multiculturalism?" The Petrie Oration, Australian Institute of Archaeology, Melbourne 2005. *Buried History* 41 (2005) 3–28. Reproduced in Judge, *The First Christians*, 619–68 and as chapter 6 of the present volume.

———. *Paul and the Conflict of Cultures: The Legacy of his Thought Today*. Edited by J. R. Harrison. Eugene, OR: Cascade, 2019.

———. "The Quest for Mercy in Late Antiquity." In *God Who is Rich in Mercy: Essays Presented to D. Broughton Knox*, edited by P. T. O'Brien and D. G. Peterson, 107–21. Homebush West, NSW: Lancer, 1986. Reproduced in Judge, *Jerusalem and Athens*, 185–97.

———. *Rank and Status in the World of the Caesars and St Paul*. Christchurch, NZ: University of Canterbury, 1982. Reproduced in Judge, *Social Distinctives*, 137–56.

———. Review of *Christianity and Paganism in the Fourth to Eighth Centuries*, by R. MacMullen. *JRH* 23 (1999) 240–41. Reproduced as "Did the 'Flood of Words' Change Nothing?" in Judge, *Engaging Rome and Jerusalem*, 61–4, and as chapter 10 of the present volume.

———. Review of *Destroyer of the Gods: Early Christian Distinctiveness in the Roman World*, by L. W. Hurtado. *Ancient History: Resources for Teachers* 46 (2016) 184–86. Reproduced as chapter 11 of the present volume.

———. Review of *Gruppenreligionen im römischen Reich: Sozialformen, Grenzziehungen und Leistungen*, edited by J. Rüpke. *JAC* 51 (2008) 188–95. Reproduced as "Group Religions in the Roman Empire" in Judge, *Jerusalem and Athens*, 32–43, and as chapter 4 of the present volume.

———. Review of *Rethinking Religion: Studies in the Hellenistic Process*, edited by J. Podemann Sørensen. *JRH* 20 (1996) 246–47. Reproduced as chapter 5 of the present volume.

———. "The Secular Jerusalem of the West." In Judge, *Paul and the Conflict of Cultures*, edited by J. R. Harrison, 159–70. Eugene, OR: Cascade, 2019.

———. *Social Distinctives of the Christians in the First Century: Pivotal Essays by E. A. Judge*. Edited by David Scholer. Peabody, MA: Hendrickson, 2008.

———. "The Social Identity of the First Christians: A Question of Method in Religious History." *JRH* 11 (1980) 201–17. Reproduced in Judge, *Social Distinctives*, 117–39.

———. *The Social Pattern of the Christian Groups in the First Century*. London: Tyndale Press, 1960. Reproduced in Judge, *Social Distinctives*, 1–56.

———. "St. Paul and Classical Society." *JAC* (1972) 19–36. Reproduced in Judge, *Social Distinctives*, 73–98.

———. "St Paul as a Radical Critic of Society." *Interchange* 16 (1974) 191–203. Reproduced in Judge, *Social Distinctives*, 99–115.

———. "Synagogue and Church in the Roman Empire: The Insoluble Problem of Toleration." *RTR* 68 (2009) 29–45. Reproduced in Judge, *Jerusalem and Athens*, 44–57, and as chapter 3 of the present volume.

———. "What Makes a Philosophical School?" In *New Documents Illustrating Early Christianity: Greek and Other Inscriptions and Papyri Published 1988–1992*, edited by S. R. Llewelyn et al., 1–5. Grand Rapids: Eerdmans, 2012. Reproduced as chapter 13 of the present volume.

———. "A Woman's Behaviour." In *New Documents Illustrating Early Christianity: A Review of the Greek Inscriptions and Papyri Published in 1980–81*, edited by S. R. Llewelyn, 18–23. Reproduced in Judge, *The First Christians*, 360–67.

Judge, E. A., and S. R. Pickering. "Biblical Papyri Prior to Constantine: Some Cultural Implications of Their Physical Form." *Prudentia* 10 (1978) 1–13.

———. "Papyrus Documentation of Church and Community in Egypt to the Mid-fourth Century." *JAC* 20 (1977) 47–71.

Kaczynski, R. *Das Wort Gottes in Liturgie und Alltag der Gemeinden des Johannes Chrysostomus*. Freiburg: Herder, 1974.

Kane, J. P. "The Mithraic Cult Meal in its Greek and Roman Environment." In *Mithraic Studies: Proceedings of the First International Congress of Mithraic Studies*, edited by J. R. Hinnells. Manchester: Manchester University Press, 1975.

Kasher, A. "Synagogues as 'Houses of Prayer' and 'Holy Places' in the Jewish Communities of Hellenistic and Roman Egypt." In *Ancient Synagogues: Historical Analysis and Archaeological Discovery*, edited by D. Urman and P. M .V. Flesher, 205–20. Leiden: Brill, 1995.

Katz, S. N., ed. *The Oxford International Encyclopedia of Legal History*. 6 vols. Oxford: Oxford University Press, 2009.

Kautsky, K. *Der Ursprung des Christentums: eine historische Untersuchung*. Stuttgart: Dietz, 1908.

Kearsley, R. A. "The Epitaph of Aberkios: The Earliest Christian Inscription?" In *New Documents Illustrating Early Christianity: A Review of the Greek Inscriptions and Papyri Published in 1980–81*, edited by S. R. Llewelyn, 177–81. North Ryde: The Ancient History Documentary Research Centre, 1992.

Keck, L. E. "On the Ethos of Early Christians." *JAAR* 42 (1974) 435–52.

Kee, H. C. *Christian Origins in Sociological Perspective: Methods and Resources*. Philadelphia: Westminster, 1980.

———. "The Transformation of the Synagogue after 70 CE: Its Import for Early Christianity." *NTS* 36 (1990) 1–24.

Kertelge, K. *Gemeinde und Amt im Neuen Testament*. Münich: Kösel, 1972.

Kinzig, W. *Novitas Christiana: die Idee des Fortschritts in der Alten Kirche bis Eusebius*. Göttingen: Vandenhoeck & Ruprecht, 1994.

Kippenberg, H. G. *Religion und Klassenbildung im antiken Judäa: eine religionssoziologische Studie zum Verhältnis von Tradition und gesellschaftlicher Entwicklung*. Vandenhoeck & Ruprecht, 1978. 2nd ed. Göttingen: Vandenhoeck & Ruprecht, 1982.

Klauck, H.-J. *Hausgemeinde und Hauskirche im frühen Christentum*. Stuttgart: Katholisches Bibelwerk, 1981.

———. *Herrenmahl und hellenistischer Kult: eine religionsgeschichtliche Untersuchung zum 1. Korintherbrief*. Münster: Aschendorff, 1986.

Klijn, A. F. J. "The 'Single One' in the Gospel of Thomas." *JBL* 81 (1962) 271–8.

Klinzing, G. *Die Umdeutung des Kultus in der Qumrangemeinde und im Neuen Testament*. Göttingen: Vandenhoeck & Ruprecht, 1971.

Kloppenborg, J. S. "Edwin Hatch, Churches and Collegia." In *Origins and Method: Towards a New Understanding of Judaism and Christianity Essays in Honour of John C. Hurd*, edited by B. H. Mclean, 212–38. Sheffield: JSOT Press, 1993.

Kloppenborg, J. S.. and S. G. Wilson. *Voluntary Associations in the Graeco-Roman World*. London: Routledge, 1996.

Knopf, R. "Über die soziale Zusammensetzung der ältesten heidenchristlichen Gemeinden." *ZTK* 10 (1900) 325–47.

Koch, H. *Quellen zur Geschichte der Askese und des Mönchtums in der alten Kirche.* Tübingen: J. C. B. Mohr, 1933.

Koester, H. "Associations of the Egyptian Cult in Asia Minor." In *Steine und Wege: Festschrift für Dieter Knibbe zum 65. Geburtstag*, edited by P. Scherrer et al., 318–18. Vienna: Österreichisches Archäologisches Institut, 1999.

Koffmahn, E. "Die staatsrechtliche Stellung der essenischen Vereinigungen in der griechisch-römischen Periode." *Biblica* 44 (1963) 46–61.

Kolb, F. "Zur Statussymbolik im antiken Rom." *Chiron* 7 (1977) 239–59.

Kornemann, E. "Collegium." In *Paulys Real-Encyclopädie der classischen Altertumswissenschaft*, edited by A. Pauly and G. Wissowa, 4:380–479. Stuttgart: Druckenmüller, 1900.

Kötting, B. "Die Alte Kirche: mehr als Genossenschaft und Verein." *IKaZ* 6 (1977) 128–39.

———. "Die Aufnahme des Begriffs 'Hiereus' in den christlichen Sprachgebrauch." In *Ecclesia Peregrinans, das Gottesvolk unterwegs: Gesammelte Aufsätze*, 1:356–64. Münster: Aschendorff, 1988.

Kraabel, A. T. "The Diaspora Synagogue: Archaeological and Epigraphic Evidence since Sukenik." *ANRW* II 19 (1979) 477–510.

Kraft, H. *Kaiser Konstantins religiöse Entwicklung*. Tübingen: J. C. B. Mohr, 1955.

Kreissig, H. *Die sozialen Zusammenhänge des Judäischen Krieges: Klassen und Klassenkampf im Palästina des 1. Jahrhunderts v. u. Z.* Berlin: Akademie-Verlag, 1970.

———. "Zur sozialen Zusammensetzung: der frühchristlichen Gemeinden im ersten Jahrhundert u. Z." *Eirene* 6 (1967) 91–100.

La Piana, G. "Foreign Groups in Rome During the First Century of the Empire." *HTR* 20 (1927) 183–403.

Lacroix, B. *Orose et ses idées*. Montreal: Institut d'études médiévales, 1965.

Ladner, G. B. *The Idea of Reform: Its Impact on Christian Thought and Action in the Age of the Fathers*. Cambridge, MA: Harvard University Press, 1959.

Lai, K., et al., eds. *Cultivating the Good Life in Early Chinese and Ancient Greek Philosophy*. London: Bloomsbury Academic, 2019.

Laks, A., and G. W. Most. *Studies on the Derveni Papyrus*. Oxford: Clarendon, 1997.

Lambert, A. "Apotactites et Apotaxamènes." In *Dictionnaire d'archéologie chrétienne et de liturgie*, edited by F. Cabrol, 2604–26. Paris: Letouzey, 1907.

Lampe, P. *From Paul to Valentinus: Christians at Rome in the First Two Centuries*. Minneapolis: Fortress, 2003.

Leadbetter, B. *Galerius and the Will of Diocletian*. London: Routledge, 2009.

Leclercq, H. "Autel." In *Dictionnaire d'archéologie chrétienne et de liturgie*, edited by F. Cabrol, 3155–89. Paris: Letouzey, 1907.

Leon, H.-J. *The Jews of Ancient Rome*. Philadelphia: The Jewish Publication Society of America, 1960.

Levine, L. I. *The Ancient Synagogue: The First Thousand Years*. New Haven, CT: Yale University Press, 2000.

Levinskaya, I. *The Book of Acts in its Diaspora Setting*. Grand Rapids: Eerdmans, 1996.

Liebenam, W. *Zur Geschichte und Organisation des römischen Vereinswesens*. Leipzig: Teubner, 1890.

Liebeschuetz, W. "The Expansion of Mithraism among the Religious Cults of the Second Century." In *Studies in Mithraism: Papers associated with the Mithraic Panel organized on the occasion of the XVIth Congress of the International Association for the History of Religions*, edited by J. R. Hinnells, 195–216. Rome: L'Erma di Bretschneider, 1994.

Lienhard, J. T. *Paulinus of Nola and Early Western Monasticism*. Cologne: Hanstein, 1977.

Lieu, J. M. "The Forging of Christian Identity." *Mediterranean Archaeology* 11 (1998) 71–82.

Lifshitz, B. *Donateurs et fondateurs dans le synagogues: répertoire des dédicaces greques relatives à la construction et à la réfection des synagogues*. Paris: Gabalda, 1967.

Lindemann, Andreas. "Der Apostel Paulus im 2. Jahrhundert." In *The New Testament in Early Christianity: La réception des écrits néotestamentaires dans le christianisme primitif*, edited by J.-M. Sevrin, 39–67. Leuven: Peeters, 1989.

Lindsay, H. M. "Characterisation in the Suetonian Life of Tiberius." In *Ancient History in a Modern University: The Ancient Near East, Greece and Rome*, edited by T. W. Hillard et al., 299–308. Grand Rapids: Eerdmans, 1998.

Locher, A. *Marii Victorini Afri Commentarii in epistulas Pauli ad Galatas ad Philippenses ad Ephesios*. Leipzig: Teubner, 1972.

Lohse, B. *Askese und Mönchtum in der Antike und in der alten Kirche*. Munich: Oldenbourg, 1969.

Lorenz, R. "Die Anfänge des abendländischen Mönchtums im 4. Jahrhundert." *ZKG* 77 (1966) 1–61.

Lorié, L. T. A. *Spiritual Terminology in the Latin Translations of the Vita Antonii with Reference to Fourth and Fifth Century Monastic Literature*. Nijmegen: Dekker & Van de Vegt, 1955.

Löwith, K. *From Hegel to Nietzsche: The Revolution in Nineteenth Century Thought*. New York: Holt, Rinehart and Winston, 1964.

Lüddeckens, Erich. "Gottesdienstliche Gemeinschaften im pharaonischen, ellenistischen undcChristlichen Ägypten." *ZRGG* 20 (1968) 193–211.

Lynch, J. P. *Aristotle's School: A Study of a Greek Educational Institution*. Berkeley: University of California Press, 1972.

MacMullen, R. *Christianity and Paganism in the Fourth to Eighth Centuries*. New Haven, CT: Yale University Press, 1997.

———. *Christianizing the Roman Empire (A.D. 100–400)*. New Haven, CT: Yale University Press, 1984.

———. *Constantine*. New York: Dial, 1969.

———. *Paganism in the Roman Empire*. New Haven, CT: Yale University Press, 1981.

———. *Roman Social Relations: 50 B.C. to A.D. 284*. New Haven, CT: Yale University Press, 1974.

———. *Soldier and Civilian in the Later Roman Empire*. Cambridge, MA: Harvard University Press, 1963.

———. "What Difference Did Christianity Make?" *Historia* 35 (1986) 322–43.

Madec, G. *Saint Ambroise et la philosophie*. Paris: Études Augustiniennes, 1974.

Malherbe, A. J. *Social Aspects of Early Christianity*. Baton Rouge: Louisiana State University Press, 1977.

Malina, B. J. *The New Testament World: Insights from Cultural Anthropology*. Atlanta: John Knox Press, 1981.

———. "The Social Sciences and Biblical Interpretation: Reflections on Tradition and Practice." *Int* 36 (1982) 229–42.
Mandouze, A. *Augustin: L'aventure de la raison et de la grâce*. Paris: Études Augustiniennes, 1968.
Manning, C. E. "School Philosophy and Popular Philosophy in the Roman Empire." *ANRW* II 36 (1994) 4995–5026.
Markschies, C. *Zwischen den Welten wandern: Strukuren des antiken Christentums*. Frankfurt am Main: Fischer Taschenbuch Verlag, 1997.
Markus, R. A. *Christianity in the Roman World*. London: Thames and Hudson, 1974.
———. "How on Earth Could Places Become Holy? Origins of the Christian Idea of Holy Places." *JECS* 2 (1994) 257–71.
———. *Saeculum: History and Society in the Theology of St. Augustine*. Cambridge: Cambridge University Press, 1970.
Marshall, P. *Enmity and Other Social Conventions in Paul's Relations with the Corinthians*. PhD diss., Macquarie University, 1980.
Marshall, P. J. "The Enigmatic Apostle: Paul and Social Change. Did Paul Seek to Transform Graeco-Roman Society?" In *Ancient History in a Modern University: Early Christianity, Late Antiquity, and Beyond*, edited by T. W. Hillard et al., 153–74. Grand Rapids: Eerdmans, 1998.
Martinez, F. G., and J. T. Barrera. *The People of the Dead Sea Scrolls: Their Writings, Beliefs and Practices*. Leiden: Brill, 1995.
Marx, K. *Capital: A Critical Analysis of Capitalist Production*. Moscow: Foreign Languages Publishing House, 1954.
Mason, S. N. "Philosophiai: Graeco-Roman, Judean and Christian." In *Voluntary Associations in the Graeco-Roman World*, edited by J. S. Kloppenborg and S. G. Wilson, 31–58. London: Routledge, 1996.
Matthews, J. *The Journey of Theophanes: Travel, Business, and Daily Life in the Roman East*. New Haven, CT: Yale University Press, 2006.
———. *The Roman Empire of Ammianus*. London: Duckworth, 1989.
———. "Symmachus and the Oriental Cults." *JRS* 63 (1973) 175–95.
———. *Western Aristocracies and Imperial Court, AD 364–425*. Oxford: Clarendon, 1975.
McGregor, N. *Seeing Salvation: Images of Christ in Art*. New Haven, CT: Yale University Press, 200.
McKechnie, P. *Christianizing Asia Minor: Conversion, Communities, and Social Change in the Pre-Constantinian Era*. Cambridge: Cambridge University Press, 2019.
McKelvey, R. J. *The New Temple: The Church in the New Testament*. London: Oxford University Press, 1969.
McLaughlin, J. L. *The Marzéah in the Prophetic Literature: References and Allusions in Light of the Extra-Biblical Evidence*. Leiden: Brill, 2001.
McLean, B. H. "The Agrippinilla Inscription: Religious Associations and Early Church Formation." In *Origins and Method: Towards a New Understanding of of Judaism and Christianity*, edited by B. H. McLean, 239–70. Sheffield: JSOT Press, 1993.
McManners, J. *The Oxford Illustrated History of Christianity*. Oxford: Oxford University Press, 1990.
Mealand, D. L. *Poverty and Expectation in the Gospels*. London: SPCK, 1980.
Meeks, W. A. *The First Urban Christians: The Social World of the Apostle Paul*. New Haven, CT: Yale University Press, 1983.

———. "The Social Context of Pauline Theology." *Int* 36 (1982) 266–77.

———. "The Social World of Early Christianity." *BCSR* 6 (1975) 1–5.

———. *Zur Soziologie des Urchristentums: ausgewählte Beiträge zum frühchristlichen Gemeinschaftsleben in seiner gesellschaftlichen Umwelt*. Munich: Kaiser, 1979.

Meijering, E. P. *Orthodoxy and Platonism in Athanasius: Synthesis or antithesis?* Leiden, Brill: 1968.

———. "Wie platonisierten Christen? Zur Grenzziehung zwischen Platonismus, kirchlichem Credo und patristischer Theologie." *VC* 28 (1974) 15–28.

Ménard, J. E. *L'évangile selon Thomas*. Leiden: Brill, 1975.

Mendel, Gustave. "Catalogue des monuments grecs, romains et byzantins du Musée Impérial Ottomande Brousse." *BCH* 33 (1909) 245–435.

Mendelsohn, I. "Gilds [*sic*] in Babylonia and Assyria." *JAOS* 50 (1940) 68–72.

———. "Guilds in Ancient Palestine." *BASOR* 80 (1940) 17–21.

Meredith, A. "Asceticism, Christian and Greek." *JTS* 27 (1976) 313–32.

Merkelbach, R. *Die Hirten des Dionysos: Die Dionysos-Mysterien der römischen Kaiserzeit und der bukolische Roman des Longus*. Stuttgart: Teubner, 1988.

———. *Isis regina, Zeus Sarapis: die griechisch-ägyptische Religion nach den Quellen dargestellt*. Stuttgart: Teubner, 1995.

———. *Mithras: ein persisch-römischer Mysterienkult*. Königstein: Hain, 1984.

Merlat, P. *Jupiter Dolichenus: Essai d'interprétation et de synthèse*. Paris: Presses universitaires de France, 1960.

Metzger, B. M. *A Classified Bibliography of the Graeco-Roman Mystery Religions, 1924–1973: With a supplement, 1974–1977*. Berlin: De Gruyter, 1984.

Meyer, M. *The Ancient Mysteries: A Sourcebook of Sacred Texts*. San Francisco: Harper & Row, 1987.

Meyer, B. F., and E. P. Sanders, eds. *Jewish and Christian Self-definition: Self-Definition in the Graeco-Roman World*. Philadelphia: Fortress, 1983.

Migne, J.-P., ed. *Patrologiae Cursus Completus: Series Græca*. Vol. 20. Paris: Petit-Montrouge, 1857.

———, ed. *Patrologiae Cursus Completus: Series Græca*. Vol. 26. Paris: Petit-Montrouge, 1857.

Mikalson, J. D. *Religion in Hellenistic Athens*. Berkeley: University of California Press, 1998.

Militello, C. *Memorie Epicuree (P.Herc. 1418e, 310)*. Naples: Bibliopolis, 1997.

Misch, G. *A History of Autobiography in Antiquity*. Cambridge, MA: Harvard University Press, 1951.

Mitchell, M. M. "'A Variable and Many-sided Man': John Chrysostom's Treatment of Pauline Inconsistency." *JECS* 6 (1998) 93–111.

Mitchell, S. "Maximinus and the Christians in AD 312: A New Latin Inscription." *JRS* 78 (1988) 105–24.

Mitthof, F. "Der Vorstand der Kultgemeinden des Mithras: Eine Sammlung und Untersuchung der inschriftlichen Zeugnisse." *Klio* 74 (1992) 275–90.

Mohrmann, C. *Die altchristliche Sondersprache in den Sermones des hl. Augustin*. Amsterdam: Hakkert, 1932.

———. "La langue et le style de la poésie latine chrétienne." *Revue des Etudes Latines* 25 (1947) 280–97.

Momigliano, A. *The Conflict between Paganism and Christianity in the Fourth Century*. Oxford: Clarendon, 1963.

———. "Pagan and Christian Historiography in the Fourth Century A.D." In *The Conflict between Paganism and Christianity in the Fourth Century*, 79–99. Oxford: Clarendon, 1963.

———. "Popular Religious Beliefs and the Late Roman Historians." SCH 8 (1972) 1–18.

Mommsen, T. *De Collegiis et Sodaliciis Romanorum*. Kiel: Libraria Schwersiana, 1843.

Mommsen, T., et al. *The Digest of Justinian*. Philadelphia: University of Pennsylvania Press.

Monachino, V. *S. Ambrogio e la cura pastorale a Milano nel secolo IV: centenario di S. Ambrogio, 374–1974*. Milan: Centro ambrosiano di documentazione e studi religiosi, 1973.

Mora, F. *Prosopografia Isiaca*. Leiden: Brill, 1990.

Morard, F. E. "Monachos, moine. Histoire du terme grec jusqu'au 4e siècle." *FZPhTh* 20 (1973) 332–411.

Moreau, J. L. "Eusebius von Caesarea." *RAC* 6 (1966) 1052–88.

Mortley, R. J. "The Past in Clement Alexandria: A Study of an Attempt to Define Christianity in Socio-cultural Terms." In *Jewish and Christian Self-Definition: The Shaping of Christianity in the Second and Third Centuries*, edited by E. P. Sanders, 186–200. Philadelphia: Fortress, 1980.

———. *Plotinus, Self and the World*. Cambridge: Cambridge University Press, 2013.

Musurillo, H. *The Acts of the Christian Martyrs*. Oxford: Clarendon, 1972.

Mylonas, G. E. *Eleusis and the Eleusinian Mysteries*. Princeton: Princeton University Press, 1961.

Nagel, M. "Lettre chrétien sur papyrus (provenant de milieux sectaires du IVe siècle?)." *ZPE* 18 (1975) 317–23.

Nagel, P. *Die Motivierung der Askese in der alten Kirche und der Ursprung des Mönchtums*. Berlin: Akademie-Verlag, 1966.

Naldini, M. *Il Cristianesimo in Egitto: Lettere private nei papiri dei secoli II-IV*. Florence: Le Monnier, 1968.

Nappo, S. *Pompeii: Guide to the Lost City*. London: Weidenfeld & Nicolson, 1998.

Neri, V. *Ammiano e il cristianesimo: religione e politica nelle "Res gestae" di Ammiano Marcellino*. Bologna: CLUEB, 1985.

———. "Ammianus' Definition of Christianity as absoluta et simplex religio." In *Cognitio Gestorum: The Historiographic Art of Ammianus Marcellinus*, edited by J. den Boeft et al., 59–65. Amsterdam: North-Holland, 1992.

Nestle, W. "Die Haupteinwände des antiken Denkens gegen das Christentum." *AR* 37 (1941) 51–100.

Nielsen, I. "Exedra." In *Brill's New Pauly: Encyclopaedia of the Ancient World*, edited by H. Cancik and H. Schneider, 5:261–2. Leiden: Brill, 2004.

Nicholson, O. "The 'Pagan Churches' of Maximinus Daia and Julian the Apostate." *JEH* 45 (1994) 1–10.

Niederwimmer, K. *The Didache: A Commentary*. Minneapolis: Fortress, 1993.

Nock, A. D. *Essays on Religion and the Ancient World, Volume 1*. Edited by Z. Stewart. Cambridge, MA: Harvard University Press, 1972.

———. "The Historical Importance of Cult-Associations." *The Classical Review* 38 (1924) 105–9.

Nock, A. D., et al. "The Gild of Zeus Hypsistos." *HTR* 29 (1936) 39–88. Reprinted omitting introduction, in A. D. Nock, *Essays on Religion and the Ancient World*, edited by Z. Stewart, 1:414–43. Cambridge, MA: Harvard University Press, 1972.

Noormann, R. *Irenäus als Paulusinterpret: zur Rezeption und Wirkung der paulinischen und deuteropaulinischen Briefe im Werk des Irenäus von Lyon*. Tübingen: J. C. B. Mohr, 1994.

Norris, F. W. "The Social Status of Early Christianity." *Gospel in Context* 2 (1979) 4–14.

O'Brien, P. T. "The Church as a Heavenly and Eschatological Entity." In *The Church in the Bible and the World*, edited by D. A. Carson, 88–119, 307–11. Exeter: Paternoster, 1987.

Oddie, G. A. *Imagined Hinduism: British Protestant missionary constructions of Hinduism, 1793–1900*. New Delhi: Sage, 2006.

Ollrog, W.-H. *Paulus und seine Mitarbeiter: Untersuchungen zu Theorie und Praxis der paulinischen Mission*. Neukirchen-Vluyn: Neukirchener Verlag, 1979.

Opelt, I. "Eunapios." *RAC* 6 (1966) 928–36.

Oppenheim, P. *Das Mönchskleid im christlichen Altertum* Freiburg: Herder, 1931.

Otto, S. *Die Antike im Umbruch: Politisches Denken zwischen hellenistischer Tradition und christlicher Offenbarung bis zur Reichstheologie Justinians*. Munich: List, 1974.

O'Sullivan, J. N. *Xenophon of Ephesus: His Compositional Technique and the Birth of the Novel*. Berlin: De Gruyter, 1995.

Oulton, J. E. L. *Eusebius: Ecclesiastical History: Books 6–10*. LCL 265. London: Heinemann, 1932.

Pagels, E. *The Gnostic Paul: Gnostic Exegesis of the Pauline Letters*. Philadelphia: Fortress, 1975.

Pailler, J.-M. *Bacchanalia: la répression de 186 av. J.-C. à Rome et en Italie: vestiges, images, tradition*. Rome: École française de Rome, 1988.

Painter, J. *Just James: The Brother of Jesus in History and Tradition*. Columbia, SC: University of South Carolina Press, 1997.

Parker, *Athenian Religion: A History*. Oxford: Clarendon, 1996.

———. "Private Religious Associations." In *Athenian Religion: A History*, 333–42. Oxford: Clarendon, 1996.

Paschoud, F. *Roma Aeterna: études sur le patriotisme romain dans l'occident latin à l'époque des grandes invasions*. Rome: Institut suisse de Rome, 1967.

Pearson, B. A. *The Emergence of the Christian Religion: Essays on Early Christianity*. Harrisburg, PA: Trinity, 1997.

Pesce, M., dir. *Annali di Storia dell'Esegesi*, vol. 18.1: *Il sacrificio nel Giudaismo e nel Cristianesimo*. Bologna: Edizione Dehoiane Bologna, 2001.

———., dir. *Annali di Storia dell'Esegesi*, vol. 19.1: *I cristiani e il sacrificio pagano e biblico*. Bologna: Edizione Dehoiane Bologna, 2002.

Peterson, D. G. "The Worship of the New Community." In *Witness to the Gospel: The Theology of Acts*, edited by I. H. Marshall and D. G. Peterson, 373–92. Grand Rapids: Eerdmans, 1998.

Peterson, E. *Der Monotheismus als Politisches Problem: ein Beitrag zur Geschichte der Politischen Theologie im Imperium Romanum*. Leipzig: Hegner, 1935.

Petit, P. *Libanius et la vie municipale à Antioche au 4e siècle après J.-C*. Paris: P. Geuthner, 1955.

Phillips, C. R. "Approaching Roman Religion: The Case for Wissenschaftsgeschichte." In *A Companion to Roman Religion*, edited by J. Rüpke, 10–28. Malden, MA: Blackwell, 2007.

Pietersma, A. *The Acts of Phileas Bishop of Thmuis (including Fragments of the Greek Psalter): P. Chester Beatty XV (with a New Edition of P. Bodmer XX, and Halkin's Latin Acta)*. Geneva: Cramer, 1984.

Pighi, G. B. "Latinità cristiana negli scrittori pagani del iv secolo." In *Studi dedicati alla memoria di Paolo Ubaldi*, edited by A. Gemelli, 41–72. Milan: Vita e Pensiero, 1937.

Pocock, J. G. A."The Origins of the Study of the Past: A Comparative Approach." *Comparative Studies in Society and History* 4 (1962) 209–46.

Podemann Sørensen, J., ed. *Rethinking Religion: Studies in the Hellenistic Process*, Copenhagen: Museum Tusculanum Press, 1989.

Pohlmann, H. "Erbauung." *RAC* 5 (1962) 1043–70.

Pöhlmann, R. von. *Geschichte der sozialen Frage und des Sozialismus in der antiken Welt*. Munich: Beck, 1984.

Poland, F. *Geschichte des griechischen Vereinswesens*. Leipzig: Teubner, 1909.

———. "Technitai." In *Paulys Real-Encyclopädie der classischen Altertumswissenschaft*, edited by A. Pauly and G. Wissowa, 2473–2558. Stuttgart: Druckenmüller, 1934.

Préaux, C. "À propos des associations dans l'Égypte gréco-romaine." *RIDA* 1 (1948) 189–98.

Price, S. *Religions of the Ancient Greeks*. Cambridge: Cambridge University Press, 1999.

Pruneti, P. "Il termine φιλόσοφος nei papiri documentari." In *ΟΔΟΙ ΔΙΖΗΣΙΟΣ. Le vie della ricerca: Studi in onore di Francesco Adorno*, edited by M. S. Funghi, 389–41. Florence: Olschki, 1996.

Qimron, E., and J. Strugnell. *Discoveries in the Judean Desert: Qumran Cave 4.V: Miqs a t Ma as 'e ha-Torah*. Oxford: Clarendon, 1994.

Quasten, J. *Patrology, Volume 3*. Utrecht: Spectrum, 1950.

Quispel, G. "L'évangile selon Thomas et les Clémentines." *VC* 12 (1958) 181–96.

———. *Makarius, das Thomasevangelium und das Lied von der Perle*. Leiden: Brill, 1967.

Rajak, T. "Jewish Rights in the Greek Cities under Roman Rule: A New Approach." In *Approaches to Ancient Judaism: Studies in Judaism in Its Greco-Roman Context*, edited by W. S. Green, 5:19–35. Atlanta: Scholars, 1985.

———. "Jews and Christians as Groups in the Pagan World." In *"To See Ourselves as Others See Us.": Christians, Jews, "Others" in Late Antiquity*, edited by J. Neusner and A. S. Frerichs, 274–62. Atlanta: Scholars, 1985.

Rathbone, D. *Economic Rationalism and Rural Society in Third-century A.D. Egypt: The Heroninos Archive and the Appianus Estate*. Cambridge: Cambridge University Press, 1991.

Rauh, N. K. *The Sacred Bonds of Commerce: Religion, Economy, and Trade Society at Hellenistic Roman Delos, 166–87 B.C.* Amsterdam: Gieben, 1993.

Reicke, B. *Diakonie, Festfreude und Zelos in Verbindung mit der altchristlichen Agapenfeier*. Uppsala: Lundequist, 1951.

Reitzenstein, R. *Des Athanasius Werk über das Leben des Antonius: ein philologischer Beitrag zur Geschichte des Mönchtums*. Heidelberg: Winter, 1914.

———. *Poimandres: Studien zur griechisch-agyptischen und fruhchristlichen Literatur*. Leipzig: Teubner, 1904.

Reumann, J. "One Lord, One Faith, One God, but Many House Churches." In *Common Life in the Early Church: Essays Honoring Graydon F. Snyder*, edited by J. V. Hills, 106–17. Valley Forge: Trinity Press International, 1998.

Reydams-Schils, G. *The Roman Stoics: Self, Responsibility, and Affection*. Chicago: University of Chicago Press, 2005.

Reynolds, J. and R. Tannenbaum. *Jews and God-fearers at Aphrodisias: Greek Inscriptions with Commentary*. Cambridge: Cambridge Philological Society, 1987.

Riccobono, S., et al., eds. *Fontes iuris romani antejustiniani*. 2nd ed. Edited by C. Ferrini and G. Furlani. Florence: Barbèra, 1968.

Richardson, G. P. "Philo and Eusebius on Monasteries and Monasticism: The Therapeutae and Kellia." In *Origins and Method: Towards a New Understanding of Judaism and Christianity Essays in Honour of John C. Hurd*, edited by B. H. Mclean, 334–59. Sheffield: JSOT Press, 1993.

Richardson, P. "Architectural Transitions from Synagogues and House Churches to Purpose-Built Churches." In *Common Life in the Early Church: Essays Honoring Graydon F. Snyder*, edited by J. V. Hills, 373–89. Valley Forge: Trinity Press International, 1998.

Richardson, P., and Heuchan, V. "Jewish Voluntary Associations in Egypt and the Roles of Women." In *Voluntary Associations in the Graeco-Roman World*, edited by J. S. Kloppenborg and S. G. Wilson, 226–51. London: Routledge, 1996.

Ridley, R. T. "Eunapius and Zosimus." *Helikon* 9–10 (1969–1970) 574–92.

Riedweg, C., ed. *Philosophia in der Konkurrenz von Schulen, Wissenschaften und Religionen: Zur Pluralisierung des Philosophiebegriffs in Kaiserzeit und Spätantike*. Berlin: De Gruyter, 2017.

Riesner, R. "Synagogues in Jerusalem." In *The Book of Acts in Its Palestinian Setting*, edited by R. Bauckham, 179–212. Grand Rapids: Eerdmans, 1995.

Rike, R. L. *Apex Omnium: Religion in the Res Gestae of Ammianus*. Berkeley: University of California Press, 1987.

Rinaldi, G. *Biblia Gentium: primo contributo per un indice delle citazioni, dei riferimenti e delle allusioni alla Bibbia negli autori pagani, Greci e Latini, di età imperial = A First Contribution towards an Index of Biblical Quotations, References and Allusions made by Greek and Latin Heathen Writers of the Roman Imperial Times*. Rome: Libreria Sacre Scritture, 1989.

Rives, J. B. *Religion in the Roman Empire*. Malden: Blackwell, 2007.

Robert, J., and L. Robert. "Bulletin Épigraphique." *REG* 84 (1971) 397–540.

Robert, L. "Bulletin Épigraphique." *REG* 71 (1958) 197–200.

———. *Documents de l'Asie Mineure méridionale: Inscriptions, monnaies et géographie*. Geneva: Droz, 1966.

Rolfe, J. C. *Ammianus Marcellinus: History. Books 14–19*. LCL 300. London: Heinemann, 1950.

Roller, L. E. *In Search of God the Mother: The Cult of Anatolian Cybele*. Berkeley: University of California Press, 1999.

Rostovtzeff, M. *The Social and Economic History of the Roman Empire*. Revised by P. M Fraser. New York: Oxford University Press, 1957. German translation: *Gesellschaft und Wirtschaft im römischen Kaiserreich*. Translated by L. Wickert. Leipzig: Quelle & Meyer, 1931.

Rothenhäusler, M., and P. Oppenheim. "Apotaxis." *RAC* 1 (1950) 558–64.

Rouché, C. *Performers and Partisans at Aphrodisias in the Roman and Late Roman Periods*. London: Society for the Promotion of Roman Studies, 1993.

Rousseau, P. *Ascetics, Authority, and the Church in the Age of Jerome and Cassian*. Oxford: Oxford University Press, 1978.

———. "Blood-Relationships among Early Eastern Ascetics." *JTS* 23 (1972) 135–44; 25 (1974) 113–117.

Rubenson, S. *The Letters of St Antony: Monasticism and the Making of a Saint*. Minneapolis: Fortress, 1995.

Rudolph, K. *Gnosis und spätantike Religionsgeschichte: gesammelte Aufsätze*. Leiden: Brill, 1996.

Runesson, A., et al. *The Ancient Synagogue from its Origins to 200 C.E.: A Sourcebook*. Leiden: Brill, 2008.

Rüpke, J., ed. *A Companion to Roman Religion*. Malden, MA: Blackwell, 2007.

———. *Gruppenreligionen im römischen Reich: Sozialformen, Grenzziehungen und Leistungen*. Tübingen: Mohr Siebeck, 2007

———. "Integrationsgeschichten." In *Gruppenreligionen im römischen Reich*, edited by J. Rüpke, 113–26. Tübingen: Mohr Siebeck, 2007.

———. "Literarische Darstellungen römischer Religion in christlicher Apologetik: Universal—und Lokalreligion bei Tertullian und Minucius Felix." In *Texte als Medium und Reflexion von Religion im römischen Reich*, edited by D. E. von der Osten et al., 209–24. Stuttgart: Steiner, 2006.

———. *Römische Priester in der Antike*. Stuttgart: Steiner, 2007.

Ruppert, F. *Das pachomianische Mönchtum und die Anfänge klösterlichen Gehorsams*. Münsterschwarzach: Vier-Türme, 1971.

Rydbeck, L. *Fachprosa, vermeintliche Volkssprache und Neues Testament: zur Beurteilung der sprachlichen Niveauunterschiede im nachklassischen Griechischen*. Uppsala: Uppsala Universitet, 1967.

Sabbah, G. *La méthode d'Ammien Marcellin: recherches sur la construction du discours historique dans les res gestae*. Paris: Belles Lettres, 1978.

Safrai, Z. "The Communal Functions of the Synagogue in the Land of Israel in the Rabbinic Period." In *Ancient Synagogues; Historical Analysis and Archaeological Discovery*, edited by D. Urman and P. V. M. Flesher, 181–204. Leiden: Brill, 1995.

Şahin, S. "Ein Stein aus Hadrianoi in Mysien in Bursa." *ZPE* 24 (1977) 257–58.

Saldarini, A. J. *Pharisees, Scribes and Sadducees in Palestinian Society: A Sociological Approach*. Wilmington: Glazier, 1988.

Saler, B. *Conceptualizing Religion: Immanent Anthropologists, Transcendent Natives, and Unbounded Categories*. Leiden: Brill, 1993.

Sampley, J. P. *Pauline Partnership in Christ: Christian Community and Commitment in Light of Roman Law*. Philadelphia: Fortress, 1980.

San Nicolò, M. *Ägyptisches Vereinswesen zur Zeit der Ptolemäer und Römer*. Munich: Beck, 1913.

Saumagne, C. "Corpus Christianorum." *RIDA* 7 91960) 437–78; 8 (1961) 257–79.

Savramis, D. *Zur Soziologie des Byzantinischen Mönchtums*. Leiden: Brill, 1962.

Schäfer, A. "Dionysische Kultlokale in Kleinasien und dem Donauraum." In *Gruppenreligionen im römischen Reich*, edited by J. Rüpke, 161–80. Tübingen: Mohr Siebeck, 2007.

Schiffman, L. H. *The Eschatological Community of the Dead Sea Scrolls: A Study of the Rule of the Congregation*. Atlanta: Scholars, 1989.

BIBLIOGRAPHY

———. *Who Was a Jew? Rabbinic and Halakhic Perspectives on the Jewish Christian Schism.* Hoboken: Ktav, 1985.

Schmeller, T. *Hierarchie und Egalität: eine sozialgeschichtliche Untersuchung paulinischer Gemeinden und griechisch-römischer Vereine.* Stuttgart: Katholisches Bibelwerk, 1995.

Schmid, W. "Epicurus." *RAC* 5 (1962) 746–55.

Schneemelcher, W. *New Testament Apocrypha.* 6th ed. Translated by R. M. Wilson. Cambridge: Cambridge University Press, 1992.

Schneider, A. *Le premier livre Ad Nationes de Tertullien: introduction, texte, traduction et commentaire.* Rome: Institut Suisse de Rome, 1968.

Schneider, C. *Geistesgeschichte des antiken Christentums.* Munich: Beck, 1954.

Scholten, C. "Die alexandrinische Katechetenschule." *JAC* 38 (1995) 16–37.

Schönborn, H.-B. *Die Pastophoren im Kult der ägyptischen Götter.* Meisenheim am Glan: Hain, 1976.

Schörner, G. "Von der Initiation zum Familienritual: Der Saturnkult als Gruppenreligion." In *Gruppenreligionen im römischen Reich*, edited by J. Rüpke, 181–97. Tübingen: Mohr Siebeck, 2007.

Schottroff, L., and W. Stegemann. *Jesus von Nazareth: Hoffnung der Armen.* Stuttgart: Kohlhammer, 1978.

———, eds. *Der Gott kleiner Leute: sozialgeschichtliche Bibelauslegungen.* Munich: Kaiser, 1979.

Schultz, C. "Sanctissima Femina: Gesellschaftliche Klassifizierung und religiöse Praxis von Frauen in der römischen Republik." In *Gruppenreligionen im römischen Reich*, edited by J. Rüpke, 7–30. Tübingen: Mohr Siebeck, 2007.

Schulz, F. *Classical Roman Law.* Oxford: Clarendon, 1951.

Schulz-Falkenthal, H. "Gegenseiteigkeitshilfe und Unterstützungstätigkeit in den römischen Handwerkergenossenschaften." *Wissenschaftliche Zeitschrift der Martin-Luther-Universität Halle-Wittenberg* 20 (1971) 59–78.

Schumacher, R. *Die soziale Lage der Christen im apostolischen Zeitalter.* Paderborn Schöningh, 1924.

Schütz, J. H. "Introduction." In G. Theissen, *The Social Setting of Pauline Christianity: Essays on Corinth*, edited and translated by J. H. Schütz, 1–23. Philadelphia: Fortress, 1982.

Schwarte, K.-H. "Die Christengesetze Valerians." In *Religion und Gesellschaft in der römischen Kaiserzeit: Kolloquium zu Ehren von Friedrich Vittinghoff*, edited by W. Eck, 103–63. Cologne: Böhlau, 1989.

Schwartz, E., et al., eds. *Eusebius Caesariensis Werke: Die Kirchengeschichte.* Berlin: Akademie-Verlag, 1999.

Schwertheim, E. *Inschriften von Hadrianoi und Hadrianeia.* Bonn: Habelt, 1987.

Scroggs, R. "The Sociological Interpretation of the New Testament: The Present State of Research." *NTS* 26 (1980) 164–79.

Seland, T. "Philo and the Clubs and Associations of Alexandria." In *Voluntary Associations in the Graeco-Roman World*, edited by J. S. Kloppenborg and S. G. Wilson, 110–27. London: Routledge, 1996

Selinger, R. *The Mid-Third Century Persecutions of Decius and Valerian.* Frankfurt am Main: P. Lang, 2002.

Seyfarth, W. *Soziale Fragen der spätrömischen Kaiserzeit im Spiegel des Theodosianus.* Berlin: Akademie-Verlag, 1963.

Sherwin-White, A. N. *Roman Society and Roman Law in the New Testament*. Oxford: Clarendon Press, 1963.
Sieben, H. J. *Kirchenväterhomilien zum Neuen Testament: ein Repertorium der Textausgaben und Übersetzungen: mit einem Anhang der Kirchenväterkommentare*. Steenbrugge: In Abbatia S. Petri, 1991.
Simon, M. *La civilisation de l'antiquité et le christianisme*. Paris: Arthaud, 1972.
Sirinelli, J. "Introduction Générale." In Eusebius, *La préparation évangélique*, edited by É. Des Places and J. Sirinelli, 8–15. Paris: Éditions du Cerf, 1974.
Smith, J. Z. *Drudgery Divine: On the Comparison of Early Christianities and the Religions of Late Antiquity*. Chicago: University of Chicago Press, 1990.
———. "The Social Description of Early Christianity." *RelSRev* 1 (1975) 19–25.
Smith, M. F. *Diogenes of Oinoanda: The Epicurean Inscription*. Naples: Bibliopolis, 1993.
Smith, R. *Julian's Gods: Religion and Philosophy in the Thought and Action of Julian the Apostate*. London: Routledge, 1995.
Sokolowski, F. *Lois sacrées des cités grecques*. Paris: Boccard, 1969.
———. *Lois sacrées des cités grecques: Supplément*. Paris: Boccard, 1962.
———. *Lois sacrées de l'Asie Mineure*. Paris: Boccard, 1955.
Souter, A. *The Earliest Latin Commentaries on the Epistles of St. Paul*. Oxford: Clarendon, 1927.
Spawforth, A. "Panhellenion, Attic." In *The Oxford Classical Dictionary*, edited by S. Hornblower and A. Spawforth, 1105–6. 3rd ed. Oxford: Oxford University Press, 1996.
Speidel, M. P. *The Religion of Iuppiter Dolichenus in the Roman Army*. Leiden: Brill, 1978.
Spickermann, W. "Mysteriengemeinde und Öffeltlichkeit: Integration von Mysterienkulten in die locale Panthea in Gallier und Germanien." In *Gruppenreligionen im römischen Reich*, edited by J. Rüpke, 127–60. Tübingen: Mohr Siebeck, 2007.
Stanton, G. N. *A Gospel for a New People: Studies in Matthew*. Edinburgh: T. & T. Clark, 1992.
Stanton, G. R. "The Cosmopolitan Ideas of Epictetus and Marcus Aurelius." *Phronesis* 13 (1968) 183–95.
———. "Marcus Aurelius, Emperor and Philosopher." *Historia* 18 (1969) 570–87.
———. "Sophists and Philosophers: Problems of Classification." *AJP* 94 (1973) 350–64.
Stark, R. *The Rise of Christianity: A Sociologist Reconsiders History*. Princeton: Princeton University Press, 1996.
Stegemann, H. *Die Essener, Qumran, Johannes der Täufer und Jesus: ein Sachbuch*. 4th ed. Freiburg: Herder, 1994.
Steinwenter, A. "Corpus Iuris." *RAC* 3 (1957) 453–63.
Stemberger, G. *Jewish Contemporaries of Jesus: Pharisees, Sadducees, Essenes*. Minneapolis: Fortress, 1995.
Stephan, E. *Honoratioren, Griechen, Polisbürger: kollektive Identitäten innerhalb der Oberschicht des kaiserzeitlichen Kleinasien*. Göttingen: Vandenhoeck & Ruprecht, 2002.
Stephanis, I. E. *Dionysiakoi Technitai*. Heraklion: Panepistemiakes Ekdoseis Kretes, 1988.
Stern, M. *Greek and Latin Authors on Jews and Judaism*. Jerusalem: Israel Academy of Sciences and Humanities, 1974.
Stockmeier, P. *Glaube und Religion in der frühen Kirche*. Freiburg: Herder, 1973.

Stowers, S. K. "A Cult from Philadelphia: Oikos Religion or Cultic Association?" In *The Early Church in Context: Essays in Honor of Everett Ferguson*, edited by A. J. Malherbe et al., 287–301. Leiden: Brill, 1998.
Strange, S. K., and J. Zupko, eds. *Stoicism: Traditions and Transformations*. Cambridge: Cambridge University Press, 2004.
Stroumsa, G. *Barbarian Philosophy: the religious revolution of early Christianity*. Tübingen: Mohr Siebeck, 1999.
———. *The Scriptural Universe of Early Christianity*. Cambridge, MA: Harvard University Press, 2016.
Swain, S. "Character Change in Plutarch." *Phoenix* 43 (1989) 62–68.
———. *Hellenism and Empire: Language, Classicism, and Power in the Greek World, AD 50–250*. Oxford: Clarendon, 1996.
Syme, R. *Ammianus and the Historia Augusta*. Oxford: Clarendon, 1968.
———. *Emperors and Biography: Studies in the Historia Augusta*. Oxford: Clarendon, 1971.
Tajra, H. W. *The Martyrdom of St Paul: Historical and Judicial Context, Traditions, and Legends*. Tübingen: J. C. B. Mohr, 1994.
Takács, S. A. *Isis and Sarapis in the Roman World*. Leiden: Brill, 1995.
Talmon, S. "'The Essential 'Community of the Renewed Covenant'.: How Should Qumran Studies Proceed?" In *Geschichte—Tradition—Reflexion: Festschrift für Martin Hengel zum 70. Geburtstag*, edited by H. Cancik et al., 1:323–52. Tubingen: J. C. B. Mohr, 1996.
Tatum, J., ed. *The Search for the Ancient Novel*. Baltimore: Johns Hopkins University Press, 1994.
Taylor, M. C. *Critical Terms for Religious Studies*. Chicago: University of Chicago Press, 1998.
Teja, R. *Organización económica y social de Capadocia en el siglo IV: según los Padres Capadocios*. Salamanca: Universidad de Salamanca, 1974.
Theissen, G. *Die Religion der ersten Christen: eine Theorie des Urchristentums*. Gütersloh: Gütersloher Verlagshaus, 2000.
———. *The First Followers of Jesus: A Sociological Analysis of the Earliest Christianity*. London: SCM, 1978.
———. *Soziologie der Jesusbewegung: Ein Beitrag zur Entstehungsgeschichte des Urchristentums*. Munich: Kaiser, 1977.
———. *Studien zur Soziologie des Urchristentums*. Tübingen: Mohr Siebeck, 1979.
Thomas, G. S. R. "Magna Mater and Attis." *ANRW* II 17 (1984) 1500–1535.
Thomas, G. S. R., and S. R. Pickering. *Papyrus Editions held in Australian Libraries: A List*. 2nd ed. North Ryde, NSW: Macquarie University, 1974.
Thomas, J. "Baptistes." *RAC* 1 (1950) 1167–72.
Thompson, E. A. *A Roman Reformer and Inventor, Being a New Text of the Treatise De rebus bellicus*. Oxford: Clarendon, 1952.
Thompson, M. B. "Romans 12:1–2 and Paul's Vision for Worship." In *A Vision for the Church: Studies in Early Christian Ecclesiology in Honour of J.P.M. Sweet*, edited by M. N. A. Bockmuehl and M. B. Thompson, Edinburgh: T. & T. Clark, 1997.
Thraede, K. "Gesellschaft." *RAC* 10 (1978) 837–47.
Tod, M. N. "Sidelights on Greek Philosophers." *JHS* 77 (1957) 132–41.

Treu, K. "Christliche Empfehlungs-Schemabriefe auf Papyrus." In *Zetesis: album amicorum door vrienden en collega's aangeboden aan Prof. Dr. E. de Strycker Gewoon Hoogleraar aan de Universitaire Faculteiten Sint-Ignatius te Antwerpen ter gelegenheid van zijn 65e verjaardag*, edited by E. de Strycker, 629-36. Antwerp: De Nederlandsche Boekhandel, 1973.

Troeltsch, E. *Die Soziallehren der christlichen Kirchen und Gruppen*. Tübingen: J. C. B. Mohr, 1912.

Turcan, R. "Initiation." *RAC* 18 (1998) 87-159.

Uffenheimer, B. *Early Prophecy in Israel*. Jerusalem: Magnes, 1999.

Ulrich, E. and J. Vanderkam, *The Community of the Renewed Covenant*. Notre Dame: Notre Dame University Press, 1994.

Urman, P., and P. V. M. Flesher, eds. *Ancient Synagogues; Historical Analysis and Archaeological Discovery*. Leiden: Brill, 1995.

Ustinova, J. "The *thiasoi* of *theos hypsistos* in Tanais." *HR* 31 (1991) 150-80.

Van Haelst, J. *Catalogue des Papyrus Littéraires Juifs et Chrétiens*. Paris: Sorbonne, 1976.

———. "Les sources papyrologiques concernant l'Église en Égypte à l'époque de Constantin." In *Proceedings of the Twelfth International Congress of Papyrology*, edited by D. H. Samuel, 497-503. Toronto: Hakkert, 1970.

Van Nijf, O. *The Civic World of Professional Associations in the Roman East*. Amsterdam: Gieben, 1997.

Vanderlip, V. F. *The Four Greek Hymns of Isidorus*. Toronto: Hakkert, 1972.

Vermaseren, M. *Corpus cultus Cybelae Attidisque: Italia-Latium*. Leiden: Brill, 1977.

———. *Corpus cultus Cybelae Attidisque: Italia-Aliae Provinciae*. Leiden: Brill, 1978.

Vermes, G., and M. Goodman, *The Essenes: According to the Classical Sources*. Sheffield: JSOT on behalf of the Oxford Centre for Postgraduate Hebrew Studies, 1989.

Vidman, Ladislav. *Isis und Sarapis bei den Griechen und Römern: Epigraphische Studie zur Verbreitung und zu den Trägern des ägyptischen Kultes*. Berlin: De Gruyter, 1969.

———. *Sylloge inscriptionum religionis Isiacae et Sarapiacae*. Berlin: De Gruyter, 1970.

Vielhauer, P. *Oikodome*. ThD diss., Karlsruhe, 1940. Munich: Kaiser, 1979.

Vogliano, A. "La grande iscrizione bacchica del Metropolitan Museum." *AJA* 37 (1933) 215-70.

Vogt, H. C. M. *Studie zur nachexilischen Gemeinde in Esra-Nehemia*. Werl: Dietrich-Coelde, 1966.

Vogt, J. *Kulturwelt und Barbaren: zum Menschheitsbild der spätantiken Gesellschaft*. Mainz: Akademie der Wissenschaften und der Literatur, 1967.

Von Haehling, R. *Die Religionszugehörigkeit der hohen Amtsträger des Römischen Reiches Seit Constantins I. Alleinherrschaft bis zum Ende der Theodosianischen Dynastie (324-450 bzw. 455 n. chr.)*. Bonn: Habelt, 1978.

Von Harnack, A. *Die Mission und Ausbreitung des Christentums in den ersten drei Jahrhunderten*. Leipzig: Hinrichs, 1902. English translation: *The Mission and Expansion of Christianity in the First Three Centuries*. 2 vols. Translated by J. Moffatt. Reprint. Gloucester, MA: Peter Smith, 1972.

———. *Porphyrius, "Gegen die Christen": 15 Bücher; Zeugnisse, Fragmente und Referate*. Berlin: Reimer, 1916.

Von Ivánka, E. *Plato Christianus: Übernahme und Umgestaltung des Platonismus durch die Väter*. Einsiedeln: Johannes, 1964.

Von Wilamowitz-Moellendorf, U. *Antigonos von Karystos*. Berlin: Weidmann, 1881.

———. "Ein Bruchstuck aus der Schrift des Porphyrius gegen die Christen." *ZNW* 1 (1900) 101–5.
Vööbus, A. *History of Asceticism in the Syrian Orient: A Contribution to the History of Culture in the Near East*. Leuven: Peeters, 1958
Wagenvoort, H. "Orare, precari." In *Verbum: Essays on Some Aspects of the Religious Function of Words; Dedicated to H. W. Obbink*, FS H. W. Obbink, edited by T. P. van Baaren, 101–11. Utrecht: Kemink, 1964. Reproduced in H. Wagenvoort, *Pietas: Selected Studies in Roman Religion*, 197–209. Leiden: Brill, 1980.
Waldmann, H. *Die kommagenischen Kultreformen unter König Mithradates I. Kallinikos und seinem Sohne Antiochos I*. Leiden: Brill, 1973.
Walker-Ramisch, S. "Graeco-Roman Voluntary Associations." In *Voluntary Associations in the Graeco-Roman World*, edited by J. S. Kloppenborg and S. G. Wilson, 128–45. London: Routledge, 1996.
Wallace-Hadrill, D. S. *Eusebius of Caesarea*. London: Mowbray, 1960.
Waltzing, J.-P. "Collegia." In *Dictionnaire d'archéologie chrétienne et de liturgie*, edited by F. Cabrol and H. Leclerq, 2107–40. Paris: Letouzey, 1914.
———. "Collegium." In *Dizionario epigrafico di antichità*, edited by E. de Ruggiero, 304–406. Rome: Pasqualucci, 1900.
———. *Étude historique sur les corporations professionnelles chez les Romains: depuis les origines jusqu'à la chute de l'Empire d'Occident*. Leuven: Peeters, 1895–1900.
Walzer, R. *Galen on Jews and Christians*. London: Oxford University Press, 1949.
———. "Galenos." *RAC* 8 (1972) 777–86.
Watts, E. J. "Academic Life in the Roman Empire." In *City and School in Late Antique Athens and Alexandria*, 1–23. Berkeley: University of California Press, 2006.
Watt, I. P. *The Rise of the Novel: Studies in Defoe, Richardson, and Fielding*. Berkeley: University of California Press, 1957.
Weber, W. "The Antonines." In *The Cambridge Ancient History: The Imperial Peace, A.D. 70–192*, edited by S. A. Cook et al., 325–92. Cambridge: Cambridge University Press, 1936.
Wedderburn, A. J. M. "Paul and the Hellenistic Mystery-Cults: On Posing the Right Questions." In *La soteriologia dei culti orientali nell'Impero Romano*, edited by M. J. Vermaseren and U. Bianchi, 817–33. Leiden: Brill, 1982.
Weinfeld, M. *The Organizational Pattern and the penal code of the Qumran sect a comparison with guilds and religious associations of the Hellenistic-Roman period*. Freiburg: Éditions Universitaires, 1986.
Weinholt, K. "The Gateways of Judaism from Simon the Just to Rabbi Akiba." In *Rethinking Religion: Studies in the Hellenistic Process*, edited by J. Podemann Sørensen, 87–101. Copenhagen: Museum Tusculanum Press, 1989.
White, L. M. *The Social Origins of Christian Architecture*. Valley Forge: Trinity Press International, 1996–1997.
Whitehorne, J. "The Pagan Cults of Roman Oxyrhynchus." *ANRW* II 18 (1995) 3050–3091.
Wiles, M. F. *The Divine Apostle: The Interpretation of St. Paul's Epistles in the Early Church*. Cambridge: Cambridge University Press, 1967.
Wilken, R. L. *The Christians as the Romans Saw Them*. New Haven, CT: Yale University Press, 1984.

――― . "Collegia, Philosophical Schools, and Theology." In *The Catacombs and the Colosseum: The Roman Empire as the Setting of Primitive Christianity*, edited by S. Benko and J. J. O'Rourke, 268–91. Valley Forge: Judson Press, 1971.

――― . Review of *Die Idee des Fortschritts in der Alten Kirche bis Eusebius*, by W. Kinzig. *JTS* 47 (1996) 271.

Wilkinson, J. *Egeria's Travels*. London: SPCK, 1971.

Williams, M. H. "The Structure of the Jewish Community in Rome." In *Jews in a Graeco-Roman Environment*, 111–24. Tübingen: Mohr Siebeck, 2013.

Williams, R. *The Wound of Knowledge: Christian spirituality from the New Testament to St. John of the Cross*. London: Darton, Longman & Todd, 1979.

Williamson, H. G. M. *Israel in the Books of Chronicles*. Cambridge: Cambridge University Press, 1977.

Wimbush, V. L. *Ascetic Behaviour in Greco-Roman Antiquity: A Sourcebook*. Minneapolis: Fortress, 1990.

Winkelmann, F. "Probleme der Zitate in den Werken der oströmischen Kirchenhistoriker." In *Das Korpus der griechisch-christlichen Schriftsteller. Historie, Gegenwart, Zukunft*, edited by J. Irmscher and K. Treu, 195–207. Berlin: Akademie-Verlag, 1977.

――― . *Über das Leben des Kaisers Konstantin*. Berlin: Akademie-Verlag, 1975.

Winter, B. W. *Philo and Paul Among the Sophists*. Cambridge: Cambridge University Press, 1997.

――― . "Rehabilitating Gallio and his Judgement in Acts 18:14–15." *TynBul* 57 (2006) 291–308.

Witke, C. *Numen litterarum: The Old and the New in Latin Poetry from Constantine to Gregory the Great*. Leiden: Brill, 1971

Woyke, J. "Depotenzierung und Tabuisierung von Göttern nach 1 Ko 10." In *Gruppenreligionen im römischen Reich*, edited by J. Rüpke, 87–112. Tübingen: Mohr Siebeck, 2007.

Wipszycka, E. "Les confréries dans la vie religieuse de l'Égypte chrétienne." In *Études sur le christianisme dans l'Égypte de l'Antiquité tardive*, 511–25. Rome: Institutum Patristicum Augustinianum, 1996.

Wright, W. C. F. *The Works of the Emperor Julian, Volume 3*. LCL 29. London: Heinemann, 1923.

Wüllner, W. *The Meaning of "Fishers of Men."* Philadelphia: Westminster, 1967.

――― . "Ursprung und Verwendung der σοφός-, δυνατός-, εὐγενής- Formel in 1 Kor 1,26." In *Donum gentilicium: New Testament studies in honour of David Daube*, edited by E. Bammel et al., 165–84. Oxford: Clarendon, 1978.

Young, F. M. *Biblical Exegesis and the Formation of Christian Culture*. Cambridge: Cambridge University Press, 1997.

Zabkar, L. V. *Hymns to Isis in Her Temple at Philae*. Hanover, NH: University Press of New England for Brandeis University, 1988.

Zanker, P. *The Mask of Socrates: The Image of the Intellectual in Antiquity*. Berkeley: University of California Press, 1995.

Zhmud, L. *Wissenschaft, Philosophie und Religion im frühen Pythagoreismus*. Oxford: Oxford University Press, 2012.

Ziebarth, E. "Orgeones." In *Paulys Real-Encyclopädie der classischen Altertumswissenschaft*, edited by A. Pauly and G. Wissowa, 1024–25. Stuttgart: Metzler, 1939.

Ziwsa, C. *Corpus Scriptorum Ecclesiasticorum Latinorum: S. Optati Milevitani Libri VII*. Vienna: Tempsky, 1893.

Index

Aberkios, 187–88
Abinnaeus, 129–30, 147–48
Abraham, 27, 83, 175, 224
Academy, philosophical school, 73, 185
activism, 23, 161, 229. *See* commitment
Africa, 68, 92, 97–99, 178, 180–81
Agrippinilla, 66–67, 186
Alexandria, 68, 89, 115–16, 122–23, 124, 130, 145–46, 154, 161, 177, 186, 188, 208, 223
alternative society, 2–4, 14, 16–17, 35–36, 42, 44, 72–73, 88, 95–96, 100, 102, 107, 109, 118, 126, 157–58, 162, 166, 218, 225–26
Ammianus Marcellinus, 3, 42, 99–100, 105–7, 125–26, 131–32, 136–37, 149–62, 225
anchorites, 206–7, 209
Antioch, 6, 34, 85, 96, 114–20, 125, 137, 155, 177
Antoninus (deacon), 129, 147, 190–93
Antoninus Pius, 177, 187
Antony, Saint 129, 140–42, 198–200, 209–210, 213–14, 223–24
Aphrodisias, 60, 82
Apollinarius (sg.), Apollinares (pl.), 108, 179, 229
Apollonius of Tyana, 112, 184
apostles, 84–87, 112
Apuleius, 47, 68–69
Arians, 19, 108, 122
Aristotle, 9, 25, 59, 73, 177, 188, 229

asceticism, 74, 100, 116–17, 129, 136, 140, 142, 190–99, 209, 213, 223. *See* celibacy, monasticism
associations (e.g. *collegia, thiasoi, eranoi*), 5–6, 16–17, 22–27, 31, 38–51, 57–71, 75–102, 130–31, 158, 184, 186, 214, 224
Athanasius, 99, 114, 16, 140, 142–43, 158–61, 197–200, 208–9, 212, 214, 223
atheism, 58, 99, 152
Athens, Attica, 58–60, 61, 63, 66, 69, 73, 115, 117, 138, 144, 186, 188
Attis, 53–54
Augustine Saint, 19–21, 82, 110, 131, 134, 137, 141–43, 153, 166, 180, 217, 221
Aurelian, 6, 33–34, 94, 106, 132
Aurelius Ammonius (lector), 128, 145–46, 228
Aurelius Heron (deacon), 148
authority, 43, 80, 86–88, 92, 100–101, 119, 144, 166, 220
autonomy, 15, 17, 218, 224–25. *See* alternative society

Bacchus. *See* Dionysus
baptism, 49, 54, 68, 89–90, 134, 177, 221
Basil, 115, 179
Bendis, 59, 61
Bianchi, Ugo, 53, 63

INDEX

bishops, episcopacy, 6, 19, 32–34, 47, 91–94, 98–100, 106, 110, 115–17, 120–24, 132–34, 136, 138–39, 146, 151, 154–61, 164–66, 177, 223, 225
Bithynia, 182–3, 187
Brown, Peter, ix

Caesarea, 7, 46, 177, 207–8
Cancik, H., 40–41, 46–49
Cantwell Smith, W., 42, 106
Cappadocia, 179
Caracalla, 165, 187, 204
catechism, catechumens, 90, 110, 123, 133, 177, 180, 202–4
Catholicism (late antique). *See* orthodoxy
celibacy, abstinence, 89, 140, 195–99, 222–23
Celsus, 16, 31, 89, 92, 99, 108, 111–13, 167, 222
cemeteries (*koimētēria*), 33, 93
Ceres, 64–65, 75
Chadwick, Henry, ix, 164
charity, benefaction, 16, 21, 47, 62, 115, 120, 123–24, 184–86, 225–26
children, orphans, 9, 16, 21, 115–16, 119–20, 170, 171–81, 206, 209
Christianization, conversion of Rome, 18, 20–21, 45, 52–53, 99–102, 127–48, 164, 215–16, 228
Chrysostom, John, 141, 179–81
church buildings, 2, 5–6, 22, 33—35, 85, 93–97, 110, 118–19, 121–24, 154, 158, 185. *See ekklēsia*, monasteries
church (corporate body), 1, 5–7, 15, 20, 22, 48, 50, 57, 83–87, 94–97, 131, 169, 196, 218, 228. *See* associations, *ekklēsia*
Cicero, 33, 46–47, 75, 155
Cilicia, 71, 85, 201
circumcision, 27–28, 49, 82, 85
citizenship, 10, 15–16, 28, 33, 58–60, 84, 93, 142, 184, 187–88, 198, 218, 222, 224
classical literature, 115, 138, 172–73, 177–79

Clement of Alexandria, 90, 107, 177, 220
Clement of Rome, 91, 176
commitment, x, 3, 13–14, 16, 32, 58, 62, 68, 80, 89–90, 93, 98, 100, 120, 139, 144, 152, 157–59, 170, 184, 210, 217, 225, 228
community (*koinonia, koinon*), 9, 59–60, 66, 114, 186
compassion, 189, 228
confessors, 92, 101
Constantine, 4–7, 18–19, 46, 91, 95–99, 105, 107–8, 114, 120–22, 124–25, 131–32, 136, 138–39, 160, 178, 209
Constantinople, 20, 129, 137
Constantius, 99, 106, 116–17, 129, 145–46, 154, 157–61
conversion, 18, 19, 29, 46, 131, 138, 164, 173, 221. *See* Christianization
Coptic, 128, 173, 195, 209–12
Corinth, 11, 26–27, 64, 81, 87, 173, 176, 219
cosmos, 25, 33, 36, 43, 113, 166, 217, 229
covenant, 79–80, 86, 90–91, 175
Culcianus, 145–46, 219–20
cults (classical), 17–18, 24, 26, 28, 32, 39–51, 53–54, 57–95, 98–102, 119, 125, 131–32, 134, 139, 153–57, 186, 222, 227–28
Cybele, 46, 48, 50, 61, 70
cynics, 73, 115, 117, 139, 201, 223
Cyprian, 91–94, 101, 178

Dead Sea Scrolls. *See* Qumran
Decian persecution, 18, 31–32, 92–93
Delos, 60, 69
Demeter, 63–65, 132
demonstration (*apodeixis*) 89–90. *See* empiricism, historiography
desert, 129, 141–42, 198–202, 208, 223
Didache, 90–91, 141, 220
Dio Chrysostom, 183, 187
Diocletian, 17, 34–36, 67, 77, 95, 112, 128–29, 145–46, 165
Diogenes of Oenoanda, 74

INDEX

Dionysius (bishop of Alexandria), 92–93
Dionysus (Bacchus); Dionysiasts, 6, 24, 46, 50–51, 60–62, 64–67, 94, 158, 186
disciples (of Jesus,) 10–11, 14, 83–84, 91, 113, 196
diversity (social), 15–19, 36, 87–88, 110–11, 113, 116, 130, 170. *See* alternative society, commitment
dogma; dogmatism, 18, 43, 49, 100, 102, 120, 134, 161, 166, 225
Donatism, 19–20, 131
Dunn, James D. G., 49

edict of Milan, 4, 95–97, 133
education, 9, 47, 70, 72–74, 87, 89, 96, 114–15, 117, 119–20, 131, 134, 136, 138, 150, 166, 169, 171–81, 185–88, 217, 228–29. *See* philosophical schools
Egeria, 133, 201–2, 206, 213–14
Ehrhardt, Arnold, 7, 95, 97
ekklēsia. 6, 22, 35, 48, 54, 57–58, 67, 84–102, 113, 128, 151, 155, 158, 169, 228
empiricism, experiment 36, 43–44, 89, 165–66, 229. *See* demonstration, historiography, science
Ephesus, 50, 184–86
Epicureans, 44, 73, 152, 186, 188, 227
Essenes, 78–80. *See* Qumran
ethics, ix, 29, 47, 53, 58, 62, 70, 73, 79, 104, 117, 160, 170, 200, 216, 225, 228. *See* virtue(s)
Eucharist, 48, 90–91
Eunapius, 105, 117, 138, 191n2, 211n42, 223
Eusebius of Caesarea, 3, 6–7, 19, 30, 33–36, 49, 91, 94–100, 105, 107–110, 112–13, 118–25, 131, 136, 138, 142, 153, 194–97, 210, 213
Eusebius of Nicomedia, 124
Evagrius Ponticus, 140

family, 9, 19, 25, 51, 57, 61, 66–67, 75, 77, 140, 174–75, 186, 205. *See* children, marriage, women

fasting, 90, 141, 201. *See* asceticism
fate, fortune, 68, 144, 216–17
firefighters, 75
forgiveness, 115, 138, 228
freedmen, 10, 26, 66, 81, 93

Gaius (jurist), 23, 25, 97
Galen, 89, 140, 196, 222
Galerius, 1–4, 6, 18, 35–37, 95–97, 102, 118, 145–46, 225
Galileans (Christians), 42, 99, 115, 117, 138–39, 178, 201
Gallienus, 6, 32–33, 74, 93, 144–45
Gallio, 27–28
Gentiles, 14, 27, 50, 52, 82, 85–87, 91, 169, 218, 221
George (bishop of Alexandria), 115–16, 159–61
Germanic tribes, 19–20, 180
gnostics, 53–54, 74, 107, 212, 220
Godfearers (*theosebeis*), 82
Goths. *See* Germanic tribes
graves. *See* tombs
Gregory of Nyssa, 179
group religions, 38–51

Hadrianoi, 182–87
hairesis, 3, 49, 71, 78–79, 85, 95, 98. *See* secta
Hegesippus, 79, 85
Hellenism, Hellenization, 9, 18, 26, 42, 44, 78, 97, 99, 107, 109, 114, 117, 133, 143, 153n7, 169
Helvidius, 223
Herculaneum, 69, 74
Hercules, 48, 75
Hermeticism, 54, 74, 125
hermits. *See* monasticism
Hierocles, 108, 112, 125
Historia Augusta, 106, 132, 137
historiography, 30, 45, 48–49, 103, 107, 113, 126, 136, 138, 166, 229
Homer, 114, 229
hospitality, 50, 62, 83, 87–88, 119, 133, 204
humility, 13–14, 134, 144
Hurtado, L. W., 167–70

Iamblichus, 73, 165
idolatry, 4, 29, 32, 43, 82, 90, 94, 228
initiation, 63–66, 68, 70, 72, 179
Irenaeus, 91, 220
Isaac (monk) of Karanis, 129, 146–47, 190–93, 199, 209, 212
Isidore (petitioner) of Karanis, 129, 140, 146–47, 190–93
Isis, 47, 50, 68–70, 75, 168

James (of Jerusalem), 85
Jerome, 111, 135, 141n45, 180, 197, 199–202, 205–6, 209, 210n40, 211n42, 213–14, 223
Jerusalem, 9, 26, 30, 77, 85–86, 88, 112, 174, 180, 189, 201
Jerusalem temple, 26, 28, 79, 81–82, 98. *See* Jewish cult
Jesus, 10, 14, 57, 83, 86, 91, 98, 107, 109–116, 135, 141–42, 168, 175, 196
Jewish cult, 26–29, 79–83, 88. *See* Jerusalem temple
Jewish tax, 28–29, 81–82
John (apostle), 13, 84–86, 91
John the Baptist, 83, 85
Jones, A. H. M., 135, 150
Josephus, 78–79, 81, 108n9
Jovian, 156
Jovinian, 223
Julian, 18, 42, 47, 99, 106–7, 113–17, 124–25, 132–33, 138–40, 153, 155, 157, 159–62, 178–79, 191n2, 201, 203n28, 213–14, 222–23, 228–29
Jupiter, 28, 39, 72, 75, 82, 160
Justin Martyr, 16, 89, 91, 113, 177
Justinian, 20, 164

Karanis, 116, 124, 129, 140, 146–47, 190–93, 199–200, 209, 212
kingdom (messianic), 14, 19, 48, 83, 86–87, 138, 140
koinonia, 9, 59, 66, 88
Kore (Persephone), 63–65

Lactantius, 3–7, 35–37, 95–96, 112, 119, 178

law (Jewish/Mosaic), 49, 54, 77–81, 85–86, 90
lectors, 128, 132, 145–46, 169,
letters of recommendation, 132–33, 202–4
Libanius, 117, 137, 165, 191n2, 201n25, 214, 223
libelli. *See* Decian persecution.
Licinius, 1, 4–7, 95–97, 112, 120–26, 129n4, 139n39
Livy, 65–66, 81, 155
logic, 89, 153, 165–66, 229. *See* demonstration, empiricism, *logos*.
logos, 25, 30–31, 48–49, 68
Lucian, 48–49, 91
Luther, 43, 228

Maccabees, 9, 27, 78, 81
MacMullen, Ramsay, 101, 163–66
Mani, Manichaeans, 34–36, 42, 95, 106–7
Marcion, 47, 220
Marcus Aurelius, 46, 73, 116, 161, 187–88
Marius Victorinus, 134, 138, 154n8, 221–22, 225, 229
marriage, 16, 19, 21, 43, 77, 79, 111, 140, 170, 198
martyrs, 6, 33, 92, 100, 101, 116, 122, 151, 155, 157–59, 199n20, 218–19, 222, 224–25
Marxism, Karl Marx, 10–12, 18, 130, 142
Maximian, 34, 145–46
Maximinus Daia, 18, 96–97, 118–20, 122–23, 125, 139n39
Melania, 140, 142
Meletians, 207–9, 212–13
Men Tyrannus, 61–62
Mermertha, 128, 144–45
Mesopotamia, 34, 77, 201
Messiah, Messianism, 9, 14, 19, 30, 37, 57, 89
Middle Ages, 5, 20, 87, 172
Milan 4, 135. *See* edict of Milan
Minucius Felix, 41, 178

INDEX

Mithraism, 39, 48, 50–51, 53, 70–72, 75, 168
Momigliano, Arnaldo, 45, 135, 165
Mommsen, Theodor, 75
monasteries, 101, 129, 139, 140, 172, 179–81, 193, 195, 198–204, 207–9, 213
monks, monasticism, 19, 73, 76, 79, 100, 105, 107, 111, 116, 117, 129, 132–33, 136–37, 139–42, 147, 155, 161, 180, 190–214, 222–24, 226
monastic dress, 202, 204, 209–11, 213, 223
Moses, 22, 54, 83–84, 89, 107, 109, 179, 222
multiculturalism, ix–x, 4, 56–57, 102
mystery religions, 38, 47, 50–51, 53–54, 63–64, 70, 91

Nag Hammadi, 211–12
nation, national values, 3–4, 15–20, 24, 28, 37, 54, 56, 76, 80–82, 86, 93, 96–98, 104–5, 107, 109, 113–15, 117–18, 131, 168–69, 218–19, 224
Neoplatonism, 18, 47, 73–74, 94, 134, 140, 142
Nerva, 28–29
new consensus, 12, 30
Nicomedia, 4, 7, 35, 75, 96–97, 124
Nile, 64, 132, 207n34
Nobbs, Alanna, x, 103, 135n18, 156n14
Nongbri, Brent, 168

oikia (household), 9–10, 94
oikodomē (construction), 15, 218
oikos (house), 6, 11, 13, 62–63, 66, 93–94
open society, 1, 37, 102, 144, 218. *See* Popper
orgeōnes (celebrants), 58–61, 64, 66, 70
Origen, 3, 10, 16, 18, 30–31, 71, 91–92, 96–97, 102, 177, 220–21, 224
Orosius, 20, 135
Orphism, 53, 72–73
orthodoxy, 3, 20, 43, 47, 49, 74, 97–98, 106–7, 116, 122, 125, 129–30,
140, 143, 160–61, 178, 198–99, 201, 208, 212, 214, 220, 225
Osiris, 54, 68
Ostia, 70, 185. *See* Portus
Oxyrhynchus, 69, 128, 140, 144–46, 202, 206, 211

Pachomius, 76, 141n45, 199, 204, 209–211
Palestine, 23, 77, 121, 177, 195
Palladas, 200n23, 224
Pantaenus, 188
Papnutius, 207–9, 213
papyri, 10–11, 69, 72, 80, 114, 123, 127–30, 132–33, 135, 144–48, 169, 190–93, 202–210, 219–20, 228
patriarchy, 21, 73
patronage, 9, 12, 16, 19, 59–60, 64, 66–67, 72, 75, 85, 87, 101, 106, 115, 123–24, 131, 133, 193, 206, 208–9
Paul (apostle), ix, 10–14, 27, 47, 49–50, 73, 83–89, 131–32, 168–70, 173–75, 185, 216–26, 227–29
Paul of Samosata, 6, 34, 94
Pegasius, bishop of Troy, x, 99, 115, 229
Persephone. *See* Kore
Persians, 6, 33, 93, 117
Peter (apostle), 57, 83–86
Petosorapis, 128, 144–45
Pharisees, 49, 78–79, 83, 85–86, 141
Philadelphia, 62, 63, 147–48, 186
Phileas, 219–20
Philippi, 26, 46, 184
Philo, 78–79, 82, 177
philoponoi, 76, 214n45
philosophical schools, 17, 44, 47, 72–74, 89, 104, 134, 154, 169, 182–89
philosophy, ix, 7, 17, 22, 32, 47, 54, 58, 70, 73–74, 93, 108–117, 125, 131, 152, 159, 166, 174, 177–78, 182–89, 222, 227–28
Photius, 109
Phrygia, 46, 54, 61, 70, 119n19, 187, 201
piety, 61, 83, 111, 150, 165,
Pilate, 119
Pionius, 30
Piraeus, 60–61, 66, 70–71

pity (*misericordia*), 152, 217
Plato, 9, 31, 59, 63, 65, 73–74, 107, 109, 114, 160, 188, 217, 220
Platonism, 31, 37, 53, 73, 109, 143, 152, 177, 179, 186, 188. *See* Neoplatonism, Plato
Pliny the Younger, 35, 78, 89, 165, 183
Plotinus, 47, 74, 113, 165, 210, 217
Plutarch, 68, 71, 165
polis, 9–10, 13, 59, 198
Popper, Karl, 37
Porphyry, 18, 94, 97, 99, 108–113, 125, 139n39, 165, 222,
Portus, 71. *See* Ostia
prayer, 4, 27, 36–37, 54, 90–91, 95, 98, 112, 123, 132, 140, 155, 206–7, 209, 225, 228
priests, priestesses, priesthood, 9, 24, 43, 47, 51, 60–61, 64–70, 77, 84–86, 91, 96, 98–99, 110–11, 115, 119, 132, 139, 154, 186, 205
Prohaeresius, 117, 138
prophets, 43, 47, 77, 83, 89–91, 125, 222
proselytization, 54, 82
proseuchai, 81, 94
providence, 98
Prusa, 97, 183–85, 187
Pythagoras, Pythagoreans, 73, 78, 140, 177, 186, 198n20

Qumran, Dead Sea Scrolls, 50, 78–80, 196,\

race, 224, 16, 37, 82, 107, 169. *See* nation
rank, 14–16, 18, 20, 39, 66, 93, 111, 121, 123, 130–31, 133–34, 141, 156, 160, 192, 195–96, 201, 204–6, 210, 213
religio, 5, 32, 39, 41, 44, 53, 75, 88, 90, 93, 95, 98, 100, 106, 150–52, 156–59, 225, 228
res publica, 2, 9, 48, 90, 95
rhetoric, 7, 117, 124, 134, 172, 174, 176, 178, 187, 221, 229

rights, 9–10, 15, 21, 31, 121, 123
ritus, 28, 81, 100, 151, 155–57, 159, 225
Rome (city, episcopal see), 4, 6, 10, 16, 19–20, 26–30, 34, 45–47, 67, 69–71, 74, 81, 87, 106, 130, 134, 136–38, 141, 157, 17–77, 184–86, 188, 221, 224–25, 229. *See* Christianization
Rufinus, 3, 195n11, 202, 206
Rüpke, J. 38–51

Sabbath, 26, 29, 39
Sabinus, 118, 206
sacrifice, 2, 4, 18, 24, 26–27, 30–33, 37, 43, 46, 51, 57, 59–62, 69, 71–76, 78–81, 90–92, 94, 96, 98, 110, 114, 116, 119, 120, 132, 152–53, 16, 201, 219, 223
Sadducees, 49, 78–79, 85
Salvian, 20
Sapor, 99, 154, 159
Sarapis, 68–70
Saturn, 50–51
Science, 36, 41, 43, 149, 165–66, 227, 229. *See* empiricism
secta, 2–3, 34–35, 90, 95, 99, 151, 157. *See hairesis*
Seneca, 28, 81–82, 152
Serapion of Thmuis, 68, 132, 198–99, 207n34
sex, sexuality, 49, 123, 170, 195, 211–12, 222
Shepherd of Hermas, 220
slaves, 13, 16, 20–21, 28, 59–62, 70, 122, 141, 145–46, 164, 174, 209, 224
society. *See* alternate society, open society, nation
Sokolowski, F. 60–63, 66
Solon, 23, 59, 75
soul, 53, 61, 71, 98, 217, 220–21, 228
status, 12, 14, 77, 87, 121–22, 125, 129, 131, 134, 172, 187, 196–97, 204–6, 219, 228
Stoicism, 50, 73, 97, 140, 177, 183–84, 186, 188, 216, 229

Stroumsa, G., 184n6, 188
Suetonius, 24, 27–28, 89, 152, 169, 217n6
Symmachus, 136–37, 194–96, 211
synagogues, 22–23, 25–26, 30, 33, 37, 52, 58, 78–83, 85, 87, 91, 93, 174, 218
synods, 6, 33, 59–60, 62, 67, 69, 74, 93–94, 100, 105–7, 122, 132, 151, 158–60, 225, 227
Syria, 34, 85, 137, 177, 179, 193, 195n12, 201
Syriac, 173, 199n21, 211–12

Tacitus, 89, 155, 217n6, 225
Talmud, 139n38, 173
temples, 26, 28, 39, 47, 54, 70, 75, 77, 79, 82, 90, 94, 98–99, 110, 114–16, 132, 136, 139, 160, 165, 202, 223, 229. *See* Jerusalem temple
Tertullian, 16–17, 29, 41, 48, 90–91, 97, 150, 178, 210n40, 220, 224
Theissen, G., 11–12, 14, 45n25, 89n170
Themistius, 117, 134, 137
Theodosius, 18, 20, 105, 117, 121
theology, 11, 44, 53, 57–58, 67, 70, 72, 99, 104, 113, 115, 151, 161, 168, 177, 180, 212, 227–29
Theophanes (lawyer), 125
Theos Hypsistos, 82
Theotecnus, 96, 119
Therapeutae, 79
Thomas, Gospel of, 211–12
Timothy, 175, 219
toleration, 1–3, 5, 7, 18, 26, 30, 36–37, 87, 96, 100, 106, 118, 136–37, 160–61, 164, 218, 225
tombs, graves, 6, 62, 99, 101, 116, 122, 160, 185, 223. *See* cemeteries
Torah. *See* law
Toynbee, A., 130
Trajan, 75–76
triumphalism, 19, 45, 163, 170

Twelve Tables, 23, 75

Ulpian, 5

Valentinian, 150, 157
Valerian, 6, 32–33, 35, 93, 144–45
Valerius Maximus, 26, 81
Valesius, H., 3, 36, 95
values, common law, 3, 14, 20–21, 25, 31, 37, 47, 92, 99, 101, 118, 151, 170, 172–73, 218
Vandals. *See* Germanic tribes
Varro, 41, 54
Vigilantius, 223
virgins, 99–100, 111, 123, 140, 154, 159, 161, 180, 197, 202, 206, 210, 213, 222–23, 225–26. *See* celibacy
virtue(s), 123, 194, 217, 220
Visigoths. *See* Germanic tribes

widows, 16, 85, 100, 123, 175, 195–97, 205, 210, 213
witness, testimony, 48, 89, 101, 225
women, 9, 16, 24, 45–46, 50, 60, 62, 65–66, 69, 72–74, 79, 100, 110–12, 116, 121, 123, 164, 170, 175, 201, 203, 205–6, 209, 213–14, 222–23, 226. *See* virgins, widows
worship, *thrēskeia*, 2, 16–18, 27, 29, 33, 46, 49, 53, 57, 60, 69, 71–72, 85–86, 88, 104, 135, 150–51, 154–55, 158, 169, 227. *See* cult

Xenophon of Ephesus, 68

zeal, 77, 151, 216
Zealots, 79, 83
Zeno, 73
Zenobia, 6, 34
Zeus, 26, 60, 62, 114, 119, 227
Zosimus, 164, 224